The House of Redgrave

The House of Redgrave

The Lives of a Theatrical Dynasty

Tim Adler

Aurum
Press

First published 2012 by
Aurum Press Limited
74–77 White Lion Street
London N1 9PF
www.aurumpress.co.uk

This paperback edition first published in 2014 by Aurum Press Ltd

A catalogue record for this book is available from the British Library.

ISBN 978 1 78131 224 7

10 9 8 7 6 5 4 3 2 1
2018 2017 2016 2015 2014

Typeset in Sabon by RefineCatch Ltd, Bungay, Suffolk

Printed and bound in Great Britain by Clays Ltd, St Ives plc

For dear friends
Harriet Wallace-Jones
Adam Cox

'Try again. Fail again. Fail better.'

Worstward Ho, Samuel Beckett

Contents

CHAPTER ONE

And Laertes Had a Daughter

More than seventy years ago, after a Saturday night performance of *Hamlet* at the Old Vic, Laurence Olivier stepped out on stage from behind the curtain to announce, 'Ladies and gentlemen, tonight a great actress has been born: Laertes has a daughter.' It was the night of 30 January 1937. Backstage, Michael Redgrave was crying as he hugged the bouquets given by members of the cast (he was prone to weeping). Old Vic students had filled his dressing room with blossoms and the note, 'Love's Labour's Not Lost'. He weaved his way through the Old Vic corridors with these floriferous tokens, kissing everybody he came across. Meanwhile, Rachel Kempson, the actress whom Michael had married in July 1935, lay recovering in a Blackheath nursing home after her long and painful labour. The couple had already decided to name the baby Vanessa.

But Olivier was not just raising the curtain on one great actress: Vanessa's younger brother and sister and both her children would also inherit what Michael described as 'the divine gift' – the ability to be spontaneous on stage and screen and to show others what one feels on the inside. Between them, Michael's children and grandchildren would go on to win four Golden Globes, a Tony Award and an Oscar. And it's not just on stage and screen that the family has touched others' lives: Vanessa and her brother Corin spent years giving a voice to those who didn't share the same privileged upbringing – refugees, gypsies and children traumatised by war. Yet just as Prometheus was punished for giving fire to humanity, so the Redgrave family has suffered more than its fair share of the most appalling unhappiness: within just over a year of each other, Vanessa's daughter, brother and sister would die. The Redgrave family story is a febrile mix of ambition, controversy and tragedy that for some of them ends in a remote country churchyard, 80 miles north of Manhattan.

Rather than struggle through the snow to be with his wife and child, Michael celebrated the birth at Le Moulin d'Or restaurant in Soho.

He entered the restaurant theatrically, distributing blooms to surprised diners. Afterwards, he travelled to the Belgravia flat of actress Edith Evans, where he went to bed with her.[1]

Michael was having an intense affair with Evans, with whom he had starred in *As You Like It* (1936). Speaking from experience, he once said that the best advice he could give any prospective Orlando was to fall in love with his Rosalind. The affair with Evans had been going for more than a year before Vanessa's birth and began after a year of being married to Rachel. However, Michael didn't have the nerve to tell his wife about the affair with Evans, one of her closest friends, until the late 1970s, when the secret was about to be exposed in a book. Rachel, whom the actress Constance Cummings once compared to a beautiful swan gliding gracefully through adversity, thought it must have been 'very wonderful' for her husband to have been in love with, and in turn loved by Britain's greatest actress. Throughout their marriage, she maintained this oddly complaisant attitude.

Michael's infidelity repeated his father's, in a pattern which would continue in the family. Vanessa's grandfather Roy Redgrave is reputed to have had at least one bigamous marriage, possibly two. He got another married woman, Ettie Carlisle, pregnant when he was married to his first wife, Judith Kyrie (née Ellen Maud Pratt), whom he deserted to be with Michael's mother, Daisy Redgrave, by 1903. 'Roy could have charmed the birds from the trees,' said one contemporary (another family trait). 'Men loved him and women went mad for him,' wrote Daisy.

Vanessa's grandparents Roy and Daisy met in the summer of 1907 in Brighton when both were acting in rep. Heart-meltingly handsome, Roy was often billed as 'The Dramatic Cock of the North'. Born in 1873, he was the eldest son of George and Zoe Redgrave and was brought up in the poor south London neighbourhood of Waterloo. George Redgrave was something of a card, describing himself variously as a publican and a billiard table maker. His wife Zoe was only sixteen when they married. Their son Roy carved out a career for himself on the Victorian stage playing splendid heroes, always in sword fights, escaping from burning buildings or being set free by his trusty horse.

Roy never made it into the West End, though. He disdained Shaftesbury Avenue as a closed shop barred to provincial actors, becoming instead a matinee idol in the big suburban theatres of late-Victorian

London. Once he even played Hamlet at the Britannia Theatre in Hoxton, a poor neighbourhood in north London. Unlike his granddaughter, who would play Shakespeare in her agonised way, Roy decided to treat the pale Dane as yet another hero. Glancing through his script, he took in the sword-fights, ghosts and derring-do. He didn't bother to read the play itself until he heard a market porter recite some lines. After that, he decided to knuckle down and learn Shakespeare's actual words.

Daisy Redgrave had an even more remarkable early life. Born in 1881, she was the youngest daughter of boat-maker William Scudamore and his wife Clara. Daisy Scudamore grew up in Portsmouth. However, it seems likely that Vanessa's great-grandmother Clara became pregnant after an affair with a visiting actor, the grandly named Fortunatus Augustus Scudamore. Known to everybody as 'Scudie', he was an actor-turned-writer of melodramas. (Confusingly, both Clara and Scudie shared the surname Scudamore.) Their illegitimate daughter Daisy inherited Scudie's acting gene. Teenage Daisy flitted to London, where she barged into a theatrical agent's office. The agent, enchanted by this blossoming young girl, signed her up on the spot. On learning her surname, he said: 'So, you must be Scudie's little girl?' He gave her Scudie's address in Barnes, southwest London. Assuming he must be talking about her boat builder father, Daisy went off to visit her distant Scudamore relative. On seeing Daisy, Scudie exclaimed in a line worthy of one of his own melodramas: 'If you are not my daughter, then I do not know whose daughter you can be!' and then clutched her to his manly bosom.

Scudie offered Daisy the use of his Barnes home. He was besotted with his long-lost daughter, putting every playbill she featured in up on his study walls. By 1904, Daisy had become the leading lady at the Pavilion in Mile End Road, known as the Drury Lane of the East End. It was during the 1904 season of creaky plays – ('Endowed by a freak of nature with the talons of a vulture') – that she had a terrible row with Scudie. Following this, Daisy stayed away from Barnes for a couple of nights. When she eventually returned home, she and a neighbour had to force their way in only to find Scudie lying dead on his study floor. He had fallen from a stepladder while turning every single picture of Daisy to face the wall. Just as he was about to turn the last one over, he had suffered a fatal heart attack.

During the glorious summer of 1907, Daisy and Roy met in Brighton and knocked about together. Then Daisy discovered that she was pregnant with Roy's child, which complicated matters. Not only was Roy already married – although he had deserted his wife and their three young children – he'd had a son with another married woman. While travelling in Scotland as one of George Seymour's Comedians in a bill of *Novelties and Sketches*, he received Daisy's 'good news'.

Michael Redgrave was born on 20 March 1908 in Bristol. At the time, Roy was working in London and sent back dribs and drabs of cash to his new wife and son. Daisy was so poor that the newborn infant soon began to lose weight. Around then, she began drinking heavily. According to Lynn Redgrave, both her grandparents were alcoholics. Touring the provinces in rep with a wife he hardly knew and an unwanted baby, Roy suddenly made a bolt for Australia. Metaphorically waving his hat, he sent them a cable – 'Goodbye, my darlings, Roy' – as his ship sailed from Plymouth. Having successfully absconded, he sent almost no money back to his little family, instead spending his wages on himself and then mostly on drink. Daisy was reduced to travelling far out of London to play bit parts on the suburban circuit. One night she was so exhausted by the time she got home that she sat down on the pavement and wept.

By now, even the besotted Daisy suspected her husband was blowing his wages on having a good time. She wangled a role with Roy's touring company out in the Australian Outback but the marriage foundered there when Michael was only two years old. Like many homosexuals, he grew up never really knowing his father and Daisy became the dominant influence in his life. Hurtfully, she later told him the marriage failed because Roy didn't love his son enough. Daisy gathered up Michael and sailed back to England. Meanwhile, Roy stayed behind in Australia, where he drank himself to death. Six years later, he bigamously married Mary Seward Leresche, another woman 'of independent means'. On the voyage home, Daisy had already earmarked the man who was to become Michael's stepfather. J.P. 'Andy' Anderson was a Maughamesque rubber planter, who was returning to England from Sri Lanka. The well-off bachelor, aged forty-seven, had already submitted to Daisy by the time they disembarked.

Daisy and Anderson now began a secret relationship. Michael once glimpsed Anderson leaving the Battersea flat, where he lived with his mother. The relationship deepened and became more complicated when Daisy realised she was pregnant again. In one of those childhood snapshots only fully understood much later in life, Michael remembered challenging his mother to a race on the lawn and being surprised when he won so easily. Daisy had been heavy and breathless. Looking back, he realised his mother must have been heavily pregnant. Peggy Anderson was born in 1911. Five years later, Michael and his half-sister moved with their mother into Anderson's Belgravia house. From then on, Daisy told Michael, 'Uncle Andy' was to be called 'Daddy'. She also explained that Peggy was his half-sister. However, she lied when she told him that she and Anderson were already married.

Roy Redgrave wrecked his life on the shoals of dissipation. In May 1922 he was admitted to the Sacred Heart Hospice for the Dying in Darlingham, Sydney, suffering from tuberculosis and cancer of the throat. He died on 25 May. As they were now free to marry, 'Mr and Mrs Anderson' went out to The Ritz to celebrate. Daisy became Mrs Andy Anderson on 27 June 1922, one month after Roy's death.

Michael went away to boarding school at the age of twelve, attending Clifton College, Bristol. He then won a place at Magdalene College, Cambridge, where he studied Modern Languages. After leaving university, he became a schoolmaster at Cranleigh School, Surrey, teaching French and English. There, he began directing school plays – *Hamlet*, *King Lear* and *The Tempest* – casting himself in lead roles. The reaction was so overwhelming that he decided to become a full-time actor and made his first professional appearance at the Liverpool Playhouse on 30 August 1934. It was as a member of the Liverpool Repertory Company that he met his future wife, Rachel Kempson.

Vanessa Redgrave inherited her slightly sorrowful beauty from her mother. Rachel, twenty-four, had already been a professional actress for a couple of years when she met Michael. She also had more professional experience, having played Juliet at Stratford-upon-Avon. Her daughter Lynn was to write a play about Rachel's fascination with Juliet shortly before her own death, seventy-five years later. Rachel was booked in as a late replacement for another actress who had dropped out of John Van Druten's play, *Flowers of the Forest*. Rachel's father Eric had been a science master at Rugby and later became headmaster of the Royal Naval College in Dartmouth. Her mother Beatrice was the youngest daughter of a homeopathic chemist. Beatrice was very beautiful in her youth, but later became bitter and disillusioned with her lot. Married life, Rachel told Vanessa, had not come up to Beatrice's expectations. Rachel had adored Eric but after he died, her relationship with Beatrice became difficult. 'If ever I become like her,' Rachel told Vanessa, 'please warn me.'

When they first met, Rachel was a virgin although she felt faint with desire at the thought of Michael. What she especially liked about him was that he didn't seem remotely theatrical or camp at all – he could have been a naval officer. Yet it was when they were discussing marriage that Michael told her frankly about the affairs he'd already had with men. This, he described as 'difficulties in my nature.'

Michael first began brooding about his homosexual impulses when he was a schoolboy. On a family trip to Paris, he allowed himself to be picked up by an Italian man but panicked after they had gone back to his room. His first flirtation, aged sixteen, had been with twenty-five-year-old Oliver Baldwin, son of prime minister Stanley Baldwin. It was Baldwin who sparked Michael's interest in left-wing politics that he would pass on to two of his three children. At Cambridge, he became engaged to an American Communist yet he also had affairs with fellow male students. Diary entries refer to nude wrestling bouts with chums – ('Changing in our room, we fought and got very hot – good exercise. D. routed') – and lots of Ryvita picnics with Geoffrey or cycling trips with Cyril to Minehead ('Paradise').

During his early days as a schoolmaster, Michael continued to have affairs with both sexes. One of his male conquests declared that Michael had 'initiated' him 'into the joys of love as if it was the most natural thing in the world'. Despite his bisexuality, Michael still wanted marriage and children. Completely besotted, Rachel insisted that what he had confided in her made no difference (for a girl of her background, she was remarkably open-minded). 'Of course,' she later told her grown-up children, 'I thought I could change him.'

For his part, Michael never deceived himself or Rachel that marriage would cure him of being gay: he was self-reflective enough to realise that bisexuality was part of his nature. The couple were married on 18 July 1935. Michael was extremely fortunate in finding someone as broadminded as Rachel. She once wrote that so many more marriages would survive if partners allowed each other a little latitude and compared being married and never experiencing another person's love to a kind of imprisonment: 'It is an extraordinary rule that once married, no man or woman should ever have some of the love that men and women have in them to give.'

Michael began cheating on Rachel within a year of marriage. He started an affair with Noël Coward in the summer of 1941, shortly before being called up. Indeed, he was so intoxicated with Coward that he spent his last night before reporting for naval duty with the playwright. Coward's pet name for Michael was 'China', after the euphemism for male genitalia used in the play *The Country Wife*. Years later, Coward told Rachel that he hadn't wished to hurt her, but he'd found Michael so irresistibly charming: 'I couldn't help but agree with him,' she wrote.

Crucified with guilt, Michael would confess his gay affairs to Rachel. One night he cried himself to sleep after telling her about a new love. The next morning, Rachel told him brightly: 'It's silly, but I feel quite happy about it.' Perhaps she was becoming indifferent to him. Eventually, she would seek comfort elsewhere, having an affair with Glen Byam Shaw, a married man, over a twenty-year period.

Rachel continued to work, even though Vanessa was a newborn. She went to Oxford for a month, playing Viola in *Twelfth Night*, despite her daughter being only four months old. Michael, too was increasingly in demand and often away from home. He began alternating Shakespearian parts with West End comedies. John Gielgud invited him to join his company at the Queen's Theatre in September 1937, where he performed Shakespeare, Chekhov and Restoration Comedy. The show had to go on. Even as an infant, Vanessa was clearly wilful. Rachel remembered how baby Vanessa once had such a temper tantrum that Edith Evans exclaimed, 'Wallop her, Rachel, and I'll stand by and bear witness that you only did it out of kindness.'

The following year Rachel became pregnant again. Her baby boy was born in Marylebone on 16 July 1939 and the couple settled on the name Corin William. Ironically, the name Corin came from a shepherd in *As You Like It*. (Years later, Corin would name his own son Arden after the forest where the play takes place.) Daisy vetoed the original idea of calling him William Corin, insisting future schoolmates would pick on the 'W.C.' initials.

On 3 September 1939, Britain and France declared war on Germany. Then, on 10 July 1940, the Luftwaffe launched a series of attacks on shipping convoys on the southeast coast of England and so began the Battle of Britain. Three-year-old Vanessa and two-year-old Corin were evacuated to Herefordshire. They were sent to stay with a distant spinster bluestocking relative. Lucy Wedgwood Kempson was a cousin of Rachel's grandfather. She lived in a large Victorian house in Bromyard, near the Welsh border. Cousin Lucy, as she was known, had been one of the first women to study at London University, eventually becoming warden of Bedford College. Vanessa later suspected the reason why Cousin Lucy had never married was because her emancipated views were unacceptable.

Vanessa's childhood in the country – isolated from the war, almost untouched by modernity – had an enormous effect on her. She remembered it as, 'full of pleasure and full of pain.' There was one night in November 1940 when she was shown Coventry in flames from a top-floor window. German bombs were pounding the city, lighting up the sky. More than 2,000 people were killed. Three-year-old Vanessa remembered a fierce red glow on the northeast horizon. The sight of Coventry burning traumatised the youngster, who would have night-mares about flames for the rest of her life. Despite this, amid the peace of country living the children were protected from the Blitz – from an upstairs window, you could see the Welsh mountains. It was a cosy, settled routine of Snakes and Ladders after high tea and *Children's Hour* on the wireless. Life was rustic and pretty basic. Cousin Lucy would churn butter herself; also gather and bottle fruit. 'All the old ways,' Vanessa remembered.

Cousin Lucy's house was full of treasures that fascinated the young Vanessa. The walls were hung with Chinese silk tapestries brought back by Lucy's father, who had fought in the Opium Wars of the 1840s. Tiny Chinese ivory figures were preserved in a beautiful glass case. Lucy also had a bookcase full of books from her childhood days. That bookcase is the Rosebud that unlocks the key to Vanessa's character. Vanessa learned to read when she was four, devouring these Victorian tomes, Kipling and *Our Island Story*. At night in her dressing gown, she read about a world divided into good and evil, truth and wickedness. Cousin Lucy's bookcase instilled in her the 19th-century values in which she still believes today: truth, hope, justice.

During those early war years, Vanessa and Corin grew close. For a long time, they rather thought of themselves as twins. They made friends with no other children, instead relying almost exclusively on the other for company. Together, they created imaginary worlds for themselves: a prince and a princess, pirates, magicians, knights and monsters. Both were tall, fair and handsome, with hypnotic blue eyes. Growing up, they complemented each other perfectly – Corin the intellectual, Vanessa the romantic; Corin the teacher, Vanessa the pupil – two halves of the same person. Sometimes it felt as if there was no real room for anybody else. Vanessa later remarked to her future sister-in-law, Deirdre Redgrave: 'I will never find for myself a man like Corin.'[2]

Their younger sister Lynn was born in London on 8 March 1943. 'An afterthought,' was how Lynn Redgrave described herself. This time, there would be no Laurence Olivier stepping forward into the footlights to announce her birth. Indeed, when going through Michael's diary to see what prescient entry he might have written for her, Lynn would be deeply hurt that he merely noted a luncheon appointment, an air raid and how he performed in a play by Ivan Turgenev. Her birth didn't warrant a mention. That same year, Corin and Vanessa joined baby Lynn back in London. The two older children had been away more than two years, seeing their parents only intermittently.

Rachel had rented a flat in Putney, southwest London, for the family to live in (Michael was now an ordinary seaman in the Navy). The children lived with Rachel for about a year before the German 'doodlebug' V-1 and V-2 bombing raids began. This time all three were evacuated back to Herefordshire, where they lived with another Kempson relative. One wet afternoon, Vanessa and Corin were in Bromyard with their nanny, who was pushing baby Lynn through the high street when they came across a crowd standing around a van, its back doors open. Inside the van was a window and another crowd beyond it. Inside the window, a woman turned and waved. Vanessa and Corin waved back. The crowd around the van burst out laughing and their nanny joined in the laughter: the newsreel was the first film they had ever seen. The war was over.

During the Second World War, Michael became increasingly well known. When the theatres reopened, he starred in a succession of hit plays, sometimes opposite Rachel. He also began to appear in films, starting with Hitchcock's *The Lady Vanishes* in 1939. By now, he was becoming the most popular actor in Britain. One cartoon showed Olivier looking nervously over his shoulder at Michael. In 1945,

Michael played his most famous screen role: the ventriloquist with the murderous dummy in *Dead Of Night*. The role of the tortured, conflicted entertainer suited him perfectly.

In keeping with his status, Michael moved his family into a sumptuous 18th-century house in Chiswick Mall, west London in 1946. Bedford House was one of several redbrick mansions running along a Queen Anne terrace. Swans glided past Vanessa's nursery window and as the cruisers ploughed up and down the River Thames, megaphones would bark that this was where 'Michael Redgrave, the film star' lived. Bedford House employed six staff, including a cook, two housemaids and a gardener. For the next eleven years, it was to become the Redgrave family home. Michael Redgrave belonged to a generation of actors who assumed they belonged on the same level as bankers and industrialists. The Oliviers, for instance, lived in Notley Abbey, a stately home at Thame, Oxfordshire. They seemed to have forgotten that they were only a few generations away from being travelling players and minstrels before that. The desire for upper middle-class respectability runs deep in the English.

Michael, meanwhile, had taken out a large mortgage that he couldn't really afford. The family's neighbours in 'The Mall' as they called it also belonged to haute bohemia and included the lawyer and painter Anthony Lousada and his stage designer wife, Jocelyn Herbert. Also, Jocelyn's father, the author and journalist A.P. Herbert and further along Upper Mall, theatre director George Devine and his wife Sophie. All would become significant figures in Vanessa's life – and more especially, her future husband's.

Growing up, Vanessa was awestruck by her parents' famous friends. Laurence Olivier and Vivien Leigh would drop by for tea and she had never seen such a beautiful couple. Ralph Richardson and Alec Guinness would also call round. Hers was a privileged childhood, evocative of King and Country, Empire and the Church of England. She even presented a bouquet to the young Princess Elizabeth at a Royal Command Performance. Governesses and chauffeurs would take her to Harrods, a shop she still visited even when at her most revolutionary.

On their return to London, Vanessa and Corin were sent to the local state primary school. Although Vanessa was far ahead in reading, she was behind at maths. Quickly, she realised that she had nothing in

common with her classmates. She thought they might have been interested in her because of her film star father but their interest swiftly
waned when they realised she didn't have any autographs to swap that
were better than theirs. In 1947, Mall residents now unhappy with
the local state school, clubbed together to hire their own teacher, a
Miss Glascot. They converted one room of the local vicarage into a
classroom. Apart from Vanessa and Corin, other pupils included the
Lousada's two daughters – one of whom (Sandra) would become the
official Royal Court Theatre photographer a decade later – and Alec
Guinness's son Matthew. The Guinnesses lived in nearby St Peter's
Square, where Vanessa, too was to reside with her first husband, Tony
Richardson.

Looking back on her childhood, Vanessa seems to have spent much
of it in a garden pretending to be somebody else. 'Like the Brontës,'
Michael remembered, 'she lived in great islands of imagination that
were entirely her own creation.' The length of time her parents spent
away meant that their arrival home was duly celebrated: Michael
would put down his suitcase in the hall, smothered by his children.
There was a kind of theatricality about it all, play-acting being a family.
'We would hug and kiss even if we were going to shop,' said Lynn.
Perhaps she sensed early on that real emotion was something reserved
for the theatre: real life was play-acting, and vice-versa.

That same year Michael and Rachel went to Hollywood, partly
because he needed the money. The family's grand lifestyle was haemor-
rhaging his actor's wages – especially as he kept turning down parts
in films in favour of classical roles. Meanwhile, the children stayed
behind. Their childhood combined the apparently secure trappings of
an affluent upper-middle-class British life and benign neglect. Vanessa
recalled: 'I missed them very much when they were away. I missed
them physically, the sound of their voices and spending time with them.
When they were around, there were stories and games and songs and
such fun but often they couldn't even make it home for the weekend.'
Ironically, she suffered similarly to her own children later on when she
left them for months at a time.

Michael's Hollywood sojourn meant there was no strong male role
model for Corin to follow. With their parents away so much of the
time, he fell into a paternal role with both his sisters and became the
man of the household, almost a substitute father.

Even when their parents were at home, the children rarely saw them.[3] When he was appearing in the West End, Michael slept late and he was often sequestered in his study. Lynn once observed that it was as if there was a sign on his door, saying: 'genius resting'. Often there would be only the telltale smell of his presence: a mix of pipe tobacco and his favourite Knize cologne. 'It was a very quiet household because my father was usually working at night and had to be allowed to sleep in the mornings before doing his matinee *Hamlet* or *Lear*,' remembered Lynn. 'My general memory of childhood is of always having to be quiet in the mornings.'

Impenetrable and aloof with his family, Michael's main means of communication was acting. Here was a man capable of expressing any emotion when it belonged to someone else, yet he was a blank canvas with his own children. Lynn once described him as a 'mask, who just vanished behind his face.' He would rashly promise Corin a new bicycle or a fishing rod, but then forget all about it. However, this wasn't maliciousness, more thoughtlessness: Michael was so self-absorbed, he seemed only vaguely aware of his children's needs.

Nevertheless, Michael invested all his artistic hopes into Vanessa and Corin. Vanessa was the one expected to be the great actress, while Corin was regarded as the intellectual. Lynn was the child of whom nothing was expected and in this dynasty of dramatic swans, she was left to feel like the ugly duckling. In family photographs, she could always be picked out as 'the glum one'. 'As a child, you eventually get the feeling that you have nothing to offer,' she explained. Because he was away so often in Hollywood or on location around Britain, Lynn also felt that she never really knew her father. A charitable interpretation might be that Michael felt shy around her.

'My father, who never liked to enter a race unless he decided to win it, seemed to give up the challenge of winning her affection,' said Corin. Or it could be that Michael was so bound up in himself, he simply wasn't all that interested. And Lynn never felt she could really confide in Vanessa since she was the child of whom all things were expected. As a small child, Lynn found herself completely immobilised in her father's presence. 'My relationship with my father was a difficult one,' she admitted. 'I was very much in awe of him and I adored him, and I was terrified of him and I hated him and I loved him, all in one go.'

Even with Vanessa and Corin, Michael made it clear his eldest daughter was his favourite. 'As we grew up, it was always assumed that Vanessa especially was pure gold and that she was going to do remarkable things,' said Lynn. 'She would dance and sing soprano to entertain Dad and whatever her future was going to be, it could never be dull.' Playing favourites is one of the worst things a parent can do. Eventually, Corin grew jealous of the relationship because it made him feel just as much of an outsider as Lynn. Vanessa was always able to tell him things about Michael that he did not know – she shared her father's secrets in a way he never could. In turn, Lynn felt on the outside of Vanessa and Corin, partly because she was too young to join in their dressing-up games. Like most elder siblings, they seldom wanted their sister to play with them and there was a six-year age difference between Vanessa and Lynn. Corin would encourage Lynn to climb trees and leave her there while Vanessa's abiding memory of Lynn as a child was of a little girl trailing behind, sobbing, 'Wait for me!' Their relationships were summarised in one make-believe game where Vanessa played the US President, Corin was the British Prime Minister, while Lynn had the part of the President's dog.

As a small child, Lynn was anaemic and suffered bronchial attacks, which left her breathless. Despite her shyness and tendency to burst into tears, Lynn always thought of herself as resilient as a piece of rubber, always able to bounce back. Around this time, she was becoming an accomplished mimic and borrowed her father's tape recorder to make her own version of the BBC radio serial *Journey Into Space*, doing all the characters. She would play the tape back to Vanessa and Corin and keep them entertained. 'Faced with such competition, my only hope of attention within the family was to do imitations and make people laugh,' Lynn remembered.

Lynn wasn't a happy child: she was very lonely because there were no children of the same age near Bedford House and her older siblings were already away at school. With her parents often on tour and being too young to tag along with her brother and sister when they were home, she resorted to secret eating as a way of distancing herself from the rest of the family. 'I was fat and had set out to be, I think, for the very reasons I had set out to be funny as a way of coping with all the brotherly and sisterly competition,' she said. 'Being overweight was a wonderful way of opting out.'

At the age of seven, Corin was sent away to boarding school. It was the first time he and Vanessa had ever been separated and he hated his new school in Malvern Wells, where the headmaster was both supercilious and uncaring. 'I missed Vanessa terribly. I minded being separated very much,' he remembered. He would lie in the dormitory listening to the other boys crying for their parents. Sometimes the crying would continue for up to a week after term began and then again after half term. Beyond his dormitory window, he would hear the steam trains travelling to Paddington at night and would think of all the happy people on board: 'I just felt beyond crying,' Corin explained, 'that awful sadness that can't even express itself in tears.' Eventually, Michael noticed how miserable his son was and took him out of school after just one year. His boarding-school experience continued to affect Corin for a long time, however. Whenever he was away from home, he felt anxious and nervous.

Vanessa too was enrolled at a new day school for girls: Miss Spalding's in Queen's Gate. 'Your husband, Michael,' Miss Spalding told Rachel, 'is one of the intelligentsia.' But Michael and Rachel never got the children up in the mornings or picked them up from school – those chores were left to Michael's male lover, Bob Mitchell. Exotically described as 'half Red Indian', Mitchell (who had his own room in Bedford House) would walk Vanessa and Lynn to school. He even went on family holidays with them, munching sandwiches on overcast English beaches. 'I knew my father's "good male friend" through all my childhood,' Lynn remembered. 'My father's lover always told me that he wanted someday to have a child who would be just like me.'

Vanessa remembered her sexual awakening. She was playing hide-and-seek and she and another boy went off to hide in the bracken: 'I can remember terribly well lying there and suddenly for the first time I could smell the marvellous smell of masculinity. Except, you know, he was just a boy. Lying there, I suddenly became aware of him. I was ten or eleven, I suppose.'[4]

Like most little girls, Vanessa was ballet mad. She was enrolled at the beginner's class of the Ballet Rambert when she was eight. Michael and Rachel surmised that their eldest daughter was going to be far too tall to be a ballerina, though. Vanessa was 5'11" by the time she reached the age of fourteen. One day, appalled at her reflection in the mirror, she burst into tears and telephoned her mother (who was weekending in the country). 'Mummy,' she sobbed, 'I looked in the mirror and I can't see my head!'

Vanessa's realisation that she was too tall to become a ballerina led to the decision to become an actress. She started appearing in Queen's Gate school plays and, aged fourteen, played a Joan of Arc so powerful that her parents were awed. In fact, Michael claimed that the whole school revolved around her personality. Somehow, Walt Disney heard about the Redgraves' talented eldest daughter – he was looking for an English girl to play Alice in Wonderland in a live-action segment of the movie he was planning. The studio asked Michael and Rachel to send a photograph of their daughter. Vanessa, still self-conscious about her height, wrote how tall she was on the back of the photo. Delighted with what he saw, Disney then asked her parents to send their daughter to Hollywood for a screen test. However, the Redgraves decided against it. At the time, they were worried about Vanessa's health: she had started having blackouts and fainting fits – possibly a sign of insecurity over her parents' absences.

Now that she had grown too tall for ballet, Michael's first idea for his beloved daughter was that she should become a musical comedy actress. His thinking was that an actress who could sing and dance would always have a career. Vanessa enrolled at a decrepit dance studio in London's Soho, but quickly realised she wanted to play classical roles. Her father's friend, Peggy Ashcroft, was her inspiration.

Central School of Speech & Drama accepted Vanessa as a student and she began on 11 January 1955. Coming home after that first day, she told Michael, 'Oh Daddy, it was sheer bliss!' Every morning for the next six years she would take the tube from home to Gloucester Road station and emerge with her school bundle: leotard, black tights, The Oxford Book of English Verse and an inch-long piece of whalebone used for voice training. By this time, Rachel (who, like Michael, usually put art before money) had joined a new theatrical company based at the Royal Court Theatre. And it was at Chiswick House that the beanpole seventeen-year-old Vanessa first glimpsed Tony Richardson, the man she was to marry some seven years later.

Notes

1. *Sunday Telegraph Review*, 17 October 1999.
2. Redgrave, Deirdre and Brook, Danaë. *To Be a Redgrave*, Robson Books, London, 1982.
3. Lynn Redgrave, *Time*, 6 February 1989.
4. Evans, Peter. 'Vanessa: The Years that Made Her What She Is', *Daily Express*, 4 October 1966.

CHAPTER TWO

Perfection Is Not an Aim

Brian Moore, the Irish novelist, described Tony Richardson as 'the finest English director of his generation.' Moore was a maverick's maverick. The playwright John Osborne, with whom Richardson enjoyed his greatest successes, believed he was, 'just a few pence short of genius.' Tall and gaunt, Tony Richardson had a face like an Easter Island statue. He had a lanky, oddly jointed and endlessly restless body. Recounting some latest catastrophe, he would double up and massage his thighs with bony fingers, while gulping with convulsive laughter. Others compared his gaunt face and dangerous beak of a nose to an inquisitive bird of prey; his claw-like hands and feet seemed designed for grasping and climbing, his vulture-like gaze unnerving as he stared deeply into you.

One of the oddest of the many queer things about Tony was his voice. He spoke in a curious nasal drawl, full of darlings – da-h-ling – once compared to a winding-down foghorn. After you had heard it, you couldn't help but imitate it. But the theatrical camp was deceptive: underneath the limp, languid nonsense, he was a tough northerner. His cruelty made people afraid of him. Sensing their fear, he would turn on them, bullying those weaker than him.

Marianne Faithfull, who acted as Ophelia in Tony's 1969 production of *Hamlet*, described him as not just a bisexual narcissist but bitchy, sarcastic and ruthless to boot – you never knew what he might be saying about you behind your back. John Osborne, who was so obsessed with Tony that he wrote a play about him, thought him irredeemably treacherous. Tony's technique was to manipulate friends into positions of mutual suspicion and they would be too afraid of him to compare notes. He liked nothing better than to stir up a drama, vampirically feeding off on-set antagonism. Happily married couples would be at each other's throats within days and if people burst into tears, he would simply look surprised.

Cecil Antonio Richardson was born on 5 June 1928 in Shipley, a suburb of the Yorkshire town of Bradford. Tony always hated the name 'Antonio', which came from an uncle who died during the First World War. He was the only son of a lower-middle-class Shipley chemist, who was also a Conservative councillor. A keen Rotarian, the Shipley Rotary Club's motto – 'Service Before Self' – might have been Bert Richardson's personal creed. The Richardsons lived at 28 Bingley Road above the chemist's shop. Tony remembered his father as a deeply good man weighed down with responsibility. In those days, poor people could not afford doctors – this was before the National Health Service – and used chemists instead for their ailments. Bert Richardson was called on for almost everything apart from prescribing: Tony remembered his gentleness and patience when woken at all hours to deal with customers.

His mother Elsi came from a more affluent background than Bert. Her family looked down on the Richardsons for being 'trade' and thought she had married beneath her. Tony's mother was a reserved woman who tried to draw her outgoing, civic-minded husband away from doing the good works that meant so much to him. 'I loved her, but she was totally enclosed and hard-worked, looking after the household,' said Tony. His bedroom was on the top floor of the house alongside his parents' and a grandmother on his mother's side. Known as Ra, his father's mother was bedridden on the floor below. Her name suited her perfectly: because Ra owned the shop and the house they lived in, she was venerated like a totemic mummy-goddess. The family prostrated themselves before her. Maiden aunts always seemed to hover at the edges of the room, parting lace curtains with witchy fingers to criticise passers-by. 'So I lived in the world of these old women, a life of total, absolute protection,' was how Tony described it. He saw little of his father, who was always busy in the shop or out on council business. Bert eventually became mayor of Shipley.

Early on, Tony felt himself – like the anti-hero of *Look Back in Anger* – damned for being lower-middle-class: 'the thing that damns us all.' He was sensitive to the subtle class gradations of being a chemist's son. Where her family stood in the world was of great importance to Elsi Richardson. Tony couldn't say that he'd grown up in some tough Salford tenement – everything in the Richardson family home was draped with lace antimacassars, serviettes and tablecloths. Daintiness (he called it his 'secret shame') was all. His mother's social climbing left

Tony with a loathing of snobbery. At lunch parties at his home in the South of France, a theatrical knight would find himself sitting next to the butcher, a film star beside the cleaning lady.

However drab it may have seemed at the time, Tony grew to regard his Shipley suburb with affection. People who lived in Shipley were a mix of town and country with a unique blend of toughness, pride and dignity. Later, he would recognise how similar northerners were to Americans. Northerners sneered at southerners, who genuflected before state pomp and the Royal Family. What mattered was money, not class. 'Places like Bradford and Leeds, bastions of self-made men in the 19th century, men with a humorous, straightforward attitude to success and money, not at all sympathetic to any kind of class barriers, are very parallel to American ways of thinking,' he said.

Tony was sent to his first school – private and therefore 'exclusive' – when he was four. Known locally as 'Mr Manning's', he remembered it as being a dull Gradgrindian institution where he learned to read and write but not much else. He steered clear of the footballs and cricket bats dumped into what was laughably called the playground for twenty minutes each day. What he really liked was going out on walks alone. A lonely boy, hating and hopeless at games, he spent hours tramping the moors and learnt to name the flowers, birds and trees. He also taught himself how to call to the owls, which would answer and come to him, feeding from his hands. Throughout his life, the natural world remained an obsession.

His cosseted childhood in the sickly atmosphere of Bingley Road taught him how to manipulate people. From an early age, he learned the art of 'divide and rule' and once told set designer Jocelyn Herbert that as an only child – living with his parents, two grandmothers and an aunt – if he couldn't get what he wanted from one, he would get it from the other. As a child, divide and rule was chiefly used to persuade relatives to house the wounded animals and birds he brought in from his walks. House-proud Elsi didn't want dying animals in Bingley Road. Tony wondered if his need to keep animals came from an unconscious desire to mimic the way he was pampered and fretted over.

His first proper pet was a guinea pig, quickly followed by lizards, grass snakes, frogs and a terrapin. He snuck his pet rabbit out of the house to have it mated, then feigned ignorance when the creature gave birth – an immaculate conception which left his father nonplussed.

Shirley Williams, the Liberal Democrat politician who would become friends with Tony at Oxford, said: 'Tony was deeply responsive to the raw nature of the Yorkshire moors. It was a strong part of his childhood. I think he saw himself as a kind of bird of prey, a hawk or an eagle.'[1]

His other great passion was cinema going – or 'going to the pictures', as it was called. Tony's maiden aunt Ethel, whom Elsi treated as a servant, used to accompany her nephew to Salford's High Street picture palace. His favourites were the screwball comedies of Preston Sturges and Frank Capra or stirring adventure movies such as *The Four Feathers*, *Stagecoach* and *The Charge of the Light Brigade* – which he would later remake himself. Tony would have his greatest success combining comedy with the period film. (Ethel left everything to Tony after she died, which wasn't much. She also left him a heartbreaking note in which she said that he'd been the only person who ever treated her as a human being.)

Mr and Mrs Richardson, sensing that Tony, aged twelve, was becoming too cosseted in a household full of women, decided he needed toughening up. They sent him away to boarding school. Ashville College in Harrogate was about twenty miles northeast of Shipley. The school's religion was Methodist – a reflection, Tony thought, of what a minor public school it was. Methodism was Low Church compared to the pomp and ceremony of the Church of England. The best English public schools were Anglican, apart from a couple of Roman Catholic establishments. Tony despised Ashville College, which he castigated for the rest of his life. This was hurtful to those who taught him there, such as his English teacher C.N. Pleasance, uncle of the actor Donald Pleasance.

The night before he left for Ashville was the grimmest he'd ever experienced – a numb dread almost anaesthetised him from what he described as the 'oncoming horror', but not for long. Left at Ashville that first night, Tony found himself in a Spartan dormitory without carpets and curtains. The dozen boys in the dorm were issued with a single blanket each. That first night was freezing cold and they crawled into bed with each other for warmth. It was all totally innocent. Tony remembered shivering against a boy nicknamed 'Whammy' because he farted a lot. The atmosphere was gelid and unhappy. Occasionally, you would hear someone snivel with homesickness.

After a few nights of this, the dorm lights suddenly flicked on: it felt like the middle of the night. Ashville's headmaster stormed in and beat everybody for what they'd been doing. Tony remained nonplussed. Eventually he asked Whammy what they'd done wrong. 'Rubbing-up, I think,' Whammy told him ruefully, but Tony had no idea what he was talking about. Later that year, Ashville's headmaster was arrested for sodomising one of his pupils but the scandal was swiftly hushed up.[2]

Back home in Shipley, holidays were not much fun either. Tony and his father were growing estranged. As John Osborne once remarked, parents and children always end up disappointing each other. What time father and son did spend together was uncomfortable. Bert Richardson silently resented that Tony did not appreciate the sacrifices he'd made for him. Meanwhile, Tony couldn't care less: after all, he had not asked to be sent away to boarding school. It was only later when he realised how hard his father must have worked to give him a better start in life.

After the evacuation of Dunkirk in June 1940, RAF Bomber Command decided to requisition Ashville College. The school moved eighty miles northwest, deep inside the Lake District, one of the most dramatic and beautiful parts of England. Ashville's new home was Royal Windermere Hydro, an old-fashioned country hotel. After the move, the school became more informal. Tony continued to do badly in all his subjects, though – which were indifferently taught apart from English. The teachers failed to stimulate his intelligence. 'The place was monstrous, and there was no education,' he remembered. 'I just read, and lived in my own world.'

The move enabled Tony to roam the hills surrounding the school. Like Colin Smith, the anti-hero of his later film *The Loneliness of the Long Distance Runner*, he would go on solitary tramps as far afield as Grasmere, Keswick or the brooding, forbidding gray scree of West Water. Never before or since did he feel nature as such a breathing, living force. 'You could go sort of quietly Wordsworthian amongst the sort of woods and hills, and forget this sort of torture hole of existence,' he said.

Tony's teenage years were one long 'V'-sign flicked at authority. School taught him to say no. No to organised team sports, which he slunk off from; no to organised religion and a God he didn't believe in and no to petty rules and regulations. 'I learned that nobody can make you do anything you don't want to. I never played sports. I realised I could just say no, and they could do two things, throw me out – which they weren't going to do because they needed the fees – or beat me to death, and they didn't quite dare do that. So they couldn't break me,' he said.

Tony directed his first play at Ashville when he was twelve. Encouraged by Mr Pleasance, and inspired by the handful of theatre productions he'd seen, he started learning about stagecraft. Soon he was producing, directing and acting in most of Ashville's school plays. Productions staged include *Richard II*, *Romeo and Juliet* and *The Faithful Shepherdess*. Tony's knack for inveigling people into doing what he wanted was evident even then: he always cast himself in the plum role. During one production of *Henry IV*, he played Hotspur in Part One, only to decide that Prince Hal was the lead in Part Two. The audience was bewildered when he walked on again as a different character. His directing career at school ended on a high when his production of *Everyman* won an inter-school competition and he was written up in the press for the first time. Tony said: 'I wasn't going to be a diplomat, or a lawyer, or a politician, as my parents hoped. I was going to be a film director, and the way to start was in the theatre.'

Back in Bradford, Yorkshire, a senior figure in London's Old Vic theatre had opened a stage school. Esme Church had worked for Tyrone Guthrie, director of the Old Vic, during the Second World War. Guthrie was close to Michael Redgrave. The Old Vic had spent most of the war years touring the provinces. Church, an imperious figure, had decided to stay behind in Yorkshire to run an amateur theatre in Bradford. The Civic Playhouse became one of the best amateur dramatic theatres in Britain. Church decided to open a stage school as well. Students included future stars Bernard Hepton, Robert Stephens and Tom Bell. Billie Whitelaw was in the children's class. Another student, William Gaskill – who would go on to become a theatre director himself – remembered how dominating Church's personality was. The one person she didn't dominate was Tony, who joined the school during holidays.

Gaskill remembered Tony's 'elongated figure and squeaky drawl' as well as his ambition. 'He was iconoclastic about anything that was sentimental or old-fashioned,' he said. Returning from trips to London or Stratford, Tony would pour scorn on Church's shibboleths. Edith Evans was written off as Cleopatra, for example ('You should see her scrawny old chest'). Tony thought Britain's theatre tradition was so old and threadbare that it frayed to the very touch. He decided the Civic Playhouse theatre school was just as superannuated. With entrepreneurial flair, he set up his own rival theatre group, Shipley Young Theatre. His real reason for doing so wasn't so much on aesthetic grounds as feeling excluded by the rest of the school – 'I wasn't terribly acceptable to a lot of people inside it, and disagreed violently with most of them,' he said.

Tony persuaded Gaskill to help him run Shipley Young Theatre. They didn't have any funds, though. At the time, Bert Richardson was campaigning to become a Tory councillor. 'You've got to come canvassing for my father,' said Tony. 'But I'm a Socialist,' Gaskill squeaked. 'Look, do you want this production or not? It's the only way to get my dad to give us the money!' And so Shipley Young Theatre got the cash to stage its first show. Tony invited Esme Church to come along to his first production of *Comus*. Asked what she thought, Church observed, 'Well, dear, it's the sort of thing we used to do in the hall for the servants.'

Tony meanwhile had some exciting news. Having been rejected by Cambridge, he'd won a scholarship to read history at Oxford University. Going to Oxford changed his life. 'For me, it was such a liberation – spiritually and socially. Until then my life was hell,' he said. Councillor Richardson drove Tony and William Gaskill (who had also been offered a place) to Oxford for the first time in the autumn of 1948. The university was full of undergraduates who had fought and seen death up close during the war. Consequently, they were far more mature than undergraduates usually are. Those who'd been called up during the war returned to Oxford to finish their degrees, which meant demand for places was at a premium. That Oxford wanted Tony badly enough to offer him a scholarship makes his achievement even more impressive. Because the new Labour government was offering higher education for all, students were much more diverse than before. 'Tony flourished in the classless atmosphere. The dominance of people from privileged backgrounds had disappeared completely,' said his friend Shirley Williams.[3]

At Oxford, Tony's contemporaries included Margaret Thatcher, Kingsley Amis and Rupert Murdoch. Future Prime Minister Harold Wilson lectured in economics. Among his friends, Tony counted future politicians Jeremy Thorpe and Shirley Williams, but the contemporary who cast the longest shadow was Kenneth Tynan. When Tony arrived, the flamboyant critic and director was in his last term (Tynan only went down in November 1948 with a second-class degree). Tony bitched that Tynan's Oxford career had just one long letter home to his Birmingham parents – but then again, thought William Gaskill, weren't all their university careers just that? 'Tynan was brilliant – superficial, but brilliant. He would surround himself with adoring acolytes in Oxford tea shops whenever he came back up,' said Shirley Williams.[4]

Tony didn't think much of the intellectual quality of the university. Then again, he never felt any responsibility to do anything aside from having a good time – certainly not any work. Instead, he threw himself into amateur dramatics and made it clear to Gaskill that he wanted to use his time preparing to become a director. In those days, anybody who wanted to go into show business had to go through theatre. There were just 14,000 television sets in the London area and film was beyond reach. Nor was there any university drama department. Instead, there were two undergraduate societies. The Oxford University Dramatic Society was the more senior of the two and put on two plays a year: one out of doors, the other at Oxford Playhouse. 'I don't think Tony was much interested in putting on outdoors productions in college quads,' said his friend Nigel Davenport. 'The company at the Oxford Playhouse were the kind of professionals Tony aspired to be.'[5] At first, Tony was wary of joining the OUDS. He preferred the more left-field Experimental Theatre Club, although the word 'experimental' really meant more light-hearted – skits and musicals – than anything challenging.

But Tony was in a tremendous hurry: as if limbering up for his main assault, one of the first things he did was present his Shipley Youth Theatre production of *Doctor Faustus* in a local church hall. The chorus was three girls in white shifts, galumphing around the stage and making expressive movements like Isadora Duncan. It may have been terrible, but the point was to show those who ran the OUDS and ETC that he didn't need them, thank you very much. His first official Oxford production was *King John*, followed by *Romeo and Juliet* that same year. Tony loved a theatrical flourish. He announced that he had found his Juliet sitting in an Oxford greasy spoon cafe.

The myth was building. His reedy voice could be heard from several tables away in the college dining room making pronouncements such as, 'I cannot *bear Antony and Cleopatra* – they are my *noirest bêtes*!' His productions were impressive enough for him to be elected president of the ETC in the Michaelmas term of 1949. In the end, Tony had to join OUDS because that was where all the best actors were. The following spring, he directed a visually stunning *Peer Gynt* featuring future film director John Schlesinger as the Troll King. Planning *Peer Gynt*, he told actor Harold Lang, 'I see it all in rope.' As the director and film critic Lindsay Anderson remarked, a feeling for effect was very much part of Tony's talent.

Peer Gynt was the breakthrough in Tony's directing career. For the first time, he wasn't just imitating somebody else. Tony's friend Anthony Curtis remembered it as, 'the most exciting undergraduate production of the time, staged against a background of hanging ropes.' The production was deemed so remarkable that Tony was elected president of OUDS, considered the second most important student job after presidency of the Union. He was concurrently president of the ETC, the first time anybody had held both positions at the same time.

Anderson – whose time at Oxford overlapped Tony's, although they didn't meet there – said that he developed a reputation for being a real one-off. Theatre critic Irving Wardle was also a contemporary of Tony's at Oxford. He often encountered his heron-like figure crossing the quad to breakfast, carrying his post-war butter and sugar rations in jam jars. Tony seemed quite impervious to ridicule – he never lost his nerve. Not only was he president of both Oxford dramatic societies, he was also theatre critic of undergraduate magazine *Isis* to boot.

Introducing its new drama critic, *Isis* described him as, 'the *enfant terrible* of Oxford theatre.' Wardle developed what he called, 'a grudging awe for Tony Richardson, as he seemed to be plugged into some source of energy denied to the common herd. He seemed never to get tired. At three in the morning, with the cast dropping with exhaustion, he would be ready to take a fencing rehearsal.'

The OUDS provided Tony with the opportunity to travel abroad for the first time. In April 1950, the company toured France, where the author John Fowles – then a provincial teacher – hosted a lunch for them. He noted that Tony was, 'tall and nervous and excitable, rather like an overgrown child in many ways. Not artificial. A weak mouth and face, but intelligent, attractive eyes.'

That summer Tony began directing *King Lear*. The attraction for him was that the production was to tour America, the mythical country that had held such a grip on his imagination. He cast Peter Parker (who would later run British Rail) as Lear. Shirley Williams was Cordelia, John Schlesinger played Oswald and Robert Robinson (later to find fame as a television quizmaster) the King of France. The problem was that Tony didn't know what to do with the play. One of his ideas was to have Lear in a yellow duffle coat against a purple cyclorama. He had lots of ideas for effects, but not much insight into what the play was about. During the scene where Lear mourns Cordelia, Tony insisted Parker carry Williams with arms outstretched, like an altar. Even though Williams was petite, the strain of carrying her proved too much and a leather harness was made to support her.[6] Eventually, the cast mutinied and David William replaced him as director.

During his final year, Tony rented a room in Wellington Street. There, he kept a caged mynah bird, which shat all the time. He used his obsession with birds in his last Oxford production, *The Duchess of Malfi*. Tony had the Duchess keep a vivid green macaw on stage in an elaborate cage. Like the wolfhounds that Gertrude kept on a leash in Tynan's Oxford *Hamlet*, this flourish was much talked about at the time. Some thought it deeply symbolic. But Tony told screenwriter Gavin Lambert that it was just to do with his passion for exotic birds. Tony cast Nigel Davenport as the Cardinal.[7] Davenport remembered the first time he met Tony: with a girlfriend, he went to a party that Tony was hosting in his rooms. Davenport arrived drably dressed in his army demob suit. Tony pulled his girlfriend to one side and asked, 'Who's that terrible old pederast who's just walked in?' Reviewing *The Duchess of Malfi*, *Oxford Magazine* puts its finger on Tony's weakness for the flashy effect, describing him as, 'one of those who cannot leave a play alone.'

Tony only scraped a Third in English, which was hardly surprising since he didn't do any work. It was all a means to an end – and that end was becoming a professional theatre director. He would invite theatre managers from London to his shows. 'His ambition was enormous,' said William Gaskill. Tony compared his time at Oxford to splashing about in a children's swimming pool – great fun and you knew you could never get out of your depth. Leaving Oxford, now it was time for him to swim out into the colder, more treacherous waters of the real world.

Tony moved to London, where he rented a room from an acting couple in Praed Street, Paddington. He remembered the room as being small, dark and smelly, with rumbling from the tube trains below. The author Olivia Manning then rented him the basement flat in her house. Nigel Davenport remembered Tony, 'boxing around for a job. Tony was very good at networking and knew all the right people.' Eventually Manning helped him to secure a position as a trainee television producer at the BBC in May 1952.

Like Ashville College and Oxford, Tony was withering in his contempt for the BBC. 'The BBC is governmental, self-satisfied, smug. Cut off from what's really happening in life, or in the world,' he once said. One of his first jobs was assistant producer on a six-part series celebrating the married life of Queen Victoria. How that must have stuck in his republican throat. Still, the BBC worked Tony hard, teaching him how to direct quickly and without frills. Over the next five years, he would direct plays by Chekhov, Sheridan, Dostoevsky and Maupassant. Actors he worked with included Denholm Elliott, Maggie Smith and his future mother-in-law, Rachel Kempson.

Tony felt that his BBC colleagues were too Establishment in their attitudes: 'It's a dreadful institution filled with the most mediocre, pompous, middle-class British idiots you could imagine.' Any moment that Tony thought he'd shaken things up, they would soon go back to where they were: 'The BBC is a curious sort of, you know, octopus-like creature, that if you think you've made a little inroad then some other department comes along, and another sort of feeler comes out and strangles you from behind.' The highpoint of his television career came on 15 December 1955, with a live production of *Othello*. Tony broke new ground by casting black singer and actor Gordon Heath as the Moor rather than have another black up, like Olivier. Rosemary Harris was Desdemona. The cast also included Robert Hardy and Tony's university pal, Nigel Davenport.

So realistic was this production, said *The Times*, that the legendary playgoer who interrupted one theatre performance by shouting, 'You great black idiot, can't you see that it's all right?' would have smashed the glass of his TV set in fury. *The Times* praised Tony for the way he, 'brought this smouldering, unbearable play to life in a more concentrated and detailed form than any previous Shakespeare play produced on television.'

By the time he left, Tony was earning £19.04d a week at the BBC. His loathing for his colleagues was apparently reciprocal. 'I don't suppose really that they liked me any more than I liked them,' he admitted. Years later and doubtless not unaware of how Tony had disparaged them, BBC executives, turned him down after he approached them for a job when his career was on the downturn.[8]

On 16 May 1954, Tony's first West End play – an adaptation of Thomas Middleton's *The Changeling* – opened for a single performance at the Wyndham's Theatre. It also marked the first time Tony directed one of his favourite actresses, Diane Cilento. The Australian beauty remembered meeting him for the first time when he asked her to be in his play. Cilento said yes, not because she recognised him as a great theatrical visionary, but because she said yes to everything at the time. 'Tony was a gangling North Countryman so out of contact with his own body that he sometimes appeared spastic,' she recalled. 'He spoke in great gasps, expelling to breathe in bursts to emphasise words. His favourite word was "marvellous!"' Although technically the play was his professional debut, it was really just another amateur production. 'It was not well enough acted and without enough style for us to take very seriously,' opined the Manchester *Guardian*. 'But the intentions of the producer Tony Richardson were imaginative.'

His second London production was an adaptation of William Wycherley's *The Country Wife*, a Restoration Comedy with fops, cuck-olds, mistaken identity and moral duplicity. Already some key players in what would become Tony's loose repertory company were coming together. Nigel Davenport was drafted in alongside William Gaskill. *The Country Wife* opened at the Theatre Royal Stratford East for a three-week run. Reviews were warm, even if *The Times* complained that his approach was too farcical (Tony later felt he was the wrong director for it). 'Outrageously funny scenes are done very well indeed,' said the *Daily Mail*.

J.B. Priestley, meanwhile, was so impressed with what Tony had done with his BBC series, *You Know What People Are*, that he invited him to direct his new West End play, *Mr Kettle and Mrs Moon*. Tony remembered Priestley's play as terrible but he didn't know what he was doing. Once again, he lost the confidence of his cast and ended up being fired – 'rightly' in his opinion – with Priestley taking over the direction himself. *Mr Kettle and Mrs Moon* opened to lukewarm reviews on

1 September 1955 at the Duchess Theatre. *The Times* observed that Tony had gamely tried to do something with a comedy that never properly built to a climax.

Tony had also begun writing for *Sight & Sound*, the influential British Film Institute magazine. He wrote a long profile of Spanish director Luis Buñuel at the beginning of 1955. Like François Truffaut, he was working out his position and working methods through criticism. He praised Buñuel for his documentary *Land Without Bread* (1933) compared to the surrealism of his work with Salvador Dalí. *Land Without Bread* documented the appalling poverty of peasants living in the Spanish mountains. Tony shared Buñuel's sense of injustice. 'Reality here surpasses the bitterest nightmares of surrealism. The very conception of "art" here seems irrelevant. It is the most profoundly disturbing film I have ever seen,' he wrote. What Tony was groping towards was that, at its highest level, art was where fiction and non-fiction met (his best films could be documentaries, they were so realistic).

Tony also used the magazine to attack Establishment cinema – the Rank Organisation and Ealing Studios, which dominated British filmmaking. He argued it was a great mistake for English filmmakers to compete with Americans. Most British films were consciously set up for the American market. The problem was that British directors thought all the time in terms of speaking the same language instead of trying to make films specifically about their homeland. 'This is a permanent revolution that we all have to fight,' he wrote. 'What is so disheartening about the British cinema is that few of the producers have any convictions at all, their products are totally without vitality.' This call to the barricades, he admitted, made him appear 'ridiculous to everyone within the industry.'

Once again, Tony was preparing to attack. Now the time had come for him to make his first short film. He'd become friendly with Karel Reisz, another *Sight & Sound* contributor, who worked as a teacher in west London. The pair wanted to make a film sympathetic to the Teddy Boy phenomenon of working-class youths with Edwardian frock coats and Brilliantine quiffs, without the usual middle-England press hysteria. Bill Haley's 'Rock Around the Clock' had just been released and the papers were full of stories about teenagers rioting in cinemas. In contrast, Tony admired the Teddy Boys' freedom and vitality. He applied to the British Film Institute's Experimental Film

Fund for a £400 grant. His view was that the Fund should be used to make, 'the craziest, wildest possible experiments. It should never be reduced to anything but people doing lunatic things.'

Momma Don't Allow was a 25-minute documentary about kids dancing in a west London jazz club. At the time, Wood Green was a working-class neighbourhood. Pupils at the school where Reisz taught told him about Friday nights at the Fishmonger's Arms. Tony and Reisz shot their documentary over nine consecutive Saturday nights. The film begins with shots of youngsters finishing work for the day – a plain girl mucking out a British Rail carriage; a butcher wrapping meat – while Chris Barber's jazz band tunes up with a slow blues. Lonnie Donegan, the band's guitarist, would go on to create the British rock'n'roll sound of skiffle.

The club starts to fill up. What's remarkable is how middle-aged these not-quite-Teds look, with their suits, ties and pints of ale. The dancing starts. It's crude filmmaking with muzzy camerawork and overlaid sound. Already, Tony's sharp eye for class distinctions becomes apparent: a posh trio turn up in a Bentley, the driver taking care to pocket the hood ornament. He juxtaposes these Mayfair interlopers, who aren't quite taking it seriously, with the orgiastic jitterbugging going on around them. The film ends with the railway cleaner's orgasmic expression, as if she can't quite believe what's just happened.

Having made their short, Tony didn't know what to do with it. The pair became friendly with Lindsay Anderson, another critic who'd made his own short: *O Dreamland*, a sardonic look at Margate funfair. The three of them went back to the BFI for money to stage a one-night screening of their films at the National Film Theatre. Lorenza Mazzetti's *Together*, a touching study of a pair of deaf mutes living in London's East End, was the other film on the programme. Tony oversaw the programme notes with input from Anderson.

Ever the self-publicist, Anderson coined the gimmicky label 'Free Cinema'. The term was meant to signal a change of attitude within British filmmaking and was a reaction to didactic political films about herring fishermen or coalmining – the dominant English documentary tradition. The trio were trying to humanise short films, which had become boring abstract documentaries devoid of human feeling. In contrast, Free Cinema was interested in people, not social conditions. Tony never thought of Free Cinema as a movement – rather, it was a journalistic label: 'We were dealing with aspects of life that hadn't been dealt with by British movies at the time. We were just bringing contemporary life back into the arts. That's all we were doing.'

The phrase from the programme notes that stuck in Tony's head was 'Perfection is not an aim' and became his personal manifesto. He believed so many things disappeared with perfection: he'd far rather have owned a Constable sketch than a Constable painting as the sketch had a freshness and vision that often disappeared from the finished work. Tony said: 'I've never wanted to make anything that's perfect. I don't believe in perfection – I don't like perfection. I don't think there's such a thing. And if there is, it's inhuman.'

The rest of the manifesto was so vague as to be almost meaningless: the filmmakers demanded 'complete freedom of the artist, a close relationship between art and society, complete subjectivity, the expression of ideas firmly and forcefully stated'. As if anyone demanded the right to weakly suggest things. The manifesto was not unlike the wildly theoretical writings of French critic André Bazin that underpinned the Nouvelle Vague. Indeed, Tony came to loathe the way Anderson tried to support his films with a scaffolding of theory and dismissed his theorising as a sort of salesmanship under a guise of intellectualism. Free Cinema certainly worked as a headline-grabbing publicity ploy. One film company executive found himself having to explain to East European film buyers that no, it didn't mean he was making presents of his movies.

It is often assumed that Free Cinema was an anaemic reaction to what was happening in France with New Wave directors such as François Truffaut and Jean-Luc Godard. After all, it was Truffaut who said French cinema was in such a bad state that it was up to the amateurs to rescue it. However, Tony screened *Momma Don't Allow* more than a year before Truffaut began making his first film, *Les Mistons*, in 1957. It was French filmmakers who noticed what Tony had achieved with his little short. And so the New Wave gathered strength in London before breaking over Paris.

The big night at the National Film Theatre happened on 5 February 1956. Dilys Powell, film critic of the *Sunday Times*, spoke of Tony and the others as the 'white hopes' of British cinema. Mazzetti said: 'After the success of the first Free Cinema evening it became evident that London was ready for something completely new.' What she didn't know was that Tony was behind another new venture that was about to revolutionise the London arts scene. Having just turned British filmmaking upside down, he was to do the same with the stage. He had just helped secure the lease on a theatre in a drab Chelsea backwater: it was called the Royal Court.

Notes

1. Shirley Williams, author interview, 25 November 2009.
2. Richardson, Tony. *Long Distance Runner*, Faber & Faber, London, 1993.
3. Shirley Williams, author interview, 25 November 2009.
4. Shirley Williams, author interview, 25 November 2009.
5. Nigel Davenport, author interview, 24 June 2009.
6. Shirley Williams, author interview, 25 November 2009.
7. Nigel Davenport, author interview, 24 June 2009.
8. Tony Garnett, author interview, 22 June 2009.

CHAPTER THREE

Ever Feel You've Been Cheated?

Back in 1956, Sloane Square was a dingy thoroughfare: it was somewhere you drove through to get to Knightsbridge. This wasn't the Swinging Sixties so much as the Fading Fifties. In those days, there were no smart shops and no restaurants. The Royal Court Theatre, standing on the southeast corner of the Square, had seen better days, too. Once grand, it now showed cheeky farces. The origins of the modern Royal Court Theatre lay in the weird collision between a wool tycoon, a Communist, a blank-verse playwright and a music-hall comedian. 'Can you imagine a more incongruous combination?' cooed Tony.

Four years previously, Tony had found a mentor in George Devine, the distinguished actor and director. The trainee BBC producer wanted to cast Devine as the lead in an adaptation of Chekhov's *The Actor's End* retitled *Curtain Down*. He'd already seen Devine on stage in a 1946 London production of Thornton Wilder's *The Skin of Our Teeth*. Mentors often recognise themselves in their protégés. Like Tony, Devine had also been at Wadham College, Oxford. He too had been president of the OUDS, where he'd given John Gielgud the opportunity to direct his first play, *Romeo and Juliet*, in 1932. Devine had gone on to act in, or been involved in all the good revivals of classical plays in the 1930s as part of the Gielgud and Old Vic rep companies. Between 1935 and 1939, he and Michel Saint-Denis ran the London Theatre Studio together.

After the war they initiated (along with Glen Byam Shaw) the Old Vic Theatre School, whose graduates included Joan Plowright. The decision by Tyrone Guthrie, who had been Esme Church's boss at the Old Vic, to shut the theatre school in 1951 provoked an outcry. Devine struggled to keep the idea of the theatre school alive while working as a freelance director at Stratford. Michael Redgrave starred as *King Lear* for Devine during the 1953 season, with Rachel Kempson also in the cast playing Regan.

Having endured her husband's humiliating adultery for years, Rachel finally turned to another man for comfort. She began an affair with Byam Shaw during that Stratford season which lasted for 50 years. Rachel wrote in her memoirs that, 'Michael, being tolerant in these matters, was understanding and in a sense relieved.' There was talk that Michael and Rachel both shared Byam Shaw as a lover.[1] From the age of twenty, Byam Shaw had an affair with poet Siegfried Sassoon. 'No one has ever been sweeter to me than Glen,' wrote Sassoon, who referred to him in one poem as, 'my glorious angel.'

Devine could have spent the rest of his life in impeccably acted revivals of established classics. Instead, success made him impatient with an English theatre that resolutely faced the past. Indeed, he was so bored with costume drama that he turned Tony down at first. He then agreed to meet him for a drink. As a result, he agreed to be in his TV play. What really surprised Devine was when Tony rang him up the day after shooting to ask what he thought had been wrong about his direction. This marked the beginning of what Devine called their 'great friendship'. Tony was impressed by Devine's openness to new ideas, Devine in turn by Tony's intelligence. For Tony, Devine really was the embodiment of Doctor Dorn in Chekhov's The Seagull, the only one in the play who appreciates what the young playwright is trying to do. Indeed, Tony would cast Devine as Dorn fourteen years later in his revival of The Seagull. John Osborne said of Devine, 'He suffered talent gladly.'

In the days and weeks that followed, Tony and Devine often met to discuss their ideas for a new English theatre. Tony agreed with Arthur Miller when the American playwright said the English stage had become hermetically sealed from life. British theatre had stagnated: most West End plays behaved as if it was still the 1930s – and the early Thirties at that. What they were planning was nothing less than a revolution. 'We both had an idea of the sort of theatre we wanted to see in London, the kind of theatre we felt there was a complete lack of. A theatre that would present new interesting work and a large number of foreign plays which otherwise couldn't be seen in England,' Tony explained.

The friendship bewildered some of Devine's old friends. Devine was, after all, forty-three to Tony's twenty-five. Furthermore, he was on first name terms with all the established names of the London stage: Gielgud, Olivier, Edith Evans, Ralph Richardson and Peggy Ashcroft.

Why should a man of Devine's authority promote an inexperienced outsider like Tony into equal partnership? Devine's own mentor, theatre teacher Michel Saint-Denis, put a finger on it: 'George is in love.' Tony's own view was that they complemented each other perfectly: 'We both are sort of good at the things the other isn't good at.'

Nigel Davenport believed that Tony was the real mover behind the Royal Court.[2] He and Devine decided to lease a London theatre and establish a small permanent company there. Tony used his emollient charm to persuade a wealthy lady addicted to both brandy and wearing artistic kimonos to support the project. This patroness assured him that she would provide all the cash but her chemical magnate husband balked at such an esoteric adventure. 'Our scheme for starting the Court fell through because we had no one to put up the money,' said Tony. Meanwhile, property developer Alfred Esdaile had acquired the lease of the Royal Court Theatre in May 1952. During the Edwardian era, the Court was famous for its seasons of George Bernard Shaw and modern British and European plays, including Ibsen.

Esdaile was what you might call a 'card': a retired music-hall comedian who sported a monocle and spats, he used to put on nude reviews. One of his innovations was having nude models recline on a revolving stage, getting round Lord Chamberlain's rule that any on-stage nudity had to be immobile. His idea for the Royal Court was to open a theatre with a supper club upstairs. Esdaile wanted to recreate something with a spicy whiff of the music hall 'good old days'. Clement Freud, the deliciously deep-voiced brother of painter Lucien Freud, would run the nightclub and restaurant upstairs.

Esdaile brought in Oscar Lewenstein to be artistic director and theatre manager. Lewenstein was a politically committed theatre producer who combined Marxism with an acute business sense. The card-carrying Communist knew all about the Royal Court's history and had a different view to Esdaile: he wanted to put on modern plays. The question was whether Esdaile would allow another theatre company to sublet the Court. Unaware that Lewenstein was of the same mind, Devine went to see Esdaile with a proposal for he and Tony to run the theatre but Esdaile wanted too much money. At the time, the Court was having a good run with another comedy.

Unbeknownst to both Tony and Devine, there was another development in the West Country. Ronald Duncan was an Establishment poet,

High Church Anglican and sometime dramatist. He was also a disciple of T.S. Eliot, who had become disillusioned with West End theatre after his one and only verse-drama success, *This Way to the Tomb*. Duncan had founded his own theatre in Devon with the rustic name of The Taw and Torridge Arts Festival. The board's chairman was Neville Blond, the theatre-struck head of Emu knitting wool. Lord Harewood, opera devotee and first cousin to the Queen, was also a board member, as was Lewenstein. Blond insisted that Duncan's theatre must be based in London. The Devon group settled on the derelict Kingsway, which was also part of Esdaile's property portfolio.

Lewenstein remembered Devine going to see Esdaile and proposed a merger. In March 1955, he nominated Devine as artistic director. Devine accepted the job, turning down an offer to run the Royal Academy of Dramatic Art, and insisted that Tony become his associate director. The distinguished actor/director then had to accept a counterproposal – that the first season must contain two new plays by Duncan. 'There'll be trouble, of course,' said Tony with relish. Devine disliked Duncan, nicknaming him the 'Black Dwarf' on account of his malevolence and short stature. Tony, too dismissed Duncan as 'part of the blank verse shit tradition of Christopher Fry and T.S. Eliot.'

On 21 July 1955, the renamed English Stage Company was launched in the derelict shell of the Kingsway. Bomb damage meant its stage was open to the sky and the auditorium was full of rubble. The Kingsway turned out to be so cratered as to be unusable. In any case, Esdaile wanted to sell it. Instead he offered Tony and Devine another of his properties: the Royal Court. Not that this was in much better shape than the Kingsway. The actress Diane Cilento said everybody warned them not to do it because the Royal Court was so rundown and shabby.[3] There were no workshops, drains flooded the stalls and playwright John Mortimer later described the dressing rooms as 'a disgrace to civilised society.' It is important to remember how at odds this High Church Anglican, ex-Music Hall comedian and card-carrying Communist were. Each had different visions of what the Court should be. Only the royal, liberal Lord Harewood supported Tony and Devine's plans for what they termed a 'writer's theatre.'

Tony and Devine started putting together a repertory company for the Royal Court's first season. Rachel was one of the first to sign up. The Redgraves had recently moved into what Michael called, 'a large, hideous flat behind Harrods.' With Vanessa still at Central, Corin at Westminster and Lynn still at Queen's Gate, 3 Hans Crescent was more convenient than Chiswick. Joan Plowright, Alan Bates and Mary Ure – then unknowns – joined her. The Court could only afford to pay them far less than the going rate, less even than subsidised theatres paid. The top salary, earned by four members of the company, was £30: four were on £20, four on £15 and another four on £10 a week. Assistant stage managers, including Lindsay Anderson and William Gaskill, earned £1 a week. The ten-year-old Arts Council awarded the fledgling ESC a grant of £7,000. They badly needed more cash to set up with.

Tony moved from Olivia Manning's basement flat to the top floor of Devine's house in Chiswick. The top floor of the 18th-century house had been converted into a modernist flat. It was a long, low studio divided by screens, with a flat roof and other features that made it resemble a ship. Tony loved it. He installed an aviary of some forty South American parakeets plus a toucan. Diane Cilento remembered evenings when they would sit round Devine's kitchen table drinking plonk. Tony and Devine would fulminate against the appalling state of British theatre. Devine suspected that West End theatre impresario Binkie Beaumont and the rest of the gay Mafia were the real problem. They would all start singing a made-up song:

A stands for Arsehole,
Poo Poo,
B stands for Buggery.
If you want to get a job
You godda sell your knob
To dirty old Binkie B.

The hypocrisy is breathtaking considering Tony's own sexuality. Not that he gave much evidence of being homosexual at this time. Devine's biographer Irving Wardle thought of Tony as being sexless; he ploughed all his sexual energy into his driving ambition. In fact, most of the inner circle of the Royal Court was gay – something Devine chose to ignore. Apart from Tony, assistant directors Anthony Page and Lindsay Anderson were both homosexual. In Anderson's case, it took a long time for Tony's friend to acknowledge the blindingly obvious. For a start, Anderson was a virgin so he could only have 'come out' in theory. His habit of singing when busy led to Tony nicknaming him 'the singing nun.' 'I think we should just push him into a Turkish bath and leave him there,' Tony once said.[4]

Meanwhile, Tony still had to earn a living. Devine employed him as his assistant director at the Shakespeare Memorial Theatre in Stratford that autumn. Two years previously, Devine had directed Michael Redgrave at Stratford, where he had scored an astonishing hat trick starring in *Antony and Cleopatra*, *King Lear* and the *Merchant of Venice* to laudatory reviews. Tony's job was to relay notes to the cast. Donald Pleasance remembered Tony used to put his head round the door and say, 'George thinks ... And we used to shout, "F**k off!"'

The Royal Court Theatre finally opened on 2 April 1956 – three years after Tony and Devine first met – with Angus Wilson's *The Mulberry Bush*. Tony hoped that Wilson would turn out to be the English Chekhov, but it was not to be. The season's second play was Arthur Miller's *The Crucible*, which Tony was eager to direct himself but the board thought him too inexperienced. He chafed at being Devine's assistant. Reviews for both plays were sympathetic, if guarded. Tony was then let loose on the Royal Court's third play, which had won a competition for new works after Devine had placed an advert in *The Stage* – this was what he and Devine meant by a 'writer's theatre.' Privately, Tony believed *The Crucible* would be the real money earner. The play that he'd been given was called *Look Back in Anger*.

Look Back in Anger went off with all the power of an anti-Establishment bomb. In Jimmy Porter, playwright John Osborne invented a contemporary malcontent with whom the younger generation could identify. The portrayal of Porter had an extraordinary impact, representing the mood of a generation disenfranchised from its past and dubious about the future. 'You've got to picture an England where young people had nothing to do and nowhere to go,' said Vanessa, who was herself in the first-night audience with her parents. 'Nothing resonated with them, nothing.' The playwright Mark Ravenhill has described the first night of *Look Back in Anger* as being the equivalent of the Creation Myth in British theatre. Before *Look Back*, the myth goes, there was only void. Kenneth Tynan said he could, 'scarcely remember the theatrical landscape as it was before George Devine set up shop in Sloane Square and called in John Osborne, the Fulham flamethrower, to scald us with his rhetoric.' Another young theatregoer with whom the play resonated was future Social Democrat leader David Owen. 'The generation of angry young men writing for the Court changed the perceptions of a post-Imperial Britain as swiftly and assuredly as any politician,' he remembered.

In August 1955, Devine placed an advertisement in *The Stage* to state that the Royal Court was looking for new writing. On 4 May that year, John Osborne – an out-of-work actor – had started writing a play. He'd written an unproduced work before. He finished his new play in six weeks and put it in the post. Around twenty-five managers and agents had already rejected the work when Osborne posted his script to the English Stage Company. One rejection letter described the play's anti-hero as, 'just another neurotic who had not the courage to take in his stride the youthful shocks and sufferings that most people experience'. *Look Back* was just one of 675 plays that flooded into the Royal Court. Osborne resigned himself to yet another rejection.

On reading the play, Devine passed the typescript to Tony, whose customary play-reading method was to read the first and last pages of any new play and then one more page at random around the middle. 'That's quite sufficient,' he would say. This particular play, however, held his attention. 'By the time I was through the first act,' he recalled, 'I knew, whatever battles to come, we'd win the war. It confirmed everything we were trying to do. Columbus knew there was something out there when he set out for America. We knew, too – and there it was when the play arrived.'

The writer Anthony Curtis remembered visiting Tony in Hammersmith one boiling hot afternoon. As he served tea on his rooftop terrace, Tony told Curtis how important he thought the play would be. Curtis, who knew Tony was prone to exaggeration, didn't take him seriously.

Osborne recalled the moment he met Tony – an exotic-seeming, loping creature, who looked about seven feet tall. At the time, the playwright was living with his friend Anthony Creighton on a smelly barge in Chiswick. As both were on the dole, it was the cheapest accommodation they could find. Posters of Marlon Brando in *The Wild One* and other Hollywood beefcake on the walls made Tony wonder if they were lovers. They were not actually lovers, although homosexual Creighton did have a crush on Osborne and behaved like a dutiful wife.[5] Creighton said Osborne was the most important person he had ever known.

'It was an idyllic period, the happiest time of my life. When he was in London, everywhere John went, I went too – if he was going to post a letter, he would say, "Are you coming?" Creighton remembered.

Tony came straight out with it and said, 'I think you've written the best play since the war.' Osborne was struck by how unequivocal he was about it. Tony then announced – 'like a confiding toastmaster' said Osborne – that he himself would direct it. He pressed Osborne to polish his vituperative dialogue and soon learned that he wasn't interested in any rewrites. 'What came out was what you got, and it was up to you to make the best of it,' said Tony.

Around this time, he began asking friends and colleagues to read the play, studying their reaction. It became a kind of litmus test: either you were for us or against us. One theatrical grande dame told Tony that the script should be thrown into the river and washed out to sea, never to be seen again. When he relayed this back to Osborne, Tony relished every syllable. Tony also expected Ronald Duncan to hate the play when he showed it to him. 'He actually likes it,' he said, unable to hide his disappointment.

Rehearsals began. Tony discouraged Osborne from talking to the actors. Neither was Osborne allowed to talk to Devine. Having had plenty of experience in Shipley, Tony was adept at divide-and-rule. He controlled an iron conspiracy that intimidated everybody into acquiescence. It was the Court's publicist, George Fearon, who came up with the phrase 'angry young man' – he hadn't meant it kindly either. Fearon told Osborne how much he disliked his play and how difficult it would be to publicise but the phrase caught the public's imagination. To drum up publicity, Tony and Devine started to take all the theatre critics out to lunch, ranking them in descending order of importance. Kenneth Tynan was first to be wined and dined. Tony explained what the Court was trying to do, but Tynan was sniffy. When Tony ran down the list of plays for the first season, Tynan stopped him at *Look Back* and told him to change the title. According to him, it sounded like a dreadful Thirties melodrama.

One day Tony and Oscar Lewenstein sat in the cafe opposite the Court making predictions about this first season. They agreed *The Crucible* would be the biggest success, while *Look Back* would be lucky to cover its costs. The cast felt just as uncertain about the play. Kenneth Haigh, who played Jimmy Porter, would omit chunks of monologue because he didn't 'feel' them. Tony witheringly observed that audiences expected, 'To be or not to be' in *Hamlet* – even if the actor was feeling decisive. On the night of the dress rehearsal, Devine sat in the stalls next to Joan Plowright watching his director and leading man argue down below. *Look Back* ends with a saccharine speech in which Porter promises to make amends to his wife – he is, after all, just a 'lonely bear' and she's his 'little squirrel'. After the final scene of mawkish reconciliation, Devine turned to Plowright and asked what she thought of, 'that squirrels' and bears' business'. Plowright admitted it made her feel a bit queasy. 'Thank God,' he replied. 'I thought it was just me getting old!'

The production opened on 8 May 1956, starring Haigh as Porter and Mary Ure as his wife, Alison. Ure was something of a name. The Scottish actress had played a truly deranged Ophelia opposite Paul Scofield's Hamlet the year before at Stratford. With her white-blonde hair and red, red lips, Christopher Isherwood thought she was even more beautiful than Marilyn Monroe. (Tony believed there was always something holding Ure back, though – possibly a Presbyterian disapproval of performance itself.) The first-night audience gasped when the curtain rose on a realistically squalid attic flat with an ironing board dead centre. Binkie Beaumont walked out during the interval; Terence Rattigan had to be persuaded to stay. Most of the audience sat in stony silence. They were, Osborne noted, 'ill at ease; they had no rules of conduct as to how to respond ... mostly they were adrift, like Eskimos watching a Restoration comedy.' The curtain descended and after two hours of Osborne gobbing at the Establishment, the audience then stood for the National Anthem.

Tony remembered the first reviews as nearly all crushing. Milton Shulman in the *Evening Standard* called the play a 'failure', condemning its 'self-pitying snivel.' The *Guardian*'s reviewer said the play made him feel numb, while the *Evening News* called it, 'the most putrid bosh.' Tony did his usual thing of affecting scorn – 'Well, what on earth did you expect? You didn't expect them to like it, did you?' He always feigned astonishment whenever he lost a battle in the war against the philistines. Privately, he thought they'd have to pull *Look Back* after just four performances. Ticket sales were so poor that the Court considered flyposting a psychiatrist's testimonial that, yes, shock, this was how some young men today really did behave and talk.

It took until the weekend for the Sunday newspaper critics to rally to *Look Back*'s defence. Kenneth Tynan in the *Observer* and Harold Hobson in the *Sunday Times* both gave rave reviews. Tynan famously wrote that he could not love anyone who did not wish to see *Look Back*, describing it as the best young play of its decade. He admitted that what Tony and Osborne had achieved was, 'likely to be a minority taste. What matters, however, is the size of the minority. I estimate it at roughly 6,733,000, which is the number of people in this country between the ages of 20 and 30'. The play also found an unexpected champion in government minister Richard Crossman, who said of Osborne: 'He has a great intuitive understanding of what people are feeling and can vomit into print bilious emotions felt by people too decent to express themselves aloud.'

In July, the audience was invited – a first for the London stage – to stay behind and discuss the play with Tony and the cast. Around 200 people accepted this invitation. Ticket sales lifted after an 18-minute excerpt was shown on television. The Court became full of young people, many of whom had never been to the theatre. *Look Back* went on to run for 151 performances in total. The Soviet Union then invited the Court to stage *Look Back* at the Moscow Arts Theatre as part of its 1957 International Youth Festival. Tony, Osborne, Anderson and others flew out to Moscow. Osborne came home early and wrote a newspaper article criticising Tony and the Court for having, 'Red Stars in Their Eyes.'

When the first-night audience gasped at the ironing board centre-stage, it was because this was the first time that a play had presented life as it then was: the saggy-with-rain gloom of a wet Sunday. Tony's production was the first time in generations this had been done on stage. English theatre had become a completely class-bound entertainment reflecting the ideas of 1930s society. None of the other plays being performed that Tuesday night even vaguely related the vast social and economic changes that had happened. In the West End, cocktails were still being shaken by men in dinner jackets ('Cigarette?' 'Thenks'). But Tony's most important achievement was putting on a new play by a fresh writer about vital contemporary issues – and to make it matter to people who didn't normally go to the theatre. As Richard Findlater put it in *At the Royal Court*: 'When people talk about the Royal Court, in the world of the arts, they don't just mean a playhouse in

London, on the eastern side of Sloane Square. The Royal Court is more than a building. It is an attitude, a discipline, an inheritance, a global constituency whose members are scattered throughout the performing arts.'

And it wasn't only the Soviets who were interested in *Look Back*. David Merrick, the New York theatre impresario who would produce all of Tony's early Broadway plays, arranged the American transfer. Tony returned briefly to London and flew on to New York. What he loved most about Manhattan was that the whole city seemed geared around theatre. If he had one reservation, it was that the moneyed Broadway audience expected foreign plays to be brought to them like exotic animals, to be prodded and poked like a circus elephant.

Merrick was so worried about what he was taking on that he decided to forgo the usual out-of-town tryout and instead open the play cold. That way, at least he could quickly cash in on the play's notoriety. He designed an ad showing a nude man and woman locked in a passionate embrace on the floor. The *New York Times* refused to run it, despite being assured no such scene took place.

Look Back opened at the Lyceum Theatre on 1 October 1957. Tony remembered being taken to Sardi's Restaurant for the obligatory first-night meal. It was as if the place was frozen until the *Times* review came in. Tony and the others sat in stasis nursing a single drink. Thankfully, the review was good. Suddenly menus were produced and orders taken. *Look Back* became a huge critical and commercial success. The New York Drama Critics' Circle awarded it Best Foreign Play of the season. Merrick, whose nickname was the 'Abominable Showman', proved himself a master promoter. One night a girl, outraged by Jimmy Porter's hostility to women, climbed on stage and hit Kenneth Haigh with her umbrella. Merrick later came clean that he'd paid an actress $250 to create some column inches.

Looking back himself, actor Michael Sheen – who played Jimmy Porter in a later revival – compared the impact of *Look Back* to another anti-monarchist revolutionary moment. 'It must have been like seeing the Sex Pistols for the first time,' he said. 'Like Johnny Rotten crouched on the edge of the stage growling, "ever feel like you've been cheated?"'

Notes

1. Danaë Brook, author interview, 8 December 2010.
2. Nigel Davenport, author interview, 24 June 2009.
3. Diane Cilento, author interview, 1 December 2010.
4. Lambert, Gavin. *Mainly About Lindsay Anderson*, Knopf, New York, 2000.
5. Brooks, Richard. 'Gay Claim Angers Osborne Family,' *Sunday Times*, 15 December 2002 and De Jongh, Nicholas. 'The Secret Gay Love of John Osborne', *Evening Standard*, 24 January 1995.

CHAPTER FOUR

A Conscience the Size
of Grand Central Station

*L*ook *Back in Anger* also provided Vanessa Redgrave with one of her earliest roles. Her first paying job after leaving drama school was with a summer season repertory theatre company in a play titled *The Reluctant Debutante* in the Essex seaside town of Frinton. The rep company had to rehearse ten plays in as many weeks and the season consisted mostly of tried-and-tested thrillers such as *Dial M For Murder* and *Witness for the Prosecution*. She found it hard-going surviving on her first wage packet of £7 a week.

Vanessa had still been at Central when she discovered her first Great Cause. There, she had chafed at her dull, uninspiring teachers and the school's drilling on elocution and deportment. It was all so colourless. Where was the meat of acting, the Stanislavsky Method, which so enthused her father? Meanwhile, she read daily newspaper accounts of the Soviet clampdown in Hungary: tanks were roaming the Belgrade streets, machine-gunning civilians to death. It was the first note of what would be a theme in Vanessa's life – fighting Russian tyranny. She badgered Cousin Lucy with political questions, although Lucy gave up when Vanessa asked her to define inflation. 'You can do that one,' Lucy wrote to Michael.

A Hungarian relief organisation was appealing for volunteers to help sort and pack clothes for refugees pouring into Austria. Vanessa told her parents that she was dropping out of drama school to become a volunteer charity worker. Training to be an actress seemed of no importance, she said. She spent the autumn of 1956 sorting out clothes at a house in Ladbroke Grove. 'Reality, in the form of the Hungarian political revolutions, had burst through the limits of my student life and my ambitions,' she wrote. Lynn suspected there was also a dramatic angle: Vanessa always thought of herself as Joan of Arc. 'A bit of the touch of the martyr,' said Lynn. All her causes were somewhere far afield, at a great distance from her own life, and always something dramatic.[1] Scrubbing old women's bed pans this was not. Lynn said: 'If politics were to enter into it, it was clear from the start she would either have to be the first woman prime minister or something very, very Far Left. Ordinariness was out.'

Vanessa inherited her sense of injustice from her parents. Both Michael and Rachel were Socialists. During the war, Michael got involved in a pacifist organisation called People's Convention until he realised it was a Communist front. In fact, the BBC banned him from appearing on radio. Unlike his daughter, he decided injustice wasn't worth damaging his career over and he went silent on politics after that. Rachel, too was a firm Socialist. Vanessa remembered an embarrassing scene at the age of eight when her mother got involved in a doorstep argument with a Tory canvasser. The blue-rinsed woman became incensed when Rachel told her she was voting Labour. The argument must have been ferocious for Vanessa to remember it so clearly. She clutched her mother's hand ever more tightly, not wanting anybody to be cross with her.[2]

Michael's career was very much on the ascendant when Vanessa was at Central. He was the lead at the Shakespeare Memorial Theatre at Stratford, where he played Hamlet, Shylock and Lear. For a moment it seemed as if he would even eclipse Olivier as Britain's pre-eminent classical actor. Corin saw his father on stage just before he started at Westminster School. The children had been taken to see him playing the Shakespearian tragedies. Rachel was also in the company, playing Octavia and Regan.

Corin, too carried the Redgrave acting gene. He fell so in love with theatre that, age eleven, he learned the whole of *Richard II* by heart in six weeks: 'I learned to love the sound of Shakespeare from my father. Like John Gielgud, he had an effortless command of the rhythms, cadences and stresses of blank verse. But it was my mother who taught me to love Shakespeare's stories.' Corin himself began acting at Westminster, where he was Portia in *The Merchant of Venice* and the lead in *The Cherry Orchard*. His English master, who directed school plays, had acted opposite Rachel at Oxford. It was the Chekhov in particular that stuck with him. Years later, he would present the Russian author's collected works as a sacramental gift to his daughter. He was given special dispensation to be allowed out of school to play a page in Bernard Shaw's *Saint Joan* at the Embassy Theatre, with Rachel in the title role.

Being the season's star at Stratford was all very well, but it didn't pay to support the Redgraves' sumptuous lifestyle. The taxman finally caught up with Michael and he was forced to sell Bedford House and move his family out to a modest Hampshire cottage called Wilks Water. There was also a studio outbuilding that he converted into a retreat for himself featuring a sitting room, bedroom and a tiny bathroom; he decorated it with posters featuring himself. Growing up, the children continued to approach Michael with respect bordering on awe. His reserve was almost supernatural. They played out the drama of the close-knit theatrical family as well as they did Shakespeare. To observers, this was as unreal as a painted stage set: the Redgraves never seemed to have rows and the absence of conflict was almost sinister. Their world was made up of lines and gestures – as Vanessa put it, of rejoicing in each other's achievements. When it came to practical proof of love, they were speechless, however.[3]

The final play in Vanessa's debut rep season was *Look Back in Anger*, a surprisingly adventurous choice for Frinton. It was a gamble that paid off; every seat was sold out. Vanessa played the part of Helena, the actress who winds up with Jimmy Porter and she was desperate for Michael's approval. Like most children, she wanted her parents' approbation and she had spent most of her formative years watching him act. He taught her, she revealed, not to run off a copy of what she did the night before, but to find a new spontaneity within herself for each performance – 'I don't think there is an actor who can touch my father,' she once declared.

Vanessa invited Michael to see the Friday-night show. After the performance, he took her out to dinner at the hotel where he was staying. Father and daughter sat in silence for what seemed to Vanessa like a quarter of an hour; Michael kept staring out of the window or at the space above her head, drinking whisky. Eventually he sighed and told her that he wanted her to play his daughter in his next movie, *Behind the Mask*. Brian Desmond Hurst, known as 'Desdemona' to his friends, was to be the director. Not exactly a procurer, Hurst saw himself as a kind of Ganymede – cupbearer to the gods. He would host male-only parties at his mews house in Kinnerton Street, Belgravia, where local army guardsmen looking to earn a bit of extra cash would consort with homosexual MPs. Michael was also a visitor. Vanessa remembered going to see Hurst in his house and thinking how expensive it all looked. In her earnest way, she asked the director what political causes he felt strongly enough to march for. Hurst promptly replied, 'That would depend on the weather.'

Behind the Mask, based on John Rowan Wilson's novel *The Pack*, was a medical drama set in a large hospital and was about an investigation into a patient's death. Michael was playing an eminent surgeon opposed to reform. What could have been a potentially involving medical drama was smothered by a saccharine romance between Vanessa and an idealistic young doctor (Tony Britton). She was given the full 1950s starlet treatment with a tight perm, tailored costumes and caked-on make-up. Michael burst into tears when he saw the rushes, assuring Vanessa that she possessed a 'divine gift.' Since the 'gift' was derived from him, in paying her the compliment he was deifying himself.[4]

Comparing his daughter to Sarah Bernhardt, Michael wrote: 'If I say she is mad, I mean divinely mad.'[5] However, Michael had not always been supportive of Vanessa's acting ambition. He once bitchily introduced her to friends as 'my daughter Vanessa – she'll never be an actress, so we're having her do languages. That way she can get a job with an airline or something.' Meanwhile, critics praised her as a major new talent while her sister Lynn said the surprise would have been had she failed.

Michael kept in touch with Hurst right up until the end of the 1970s. During this time, his sexual tastes became increasingly kinky and he enjoyed clanking around naked inside a suit of armour so that it cut him.[6] By now, Hurst was procuring teenage boys for London show-business figures. One teenager who visited Hurst remembered Michael being there with a man in black leather called 'Big John.' After some conversation, Michael left on the back of Big John's motorbike. Once they'd left, Hurst told this teenager that Michael's particular kink was to have a thread sewn through both nipples and his penis, forming a triangle. Big John would then have to fire ping-pong balls at the cringing actor.[7]

Of course, one must ask what Rachel was doing in staying with a partner who was repeatedly unfaithful to her with both sexes. 'My father's affairs must have made my mother very unhappy,' conceded Lynn. 'I think she was a saint. I cannot imagine how my mother and father weathered what they did, something bound them together. There are different kinds of love and different kinds of needs. They must have needed each other very much or they wouldn't have stayed together all those years.'

Rachel seems to have ignored Michael's infidelity, perhaps partly for the sake of the children and partly because she may have been too cowardly to start again. After all, it takes more energy to smash up a marriage than it does to ignore what's wrong with it. In the mid-1960s, Rachel explained in a conversation with her future daughter-in-law Deirdre that although the Redgraves were brilliant, they were also selfish people who always put themselves or their causes first. She herself was no longer able to strike out on her own. Lynn advised her mother to leave Michael – 'I thought she'd be happier if she didn't stay,' she explained, 'but it's her life. Perhaps she didn't make the decision to stay so much as she didn't know how to take the next step.'[8]

Michael had by now been knighted for his services to theatre. Rachel certainly enjoyed the trappings of being the wife of a theatrical knight. It took her three years before it occurred to her to tell Deirdre to stop addressing her as 'Lady Redgrave'.

Growing up, Vanessa and Corin never talked about their father's bisexuality, although they had an unspoken understanding. They knew something odd was going on. For a start, Michael and Rachel had completely different circles of friends. 'From my early days I sensed there was something odd about their marriage,' said Lynn. 'Tension was ever-present in our house. I saw that my parents maintained separate rooms, and that my friends' parents shared a bed.' Even if the family spent an evening together, Michael would inevitably announce that he was going out. He would always be vague as to where he was going. According to Oscar Lewenstein, Vanessa only discovered that her father was bisexual when she was 20.[9] Behind the façade of family Sunday lunches and the idyllic country cottage, Michael had been living a secret double life.

Vanessa made her West End debut on 31 January 1958, again playing opposite her father. Frith Banbury and Binkie Beaumont cast Vanessa as Michael's daughter in *A Touch of the Sun*, a new play by N.C. Hunter. She found herself staying in the same digs where Michael had first lived with Rachel. 'Vanessa a distinct hit with audience (and Binkie),' Michael noted in his diary on the day when the play opened during its Liverpool tryout run. Beaumont reminded Michael of Olivier's portentous words on the play's opening night at London's Saville Theatre: 'Tonight a great actress has been born.'

Vanessa might have been a great actress but that Christmas she was back to playing Jack, the principal boy in the pantomime *Mother Goose* at Leatherhead Theatre in Surrey. There was lots of thigh-slapping and on-stage knockabout. However, Vanessa was accepted to join the Royal Shakespeare Company in the spring 1959 season. Meanwhile, she had fallen in love with a man nearly twenty years older than herself. Gavin Welby was forty and divorced from his wife Jane Portal, former private secretary to Winston Churchill and niece of Rab Butler, the former Tory minister.

She broke the news of the relationship in a letter to Michael in June 1960, announcing she was to marry Welby. At the time, Michael was on holiday in Athens with his boyfriend Fred Sadoff, staying at the luxurious Hotel Grande-Bretagne. In her letter Vanessa described Welby as a 'sweet, darling man'. Vanessa knew that her news would come as a shock: Welby was not an intellectual or an artist as they were used to – 'He isn't in the theatre. He is one of Lloyd's insurance syndicates and has shares and that sort of thing.' Rachel also wrote to Michael after Vanessa and Welby stayed at Wilks Water, describing Vanessa's fiancé as 'a no-good type with God knows what sort of background.'

Michael and Rachel were alarmed when they realised Welby wanted her as a stay-at-home wife (already, he had persuaded her to stop using contraception). Rachel wrote to Michael saying they had to prevent the marriage. Lynn too wrote to her father, telling him the match would be 'wrong' and 'disastrous'. 'I think when you've met him you'll see that though he is attractive, he is not the sort of person anyone could live with for more than a month or two,' she wrote. Vanessa, however, was completely infatuated.

Welby had custody of his four-year-old son Justin. Rachel suspected his primary motive was to find someone to help him take care of the boy. The Redgraves pressured Vanessa into breaking off the relationship, appalled she might marry a man they privately believed to be a 'rotten piece of work'. Welby had suggested, perhaps flippantly, that Vanessa might benefit from being 'knocked about a bit' to bring her down to earth. In the end, she too began to have doubts and talked of her misgivings one evening at Wilks Water. Rachel put across the family's point of view most strongly and Vanessa, perhaps secretly relieved the decision had been taken out of her hands, ended the relationship. Being Vanessa though, she felt guilty about letting Welby down. Meanwhile, the family breathed a sigh of relief.[10]

Vanessa was still playing an extra in crowd scenes at Stratford when Michael wrote to her in the autumn of 1959. He had been asked to play the lead in Robert Bolt's anti-nuclear bomb play, *The Tiger and the Horse*. Bolt's play focused on the family of an Oxford Don split apart by the atomic bomb question. One of the founders of the Campaign for Nuclear Disarmament (CND), Bolt was eventually jailed for protesting on 12 September 1961. Director Frith Banbury had sent the play to Michael with the suggestion that Vanessa might be perfect for playing his stage daughter.

But Michael was anxious for his daughter's sake about the wisdom of them playing together again so early in her career. It was the second instance of the Redgraves appearing together on stage, something for which the family would increasingly be criticised because it seemed a gimmick. (Michael's boyfriend Fred Sadoff later tried to put together a stage adaptation of Henry James's *Washington Square*, starring Vanessa or Lynn opposite Michael.) For now, though, the idea seemed fresh. Michael admitted to Bolt that the role of earnest hand-wringing Stella would suit Vanessa down to the ground – 'She has a conscience, like her mother's, the size of Grand Central Station,' he wrote.

The Tiger and the Horse opened at the Queen's Theatre on 24 August 1960. Michael was drinking heavily during the run and messed up his part. 'Michael Redgrave fucked it up,' was Banbury's blunt verdict. Meanwhile, Vanessa was judged to be the best thing in it. She certainly enjoyed acting opposite her father. She wrote to Michael: 'It has been so wonderful for me, playing with you and learning from you, however much of a stubborn mule I expect to have seemed to be at times.'

In the spring of 1961, Peter Hall asked Vanessa to rejoin the Royal Shakespeare Company and play Rosalind in *As You Like It*. Ian Bannen, with whom Tony would have a horrendous time later, was cast as Orlando. Vanessa was to fall in love with Bannen just as Michael had fallen in love with his Rosalind, Edith Evans. Even in rehearsal, Vanessa was a revelation. Hall recounted how French director Jean Renoir reacted to her sudden magic: 'Like most directors, he was always reluctant to watch other people's work but I persuaded him to stand at the back of the theatre for a minute or two. On came Vanessa and he asked with proper Gallic enthusiasm, "Oo is that girl?" He stayed for the rest of the play.'

The woman in boy's clothing, walking through the Forest of Arden swinging her velvet cap, became one of the defining images of the Sixties.

Fathoms deep in love, Vanessa created the most extraordinary effect when she removed her Ganymede cap, letting her golden locks tumble down with a noble toss of her head. And Rosalind's reappearance in a gleaming white dress, triumphantly being a woman, was one of the great moments of 20th-century theatre.

Vanessa's acting turned the critics upside down. 'A creature of fire and light,' gushed Bernard Levin, theatre critic of the *Sunday Times*, 'her voice a golden gate opening on lapis lazuli hinges, her body a supple reed rippling on the breeze of her love. This was not acting at all, but living, breathing, loving.' The rest of her family was amused when Levin wrote an article in which he stated that the best thing Michael had ever done for theatre was to give birth to Vanessa. Playwright Caryl Brahms also went, in Lynn's words, 'a bit over the top.' Brahms said that, 'had Shakespeare been alive to see Miss Redgrave's Rosalind, he would have written a Rosalind into every play thereafter.' Indeed, all the praise felt a little overwhelming. The production was such a success that Hall announced it would transfer to the West End's Aldwych theatre in 1961.

Notes

1. Adams, Cindy. *Daily Mail*, 21 February 1991.
2. Redgrave, Vanessa. *An Autobiography*, Hutchinson, London, 1991.
3. Redgrave, Deirdre and Brook, Danaë. *To Be a Redgrave*, Robson Books, London, 1982.
4. Conrad, Peter. *Feasting With Panthers: Or, the Importance of Being Famous*, Thames & Hudson, London, 1994.
5. *Guardian*, 5 June 1995.
6. Robbins, Christopher. *The Empress of Ireland*, Scribner, London, 2004.
7. Author interview, 26 June 2009.
8. Moore, Toby. 'Play Turns Redgraves Into a Family At War', *Daily Express*, 13 March 2001.
9. Lahr, John. *The Orton Diaries*. Methuen, London, 1986.
10. Hastings, Chris. 'Archive Letters Reveal The Actress Gave Up On Her Love After Tensions In the Family', *Sunday Times*, 13 September 2009.

CHAPTER FIVE

The Right to Fail

Marilyn Monroe provided the catalyst for Tony's next collaboration with John Osborne. In July 1956, the actress and her new husband, the playwright Arthur Miller, arrived in London to film *The Prince and the Showgirl*. This was a piece of Hollywood-meets-Ruritania nonsense in which she starred opposite Laurence Olivier. Paparazzi were laying siege to the couple in their hotel. Miller, meanwhile, was going crazy with cabin fever and was desperate to get out and discover what was happening on the London stage. Olivier promised to organise it. Scanning the listings, Miller came across *Look Back in Anger* at the Court. He didn't know anything about the play, but he liked the title. Everything else in the West End seemed, 'that awful English polite stuff.' Olivier, who had already seen *Look Back*, warned him off, describing it pompously as, 'an affront to England,' which whetted Miller's appetite even more.

The Royal Court was discreetly warned about the near-royal trio's visit and three seats were kept empty in the back row. On arrival, the car circled Sloane Square while Monroe kept her head down. Olivier waited for the crowd to go in: curtain up was held back for a couple of minutes as the three slipped into their seats. Similarly, the theatre was kept in the dark at the end of Act One until they could scamper upstairs for a private drink with Devine.

Miller found the play a revelation, but Olivier couldn't see what it was that Miller liked so much about it. He twice asked Miller – once during the interval, and again at the end – why he thought *Look Back* was so wonderful. They then met Osborne after the final curtain. Miller told him how much he admired the play. Olivier respected Miller and the theatrical knight made it clear that if he, Osborne, were ever to write something suitable, then he, old Larry, would be much obliged if he could take a look (later, Miller said Olivier was laying on the charm so much that he could have convinced him to buy a car with no wheels from him for $20,000).

On a deeper level, Olivier had an urgent need to do something different. Both he and Miller were trapped in unhappy marriages to unbalanced women. For the past six years, his marriage to Vivien Leigh had been a cage. Leigh's envy, together with her manic depression and heavy drinking, led to a mental disturbance which shock therapy did not cure. Alone in bed at night, Olivier knew he was in a stew: he needed a change – he was boring the public. Worse still, he was even boring himself. He was now so desperate to get out of this prison of his own making that he rejected a $300,000 movie contract to star opposite Leigh in favour of the Court's £50 a week. 'I had reached a stage in my life that I was getting profoundly sick of – not just tired – sick ... I was going mad. I really felt that death might be quite exciting compared with the purgatorial, amorphous, nothing that was my existence,' he wrote.[1]

In fact, Osborne had already started writing a new play even before *Look Back* opened. It was about a music-hall entertainer crucifying himself twice nightly in Gethsemane-on-Sea. He based the character of Archie Rice on a third-rate comic he'd once seen at the old Chelsea Palace music hall dying a death on stage doing an impression of Charles Laughton's Quasimodo. Osborne responded to the comedian's poetic awfulness: the dreadful comedian and the tatty music hall would be a metaphor for Britain following the ignominious defeat over the Suez crisis in which the Conservative government's botched, covert invasion of Egypt had ended in humiliation. The Empire was crumbling. The title came from Scott Joplin's elegiac ragtime tune.

Devine sent Olivier the first act of *The Entertainer* in New York as soon as Osborne had ripped it out of the typewriter. Olivier cancelled what he was meant to be doing and settled down to read the typescript. According to him, 'Archie leapt off the page at me and he had to be mine.' Olivier identified completely with the opportunistic and seedy Archie. He immediately telephoned Devine to tell him that he wanted to do it. Just like the music halls being demolished by the wrecker's ball, Archie's number is also up. Archie's chirpy knowledge of his own inadequacy as he soft-shoe shuffles towards his fate struck a deep chord within Olivier. 'It's really me, isn't it? It's what I really am ... I know the creature, I know him better than he knows himself,' Olivier said within Tony's earshot.

In the meantime, the Court ploughed on with groundbreaking theatre. *Look Back* prompted all sorts of young people to start writing plays, who wouldn't have thought about writing them before. Becoming a playwright became expressive of a whole generation, in much the same way as rock or rap did later. Harold Pinter, Arnold Wesker and Shelagh Delaney were all inspired by *Look Back*, seeing it was possible to write a play that said something real and still be successful. Doris Lessing, then a young novelist, submitted a political play she had written, *Each His Own Wilderness*. Tony and Devine invited her out to lunch and enthused about the play. 'Just as good as *Look Back in Anger*, da-hling,' Tony drawled. Of all the people involved in the Royal Court Theatre – who were an extraordinarily gifted lot – Lessing thought Tony stood out the most. In the end, though, Tony lost interest and Lessing felt stung by his betrayal. 'You made a promise and didn't keep it,' she thought.[2]

Cards Of Identity was the next play to open at the Court after *Look Back*, with Tony again directing. Going through his list in the cafe with Lewenstein, Tony was convinced that *Cards* would be a hit. 'The idea was that *Look Back in Anger* would be nursed in its shadow. As it turned out, of course, it was exactly the other way round. *Look Back* paid for the huge losses on my play,' said playwright Nigel Dennis. Tony had persuaded Dennis to adapt his hit 1955 novel for the stage. One of the Court's early aims as a 'writer's theatre' was to turn novelists into playwrights, believing they were an untapped source of creativity. Dennis' novel was a cold, brilliantly executed comedy about the malleability of human identity. Tony assumed he would be thrilled to adapt his work. Instead, Dennis was disappointed that he hadn't been asked to write an opera libretto – opera being his real love. Dennis had spent five years writing *Cards* and was thoroughly sick of it. Nevertheless, like many others throughout Tony's career, he found himself doing what this new director wanted.

Cards Of Identity opened on 26 June 1956. The cast was made up of Court regular players, including Rachel, Joan Greenwood, Joan Plowright and Devine, playing a former Communist secret agent-turned-alcoholic priest. The work aroused far more hostility than *Look Back* ever did: reviews were scathing, although the *Observer* admitted that Tony's production, 'brings Mr Dennis' nightmare to pungent life.' The high point of the play was the 10-minute anti-religious monologue given by Devine's chaplain. Audience members shouted 'Get off!' and 'Rubbish!' There was a lot of seat slamming as people got up and walked out. Alan Bates, who appeared in both plays, said that whereas individuals would head for the exit with *Look Back*, in this case whole sections of the audience would get up and leave – mostly from the better seats.

In May 1957, Tony directed Eugène Ionesco's *The Chairs* and it was the first time that the Romanian author had been performed in London. Tony's regular collaborators were coming together: *The Chairs* was the first Court production for which John 'Jock' Addison composed the music with production design by Jocelyn Herbert, Vanessa Redgrave's next-door neighbour in Chiswick. Herbert pioneered a design style that was austere and uncluttered. She and Tony would collaborate for many years, although his enthusiasm for elaborate settings threatened to overwhelm her spare aesthetic. In *The Chairs*, an old man and woman review their long life together. As they do so, they begin welcoming an imaginary throng of acquaintances, represented by an increasing number of empty chairs on stage. Finally comes the arrival of the Orator, who is to deliver the Old Man's message, the wisdom of his lifelong experience to the throng but the Orator is struck dumb when he opens his mouth.

Watching Tony rehearse down below from the circle, Lewenstein remembered turning to Herbert and saying, 'This is the real thing.' Herbert agreed. Devine and Plowright, however, got used to the sound of slamming seats as people walked out, deeming it, 'surrealist rubbish.' 'What was that?' they would ad lib to each other, pretending it was all part of the invisible throng around them on stage. The reviews, though, were approving. 'By turns, hilarious and terrifying, *The Chairs* is a unique theatrical experience,' wrote the *Evening Standard*. 'M. Ionesco's theatre is not designed to have any popular appeal, but *Les Chaises* might well amuse and touch a public larger and less committed to the latest new drama than the Court Theatre regulars,' admitted *The Times*.

The following year, *The Chairs* transferred to Broadway in tandem with another Ionesco one-act play, *The Lesson*. This time Plowright played a pupil whose obtuseness drives her teacher to murder. The *New York Times* judged Tony's ingenious direction as 'brilliant' – the astonishing theatrical effects he achieved were better than Ionesco deserved, the paper said.

Meanwhile, Nigel Dennis was given another chance at becoming an established playwright with *The Making of Moo*, a religious satire he wrote especially for the Court. *Moo* follows a down-to-earth engineer working in Africa who becomes high priest of a bogus religion. It was really a satire of the then hugely popular novels of Graham Greene – both Dennis and Devine thought Greene's books were superstitious nonsense. Dennis attacked the mumbo-jumbo of 'naked ladies being eaten on ant-hills for the greater glory of God.' Kenneth Tynan called *Moo* a historical milestone: the first outright attack on religion ever to be performed on the English stage.

The production sparked a row between Tony and Jocelyn Herbert, though. She hated the way he was directing the play as a farce. Court chairman Neville Blond also criticised Tony's direction. Herbert subsequently went on strike and refused to paint the set; Tony didn't speak to her for almost three years.[3] *Moo* provoked outrage in audiences and mainly derision among the critics. When he tried to explain the play on the first night, Devine was actually booed off stage. The *Evening Standard* printed a picture of his co-star Joan Plowright under a thick, black headline: 'BLASPHEMY'. The *Manchester Guardian* thought *Moo* was thin, while the *Standard* described it as not so much a play as a revue sketch directed by Tony at a lively knockabout pace.

What kept the Royal Court afloat financially during this period was not the new works such as *Cards* and *Moo*, but revivals of classics such as *The Country Wife*, the play Tony first directed in 1955. The new Court production transferred profitably to the West End. By the end of its first year, the Court had almost broken even, ending the first twelve months of its existence with a deficit of just £1,562. More importantly, it had established itself not just as a theatre but an attitude, too.

Yet *The Entertainer* almost never happened. The Court's artistic council vetoed the production for being too commercial. At the time, the Council had three members: Oscar Lewenstein, Ronald Duncan and Lord Harewood. Lewenstein and Duncan voted against the play for different ideological reasons: Lewenstein was a Communist who didn't want Olivier turning a Court ensemble into a star vehicle; Duncan, meanwhile, was a Conservative Christian who was offended by Archie's immorality and cynicism. 'Well, that makes three in favour and two against,' Harewood blithely announced, trying to railroad the play through and counting Tony and Osborne's vote in absentia.

However, Duncan and Lewenstein interrupted that the Court's co-founder and star playwright didn't actually have a vote. It took chairman Neville Blond's wife Elsie, the Marks & Spencer heiress, to bang heads together: she said they'd be 'barmy' to turn down a play starring the theatrical knight and that settled it. Elsie was proved right when the four-week run sold out ten days after the production was announced.

Tony and Osborne visited the Oliviers in the elegant drawing room of their Connaught Hotel suite to discuss who should be cast as Archie's blowsy wife. After running through some names, Olivier suddenly suggested his own wife. Of course, Vivien Leigh was far too beautiful in real life: she could wear a rubber mask, Olivier suggested. Clearly, Leigh had pressured him into putting her name forward. Olivier's astonishing suggestion caught Tony off-guard. 'Machiavellian and master-technician though he might be, [Tony] could dissemble no better than myself,' said Osborne. After a few minutes of cautious discussion, the idea was dropped. Brenda De Banzie, something of a *monstre sacré* herself, became first choice. Hitting the cold February air as they went through the hotel's revolving door, Tony screamed with laughter: 'What about that? Rubber masks! Oh, my dear God – rubber masks!'

Tony visited the last few remaining music halls with Olivier, accompanied by Osborne and Jock Addison. It wasn't just Lewenstein who was wary of the titled interloper, though. Tony said that the Oliviers' home, Notley Abbey, was emblematic of the kind of grandeur and snobbery to which all British actors of the period aspired; the Oliviers represented everything that was wrong with the profession. At this point, Michael Redgrave was still strangling himself with the debt of running Bedford House, with its maidservants, cooks and gardeners. Joan Plowright said: 'We thought that to act, you had to wear jeans. Anybody well groomed or too well dressed for their own good, we suspected all that.' But Olivier overwhelmed the company when he began rehearsals – 'You can't argue with someone who can act you off the stage whenever he feels like it. You just can't argue with that sort of talent.'

As it turned out, Archie's marriage to a drunken wife whom he plans to leave for a girl half her age would prove a painful counterpart to what was happening offstage. Olivier recommended Dorothy Tutin for the part of his daughter Jean. They'd had an affair several years before:

he found her gentleness a refuge from Leigh's hysteria. Tutin was duly cast and Olivier resumed the affair. Olivier wanted to marry her, but Tutin was afraid of driving Leigh to suicide.

Tony enjoyed telling the tale of how, when somebody asked Olivier how he managed to catch so exactly Archie's second-rate hoofing, he had replied, shocked, 'But I'm trying as hard as I can!' Act Two ends with Archie remembering a black blues singer he once saw on a vaudeville bill. He realises how pathetically small his talent is compared to this artist. Staggering against the proscenium arch, he collapses entirely. During rehearsals, Tony got the sense that Olivier was holding something back. Finally, on the day of the final run-through – before the technical rehearsal, before the dress rehearsal – he gave it his all. As he slid down the wall, Olivier made an unnameable keening sound. Tony was transfixed – it was the single most thrilling moment he'd ever seen in the theatre.

Vivien Leigh, meanwhile, became a baleful presence during rehearsals. She would drop in without warning and sit in the dress circle with her chocolate-uniformed chauffeur. Her presence made Tony nervous and he was forced to appeal to Devine when she began interfering with his direction. Devine reluctantly banned the star from the theatre on the morning of the dress rehearsal. Tony noticed that Olivier had backed off from totally collapsing at the end of Act Two: what he presented at the dress rehearsal was a very much watered-down version – it was almost as if he was afraid of what Leigh might think. She swept into his dressing room after the second-act curtain. 'You disgust me!' she announced to a roomful of people and accused him of upstaging Brenda De Banzie. Olivier went home to Notley that night, no doubt dreading what he would find. Leigh had taken a hammer to her own home: this deeply materialistic woman had smashed all the possessions she set such store by – lamps, vases, ornaments and mementoes.

The Entertainer opened on 10 April 1957 to ecstatic reviews. Olivier's Archie Rice caught the nation's mood, just as his Henry V had also done thirteen years earlier – except this time Olivier personified tatty Britannia sinking into decline rather than England's defiance during the Second World War. Tony and Osborne rubbed people's noses in national failure. 'Don't clap too hard,' Archie calls into the silence. 'It's a very old building.' Yet Olivier was still Establishment-minded enough to demand that Tony cut 'all that anti-Queen shit' from the play (he was referring to Archie's line about 'the gloved hand waving at you from the golden coach'). 'The audience freezes,' Olivier told Tony, 'it's disloyal.'

The play also implicitly attacks the Tory government and the disastrous Suez invasion (Archie's infantryman son is killed in Egypt). But Tony flatly refused to make any cuts – the Court hadn't been founded to sacrifice authors on the altars of stars, he told Olivier. Later, when *The Entertainer* transferred to the West End, Olivier imposed the cuts himself. Tony's own view was that they didn't make much difference, 'but Larry felt he'd bravely defended the Queen.'[4]

The West End transfer played for six months at the Palace Theatre in London. Joan Plowright took over the role of Jean. Olivier and Plowright had first met backstage at Tony's Court production of *A Country Wife* – she'd eyed the theatrical knight askance as he went round patronising the 'young people.' As more and more of 'George's children' filed in to meet the Great Man, Olivier found he only had eyes for this brassy girl from Lincolnshire and they fell in love during *The Entertainer*. The down-to-earth appeal of this actress some twenty-two years his junior steeled Olivier to face Leigh's hysteria.

In May 1958, Tony pushed the boundaries again, directing the first West Indian play produced in London. As with *Look Back in Anger*, *Flesh to a Tiger* had also won a playwriting competition (Barry Beckford had never written a play before) and the prize was to be performed at the Court. *Flesh to a Tiger* was about a young Jamaican woman forced to choose between Western medicine and local voodoo to save the life of her young child (the village thinks her voodoo lover has cursed the child because he doesn't like the way she's been influenced by the West). She is also caught in a romantic triangle between her lover and a white doctor. Eventually, she kills the voodoo priest to free her village from his superstition.

The play suited Tony's evolving theatrical style: a combination of showman-like spectacle and social consciousness. However, there were no young West Indian actresses in London at the time. Cleo Laine, then a young singer with no acting experience, auditioned for a part. Laine thought she was just going to be an extra. At her Court audition she was ushered on stage, where she read her lines. There was an uncomfortable silence and then she heard mutterings. 'Suddenly a voice from the dark said, with a distinguished sound that he made when he spoke – a petulantly plummy, hoity-toity sound, ripe for imitators: "I sey, ahn't we lacky to hev a name, too!"' Laine was amazed to find herself given the lead – the rest of the cast was made up of experienced black actors including Pearl Prescott. The six-foot actress had such a powerful voice that Tony was forever telling her from the stalls, 'Pawul back a bit, Pourll, pawul back!'

As the play toured the provinces, Beckford continued to do rewrites. Meanwhile, some at the Court thought Tony was pushing Laine too hard. The inexperienced actress was hardly ever off stage yet she had to keep memorising new lines and even new scenes daily. *Flesh to a Tiger* was a financial and critical flop. For all the opportunities offered by crowd scenes and pagan rites, the production lacked excitement, said the *Daily Telegraph*. 'This impassioned allegory gives director Tony Richardson a rich opportunity for staging a series of bizarre religious ceremonials, succulent and rhythmic native dances. Yet this thick production camouflage fails to disguise the play's basic melodramatic weaknesses,' sighed the *Evening Standard*.

But Tony wasn't yet done with furthering the cause of black actors. Early in 1958, Glen Byam Shaw, general manager of the Shakespeare Memorial Theatre, invited Tony to direct his first play at Stratford. Tony jumped at the chance – *Pericles* would be the first time he had directed Shakespeare since Oxford. He cast Richard Johnson as Pericles and Rachel as Dionyza, but his great inspiration was making Gower – the play's chorus figure – a Negro storyteller. He envisaged Gower recounting Shakespeare's strange tale of incest at Antioch Court to a bunch of incredulous sailors and he wanted Paul Robeson, the American singer and political activist, to play the part. This was problematic because the American government had withdrawn Robeson's passport because of his Communist sympathies. Thinking it would give him leverage with the US State Department, Robeson immediately accepted the role. Tony met him in New York for further discussion. Excitement and anticipation, Tony reported, were keen but the State Department refused to budge. Robeson had no choice but to turn down Tony's offer of directing him in Shakespeare – at least, for the time being. Edric Connor was cast instead.

Rehearsals at Stratford began in June 1958. Tony sat behind a table munching an apple. He held a knife in his hand that he kept stabbing into the table in front of him. 'Now my darlings,' he said, 'this play is terribly, terribly sexy, and you mustn't forget it.' Cast member Zoe Caldwell thought Tony was brilliant, if perhaps a little mad. The first time he met Caldwell, he greeted her with, 'I want you to play the incestuous Daughter of Antiochus – it's going to be absolutely marvellous! You will be carried naked on a bier, painted green. *You* painted green, not the bier.' Indeed, Tony went to town with the theatrical effects. He staged the play on what resembled a vast ship, filling the stage with masts, tarpaulins, ropes and rope ladders reminiscent of his Oxford *Peer Gynt*. Writing in the *Observer*, Kenneth Tynan said that Tony's Stratford debut would have been as impressive as Peter Brook's, had he not been let down by the acting. He called the production, 'pictorially magnificent, a restless Oriental kaleidoscope … Tony Richardson deploys a visual imagination of Reinhardtian fertility'.

The following February, Tony returned to Stratford to begin rehearsals on *Othello*. This was to be the opening production in the centenary season of the Shakespeare Memorial Theatre. By now, Robeson had permission to come to London and this would be the first time that a black had played Othello at Stratford. Tony cast Mary Ure as Desdemona and Sam Wanamaker as Iago. With his usual flair for casting, he rounded out the rest of the cast with actors who would go on to become famous such as Albert Finney, Ian Holm and Roy Dotrice. Robeson, however, was in a hospital bed in Moscow suffering from exhaustion. He told Byam Shaw that he was too ill to start rehearsals. Byam Shaw cabled Robeson back, begging him to reconsider; he promised to adjust rehearsals and schedule performances to minimise the strain. Otherwise, he said, the Stratford season would be ruined. Feeling stronger, Robeson accepted: his performance would concentrate on words rather than movement. On 9 March, he flew to London, telling reporters that his performance as Othello would now have to be a 'muted' one. Advanced booking was remarkable, even by Stratford standards – there was excitement in the air. But Robeson found Ure 'cold' in rehearsal and didn't enjoy acting opposite her … nor did he think much of Tony according to his friend Silvia Schwartz, who told Robeson's biographer as much.

Tony's interpretation of *Othello* was the traditional one: he saw the play as being about a noble Moor brought down by the machinations of Venice society. However, he then filled the show with dazzling stagecraft: Great Danes dashed across the footlights and there were rock'n'roll drums. His three leads seemed to be acting in different plays, though – Robeson portrayed Othello with his customary gravitas and reserve, Ure played Desdemona as if she was still ironing Jimmy Porter's shirts and Tony allowed Wanamaker to keep his Midwestern accent, portraying Iago as a slick huckster. The play opened on 7 April 1959 and the audience reception was so ecstatic that there were 15 curtain calls. Sam Wanamaker pushed Robeson to one side and led the cast in applauding him. Vanessa was one of those clapping, standing beside Diana Rigg. She was understudying that summer and had especially rehearsed Desdemona, longing to show Tony what she could do. The *Daily Mail* admired the production's liveliness although the reviewer also commented, 'Richardson's production seemed determined to make the whole tragedy as un-Shakespearean as possible. I admired the pace and resource of the production but I wish rather more of Shakespeare's *Othello* had survived the treatment'. Tony's *Othello* sold out of its seven-month run – long queues formed nightly in the hope of any returns. The *Daily Telegraph* observed: 'Advanced booking is remarkable even by Stratford's standards and there is excitement in the air. And the quality of the opening performance, which has a tremendous reception, justifies all this anticipation. Tony Richardson's production, admirable on the whole in its speed and liveliness, has some ineffective patches.'

Tony's next production for the Court couldn't have been more different – or Establishment. *Looking After Lulu* was a French farce adapted by Noël Coward and starring Vivien Leigh. It was just the sort of soufflé-light nonsense the Court was meant to be against. Tony later admitted *Looking After Lulu* was brought in as a 'sure-fire' hit attempt to keep the otherwise radical Court in business. Georges Feydeau's work was first performed in 1908. After Olivier's triumph in *The Entertainer*, Leigh was anxious to one-up her husband: now she, too wanted to star in a Court production. Devine and a young Peter Sallis were also cast.

Tony began rehearsing the play for short try-out runs in the provinces. He fell on Osborne when his friend came to see the play in Nottingham in mid-July 1959. 'Thank God you've come! I think I'm going mad,' he said. 'Vivien's gone to pieces because of Joan, George is in a state and Noël insists on being fucking witty all the time!' Coward and Leigh would end up screaming at each other after they'd had too much to drink. 'Thank God you and Larry had a miscarriage,' Coward shrieked. 'Any child of yours would be a monster three times over!'

Looking After Lulu transferred to the Court the following week. Watching rehearsals, Osborne felt as if he'd suddenly been transported from Sloane Square to Shaftesbury Avenue. Despite the bad reviews, the farce sold out its 45-performance run because of Leigh but its West End transfer – when it was supposed to bring in the big money – faltered and closed early. The critic Irving Wardle wrote that *Lulu*, 'became a byword among experimental companies on the folly of selling out for fairy gold.'

Despite this, Kenneth Tynan reported that the Court had given the modern repertoire a permanent London home: it had reached out and captured popular audiences in the West End and Broadway and on television. Yes, the Court had quite spectacularly fallen on its face once or twice, but that was one of the occupational hazards when you set out to climb mountains. Devine once asked Tony to define what they'd established at the Court. Tony replied: 'I'll tell you what: the right to fail.' It soon became the Court's catchphrase. What Tony meant was that not every play needed to be a sure-fire hit – they should not be afraid to lose money on the occasional worthy misfire. It marked the beginning of what would become subsidised theatre in Britain (the National Theatre was still five years away). Not every ESC board member agreed with Tony's credo, though. Lord Drogheda fulminated: 'Nothing is admitted on the boards of the Royal Court unless it is calculated to put the audience into a suicidal frame of mind (or give them a list of pot-boiling 18th-century smut).'

But Tony and Devine did not always agree. Devine stood for tradition, craftsmanship and nurturing talent, while Tony was all for enterprise, new ideas and exploitation of success. He was also ambitious for a movie career. As far back as Ashville College, he'd always wanted to become a successful film director and theatre was just a stepping-stone. Tony told Wardle that film was far more important to him than theatre. 'It was a medium he was much more in control of once he'd got the capitalisation,' explained Wardle. 'The Royal Court was close to the heart of many people, including me, but in a curious way, I don't think it was close to his.'

In the summer of 1957, Tony, Osborne and Devine had all gone over to New York to supervise the Broadway opening of *Look Back in Anger*. In the July, Tony flew back to London to direct the Moscow production, leaving his friends behind. Soon, letters began arriving about the marvellous character they'd met, who was going to conjure up a private bank of gold for the Court. Meanwhile, this magician was giving Osborne and Devine the time of their lives in Manhattan jazz cellars. The showbusiness Midas was Harry Saltzman, a Canadian entrepreneur who'd already left behind him enough careers for several men. In a business not so far removed from its medieval origins in bands of travelling players, Saltzman was the real thing. Moving from America to France and back again, he'd worked in vaudeville, advertising and television – in fact, in anything which attracted his gambler's instinct and feel for popular culture. 'Harry was a very charming, exuberant sort of rascal, really,' explained Karel Reisz. 'He had never made a feature film before in his life, but he had any amount of energy and cheek.'

Tony went back out to New York to discuss the Broadway trans-fer of *The Entertainer*. Saltzman arranged for him to be met at the airport by a limo, which whisked him to Saltzman's vast, gloomy Manhattan apartment. Tony was suitably awed. 'Harry was a hard bastard, extremely brusque. If he saw no advantage in having a conversation with you, then likely he wouldn't reply to "Good morning,"' said producer Michael Deeley.[5] Saltzman was forever unrolling the same threadbare carpet, tempting the unwary to buy – sometimes the carpet wasn't even his to sell. Tony, meanwhile, was being wined and dined and even threatened with never working again in New York unless he gave *The Entertainer* to one of the impresarios competing for his attention. To his credit, he loyally stuck with David Merrick, who'd taken such a risk with *Look Back in Anger*.

Slowly, it dawned on Tony that Saltzman didn't actually have any money. As a movie producer, he was a hustler. In many ways, he and Tony made an odd couple: Saltzman was short, round and loaded with aggression while Tony was tall, stork-like and imperious. Rather than be swept up in another of Saltzman's crazy schemes, Tony decided to harness his carnival-barker energy for his own ends. What he wanted was to make a film version of *Look Back in Anger* – and Saltzman was to help him to achieve this.

Notes

1. Holden, Anthony. *Olivier*, Weidenfeld & Nicolson, London, 1988.
2. Lessing, Doris. *Walking In the Shade*, HarperCollins, London, 1997.

3. Little, Ruth and McLaughlin, Emily. *The Royal Court Theatre Inside Out*, Chevron Books, London, 2007.
4. Heilpern, John. *John Osborne: A Patriot For Me*, Chatto & Windus, London, 2006.
5. Deeley, Michael. *Blade Runners, Deer Hunters and Blowing the Bloody Doors Off*, Faber & Faber, London, 2008.

CHAPTER SIX

The Ugliest Girl in the World

Three years after *Look Back in Anger* opened at the Royal Court, Tony began adapting it as a film. His problem was that *Look Back* had become something of an institution itself. Vanessa had already played Helena in Frinton rep and Jimmy Porter's shaking fist had become thoroughly assimilated; what lay behind Porter's anger had been so much raked over by newspapers, it now looked like petulance. Certainly Nigel Kneale, the television scriptwriter brought in to 'open the play out' because John Osborne was sick of the sight of it, believed Porter's anger was more to do with Osborne being rejected by the theatrical establishment than anything concerning the state of the nation.

Dirk Bogarde sniffed the film rights after *Look Back* was such a success on Broadway but Osborne stuck with Tony. Together, the pair set up a company for their film projects. Woodfall was named after the pretty Chelsea street where Osborne was living with Mary Ure (Tony just looked out of the sitting-room window). He founded the company in April 1958, shortly after the Broadway opening of *The Entertainer*. 'Neither John Osborne nor myself originally set out to get embroiled in this production business, but it really did become the only way if we were to make films we wanted to in the way we wanted,' Tony explained.

For Doris Lessing, Tony and Osborne were brothers, 'and, as with any siblings, behind everything said or not said were suggestions of long, intense entwined experience.' The joke among their circle of friends was that Osborne played John the Baptist to Tony's Jesus Christ.[1]

Tony reflected on the difference between his and Osborne's roles at Woodfall: 'I am much more of a politician than John Osborne. John is a writer and he, basically, has only to have a relationship with a sheet of paper in his typewriter. I have to deal with people, with actors and artists and financiers ... I have to be more of a diplomat.'

Woodfall first pitched *Look Back* to Ealing Studios, where Kenneth Tynan was working as head of development. Michael Balcon, who ran the studio and would later invite Tony onto the board of distribution company British Lion, wouldn't take the risk on a first-time director and his timidity irritated Tynan. Tony, meanwhile, persuaded the mesmerisingly handsome Richard Burton, whose career had been foundering of late, to play Porter. His most recent films had mostly been toga epics that didn't give him the opportunity to do much acting. Burton wasn't Saltzman's first choice, though: the Canadian producer later called the casting, 'a monumental miscalculation.'

Warner Brothers agreed to put up the £250,000 cost of the film because it had what is known as a 'pay or play' deal with Burton. This meant the studio would still have to pay him regardless of whether or not he made a film. Either the Hollywood studio fully financed *Look Back* or Burton could still walk away with £125,000. The quid quo pro was that Tony and Osborne had to defer their combined fee of £2,500. They would be paid out of later profits and meanwhile, Warner Bros gave the pair a couple of thousand pounds to live on. Five years later, Warner had the temerity to ask for its loan back.

Osborne and Kneale started work on the script over a ten-day stint in the South of France. Tony wanted to show the rain-swept Midlands townscape where Jimmy lived: railway lines, gasworks and the Salvation Army band; he also wanted to depict the sweet stall run by Porter and the jazz club where he plays trumpet at night. This last change made Porter's character even more inexplicable: market trader by day, hot Bix Beiderbecke by night. Osborne added a few extra characters, notably Jimmy's former landlady Ma Tanner, played by Edith Evans.

Tony's worst innovation was to introduce the bullying of an Indian market trader as the reason for Porter's anger. Focusing on a single issue weakened the force of the original. Many speeches, too, stopped short of their original climax. References to Christianity and atomic weapons were cut, while Jimmy's speech about there being 'no brave good causes' left was dropped. Tony's argument was that the politics dated the script. The censor still put his blue pencil through some of the finished screenplay, though. Words such as 'Christ', 'bitch' and 'bastard' were deleted. Showing Porter and his wife Alison in bed together was also forbidden.

Mary Ure was the only cast member retained from the original Court production. Claire Bloom was cast as her odiously crisp girlfriend, Helena. Other cast members in what would become Tony's repertory company included George Devine and Glen Byam Shaw played Alison's father.

On the first morning of shooting in September 1958, Tony addressed the crew: he told them that he was a beginner and therefore largely in their hands, which won him their goodwill. He filmed the play over eight weeks at Elstree Studios and on location around outer London. Sequences were shot in Kensal Rise Cemetery, a disused railway junction at Dalston and a Romford street market. Cinematographer Oswald Morris was impressed by how quickly Tony picked things up, while Bloom remembers him as being the first director who ever gave her freedom to try things out – all her previous directors had simply ordered her what to do. Consequently, she felt that Tony was creating a reality, a living thing. Jocelyn Rickards, the film's costume designer, loved working with Tony in those early days. Although already a skilled manipulator, Rickards said he hadn't as yet developed his full-blown Machiavellian techniques.[2]

Tony moved into the Chelsea house that Saltzman was renting – the previous occupants had been Laurence Olivier and Vivien Leigh. He would come back from shooting and find himself having dinner with Kirk Douglas or Burt Lancaster. It was a crazy, heady world and it never once occurred to him to ask how Saltzman was paying for it.

Tony was directing Shakespeare at Stratford when he had an opportunity to screen the finished film. Vanessa, then aged twenty-two, remembered watching the preview in Stratford's small, old cinema. What he had done, she felt, represented a big break not only with English films but with American films, too. Vanessa may have thought that *Look Back* was about to shatter England's stifling philistinism but director Carol Reed was completely aghast. 'Why should we drag the audience to the cinema to look for an hour or two at a kitchen sink, a one-set film, the greasy dishes and the mental and moral miasma of certain elements in society?' he asked.

Bizarrely, *Look Back* was given a royal premiere on 28 May 1959 in front of Princess Margaret. Trumpeters of the Life Guard heralded the royal arrival and the Band of the Royal Marines played on stage. It just showed how Establishment *Look Back* had become. Fortunately, one peer stood up in the House of Lords to denounce the film as 'unadulterated filth.'

Richard Burton plays Jimmy as a kind of skiffle-group Hamlet with the vibrant elocution of an experienced Shakespearian actor. Like the play, the film shows Jimmy Porter's nagging love-hate marriage with his drained middle-class wife, his tortuous affair with her icy girlfriend and his own corrosive bitterness. Fifty years on, his over-literary ravings seem like the tantrums of a spoilt adolescent. 'What do you really want, Jimmy?' asks Ma Tanner during a tender cemetery visit. 'Everything. Nothing,' Porter shrugs. You can imagine the hair-netted matrons watching the film turning to each other and saying, 'He's not right in the head, you know.' Moments where Jimmy and Cliff (Gary Raymond) ham it up as a music-hall double act would have gone down well at one of Binkie Beaumont's Mayfair parties – you keep expecting Burton to reappear at any moment dressed as a Roman Centurion.

On the whole, the reviews were mostly good. The *Daily Telegraph* wrote, 'Tony Richardson, the stage director, shows again that in filmmaking, intelligence and flair are more important than long experience.' *The Times* called it an 'outstanding first film', while the *Evening Standard* said Tony had made, 'an auspicious debut.' Its critic John Waterman described *Look Back* as a grenade lobbed into the laps of those in the British film industry who wanted an endless future of Cinemascope epics and costume dramas. But the *Sunday Dispatch* humphed that Jimmy's rebellion was about as shocking as eating baked beans straight out from the tin with a knife. Tony himself thought that he'd stuck too much to the play – he always believed one of his greatest weaknesses as a director was reverence for the script.

Westminster Council slapped an 'X' certificate on the film, banning the under-16s from seeing it. *Look Back* opened on 29 May 1959 during a heatwave that turned London into an outdoor city for a fortnight – it was so hot that people were sleeping in the parks at night. Nobody wanted to be stuck inside a sweltering cinema. Financially, the film was a disaster – at least in the short term. Most Hollywood movies do eventually make their money back once they've been repeatedly sold to television. Tony never found out whether *Look Back* ultimately made a profit or loss, though – 'American film accounting is so mysterious,' he said.

Woodfall's second film was to be the film version of *The Entertainer*. Saltzman sewed the £200,000 budget together from a variety of sources. Although more ambitious than *Look Back*, *The Entertainer* would be cheaper to make. This time around, Olivier deferred his salary, as did Tony and Osborne, and all three would be paid out of nebulous profits. Bryanston, the production arm of independent distributor British Lion, advanced 75 per cent of the budget. Michael Balcon was chairman of Bryanston, who by now realised what a talent Tony was (government funding body the National Film Finance Corporation came up with most of the rest). Walter Reade Jr, the US distributor and cinema circuit, had a standing arrangement with Bryanston to cover 25 per cent of its exposure. Saltzman was convinced that Bass the brewers would also come in, given the number of times Olivier mentions the beer, but the company wasn't interested.

Nigel Kneale was once again hired to work with Osborne on the script, adding new characters such as beauty pageant winner Tina Lapford. Osborne's eviscerating dialogue – based on rows with his barmaid mother – was mostly kept intact, although references to the Suez Crisis were trimmed.

Tony and Osborne visited Brenda De Banzie at home to try and persuade her to recreate her stage performance. Osborne remembered sitting glumly on the settee next to De Banzie's husband and her would-be pop-star son. Dainty drinks were served as De Banzie made imperious demands – chiefly, that her part should be built up. Tony nodded vigorously. Later, he shot most of her improvised suggestions with a camera devoid of film. Jean Simmons was originally to play Archie's daughter Jean until Tony changed his mind and gave the part to Joan Plowright.

Shirley Anne Field, a starlet who'd made headlines after catching he eye of Frank Sinatra, was cast against type as Tina. Field was brought up in Lancashire and like Tony, had elocution lessons to iron out her northern accent. What won her the part was when Tony noticed at the audition that one of her shoes needed mending – she clearly needed the work.

That autumn, Tony began filming *The Entertainer* on location for six weeks in Morecambe, the northern seaside town where he'd spent wartime holidays with his parents. As a child, he'd hated the mean boarding houses and moribund variety shows. By 1959, Morecambe had become a failed resort with decaying piers and crumbling theatres. Tony wanted to shoot completely on location – his view was that studio-bound Hollywood films only increased their artificiality. He wanted realism. But while he thought he was becoming liberated, his cameraman Oswald Morris believed he was being irresponsible. The two rowed because Tony didn't care about minor imperfections nor did he insist on take after take, ensuring there would be plenty of material for the editing suite later. Tony's attitude was that a film could be technically appalling, but still be wonderful; you could get something truer onscreen by improvising your way out of real conditions than by doing something contrived on set.

Meanwhile, Saltzman was still convinced that Bass would put money into *The Entertainer* once the company saw the finished film. With this in mind, he had the art department construct a 20-foot high cutout of some bottles of Bass, which he tried to sneak into shot behind Olivier. The theatrical knight was not amused. Physically and emotionally, the 52-year-old actor was under enormous strain: he still hadn't summoned up the strength to tell his wife about his affair with Joan Plowright and he was also starring in *Coriolanus* every night in Stratford, which meant travelling 150 miles each day between Morecambe and Stratford for the evening performance and then back again. Olivier hired an ambulance to get himself to Stratford and back. Stretched out in the back, he would try and get some sleep. The only respite from this punishing merry-go-round came after Tony asked him to do 'just one more take' while filming a tap dance. 'Snap,' as Olivier put it, 'went the old cartilage.' He was subsequently out of action for several days.

The cast would sometimes have dinner together after filming and Tony would instigate psychological truth games, getting his actors to reveal uncomfortable facts about themselves. Field remembered how some of these get-togethers would end in tears. Nevertheless, she felt at home with the Court: 'They were a group of rebels at that time, experimenting with something new and exciting in the film industry. They were intellectuals, with egos to match, and they were also a sensitive and caring group of people.'

The censor insisted on giving *The Entertainer* an X, which again meant only those over sixteen could see it. Tony chopped eight minutes out and re-dubbed one reel. After seeing the film three times, censor John Trevelyan still insisted on X. Tony agreed to make more cuts, this time to the scene where Archie sleeps with Tina in his caravan. Rumours began to circulate that every cinema circuit had rejected *The Entertainer* – adult cinemagoers might be put off by the lurid X certificate. A restricted audience didn't bode well for takings: not only was the film not going out on general release, but distributor Rank didn't plan to show it in London's West End. Saltzman said he practically had to 'blackmail' conservative Rank into releasing it. Rank then cancelled the Odeon Leicester Square premiere a couple of days before the film was due to take place: it insisted on parts of the soundtrack being re-dubbed (seagulls screaming overhead made Olivier's dialogue difficult to hear). Tony's insistence on location shooting almost scuppered its chances.

The Entertainer remains a fascinating glimpse of grin-and-bare-it life in late-fifties England. Archie, with his terribly chirpy knowledge of his fate as he soft-shoe shuffles through songs such as 'Thank God, We're Normal', is a brilliant creation. According to the critic Alexander Walker, Olivier suggests the eroded soul of a man making a martyr of himself twice-nightly. A Catholic priest, reviewing the film anonymously, wrote one of its most perceptive reviews: 'This is world without God and yet in the midst of all the emptiness and smallness of it, the hunger for God emerges.' Most reviewers agreed the problem with 'opening out' *The Entertainer* was that it was a play about theatre – the audience was one of the characters within it. Archie's final line is addressed to the stalls: 'Let me know where you're working tomorrow night and I'll come and see *you*.'

Tony never managed to overcome this basic contradiction: he and Saltzman both wanted to free the play from the stage, yet at the same time record Olivier's tour de force as Archie. Tony's desire for naturalism clashed with Olivier's theatricality. Later, he admitted that *The Entertainer* didn't quite work: 'One of the difficulties of bringing a play to the screen, as I discovered then, is that a play is too static, too set in one mould, and doesn't have the movement needed for the screen.' The *News Chronicle* published a damning review, declaring the play didn't deserve to be shown anywhere, while the *Daily Express* described Tony's direction as 'amateurish'. At the same time, the *Sunday Express*, then the most powerful paper in Fleet Street, also tore into the film, calling it, 'a deadly blasphemy ... badly made, pretentious, slovenly and pointless.' And the American reviews weren't much better. The *New Yorker* described *The Entertainer* as, 'very depressing.' Playwright Arnold Wesker rushed to the film's defence, saying it was one of the few works to herald a change in the British film industry. Meanwhile, Paul Dehn in the *News Chronicle* wrote: 'The film's virtues so shine that they blind one to its defects; and Mr Richardson as well as the author and his cast must take credit for that.'

Woodfall was now looking for its third project and rather than direct, Tony wanted to produce this one himself. According to Saltzman, he'd been hurt by the critical response to his first two films. Meanwhile, George Devine was pressurising him to come back to the Court rather than play around in the movies. The director Lindsay Anderson – who believed he was one of the first people in the country to read David Storey's novel, *This Sporting Life* – took it to Tony, telling him that he wanted to make it into a film. Tony read the book and counselled Anderson that it wasn't the right subject for him. Only later did Anderson discover that Tony had gone behind his back and tried to buy the rights for himself [3] – Tony ended up being outbid.

Instead, Woodfall bought the rights to an Alan Sillitoe novel, which the producer Joseph Janni had failed to turn into a film. Janni reluctantly sold *Saturday Night and Sunday Morning* to Saltzman for £2,000. When Tony said he didn't want to direct, Saltzman turned to Karel Reisz, who badly wanted to make his first feature. Saltzman then had problems raising the budget: Wardour Street told him that the story was too miserable – audiences wanted to see comedy or adventure – and so Saltzman reassembled backers from *The Entertainer*. The meagre £116,000 budget was even tighter than Woodfall's previous two films. Tony suspected the only reason why financiers got involved was because the script had lots of sex in it.

Tony overruled Saltzman's first choice for Arthur Seaton (the Canadian had wanted Peter O'Toole for this beer-and-sex-in-the-Midlands story). Instead, Tony picked Albert Finney, a young actor with whom he'd worked at Stratford. Reisz was flabbergasted, though when Tony and Saltzman both pushed for Diana Dors to play Seaton's married lover – usually, Tony had perfect pitch when it came to casting. In the end, Dors considered the role beneath her and Rachel Roberts got the part. Tony recommended Shirley Anne Field to play Seaton's pretty-but-bland fiancée – at the time, Field was already appearing in the play *Lily-White Boys* with Finney. He also cast television comedienne

Hylda Baker ('She knows, you know') as a backstreet abortionist. Norman Rossington, who played Seaton's best friend Bert, considered Tony's casting was first rate – 'The whole cast was exactly right,' he said. He also remembered Tony saying they were going to make the film on location: 'Of course, back then all the sound equipment was in huge lorries – now it fits into an attaché case.'

Filming began in Nottingham in the autumn of 1959. The exterior of Seaton's house was, in fact, the very home where Alan Sillitoe had grown up and the funfair where Seaton gets beaten up was in Wimbledon; interiors were filmed at Twickenham Studios. Calamity struck when Walter Reade, the US exhibition chain, suddenly withdrew its 25 per cent share of funding one week in. 'We finished the picture with arms linked in a human rescue chain,' said Saltzman.

Tony said *Saturday Night and Sunday Morning* was about the release of the weekend. The story centres on Seaton, who works long days at his lathe in a Nottingham bicycle factory. He is very much 'I'm all right, Jack' and nobody's going to stop him being that way – 'Don't let the bastards grind you down, what I'm out for is a good time,' he declares. Seaton wrongly believes that he's different from his mates, who are all, 'dead from the neck up.' But his affair with a married woman (Rachel Roberts) leads to a beating. Seaton settles for marriage with a pretty, but shallow girl his own age. Caught in the vast interlocking grind of industrial life, she looks ahead to the shiny appliances of their still-being-built housing estate – for her, this is the good life. The film ends with Seaton's final act of rebellion – throwing a stone towards the estate where he'll probably live one day. 'It's about work – the whole business of work in those towns, the sort of tensions it produces,' said Tony.

Woodfall showed the finished film to Columbia Pictures, which opined that Finney looked tubercular, the women most unappetising, the factory locations some of the ugliest ever recorded on celluloid. No cinema was prepared to book it: none of the bookers would take *Saturday Night and Sunday Morning* on a solitary screen, let alone a whole chain. It was only the surprise failure of a Warner Bros release in its showcase Leicester Square cinema that created an opportunity. Suddenly, Warner Bros had a window and because of the British quota system, it made more sense to show a small British film than one of their own. So, in late October 1960, *Saturday Night and Sunday Morning* was given an impromptu premiere – Field remembered having to get herself together in a hurry. The film's marketing budget was one third of the £5,000 minimum distributors usually spent. Saltzman borrowed the cash from a relative.

Saturday Night and Sunday Morning remains the least dated of all British films made during this fertile period; a near-perfect weave of cast, script and direction. Critics and cinemagoers alike responded to Karel Reisz's confident and unpretentious direction. The film was incredibly successful, earning its budget back within two weeks of release at Warner Leicester Square. It eventually made more than half a million pounds profit, winning three BAFTAs and instant fame for Finney (Columbia Pictures rang back, wondering if he might be available for *Lawrence of Arabia*). Freddie Francis' photography captured the dreamy, clanging monotony of factory life. *The Times* proclaimed: 'Here – if British producers have the wit to take it – is a chance for our own New Wave.' Perhaps unsurprisingly, the *Daily Worker* said Tony had produced the best British film yet, while the *New York Times* declared: 'There is solid human fibre and a sense of hopefulness which Tony Richardson has produced with fine economy.'

Not everybody thought well of *Saturday Night and Sunday Morning*, though. Lieutenant-Colonel John Cordeaux, Conservative MP for Nottingham, said it gave the impression that the young men of the city were a bunch of ill-behaved, drunken teddy-boys: 'The most distressing part is that the film is set in our city but the principal character could hardly be less typical of the young men of Nottingham. We produce as good a type as anywhere in the country.' Meanwhile, Warwickshire County Council banned the film: distributor British Lion refused to make cuts demanded by the Warwickshire Cinematograph and Stage Plays Licensing Committee. 'It is fortunate for the world that Warwickshire's greatest and often bawdy son, William Shakespeare, was not subject in his day to the Mrs Grundys of the council,' said British Lion. 'Old fogies,' was how Tony described the local councils banning the film.

Alan Sillitoe believed *Saturday Night and Sunday Morning*'s success came from its freshness. Tony had never produced a film before, nor had Karel Reisz ever directed one. It was Sillitoe's first screenplay and Finney's debut film. Tony thought *Saturday Night*'s success originated from audiences recognising themselves onscreen for the first time: they were not watching some kind of unreal, over-glamorised world – here, were working-class people with whom they rubbed shoulders every day. Television producers had been thinking the same way and a new drama serial titled *Coronation Street*, depicting a similar world to Arthur Seaton's Nottingham, began showing on TV a fortnight after *Saturday Night*'s release.

By now Tony had pinged on Hollywood's radar. He was duly summoned to Paris to meet Darryl F. Zanuck, the Hollywood mogul who ran 20th Century Fox. Zanuck wanted him to direct *Sanctuary*, based on William Faulkner's scandalous 1931 bestseller. *Sanctuary* tells the story of Temple Drake, a rich and spoilt college girl who is kidnapped and raped by a gangster, Candyman. He sets her up in a brothel, where she discovers a taste for the sordid. Eventually, believing Candyman to be dead, she returns home and marries her college boyfriend. She employs Nancy, a black prostitute who worked in the brothel with her, as her maid. However, Candyman turns up alive, Drake agrees to run away with him and it takes the shock of Nancy murdering Temple's baby to bring the young mother to her senses. 'When you are approached to do an American film, it is really like Lucifer taking you up to the top of the mountain and showing you all the wonders of the world,' said Tony.[4]

It was not the first time that he had visited Yoknapatawpha County. Back in November 1957, Tony had staged the English-language premiere of *Requiem for a Nun* there. Based on Faulkner's 1951 novel, *Requiem for a Nun* was the sequel to *Sanctuary* and was released to laudatory reviews. It was not the first time *Sanctuary* had been filmed, either: a 1933 version of Faulkner's lurid tale created such uproar that it led to the introduction of movie censorship.

Doris Lessing, the novelist whom Tony had previously treated so cavalierly, was hired to adapt the script. Tony flew out to Los Angeles in August 1960. On arrival, however, he realised Fox had hired its own screenwriter James Poe to write another screenplay. Once again, Lessing was duly dumped. Fox wanted Lee Remick, whom it was pushing as a sex symbol, to play Temple Drake and gave Tony the choice of either Laurence Harvey or Yves Montand as Candyman. Tony plumped for Montand, whom he later described as the vainest man he had ever met.

Meanwhile, David Merrick had bought the Broadway rights to Shelagh Delaney's *A Taste of Honey*. Delaney, a Lancashire bus driver's daughter, was eighteen when she wrote the play. Joan Littlewood first staged *A Taste of Honey* at the Theatre Royal Stratford East in 1958. Delaney's play tells the story of boozy semi-whore Helen, who drags her daughter Jo through a trail of squalid lodgings before abandoning her for yet another unsuitable man. When her black sailor boyfriend returns to sea, Jo finds herself pregnant and alone. She befriends Geoff, a gay art student, who moves in with her. In its sympathetic portrayal of black and homosexual characters – and in particular presenting the love of a mixed-race couple on stage – the play confronted contemporary taboos head-on. Most of all, *A Taste of Honey* was a celebration of being different.

'Once, authors wrote good plays set in drawing rooms. Now, under the Welfare State, they write bad plays set in garrets. Shelagh Delaney worked in a Salford factory until she saw Terence Rattigan's new play and decided she could write a better one. If there is anything worse than an Angry Young Man, it's an Angry Young Woman,' fulminated the *Daily Mail*. Meanwhile, Woodfall had already optioned the film rights for £30,000. The actor Victor Spinetti ran across Tony in New York at a gay tea dance being given by a World Heavyweight boxer for his Canadian lumberjack boyfriend. 'Joan Littlewood ruined Shelagh Delaney's beautiful play,' drawled Tony. 'It's not a play. It's a poem set to jazz.'[5]

But Tony had trouble raising the budget. When Merrick asked him to direct the Broadway version, Tony believed that he would never raise the money if the American version proved a flop and so he'd better put it on himself (Angela Lansbury was already cast as the blowsy, gin-sentimental mother and Joan Plowright was later cast as Jo). He told Nigel Davenport, who he cast as Lansbury's boyfriend, that he saw the play as a romantic comedy.[6] In September 1960, the play opened in Los Angeles before transferring to New York. Tony's plan was to film *Sanctuary* during the day and somehow rehearse *A Taste of Honey* at night. Sometimes he could be ambitious to the point of madness.

Tony rented Zsa Zsa Gabor's home at 110 Montana Street in Westwood. The house was furnished with cast-offs from television talk shows. Christopher Isherwood compared the goings-on at Montana Street to a Feydeau farce – there were parties every weekend. John Osborne came from New York to stay with Mary Ure. Plowright was already installed in the swimming-pool toolshed. Osborne remembered visitors wandering in day and night – mostly tanned young men in tee-shirts and shorts of indeterminate sexuality (the boundaries between straight and gay were far less rigid in Los Angeles). Other guests included Vivien Leigh and gay actor Tom Tryon, who would attend the Broadway opening on Tony's arm.

The screenwriter John Mortimer once observed that the point of Tony's famously overcrowded house parties was that in the end everybody slept with everybody else. Tony would feign his usual astonishment, pretending they had all invited themselves: 'I mean, I don't know *why* he's/she's here! They just *arrived*! They won't say when they're going!' Zsa Zsa's black maid only added to the bizarre atmosphere: she would turn up for work after 10pm, open everybody's mail and sell any juicy stories inside to Hollywood gossip writers Hedda Hopper and Louella Parsons. She also disliked other black people. Whenever Tony was entertaining a black friend, she would come in and turn off the lights, music or television in whatever room they were in.

What wasn't so amusing was the night when Mary Ure tried to commit suicide. At this time, Mr and Mrs Osborne were fighting bitterly over the playwright's call-girl mistress. Most evenings would end with Ure crying hysterically. One night she jumped naked into the swimming pool, saying she'd just swallowed half a bottle of sleeping pills. According to Tony, he and Osborne were both lying on sun-loungers watching the histrionics. Both were pretty smashed. 'Don't you think we should do something?' Tony asked languidly. Osborne shrugged – as far as he was concerned, she was just creating a scene. According to Tony, it was he who dived in to save her but according to Joan Plowright, it was she who fished Ure out – fully-clothed this time – put her under the shower and finally, still sobbing, to bed. Only then, according to Plowright, did Tony arrive home.

Osborne and Tony began cackling with laughter over Ure's suicide attempt – 'Tony, of course, loved dramas like that which "jolted people out of their complacency,"' explained Plowright. However, Tony did go in to check if Ure was all right. (Eventually, Tony became so exhausted by the constant partying that he ended up fleeing his own house. He rented another apartment in Westwood, but found he was too tired to sleep.)

Plowright remembered the sense of growing excitement as opening night drew nearer. Meanwhile, Oscar Lewenstein found David Merrick to be difficult and stingy. Tony, however, always stood up to him. One day Merrick arrived to keep an eye on his investment. He demanded that Tony drop Andrew Ray (who'd been cast as Geoff) because it turned out that Ray had a stammer, but Tony refused to do so. Merrick and his cohorts reminded Plowright of Al Capone and his gang – 'I've never seen such a crooked-looking bunch in my life,' she wrote to Laurence Olivier. 'I expect them to pull a gun out every time they are contradicted in an argument.'

A Taste of Honey transferred to New York's Lyceum Theatre, where it opened on 4 October 1960. Merrick's instinct was to squish a nickel till it squeaks and shortly before the first night, he wanted to cut the small jazz group which was part of the production. Tony resisted and won. The New York Times' review was unfavourable despite praising Tony's 'fluid, imaginative' direction. Lewenstein remembered everybody melting away from the obligatory first-night party at Sardi's – failure might be contagious. Despite this, it went on to run for 376 performances. Once again, Tony's little play about loneliness had caught the public mood.

Tony's Hollywood experience was summed up when he said he wanted to use some of Sanctuary's actual dialogue only to be told, 'The only reason you want to use that is because Faulkner wrote it.' It was the old story of the studio hiring someone to bring in a fresh outsider's eye, then doing its damnedest to make him fit in. Tony soon found himself fighting a losing struggle against being subsumed by the studio and every day became a battle not to succumb to the worst compromise. Quickly gaining a reputation for being 'difficult', he fought studio casting directors and the art department.

Zanuck's son Richard was his nominal producer but Tony found him indecisive. Every day Zanuck Jr would wait by the phone for his father's call, during which he would then endure a tirade of abuse. Next day, the same thing would happen again. A studio censor sat in the projection room with Tony watching the dailies. Occasionally, he would tell him certain scenes had to be re-shot. 'It was terrifying,' Tony remembered. Executives forced him to shoot scenes that they assured him would never end up in the finished film. Of course, they eventually appeared in the final cut.

When studio chairman Spyros Skouras saw the rushes he cabled Zanuck Jr to close the production down – no right-minded person would want to see it anyway, he fumed. It was not long before everyone lost confidence in what Tony described as this 'shame-making' feature. Fox had promised him the earth and so he'd gone in, thinking he was about to beat Hollywood at its own game. Instead, Hollywood had defeated him.

The studio system left Tony thoroughly disenchanted. He compared the studios to extinct dinosaurs, mastodons gasping their last breath – the whole industry was weighted against an artist getting his signature on a film. *Sanctuary* left him vowing never to make another movie shackled to a sound stage. He believed that studio filming encouraged artificiality as remote from life as kabuki. 'It is impossible to make anything interesting or good under the conditions imposed by the major studios in America,' he declared. 'It is a totally impossible creative set-up; even after the film is made, so much mutilation goes on, and it becomes the product of many different people.'

After the Broadway opening of *A Taste of Honey*, Tony flew back to London. He threw himself into his next project, a television drama written by John Osborne for the BBC. *A Subject of Scandal and Concern* was, in many ways, a sketch for their next theatre collaboration, *Luther*. It was based on the true story of nonconformist George Holyoake, who, in 1842, was the last man in Britain to be jailed for blasphemy after scandalising a Cheltenham Social Missionary Society with his views. Richard Burton, by then one of the most in-demand actors in the world, agreed to star as Holyoake. Tony had just three weeks to rehearse with him. Meanwhile, the press kicked up a fuss about television licence fee money going to the Hollywood star. Together with Burton and Osborne, Tony held a press conference in which he defended the Corporation for paying the actor £1,000 (twice the amount usually paid by the BBC). The irony was that Burton had turned down $350,000 to play Christ in Nicholas Ray's *The King of Kings* (1961) in order to be in the television play.

Holyoake had a dreadful stammer, which meant that he was unable to defend himself at his trial. Osborne's version builds up to the moment when Burton at last breaks through his impediment to give a long, impassioned speech. In those days, television tape recording was so primitive you couldn't cut or edit tape – you had to film the whole thing in one go. The actor playing the jury foreman only had one line – 'Guilty, my lord' – but he got so carried away by Burton's peroration that he shouted out, 'Not guilty!' Tony had to stop and re-shoot the entire play. Immediately after filming, Burton left for Broadway to star in *Camelot*. Back in Britain, the BBC solemnly warned viewers that it was deliberately putting on the *Sunday Night Play* late at night because it was about an atheist.

Meanwhile, Tony had found the £120,000 needed to make *A Taste of Honey*. Based on the enormous success of *Saturday Night and Sunday Morning*, British Lion-Bryanston went with his vision. Tony wanted to go even further with location shooting: this time around, the entire film including interiors would be shot on location. He regarded working in a studio as akin to being in prison. Location shooting may have imposed tremendous limitations, but at least they were stimulating – that cramped way of working might produce something you could not get any other way. It's important to remember how heretical this was. Today, we're used to jerky, handheld camerawork in TV documentaries about sink estates. What Tony was doing was revolutionary, especially for technicians used to working in the Pinewood dream factory. It was the first time anybody had attempted location shooting on such a grand scale.

Tony never really thought of *A Taste of Honey* as being based on a play he'd already directed. Before the Broadway version opened, he and Shelagh Delaney had already written the script. Its cracking dialogue – 'I dreamt of you last night and I fell out of bed twice' and 'The dream's gone but the baby's real enough' would be appropriated more than twenty years later by rock band The Smiths. At one point, Jo taunts Geoff for being a 'pansified little freak', something the censor strongly objected to. The British Board of Film Classification made it clear that, 'Geoffrey should not be an exaggerated nancy boy.'

Many thought that Tony's greatest flair was for casting and in this case, he wanted Lancashire comedienne Dora Bryan to play Jo's blowsy mother. Bryan had never seen the play and had no idea who Tony Richardson was. Indeed, she thought, 'it all sounded very precarious.' Her agent recommended she take £1,500 up front rather than a share of the profits. Bryan later regretted her decision. Robert Stephens was cast as her shifty, sweaty fancy man. Murray Melvin, who had been in Littlewood's original stage production, recreated his role as Geoff.

Tony liked working with people who had never acted before – experienced actors were like old worn coins, he said. He picked a young lawyer with no acting experience to play Jo's black sailor. Paul

Danquah was the son of Ghanaian Opposition leader Dr Joseph Danquah. Tony had met him through a circle that included Francis Bacon and Danquah would take his fellow actors to meet Bacon at his favourite dive bar, Muriel's.

The casting of clumsy, wilful Jo triggered the flashpoint for Tony and Saltzman to fall out. One Hollywood producer offered to fully finance the film provided Tony cast Audrey Hepburn as Jo. His one precondition was that Jo should have a miscarriage – that way, the film could have an optimistic, happy ending. For his part, Saltzman thought the film should be set in France with Leslie Caron and Simone Signoret as the leads. Meanwhile, Tony said absolutely not.

The truth was that Woodfall had reached the point where it was unable to accommodate two impresarios. Saltzman had taught Tony the complexities of film finance but the pupil had outgrown his teacher – Woodfall's success meant Tony was now regarded as 'bankable' and Saltzman's finagling to find cash was no longer needed. Indeed, there had always been a vulgarity about Saltzman that didn't sit well with Tony. Shortly after the release of *Saturday Night and Sunday Morning*, Woodfall announced that Saltzman was to quit the board. Producing as well as directing meant Tony felt completely free for the first time. Saltzman grumbled, correctly as it turned out, that there was no longer anyone to say 'no' to Tony and he had become impervious to criticism. 'Telling him was useless,' said Saltzman. 'No mother ever believes her own child is ugly.'

One footnote to Tony's falling out with Saltzman was how he came to acquire his devoted chauffeur Jan Niemeynowicz. Saltzman had been living in high style at Woodfall's expense. He'd taken on full-time staff and sent Woodfall the bill. Tony now had the job of telling his staff that they could either stay with Saltzman or, very generously, carry on working for him. Given the way Saltzman used to bully and humiliate them, Tony thought this would be a no-brainer. Apparently this was not the case and apart from his Polish driver, everyone opted to stay with Saltzman.

Woodfall placed an advertisement in the *Daily Express* – then Britain's best-selling newspaper – looking for an 'Ugly Unknown' to play Jo. Reckoning she was both, two brothers of an eighteen-year-old dogsbody at Liverpool Playhouse pushed their younger sister to apply. Rita Tushingham's only acting experience had been playing the rear end of a panto donkey. In early 1960, she travelled down to London with her mum and along with 500 other young hopefuls, auditioned at Chelsea Town Hall. 'Don't look, don't look!' she remembered her mum hissing as they passed a cross-eyed nun on the King's Road – her Liverpudlian mother considered the nun to be bad luck.

Tushingham had never been to London before and took it as an opportunity to do some sightseeing. Tony didn't think much of her audition – she looked like the product of an unlikely coupling between Audrey Hepburn and Pinocchio. Tushingham forgot all about her day trip to London but Tony found himself haunted by this little hedgehog with her expressive eyes. One day, Tushingham was called to the Playhouse's stage-door telephone only to hear Tony's languorous drawl telling her that she had got the part. She thanked him and then went back to knocking on actors' doors, telling them they had half an hour to be on stage. 'Then I thought, hang on, did he say I've got the part or that I haven't got the part?' she remembered.[7] In fact, she signed her contract on 26 April 1960.

Naturally, the press went to town. The *Sunday Pictorial* splashed a huge picture of Tushingham across six columns underneath the headline: 'THE UGLIEST GIRL IN THE WORLD'. Osborne, who was nominally co-producing the film, retorted: 'This apparently ugly duckling has more expression and beauty when she crooks her little finger than most of these damned starlets have if they waggled their oversized bosoms and bottoms from here to eternity!' In hindsight, this was a brilliant choice. At the time, some thought it indulgent and not a little mad.

In April 1961, shooting began in a poor area of Salford, Manchester. The film starts off with street urchins playing in Hancock Street, which was later demolished as part of a slum clearance project. One of the children playing, Hazel Blears, grew up to become a Labour Cabinet Minister. The unit spent three weeks shooting in Manchester before moving down to London. Woodfall rented a shabby fourteen-roomed house at the wrong end of the King's Road, converting it into a combined studio and offices. The final bonfire scene was shot outside the English Stage Company's workshop in Fulham, southwest London.

'The way we are shooting the film, we are at the mercy of real life. If it's raining, we don't wait for the sun to come out, we just play the scene in the rain. If there's a wind blowing which gets the leading actress's hair untidy, we shoot her looking untidy,' said Tony. 'Of course, if we had a big female star in the film we couldn't do this – we haven't the time nor the inclination to bother about obtaining the most flattering shots.' Meanwhile, Tushingham recalled: 'He was marvellous at establishing a community around him. It was important to him to have everyone, cast and technical crew, working towards the same goal – he knew that you need to have everyone's enthusiasm.'

Tony roped the composer Jock Addison into playing the piano in the pub scene where Dora Bryan sings. Unlike other directors, who normally brought in the composer once editing was nearly finished, Tony liked Addison to visit the unit on location: that way, he could absorb the atmosphere. Tushingham said that Tony guided the actors in a subtle way – he knew what he wanted, but he would let them work at it, discovering it for themselves as if tugging slightly at their reins. 'There was something infectious about him. He had an enormous energy and he was an extremely generous man professionally,' she said. 'He was so keen on giving people an opportunity, which people in this business are reluctant to do. He nurtured so much talent and he allowed you to develop.'[8]

By the time shooting ended, Tony still had no regrets about taking on everything himself. He was usually exhausted by this stage and told the BBC, 'I'm having injections of all sorts. I've no energy left.' However, being his own master also energised him, he claimed.

What was so marvellous – to use Tony's favourite word – about his direction is that Jo is not just a pitiable victim. She too can be wounding, brutal and capricious. Dressed up like Widow Twankey, Jo spends a ghastly day out at the seaside with Stephens and his grotesque friends. Tony brilliantly captures the wet matey-ness of Blackpool pier and romance flowering beneath the gasometer. Jo and her black sailor lover walk past rain-soaked tombstones and filth-throttled Manchester canals. The emotional highpoint comes when Jo exults, 'What is my usual self? My usual self is a very unusual self, and don't you forget that, Geoffrey Ingham. I'm an extraordinary person. There's only one of me, like there's only one of you.' 'We're unique,' Geoff joins in. 'Young!' cries Jo. 'Unrivalled!' 'We're bloody marvellous!' It's a truly wonderful moment that the rest of the film never quite recaptures.

Paul Dehn in the *Daily Herald* praised *A Taste of Honey*'s 'unforced poetry,' while the *New York Times* decided, 'in being transported out of the theatre, this *Honey* has been enriched.' The *Evening News* predicted great things for Tony: 'Put his name up with Carol Reed and David Lean. Even higher. If his progress remains constant, he is destined to outstrip them both.' The *Daily Mail*, though, dismissed him as, 'our number one life-is-real, life-is-earnest boy wonder.' *A Taste of Honey* was selected for the Cannes Film Festival, where Bryan and Tushingham played up the angle of a couple of no-nonsense girls from Lancashire. They gave the reporters some good copy bemoaning the lack of fish and chips – although Tushingham really did ask the waiter to take the crudités away because the vegetables weren't cooked. Tushingham and Melvin won Palme d'Ors for Best Actress and Best Actor.

At one point in the film Jo exclaims, 'I'm not just talented, I'm genius-ed.' For his next production, Tony would portray the life of a true genius – Martin Luther, the founder of Protestantism – but first, a run-of-the-mill theatre visit led to him re-encountering Vanessa Redgrave, the woman he was shortly to marry.

Notes

1. Diane Cilento, author interview, 1 December 2010.
2. Rickards, Jocelyn. *The Painted Banquet*, Weidenfeld & Nicolson, London, 1987.
3. McFarlane, Brian. *The Autobiography of British Cinema*, Methuen, London, 1997.
4. *Frankly Speaking*, BBC Radio, 16 June 1962.
5. Spinetti, Victor. *Up Front…* Robson Books, London, 2006.
6. Rita Tushingham, author interview, 8 December 2010.
7. Rita Tushingham, author interview, 8 December 2010.
8. Rita Tushingham, author interview, 8 December 2010.

CHAPTER SEVEN

Mr and Mrs Wood

People who knew Tony said that he was so full of energy he would be planning his next film while directing a play and overseeing another Woodfall production. He loved keeping all these plates spinning in the air, seemingly recharging himself out of the energy he expended. However, now it was as if his subconscious was telling him to take time off and indulge the sybaritic side of his nature. For the past five years, he had done nothing much apart from work. On 4 July 1961, he went to see *As You Like It* at the Aldwych, not expecting much. He told his future sister-in-law Deirdre Redgrave that the moment he saw Vanessa on stage, he knew she was the woman for him; the world shifted a little on its axis before righting itself. He compared Vanessa to a sinuous golden flame: the beanpole seventeen-year-old he had glimpsed seven years previously at Bedford House had become an intoxicating, radiant woman. He had to have her. After the play, he went backstage to re-introduce himself. Rachel was also there and witnessed their meeting; she had the feeling this was love at first sight.

A couple of nights later, Tony spotted Vanessa having dinner with Bernard Levin, the critic, who was infatuated with her. Tony gave the headwaiter a note to hand to Vanessa, but it never occurred to him the famously shortsighted Vanessa had forgotten to bring her spectacles. She handed the note to Levin, who read it aloud to her: Tony's billet-doux ended with, '... and tell Mr L to go f**k himself'. Levin's presumably apoplectic reaction is not recorded, but he never asked Vanessa out again. She wrote to her father just before Christmas 1961, saying, 'He is a very interesting person to talk to and I've enjoyed myself thoroughly, but alas! My heart is engaged elsewhere.'

Tony and Vanessa began seeing each other. At the time, he was sharing a flat in Mayfair with John Osborne. One day, Osborne arrived home to be confronted by a furious porter, who complained that an orgy had taken place while he was away. Looking around at the damage, the fastidious Osborne was shocked. Tony and Vanessa's mutual ardour, he recollected later, had wrecked the place. There were cigarette burns in what furniture was still intact, a length of curtain was hanging down as if a chimpanzee had swung from it, empty champagne and whisky bottles rolled on the carpet. Worse, there were tiny piles of dog excrement everywhere. 'Burglars?' Osborne suggested cautiously. 'With small dogs!' the porter shrieked.

The idea that Tony the homosexual had now become miraculously heterosexual must have arched an eyebrow or two among those who knew him. In any case, the theatrical world was much more camp in those days. Tony was far too intelligent not to realise that sexuality is not a fixed thing – rather, it's a sliding scale. Even Michael Redgrave's lover Nöel Coward reckoned himself to be 5 per cent straight, while Alfred Kinsey, in his groundbreaking 1948 report on male sexuality, calculated that 11.6 per cent of white males aged between 20 and 35 were equally attracted to both sexes. Like many men who have had homosexual experiences when young, perhaps Tony thought this was just something he'd grown out of. Besides, he already knew that it's what's between the ears that makes someone truly attractive.

Tony confessed to Rachel that he was so in love with Vanessa, he didn't quite know what to do. Rachel suggested they get married. There was a calculating side to Tony's passion for Vanessa, though. '*Really*!' said Olivia Manning, who had let Tony move into her flat when he was job hunting and had by now been resoundingly dropped, 'It's as if he'd become a member of the Royal Family.' Rachel might have suggested the two get married, but the first she or Michael knew about it was when Vanessa phoned them to say the ceremony was taking place the next morning: 28 April 1962. Vanessa wore a navy-blue skirt and blouse for the Hammersmith & Fulham Register Office wedding. The Redgraves then went back to Tony's flat.

Despite her surface sweetness, there was a cold side to Rachel, too. 'How long do you give them?' Michael wondered. 'Five years at a guess,' Rachel replied. The joke in Hollywood, where Tony's sexual proclivities were well known, was that he only married Vanessa because he could fit into her clothes.[1] Vanessa was back on stage that very night playing Rosalind at the Aldwych, while Tony spent his wedding night watching *Chips With Everything* at the Royal Court with his new brother-in-law, Corin, in one of the roles.

The honeymoon proper began on 29 April 1962 when 'Mr and Mrs Wood' flew into Athens to join a ten-day Aegean cruise. However, the strain of neither wanting to compromise their career was apparent right from the start. On their return, Tony immediately rushed off to the Cannes Film Festival before leaving for a week in America. Vanessa was also appearing in *Cymbeline* at Stratford as well as the West End run of *As You Like It*, leaving her exhausted.

Mr and Mrs Richardson moved into a charming mews house in Eaton Mews North. Strangely, the newlyweds invited John Osborne and his new lover Penelope Gilliatt to share their doll's house. Vanessa joked that the Belgravia mews was far too small for a couple of giraffes like them, let alone four people; she also confessed to not being much good in the kitchen. The only meal she ever prepared was breakfast and that consisted of coffee and orange juice. No sooner had Osborne moved in, than, according to Osborne, Tony and Vanessa once again started smashing the place up with their passionate lovemaking. This time, however, the owner sued Tony for all the damage caused. 'I mean, Johnny,' Tony protested indignantly, 'don't you think it's a disgrace?' He and Vanessa struck Osborne as a bizarre couple. 'Similar in some tangled, physical way, they seemed to compound a piranha-toothed androgynous power within each other,' he wrote.

Not that Tony had much time to play newlywed. He was battling with the Lord Chamberlain, the theatre censor, over the script for Osborne's new play, *Luther*. The Lord Chamberlain refused to license *Luther* because of many scatological references in the script. Much of the tone was to do with excrement because Luther was obsessed with his bowels. Meanwhile, Osborne said he would rather withdraw the play than censor himself. Tony and the Lord Chamberlain argued it out point by point and by April 1961, the censor had ceded his eight most important objections.

Luther was a muscular Brechtian drama which, according to Osborne, concerned 'the nature of religious experience.' Eleven scenes follow Luther as he develops from neurotic student to angry young man and finally, reflective middle age. The centrepiece of the play comprises three Lutheran sermons delivered from the pulpit directly to the audience as congregation. Reading the play, Tony realised it was a sort of master-piece; he also knew Osborne regarded his work as finished and he was becoming increasingly irritated by Osborne's refusal to rewrite anything.

Once again, Tony assembled his core team, including Oscar Lewenstein and production designer Jocelyn Herbert around him. Albert Finney was always going to play Luther. Tony built a theatrical cathedral around Finney, with Jock Addison as the choirmaster. Peter Bull was a new member of Tony's repertory company. Bull was completely flabbergasted when, being interviewed for a role, Tony knew the exact remote Spanish *pensione* from whence Bull had just returned – 'I couldn't imagine Mr Richardson there with all those hens and pigs, who tend to roam about at whim. But now he was regaling me with some splendid gossip about the local inhabs,' Bull remembered.

Tony spent days casting dogs – he needed to find just the right ones to accompany the entrance of the sporting Medici Pope. He then took one of the Pope's falcons out into an alley to teach it to fly. After losing the bird, he spent several hours knocking on people's front doors to ask, 'Do you have my hawk in your garden?'

Luther opened at the Theatre Royal, Nottingham, on 26 June 1961. It started to rain on opening night – a cold, gray drizzle, which a few in the cast took as a bad omen. Everybody was feeling jittery. Some of those mingling in the foyer had come up from London – there had been so much anticipation of Osborne's new play that *Time* magazine had reviewed the script. You could hear the West End crowd talking to each other, with 'Tony' this and 'Johnny' that. Worried that many of the local first-nighters might be expecting Finney to be Arthur Seaton again, Tony scrutinised the audience through the curtain and tried to gauge the mood. When they found out Finney was now Martin Luther, the 16th-century Protestant revolutionary, they might 'turn ugly.' Instead, the first-night applause was tremendous. *Luther* marked Osborne's zenith as the hell-fire preacher of national conscience. And for Tony, Finney played Luther with a passion he'd never achieved before or since. The company took several curtain calls.

Kenneth Tynan described Tony's direction as 'simple and dramatic'. 'Tony Richardson has surpassed himself as director with a production of magisterial grandeur and theatrical pageantry. Every stage picture seems to have been cut from a frame in the Uffizi and set into motion,' agreed the *Sunday Telegraph*. '[It] remains a hammer-blow of an evening.'

Luther went on to Paris and Amsterdam before returning to the Court for a short run of 28 sell-out performances; it then travelled to the Edinburgh Festival for a fortnight before transferring to

London's Phoenix Theatre. There it stayed for a long and successful run. 'Richardson's direction is a model of gravity and style,' wrote *The Times*. On 25 September 1961, David Merrick opened *Luther* on Broadway, with Finney recreating his starring role. Merrick had to battle US immigration authorities to get him into the country, though – American Equity objected to an English actor getting a work permit. '*Luther*,' said the *New York Times*, 'makes the theatre ten feet tall'.

That summer, Tony rented La Baumette, an old farmhouse in the South of France, for the very first time. Vanessa said it was the kind of holiday she'd never dreamed of. La Baumette was beautiful. Set amid a vineyard, olive trees and a pinewood, it was an old stone farmhouse with a built-on modern wing. The living room was huge, with glass doors leading onto to a terrace where everyone ate meals shaded by the overhanging trees. One Monsieur Voisin looked after the property, tending the olives and the vines. According to Jocelyn Rickards, the lavender hedge was turned into the sweetest-smelling oil of lavender she had ever known. Grapes were crushed into wine. Vanessa remembered sun on hot stones, aïoli and fireflies.

Osborne, however, noticed that newlywed Tony kept driving off in his red Thunderbird for mysterious assignations on the beach at Cannes or to parties in Terence Rattigan's suite at the shocking-pink Hotel Negresco. Christopher Isherwood, another La Baumette guest, mentioned Tony attending one of Rattigan's all-male parties along with his father-in-law, Michael Redgrave. Seven years later, Osborne would look back with disgust at this holiday: 'Luxury, spoiled people ... lounging together, basting themselves with comfort, staring into pools. A swimming pool is a terrible thing to look into on a holiday. It's no past and no future.'[2]

Vanessa would have objected to this portrait of herself as one of the idle rich. She once listed her hobby in *Who's Who* as, 'changing the status quo.' There has been much speculation as to what made her become such a political animal. One theory is that it coincided with her realising that Michael was bisexual. The argument runs that she identified him as one of the 'oppressed' and resolved there and then to dedicate her life to fighting oppression. Or perhaps it was that her intellectual insecurity about emphasising arts over academia – and her rivalry with Corin – forced her to overcompensate, turning to politics as proof of her seriousness. She herself has said that her political education came first from family friends such as Peggy Ashcroft, and from Paul Robeson, whom she met during *Othello*. Robert Bolt convinced her to join the Campaign For Nuclear Disarmament (CND), but it was Tony who was the biggest influence on her politically. 'He was the real [political] shaker and iconoclast of the family,' she said. 'I was a very conservative and somewhat ignorant lady compared to him.'

Vanessa's earliest act of political subversion chimed perfectly with her background as a well-brought-up gel: she slipped 'Ban the Bomb' leaflets in between glossy pages of magazines lying on antique tables in London's most exclusive hotels. Vanessa would walk into the Connaught, Ritz and Savoy dressed in twin-set and pearls, leaf idly through *Country Life*, *Vogue* and *The Tatler*, then get up and leave. She was never caught. Rachel complained to Michael that their Knightsbridge flat had, 'become a sort of Committee headquarters.'

The day after she came back to London from her honeymoon in May 1961, Vanessa stood on a soapbox in Trafalgar Square urging the crowd to ban the bomb. Tony was tolerant of his wife making speeches at Hyde Park and going on ban-the-bomb demonstrations. However, friends and family, especially Michael, warned that she might damage her career. On 17 September 1961, some 15,000 people jammed Trafalgar Square in protest against nuclear weapons. Already that same day, Russia had exploded a nuclear weapon in the twelfth test of its current series – it was as if Moscow was rehearsing the apocalypse to come. Clashes came as 3,000 police officers struggled to arrest demonstrators staging 'sit down' protests.

Nearly 850 people, including Vanessa and Osborne, were arrested during the rally. Vanessa was bundled into a Black Maria, where she was transported to Ealing police station. Shelagh Delaney was arrested with her. Vanessa and Delaney shared a cold and dirty police cell. The next day, she appeared at Marlborough Street Magistrates Court. Following this, she began donating to several radical peace bodies, including the CND-linked Committee of 100. Osborne, who was arrested that same afternoon, was fined twenty shillings at Bow Street Magistrates Court.

In February 1962, Vanessa gave evidence at an Old Bailey trial in support of two disarmament activists, who later helped Soviet spy George Blake to escape from Wormwood Scrubs. It was claimed she unwittingly helped finance the 1966 operation – her money was used to buy the Dormobile that smuggled Blake across the Iron Curtain to Moscow.[3]

Unilateral nuclear disarmament was one thing Vanessa and Tony disagreed about: he maintained that a film could change more people than Vanessa sitting down in Trafalgar Square. In any case, he believed in having nuclear weapons as 'the only realistic way.' Unlike Vanessa, who believed all good art was about social change, Tony's attitude was ambivalent and some accused him of trying to have it both ways. Sometimes he never felt an artist had any difficulty in trying to preach political doctrine: the artist's political attitude would be there in his work anyway; it would be woven into the fabric of the person making it. Other times, he was convinced cinema had a polemic role. His later films, *The Charge of the Light Brigade* and *Loneliness of the Long Distance Runner*, indicted the Army and the Borstal system. He felt strongly enough about apartheid to have his films banned in South Africa. Possibly trying to give his hosts at a Cuban film festival what they wanted to hear, he told *Cine Cubano* magazine in July 1963 that the Royal Court was a theatre of the Left protesting against social conditions, although not in a propagandistic sense.

Tony described himself as a Communist, although he never joined the party. He wanted to see the red flag fly from the tops of Oxford colleges, a position he gradually arrived at. During the 1960s, he leaned ever further towards the Left, although he believed all artists were basically apolitical. His champagne Communism irritated Doris Lessing. Tony made sure that Carlo Levi's novel about poverty in southern Italy, *Christ Stopped at Eboli*, was always prominently displayed on his desk. Lessing described Tony as putting on Communism like the latest jacket – he enjoyed shocking people. Film director Ken Loach also accused him of dilettantism. According to him, Tony had used the North of England and the working-class merely as a location before they went out of fashion.

Vanessa's own views were well known enough for the BBC to ask her to sing her self-composed song, 'Hanging On A Tree', on the radio on Christmas Day, 1963 (she had written the song in protest against the imprisonment of Nelson Mandela and other anti-apartheid activists in South Africa). A group of businessmen was so moved by her lyrics that they tried to publish them in a full-page advertisement calling for sanctions against South Africa in the *Financial Times*. It was a curious thing. She once. Lynn that she felt much more strongly for a group of people she didn't know than those closest to her.[4] 'My paradox is that although I care a great deal for the masses – the orphans in Vietnam, the starving in India – I seem to care little about the individuals around me. I've resisted that accusation. But quite bluntly, it's me.'[5]

Tony's final play at the Royal Court was, with pleasing symmetry, the very first Shakespeare play he'd seen as a child. *A Midsummer Night's Dream* had made him want to become a theatre director in the first place; it remained his favourite Shakespeare play. Rehearsals started at the beginning of 1962. He assembled his usual team of set designer Jocelyn Herbert and composer Jock Addison. Tony also gave Lynn Redgrave her first break, encouraging his eighteen-year-old sister-in-law to drop out of drama school.

Unlike Vanessa, Lynn didn't set out to become an actress. 'To an outsider, it probably seemed inevitable I should have followed the rest of the family in choosing a career,' she said. 'But it wasn't by any means a foregone conclusion.' Lynn, who had been mad keen on riding since the age of six, had dropped out of Queen's Gate school hoping to train as a professional show jumper under equestrian Pat Smythe. Her godmother (Edith Hargreaves, who had been Michael's first secretary) gave her a pony named Rosalinda. 'As far as I can recollect, show jumping and hours of riding were all I ever did until I was sixteen,' she admitted. Indeed, the glittering trophies she won all said the same thing: Lynn could do something the others couldn't. She then enrolled in a cooking course at Rupert Street Polytechnic, planning to finance her show jumping career through serving gourmet meals to the wealthy. Quickly realising this was an impractical idea, she gave it up: 'I suddenly realised that my lifelong ambition to show jump wasn't very practical. I found I didn't have the nerve to jump as high as I had to. I got into a terrible depression – having known from a child what I was going to be and now not knowing what I was going to do.'

Lynn decided to become an actress at the age of fifteen after watching Dorothy Tutin's performance in *Twelfth Night* at Stratford. It was 1958, the year in which Michael was doing his third *Hamlet*. The rest of the family were amazed by her decision, which they regarded with a kind of suppressed shock. Michael didn't think much of her ambitions – it was Vanessa who had inherited his 'divine gift,' as he called it. Lynn was the ugly duckling. He wrote in his diary, 'This strange, shy pudding of a child thought she was going to be an actress.'

When she was little, Michael used to pat Lynn's bulging waistline and make cruel remarks, often in front of guests. He hadn't helped her self-confidence either by walking out of the school play in 1959 after her first scene: watching through a hole in the curtain, Lynn was deeply hurt. Nevertheless, her mother coached Lynn in drama-school audition speeches. 'I think we have got another tip-top actress in her,' Rachel wrote to Michael.

Lynn auditioned for the London Academy of Music and Dramatic Art (LAMDA), but they turned her down, suggesting she was wasting her time. Instead, Central – where her sister had trained – offered her a place. Other students resented her for getting in on the family name. 'When I was a teenager at drama school, I was sensitive about that and occasionally had a weep,' Lynn recalled. 'A lot of people seemed to think I would have it easy.'

Accepting Tony's offer of a part in *A Midsummer Night's Dream* would mean dropping out of Central with six months to go. Unsure as to what to do, Lynn called her father, who was in New York at the time. Michael was doubtful. Over a muffled transatlantic line, Michael – who wasn't very enthusiastic about Tony as a director, either – advised her to stay put. Lynn also asked Vanessa for her advice. Remembering that Tony had rejected her for the film of *Look Back in Anger*, Vanessa reassured Lynn that her husband wouldn't have offered her the part if he didn't think she was ready.

What Michael hadn't understood during the transatlantic phone call was that Lynn had already auditioned for Tony. On 20 November 1961, Lynn wrote to Michael telling him that she'd decided to accept the part. Describing herself as being in 'a torrent of turmoil', Lynn had telephoned Tony, telling him she wasn't ready. He in turn had been 'fairly demented' about her doing it. 'What upsets me more than anything is the fact that I possibly do not have your support in this,' she told Michael.

Keeping things in the family, Tony also cast Corin as Lysander. Corin felt pressure to succeed at something: growing up surrounded by his parents' famous friends – Laurence Olivier and Vivien Leigh, John Mills, Ralph Richardson and the rest – it was almost expected of him and he became schoolboy national fencing champion at Westminster.

'I was fairly bookish, rather self-sufficient and independent-minded. I was also one of the best fencers of my generation,' Corin remembered. He too was stage-struck watching Michael's 1958 Stratford season – partly because he became hopelessly infatuated with Tutin. 'I was good enough to beat anyone in England, but not all the time,' he said. 'I had to make a choice between acting and fencing, and I chose acting.'

Corin never considered that he would do more than get a place at university and it was his Latin master who told him he was underestimating himself. 'That can make all the difference to a child,' said Corin. Michael was understandably thrilled when his son won an open scholarship to read classics at Cambridge (noted in big, bold letters as a single entry in his diary). Over the years, he had grown distant from Corin, just as he had with Lynn (the two hardly ever talked, but would leave notes to each other if they wanted to communicate).

Corin achieved a First in English at Cambridge, where his friends included Trevor Nunn and Ian McKellen, stars of the Marlowe Society production of *Henry IV* directed by him. Other university friends included Peter Cook, David Frost and Margaret Drabble. More than anything, Cambridge gave Corin time to ponder what he wanted to do with his life. 'I found this hiatus as an undergraduate at Cambridge invaluable,' he said. 'Because I knew I wanted to be involved in the entertainment world in some way, I didn't know what I particularly wanted to do.'

In June 1961, Corin had come down from Cambridge and did a variety of jobs for the Royal Court, including assisting George Devine and reading scripts. Tony asked Corin if he could act, whereupon Corin launched into Hotspur's speech – 'My liege, I did deny no prisoners' – before Tony waved him down. 'OK, you can play Lysander,' he shrugged. As with Lynn, Michael didn't encourage his son into acting. Perhaps the schoolmaster in him was disappointed Corin did not stay in academia or maybe he was too unsettled by his family encroaching onto his turf. When Corin was a teenager, Michael told him that his acting was, 'very good, but his eyes are too close together.' As for Corin himself, 'somehow acting seemed the right thing to do.'

The rest of the cast of *A Midsummer Night's Dream* were mostly unknowns fresh out of drama school. Tony also wanted to give working-class actors the chance to do Shakespeare for the first time. It says something for his uncanny ability to spot talent that most would go on to become famous: David Warner, Nicol Williamson, Ronnie Barker, James Bolam and Samantha Eggar. The play opened on 24 January 1962 to terrible reviews. 'And so we arrive at the true horror of this production; neither Mr Richardson nor his mostly very young cast has the faintest notion of the power of the word. As much like the real thing as an errand-boy's whistle is like a fine orchestra,' said the *Sunday Times*.

The young cast read the poor reviews aloud, trying to outdo each other as to who had the worst billing. In the end, Tony summonsed everybody to the stalls, told them to ignore the audience and promptly ordered champagne.[6] However, *A Midsummer Night's Dream* closed after 29 performances. Vanessa noted that critics who only five years before had ridiculed Tony for introducing the kitchen sink into drama were now equally incensed that the home of kitchen sink should be invaded by fairies and magic.

It was during *A Midsummer Night's Dream*'s brief run that Corin met his future wife Deirdre. She remembered going to the Royal Court on a black evening when the London streets were drenched with rain. After dinner, she and her friend Jonathan Benson went back to Knightsbridge, where Corin (an accomplished pianist) serenaded her with a song from Michael's favourite musical, *Guys and Dolls*. Proust said we fall in love with a fascinating shoulder or a delicious glance. Deirdre, a rebellious part-time model from a well-off background, said she fell in love right then. 'It was that simple. And that complicated,' she remembered. They were married within six months, with Michael's boyfriend Fred Sadoff inexplicably in the role of Corin's best man. There was a moment of high farce when Corin proposed one night at Hans Crescent. Knowing what he was about to say, Deirdre was so nervous that she dropped her glass, spilling champagne onto the head of a passer-by below. Michael, disturbed by the shouts from the pavement, stormed in and bawled the pair out, ruining the romantic moment.

Given the success of *Saturday Night and Sunday Morning*, Tony decided to base his next film on another Alan Sillitoe tale. *The Loneliness of the Long Distance Runner* was a 40-page story about a working-class lad sent to Borstal for theft. The Borstal governor is a sports enthusiast, who arranges for his boys to compete against a nearby school in a cross-country running match. The narrator, whose long-distance prowess has already been spotted, becomes the Governor's pet. On the day of the race, the narrator stops before the finishing line, deliberately and mockingly allowing his rival to pass. With this two-finger salute, the narrator shows that he hasn't been reformed.

Tony and Sillitoe got down to working on the screenplay. Being a short story and not a novel, the first draft came in much too short and new material had to be added. Sillitoe found writing the script less satisfying than he had for *Saturday Night and Sunday Morning*. Before, it had been difficult to know what to take out, whereas *The Loneliness of the Long Distance Runner* always seemed, 'a bit padded.' Because it was a short story, there was plenty of room for Tony to move things about. 'He did the Yiddish trick of straying from the main plotline, interleaving scenes, and he did it very well,' Sillitoe observed.

Sillitoe's screenplay, supervised by Tony, makes the hero – now called Colin Smith – a lot more aware of class barriers than he was in the short story. The schoolboy opponents in the novel are unnamed; in the film they come from a local public school. Colin also becomes a far more conventional, misunderstood hero. In the story, he and his mam squander his father's death benefit on clothes and booze. One of the happiest moments in his life is watching the brand-new telly downstairs while Mam is having it off with her fancy man. Colin's fantasy about living it up with some tarts becomes a poignant love affair in an out-of-season seaside resort. In Tony's version, he burns the death benefit given him by his mum.

The critic Raymond Durgnat sensed Tony's hypocrisy here: it was all right for him to allow himself an affluent lifestyle, 'but we mustn't let the spartan workers get affluent, must we? Let them lie on their beds burning their pound notes – for we, the sentimentaligentsia, just love the thought of their being a vast reservoir of simple folk living as frugally as woodcutters always did in fairy stories'. The British Board of Film Classification was even more alarmed by Sillitoe's latest script than it had been for *Saturday Night and Sunday Morning*. This time, the censor sent Tony a two-page closely typed letter complaining of excess 'language'. Such words as 'bugger', 'sod' and 'Christ' weren't acceptable either. 'Bleeding' had been used 32 times in all, while 'bastard' appeared 11 times. One censor, Audley Fields, described the script as, 'Communist propaganda ... it is true Party-line stuff.' Fields was particularly concerned about one scene where the police beat up a

Borstal boy they've recaptured (the scene is still cut whenever the film plays on television).

Once the script was deemed acceptable, Tony had to go out and find his lead actor. Once again, he wanted an unknown. It was Osborne who spotted Tom Courtenay in an Old Vic production of *The Seagull* at the Edinburgh Festival. He told Tony, 'I've seen your Runner.' Unlike Finney, Courtenay really was working-class: his dad chipped paint from fisher-trawlers in the Hull dockyards. Courtenay used to joke about the contrast between his proletarian looks and the pretensions of his aristocratic-sounding name (although in its original French derivation, Courtenay merely meant 'short nose'). He described getting a phone call from Woodfall as being a little like being summoned by Harvey Weinstein today: 'It was amazingly exciting to see Tony Richardson a few weeks after leaving drama school.' Tony, with his usual instinct for casting – 'it's in the eyes' – made up his mind within ten minutes.

Michael Redgrave agreed to play the Colonel Blimp-ish Borstal governor and it's a testament to his acting that he never allows his part to become a cutout. Rather, he shows a man who has vainly tried to graft Arnold-of-Rugby good intentions onto the Borstal system. In Colin, the Governor sees a chance to regain his self-respect. James Fox, whose father was talent agent Robin Fox, was cast as Colin's public-school rival. Robin Fox – who would become Tony's own agent – was angry with Tony for encouraging his son's acting ambitions rather than to go into banking as he himself wished. Later, Fox's youngest son Robert would marry Tony's daughter, Natasha.

Meanwhile, Tony found it wasn't so easy getting into Borstal: his applications for permission to visit an institution were turned down (the authorities were concerned about the film becoming an exposé). Their reaction confirmed Tony's own view that British institutions such as prisons and the police were guarded from scrutiny with an iron curtain as hard and tough as any imposed by the Soviet bloc. He fumed: 'How can I make a film about Borstal if I don't know what one looks like?' Eventually, he found a large country house in southwest London that looked like a Borstal exterior. He had to make do using the interior as well.

Filming began in February 1962. Courtenay remembered being collected from his digs in a large old Rolls, which Woodfall had bought on the cheap. Its beige felt interior had seen better days and it had a musty smell. Courtenay wasn't impressed. Tony remembered *The Loneliness of the Long Distance Runner* as being a great pleasure to make and he made things as easy as possible for his young lead – there were rarely any more than two takes of a shot. Courtenay got the impression that he was being allowed to do whatever he wanted, even ad-libbing dialogue. Tony liked to work fast because he got bored working slowly; he used to say that he couldn't plan or imagine things until he got on set. In this, he was the exact opposite of Alfred Hitchcock.

Tony once sat next to Hitchcock on a plane and the great director told him that, because he planned everything in his head before walking on set, shooting the film was something of an anti-climax. Tony thought there were two kinds of directors: the planners and the improvisers. He was definitely the latter. 'He loved shooting,' said Karel Reisz. 'Preparation was a necessary evil, and editing was something that he mainly subcontracted to editors. He loved shooting, he loved activity.' Indeed, Tony preferred the spontaneous – after all, he could control the film in the cutting room. 'It was a very good filming atmosphere, totally different from anything that had belonged to the studio system in Britain,' said James Fox. 'I think everyone who worked on it with Tony knew it was a special experience.'

Tony brilliantly amplified Alan Sillitoe's short story. We see Colin's life in a series of flashbacks as he trains for the race: his mother splashing out on a TV with the cash Colin's dad has left her; Colin and his mate breaking into a warehouse and the Borstal psychiatrist nonplussed as Colin blankly answers his questions. The problem is there are too many styles – from the dreamy winter silhouette of an early morning training run to the speeded-up Chaplinesque bakery theft. Tony's evolving style combined the sooty live-from-the-slums look of Italian neorealism with a grab-bag of cinematic tricks (jump cuts, freeze-frames, slow and speeded-up motion) shamelessly filched from others. There's a lot of bad Truffaut in the film, a little Godard, a bit of Keystone Cops … On the other hand, *The Loneliness of the Long Distance Runner* is full of poetic moments: the savagely ironic cross-cutting between police brutalising a Borstal escapee and the rest of the school singing 'Jerusalem' and the bleak final image of boys dismantling gas masks.

'The remarkable thing about *The Loneliness of the Long Distance Runner* and *A Taste of Honey* is not that they treat working-class people, working-class problems, but that they have a very poetic view of them,' observed Tony's cameraman, Walter Lassally. Like Colin, Tony suddenly throws his own film as his hero nears the finishing tape. Colin's stream of consciousness is suggested with machine-gun bursts of flashbacks riddling him with bitter memories. But we've already seen all this – the final moments betray Tony's anxiety that the audience won't get 'the message.' *Loneliness* proved another hit for Woodfall despite *Time* reviewing the film as 'a piece of skilful but specious pleading for the British proletariat ... the hero is palpably too prolier-than-thou, his case is too obviously rigged'.

Having finished shooting *Loneliness* in the summer of 1961, Tony now cast about for his next project. He realised that he had exhausted the seam of gritty working-class drama and was now in danger of repeating himself. Worse still, he was in danger of boring the audience. Around then, *Time* magazine had run a cover story on the new wave of realistic films set in the North. It claimed cinemagoers were 'getting a bit bugged by the same scummy roofscape and the eternal kitchen-sinkdrome. They sometimes find it a bit hard to believe that things are really all that bad in Merry England'.

That 'Long Shot of Our Town from That Hill In the Rain' had superseded Kenneth More's jutting jaw on the bridge of a Destroyer as the defining image of British cinema. Other companies had jumped on the kitchen-sink bandwagon as the moneybags of Wardour Street cottoned on to the formula. Rival producers announced projects such as *Every Night and Every Morning* and *A Taste of Money* – 'It's the dirt that brings in the cloth caps and muffler trade,' said the boss of one. Meanwhile, Tony rented La Baumette again that summer and began hatching another Woodfall project with Osborne and Devine. Adapting the 18th-century novel *Tom Jones* was a world away from the damp cobbled gloom of the Midlands. He decided to call this next project his 'holiday film.'

Notes

1. Gerber, Gail and Lisanti, Tom. *Trippin' With Terry Southern: What I Think I Remember*, Jefferson and McFarland & Company, Inc., North Carolina and London, 2009.
2. Osborne, John. *The Hotel In Amsterdam*, Evans, London, 1973.
3. Penrose, Barrie. 'Spy's Escape – Did Vanessa Redgrave Pay?' *Sunday Times*, 8 November 1997.

4. Simpson, Anne. 'How Fiery Vanessa Ruffled Comfy Lynn', *Glasgow Herald*, 31 May 1978.
5. Evans, Peter. *Daily Express*, 23 March 1966.
6. Rita Tushingham, author interview, 8 December 2010.

CHAPTER EIGHT
Mad About the Boy

The 36th Academy Awards, held on 13 April 1964, started out with that most Los Angelean of events: a gridlock on the freeway. Highway construction kept limousines bumper-to-bumper all the way from Beverly Hills to the Santa Monica Civic Auditorium where the Oscars were being staged that year. The first nominee to arrive was Best Supporting Actor hopeful Nick Adams, who showed up at 5.30pm – an hour-and-a-half before the ceremony was due to begin. Watched by a bemused usher, Adams practised walking, skipping and trotting down the aisle. At least he got there – many nominees didn't show up at all. In fact, fifty-seven of those short-listed to win awards simply gave up and went home.

The tension of sitting in a car edging along the Santa Monica freeway meant most nominees stampeded for the bar on arrival. Among the throng were Leslie Caron and her boyfriend Warren Beatty, Eddie Fisher and his date (identified only as Jackie Kennedy's secretary), who was wearing her hair in the bouffant style made fashionable by her boss and Rock Hudson, who was hosting the telecast. The crush meant that Shirley MacLaine's husband ruined the train of her evening gown. Squeezing his way out of the jammed bar, *Cleopatra* producer Walter Wagner grumbled, 'There, the preliminary bone-breaking is over – when do they operate?'

And it was worth the wait: the audience applauded when they saw the set, which vividly depicted the night-time circuit board sprawl of Los Angeles from the Hollywood Hills. Jack Lemmon, that year's Master of Ceremonies, walked on stage and announced, 'It's magic time!' Many of Lemmon's jokes that night were aimed at one Best Picture nominee in particular, *Tom Jones*. The small English film had been nominated for 10 Academy Awards, including Best Director and Best Adapted Screenplay. 'Our British cousins found out that just plain eating can be very sexy,' he said, referring to the infamous scene where

Tom tears lustily into a chicken as a prelude to sex. 'We've revised the Production Code and now you can't show a couple eating unless they're married.'

Meanwhile, Hollywood columnists fumed about the English upstart being nominated so often. 'The British have their own Oscar race,' cried Hazel Flynn. 'Why are they trying to run away with ours? It took them until after World War II to even make a few good pictures!' Hedda Hopper, the dragon lady of studio gossip, was appalled by the number of *Tom Jones'* actors up for awards, including Albert Finney, Hugh Griffith, Edith Evans, Diane Cilento and Joyce Redman. 'I'm not going to be narrow enough to claim these fellows can't act,' she wrote. 'They've had plenty of practice. The weather's so foul on that tight little isle that, to get in and out of the rain, they all gather in theatres and practice *Hamlet* on each other.'

Despite Hopper's vitriol, Finney was the favourite to win but he did nothing to help the film's Oscar campaign by doing the rounds of television talk shows. Instead, he dropped out of the Broadway production of *Luther* and went on holiday in the South Seas.

Actors presenting awards included James Stewart, Sidney Poitier and Julie Andrews. Sammy Davis, Jr. floored the audience with his machine-gun delivery of jokes, impressions and songs before presenting the Best Soundtrack Oscar (Jock Addison won for *Tom Jones*). Lemmon walked back on stage during Davis Jr's longstanding ovation to declare, 'He's a genius, that boy!' Now it was Edward G. Robinson's turn to present the screenwriting awards. John Osborne won Best Adapted Screenplay, the film's second award of the night – the irony being that Tony had rewritten most of the script himself on location. Next up was a bouffanted Rita Hayworth to present Best Director. Hayworth, who was extremely short sighted, was so nervous about reading names aloud in public that she had asked for an envelope containing the winner's name written in large type but the envelope was missing when she reached the podium. She tried to read nominees from the teleprompter, but Tony Richardson came out as 'Tony Richards'. A breathless Lemmon rushed up with the large-type envelope, whereupon Hayworth became even more nervous. She opened the envelope and proclaimed the winner, 'Tony Richards for *Tom Jones*.'

(Hayworth was indeed so mortified about getting Tony's name wrong that she talked backstage about disappearing into the nothingness, as described by Buddhists. 'Is it the Taoists who practice disintegration?' she asked. 'I think I'll try that and just disappear into the fog!')

Frank Sinatra sauntered on to present the final award of the night, the Best Picture Oscar. Sinatra reminded viewers at home that Best Picture, 'is still, after 36 years, the highest honour given a motion picture.' The audience sat through a compilation of clips from the five movies nominated, including *Cleopatra* and *How the West Was Won*. The clip from *Tom Jones* showed Albert Finney retrieving Susannah York's pet canary. 'She nearly lost her bird,' Sinatra quipped. The winner was once again Tony for *Tom Jones*. It was the little English film's fourth Oscar of the night. Tony, however, felt himself so far above the cigar-chomping ex-furriers and scrap metal merchants of old Hollywood that he couldn't be bothered to attend the ceremony. 'I've had quite enough of prize giving at school,' he said. Afterwards, he used one of his *Tom Jones*' Oscars as a doorstop.[1]

All feature films have a party when production ends to celebrate the finish of shooting. Cast and crew raise their glasses to the last couple of months. No more night filming or wake-up calls at five in the morning. The best advice you can give a novice director is to wear comfortable trainers. Therefore, it was typically perverse of Tony to have a party at the start of production before a frame of his new project was even in the can.

Tom Jones follows the misadventures of Tom, a foundling who, after a series of scrapes and escapes, is eventually reunited with Sophie, his childhood sweetheart. Tony had loved Henry Fielding's novel since reading it at Oxford and he wanted to adapt it without the great weight usually attached to literary classics. He gave the book to Osborne, who became similarly enthused. Tony wrote a breakdown of the main events, characters and even scenes they could use. Osborne then wrote up the script with his usual brio and an astonishing turn of phrase. The two agreed to make a film that would be pure pleasure – a kind of holiday from social earnestness. However, Tony did not want to abandon the have-a-go-Joe camerawork and up-to-the-minute editing techniques he had developed on his recent films: what he hoped to capture was the feeling of the age of which Fielding wrote, applying the same keen sense of realism used in *The Loneliness of a Long Distance Runner* and *A Taste of Honey*. Tony announced that he wanted to stay away from, 'those terrible period pictures in which everything is lavish scenery and static actors. I want to make a picture that is entertaining, funny, and yet faithful to the spirit of Fielding, which was, after all, not in the least reverent.' After what one actor remembered as a splendid blow-out at Mayfair restaurant The White Elephant, Tony raised his champagne glass. 'Now, let's all go and have a lovely ten weeks' holiday in the West Country!' he declared.

Tony's original plan was to make the film for around £300,000: Woodfall sewed together a patchwork of cash from a variety of sources including Michael Powell's Bryanston film company, Canadian distributor Seven Arts and a loan from the British Government's National Film Finance Corporation. Columbia Pictures agreed to come in with the rest. All parties met in Columbia Pictures' hotel suite during the Cannes Film Festival of May 1961 to celebrate the deal. In the midst of the party, Tony took a call from Woodfall. What he came back and whispered in the ear of Bryanston managing director Max Setton made, in Setton's words, 'the champagne go flat' in his glass. Three hundred thousand pounds was not going to be enough, it seemed. Tony needed at least another £50,000 to £60,000. Setton promised to find him the extra cash, but Columbia balked at putting in another cent. By now the clock was ticking: Woodfall had spent every penny it had in developing the film and preparing for production.

Tony faced financial ruin if the cameras didn't start rolling soon. As producer as well as director, he would only get paid on the day that shooting began. In the meantime, he was using the cash just coming in from *Saturday Night and Sunday Morning* to pay the most pressing bills. Tony recalled, 'I'd just started my film company, and although we'd had some films that were reasonably successful, some were not, and we were on the point of bankruptcy.' It was Cecil Tennant, Tony's agent, who suggested he go and see United Artists – the studio had a new fellow in charge of production at its London office. After all, what did he have to lose?

The new man at United Artists was George Ornstein, a tough operator whose first job at the studio had been selling British films to cinemas in Brooklyn-Irish neighbourhoods. Whenever the Rank gong appeared, they started throwing beer bottles at the screen. Ornstein read Osborne's screenplay and telephoned the head office in New York. With wearisome insistence, he badgered his bosses into sending over David Picker, a young production executive who had just started working for the company. In fact, Ornstein's extreme persistence almost got him fired. Tony met Picker and the two men hit it off; Picker read the script overnight and the next day, the deal was made.

Picker told Ornstein, 'Move your head over on the block and I'll lie down with you!' Somehow he had persuaded the head office in New York to approve the £425,000 budget. But Tony's first reaction when Ornstein broke the good news was why should Hollywood share the profits equally with him? After all, it had been his idea and all the hard work would be his. Tony said: 'United Artists took over with a totally unreasonable financial view.' With the shrewdness that made Tony for many people a far better producer than director, he renegotiated the deal. When United Artists' profit had covered the cost of making the picture, he was assured with a certain sardonic inflection, then sure, he could have 75 per cent to their 25 per cent. This deal point would make Tony a millionaire throughout the Sixties.

Now that Tony could count on United Artists' funding, he went out and made offers for the cast he wanted. Albert Finney, fresh from *Luther*, was to play the hero, Tom. The rest of the cast would be filled out with actors Tony had already worked with, including Edith Evans, Joan Greenwood and his mother-in-law Rachel. The film might almost be described as the Royal Court on holiday.

Tony was able to assemble such a magnificent cast partly because the actors appreciated that he was willing to trust them – occasionally, thought actor Peter Bull, to the point of lunacy. Bull remembered Tony encouraging him and another actor to improvise, telling them, 'Don't think what you are saying now is very funny. Go off dahlings and make up something and we'll shoot it!' On another occasion, Tony asked an actress to improvise her disapproval of gamekeeper's daughter Molly emerging from church unmarried and heavily pregnant. The actress asked Tony what she should say. 'It doesn't matter, dahling. Whatever you say will be just right, I know it!' Tony grinned, rubbing his hands up and down his white Levis in excitement. (Playwright Charles Wood noted that Tony was only truly happy on set.) The cameras started rolling and the actress emerged from behind a tombstone, threw a clod of earth at Molly and shouted, 'Take that, you 18th-century c**t!'

Casting Tom's sweetheart, Sophie, proved problematic, though. Susannah York turned down the role five times. Tony and Vanessa took her out to two expensive lunches at the Savoy Hotel, but York kept telling them 'no' – she felt theatre was the place to be. The reason why Tony was so persistent was that New York made clear that casting an up-and-coming star such as York meant the difference between shooting in black and white or in colour.[2] Eventually, York felt so embarrassed by Tony spending vast sums on her that she invited them both for lunch at her flat. The lunch turned out to be a disaster: York put sugar in the casserole instead of salt and managed to burn the meringues three times. The twenty-two-year-old actress was so mortified that she blurted out she would do the film after all.

Although Picker had approved the filming schedule, the tight budget still meant Tony had to shoot at a clip. Ninety cast and crew members went down by train to establish headquarters at Weymouth. Filming began on 27 June 1962. In all, Tony would film in a dozen locations around the West Country, including Cerne Abbas in Dorset and Beaminster and Nettlecomb in Somerset. He had just 14 weeks to make this complicated period picture, which involved fussy production design and working with animals. (One call sheet, with typical eccentricity, asked for, 'Flowers to be eaten by horse, a decanter of Madeira wine, a dead crow and ball for dog'.)

Tony originally wanted to work with Oswald Morris, his camera-man on *Look Back in Anger*, but Morris felt that he was being too demanding: Tony wanted to shoot in 'forbidden' light conditions, filming from helicopters while using a lot of handheld camerawork. Instead, Tony turned to Walter Lassally, his cameraman on *Momma Don't Allow*. Lassally's luminous camerawork blended perfectly with Tony's way of doing things – he made *Tom Jones* look like the softest English watercolour. After all, Tony preferred the quickness of a water-colour sketch to a worked-over oil painting.

Meanwhile, Albert Finney said the idea was not to ponder too much, but to leap straight in: Tony wouldn't bother to rehearse a scene, just plunge haphazardly on with the cameras rolling. His method turned an unread yellowing classic into something vibrant and unpredictable. Finney said, 'Tony was in his element, picking, blending, substituting, re-arranging – if a scene took two days to shoot, the odds were he would change it all on the second day.'

Lassally achieved the film's Canaletto freshness by masking his camera lens with an extremely fine piece of 1920s veiling (the sort used to decorate women's hats) from veteran French cinematographer,

Georges Périnal. The problem was that Lassally only had two small squares of this material, just enough to cover the short- and long-focus lenses respectively. Lassally admitted that United Artists would have had a fit, had they known their entire £425,000 investment depended on these two flimsy silk squares.

One sequence where Lassally's camerawork really came into its own was the exhilarating hunting episode. Tony wanted to give his audience the visceral experience of being in at the kill: he hated blood sports and felt he could point up the mindless brutality involved by making the sequence as realistic as possible. One close-up shows the horse's bloody flanks as spurs dig in. Local huntsmen, rightly sensing these arty London types were against blood sports, refused to cooperate. Tony's solution was to round up as many old mangy hounds as possible and have his own dog pack. The dogs would be shown tearing into a deer at the climax of the chase (18th-century huntsmen hunted deer, not foxes). Tony's old dogs were then fed on venison to give them a taste for it and the dogs were to be kept hungry the night before they were needed. That night, the local hunt broke into the kennels and stuffed the hounds with meat. Next day, the dogs were too bloated to do much more than sniff the deer carcass and back away.

One of Tony's innovations was to shoot the hunt scenes by helicopter – he thought that Lord and Lady Ilchester, on whose land they were filming, might enjoy the novelty of seeing their vast property by air. After they'd touched down, Tony asked Lady Ilchester if she'd enjoyed the experience. 'Very interesting,' she replied. 'It enabled one to see which of the trees were dead and needed to be taken away.'

Diane Cilento, who played Molly the gamekeeper's daughter, remembered the shoot as, 'a fantastic summer.' The cast would drink champagne from crates that filled the boots of the Fifties Cadillacs laid on by Tony. 'Tony was a terrific director, so enthusiastic. He'd never constrict you, but egged you on to do your best,' said Cilento. Tony nicknamed Cilento 'WC', standing for 'Weather Cover'. Because most of Cilento's scenes involved her rolling around in the hay with Tom, hers were the few that they could shoot indoors while on location. Cilento remembered the local nobs crowded round her, sitting on their shooting sticks while she filmed her love scene. Throughout that glorious summer Cilento was on hand: 'I think he thought of me as being his sort of lucky charm,' she said.[3]

What Susannah York remembered about the shoot was the amount of spontaneity. One day, it was pouring with rain and Tony said, 'Let's go out and do something.' So they shot part of the montage where Tom and Sophie fall in love, playing in the rain and picking water lilies from the pond. York said: 'He was very sudden and impetuous. I hadn't really done much improvisation before then, so that was a novelty although rather terrifying. Tony was always very engaging in his enthusiasm, which is always attractive.'[4] Indeed some cast members felt that Tony started out a little too relaxed during filming. One actor complained that he was off taking horseback-riding lessons a good deal of the time – 'Imagine, horseback-riding lessons!'[5]

The raunchy, country-wedding atmosphere extended off-screen as well. One night, Tony found himself being given head by a to-be-famous lady writer while he drove through steep, one-way Dorset lanes (her husband was following in the car behind). Tony had to keep out of his headlights while facing a certain crash had he met any vehicle coming the other way.

The grind of early starts and night shooting was beginning to wear Tony down, however. Sitting there, crunching a glucose tablet, he realised what a huge job he had taken on: he was doubling up again as producer and director. Albert Finney had the feeling that nobody really knew what was happening – the production was short of money and the script kept being rewritten. Osborne's first draft may have had all the infectious vitality and some of the wit of a Vanbrugh comedy, but it still needed work. Tony carped that although Osborne loved the money and glamour of movies, he never understood and resented the process of rewriting; he found himself having to rewrite the script himself. Despite this, the two rubbed along together even if, as in many a marriage, there was increasing unspoken resentment on both sides.

Another problem was Finney himself. Tony said that Finney didn't think his starring role stretched him enough – 'He wanted something where he could rage and tear things in tatters, emote and be a big tragic actor,' Tony remembered.[6] In fact, Finney only took on the role after being promised a producer credit: Tony and Osborne agreed to make him an equal partner in the project. Finney would be an associate producer, participating in all the problems of mounting such an ambitious production, but when problems cropped up, he was nowhere to be found. Instead, he complained. He then negotiated away his producer credit in favour of a lower percentage of the profits. Even so, Finney's first cheque would be for over a million pounds. Susannah York was not so lucky: in a business where future profits are called 'monkey points' (because you'd have to be a monkey to believe you're ever going to see any), York's agent urged caution and strongly advised her to go for a bigger $10,000 fee.

Adding to Tony's problems, Finney had sworn never to speak to his co-star Hugh Griffith again. Griffith, playing Sophie's irascible father, was drunk from morning till night – Tony never knew whether he'd make it on set or be lying in a ditch. The Welsh actor had already caused horror by hanging a barmaid upside down out of a window in Weymouth, the sedate seaside town where he was billeted. Another time he tried to kill Edith Evans by stampeding the coach she was in. On one occasion, he got his hands on a shotgun and fired it at the crew as they were trudging off home to sleep – he discharged one barrel into the roof of Tony's beloved red Thunderbird sports car before being overpowered.

One of Griffith's drunken accidents is captured in the finished film. At the end of one scene, he yanked his horse's reins so sharply that the creature turned in a circle and fell over, leaving Griffith pinned underneath. 'We thought he had killed himself – the horse fell right on top of him,' said Tony. 'If you stop the film and look at the frame, you can see the hands of the crew reaching to save him. We thought he was dead.'

The flashpoint for Finney was the scene where Griffith chases him, brandishing a whip. Tony warned Griffith not to touch his star; Finney himself warned there would be trouble if the whip touched him. Tony had taken the precaution of securing the tip to its handle. Unbeknownst to him, Griffith had maliciously unpicked the stitching. As the cameras started to roll, Griffith lashed out. The actor was only wearing a lightweight shirt and the whip tore his back open. Finney turned around and shouted, 'I can't abide to be whipped, Squire!' then punched Griffith squarely in the face, cutting his lip open.

One weekend, Vanessa came down to visit Tony and donned make-up, wig and costume to play a young boy in the jail scene. To tease her husband, she deliberately took wrong positions and slowed up shooting until in exasperation, Tony shouted to his assistant, 'Tell that f**king idiot to lose himself at the back – he's ruining my picture!' Although the couple had only been married a year, tensions were already beginning to appear. Jocelyn Herbert remembered Vanessa coming on location and longing for a quiet time with her husband and instead he was surrounded by cast and crew. The only time they could really see each other was weekends at Wilks Water. Away from the pressures of work, they were so in love they were difficult to be around. Their burning intensity could be overwhelming for others – 'She was starry-eyed, besotted by him, and it was tough on her. It took her quite a while to realise that Tony would always be surrounded by people, and that life was not going to be as she'd imagined.'[7]

Another location visitor was James Bond himself, Sean Connery. Diane Cilento's husband arrived on Midsummer's night to find everybody swigging powerful homemade cider as they waited for a whole hog to be roasted. Tony challenged Connery to a game of chess and the crème de la crème of British theatre gathered to watch, assuming he would trounce the brawny Glaswegian ex-bodybuilder (Connery had only just been cast as Bond). Instead, there were a few raised eyebrows when Tony turned his king over and hunched up his shoulders like a disappointed vulture.

The most notorious scene in *Tom Jones* takes place in a tavern, where Finney and Joyce Redman (one of three actresses whose performances were nominated for an Oscar) make clear over dinner that their appetite is really for the other. The scene proved hellish to film: when Finney and Redman started to disembowel the chicken, Tony discovered that being a battery chicken, its bones were so gelatinous as to be practically nonexistent. Prop men had to construct a fake wishbone out of matchsticks before they could start filming again. Buckets were then strategically placed beside Finney and Redman so they could vomit in-between takes. 'I always wanted to do a seduction-over-eating scene,' said Tony, 'but it was tough for the two of them because they were throwing up all the time. It was physical torture of the worst kind.' But when United Artists watched the eating scene, it sat up and took notice. One executive, who had seen the edited sequence, cabled back to New York, 'Holy smokes! We've got something on our hands. I'm not sure what it is, but it's very unusual.'

United Artists may have got excited about what Tony was doing, but he himself was not. As filming staggered over the finishing line, he was exhausted and depressed – he'd spent so long with his face jammed up against the project, he couldn't see it anymore. In the editing suite, he panicked that things just 'didn't hold.' He decided none of the jokes were working, so he speeded everything up: he changed the whole beginning, shortening scenes by starting them somewhere in the middle, intercutting scenes which might have been better to run their whole course. Assistant editor Gerry O'Hara thought there was a much better film on the cutting-room floor than the one that finally emerged. Lassally also believed Tony was wrong to use freeze frames, zany silent-movie effects and voice-overs: 'The one thing that Tony never learned, I believe, was that in the editing process there can very easily come a point where a producer needs to get you by the scruff of the neck, remove you from the Moviola and send you somewhere for a holiday. You get too close to the material; you are tempted to rejig it. The first half of *Tom Jones* was very roughly, even violently re-edited because of this fear that it wasn't working. Some of Diane Cilento's best scenes were cut entirely – at least half of them.'

Looking back, Tony felt that Cilento should have been a great star: 'She had those fantastic looks. Wonderful long hair, blue eyes – she had a freedom about her. But at that point English movies were casting actresses as repressed nurses or tarts. No one knew how to use Diane. She just came along at the wrong time.'

Tony now had to get his sexy comedy past the censor. John Trevelyan, head of the British Board of Film Classification, thoroughly enjoyed the film – 'clean bawdy, not dirty bawdy' the censorship board agreed – but insisted on a couple of cuts. First, there was a shot in the eating scene, where oysters were obviously used to suggest fellatio. That would have to go, even if *Tom Jones* was to be X certificate. Then there was a bedroom scene between Finney and Joyce Redman, which, if cut, would pave the way for an A rating. Tony, perhaps mindful that an X certificate would splash some extra box-office sauce, refused to do as the censor requested: an American cinema owner had already told United Artists that *Tom Jones* would have to be X-rated, if it was to attract any customers at all.

Any enthusiasm United Artists might have had evaporated once they saw the finished film. According to Osborne's lawyer, Oscar Beuselinck, the studio hated the movie and thought it had lost every cent. Indeed, the head of British distribution pronounced disaster: *Tom Jones* would be lucky if it made £40,000 worldwide, he predicted. (It was around this time that Ornstein told the same distribution executive that he'd signed the Beatles for their first film. The distributor replied: 'Yeah, but who's going to star?') Osborne didn't think much of *Tom Jones* either – 'The actors saved that film. Jock's music covered up some holes too,' he wrote.

When the film opened in June 1963, the critics were equally damning. Tony remembered Vanessa was in the kitchen as he read the first reviews. Bearing mugs of coffee, she asked how they were. 'Listen to this,' he told her, opening *The Times*. '"There is nothing in this film that could give any member of the audience one moment of enjoyment."' Alexander Walker in the *London Evening Standard* was also dismissive: 'Tony Richardson has proved himself a clever director in the past. It saddens me that this time he shows himself to be merely clever however,' he wrote. The *Sunday Telegraph* held its nose at the film's breast-and-bum anticry, describing Tony as a director who assimilated other men's styles as easily as a schoolboy catches measles. *Tom Jones* was a failure, it declared, squandering reputations and money in the most costly way.

It's true that on one level *Tom Jones* is a bosom-jiggling, upstairs-downstairs, in-my-lady's-chamber romp. Also, that the film revels voraciously in the physical world. Tony conveys the finery, coarseness and cruelty of the age, opening his usual dictionary of up-to-the-minute French New Wave cinematic tricks, which are almost cheeky in their virtuosity. He attacks Fielding's book with the abandon and zest of an action painter, throwing everything he has at his new, bigger canvas short of riding over it on a bicycle. Clearly, he takes enormous pleasure in actors and their gifts. Arriving just on the eve of Beatlemania and the British Invasion, Tony helped make an international star out of Albert Finney, whose smouldering, slightly loutish lubricity encouraged the mould for a whole new generation of English rock stars. Susannah York lifts her crinolines and picks her way through a difficult part as the wilful heroine, Diane Cilento oozes from her dress like cream from a meringue, while Edith Evans flutes her lines with all the resolution of a tipsy swan.

In one scene, a bony highwayman levels his pistol at Evans' stage-coach. 'Stand and deliver!' he cries. Evans summons up a glance of withering scorn. 'Stand and deliver, sir?' she thunders. 'What do you think I am – a travelling midwife?' And drives on. Indeed, everybody seems to be having such a good time that even the most sceptical critic must think, 'Ah, the hell with it!' and snap his pencil in two. Most of all, the film flaunts a full-blooded sensuality, a quality rarely found in British films.

With its satirically edged portrait of sexually liberated youth triumphing over sour-faced prudes, *Tom Jones* anticipates the hedonism just around the corner. Until then, sex in British cinema had mostly been confined – even in Tony's own films – to women bracing themselves up against the factory wall before the inevitable trip to the abortionist. What was different about *Tom Jones* is that women actually appeared to be enjoying sex. Its subliminal message seems to be that if 18th-century English life used to be so much fun, why shouldn't it be this way again? One cinema projectionist remembered: 'It was such a voluptuous film. After all that gritty realism, it glowed on the screen. It was a vision of plenty after the 1950s. To me, it was what got the 1960s started – forget all that hippy nonsense.'

In the words of the Dinah Washington hit, the British public went 'mad for the boy'. Queues to buy tickets formed outside the London Pavilion cinema. Here was a lusty, slap-and-tickle version of a dusty English classic we could all lap up. Long, sprig-printed dresses turned up in shop windows and women started to pull back their hair in big black velvet bows. In white stockings and buckled shoes, Cathy McGowan appeared on *Ready, Steady, Go!* Meanwhile, pop star P. J. Proby, bless him, adopted full Restoration drag of frilled shirt, britches and tricorn hat.

Three months later, United Artists released *Tom Jones* in America. Picker dropped Tony's witty pop-art advertising campaign in favour of a poster that was all bonnets and bosoms, with the leading ladies clutching Finney's splendid thighs. The *New York Times* wrote, 'Prepare yourself for what is surely one of the wildest, bawdiest and funniest comedies that a refreshingly agile filmmaker has ever brought to the screen. Mr. Richardson gives his film the speed and the character of a Keystone comedy'. The New York Film Critics awarded the film its Best Picture and Best Director Awards. So popular was it that a *New Yorker* magazine cartoon showed a patient moaning to his analyst, 'Doctor, what's my problem? *Tom Jones* depressed me.'

Arthur Knight, critic in the *Saturday Review*, realised the scale of Tony's achievement on such limited resources. Imagination, it seemed, did not cost much. 'While such mundane matters as money should be the last of a critic's concerns,' Knight wrote, 'I find it impossible not to add as a footnote that this sumptuous, satisfying production cost only 1,300,000 dollars. In this age of super-budgets, such a modest statistic might prove sobering. The race is not to the rich, it seems to imply, but to the talented.'

Tom Jones, which had cost less than half a million pounds to make, went on to gross £25 million (the equivalent of £250 million in today's money). Its success caused Tony's name to be hallooed like a hunting cry all over the world. According to Kenneth Tynan, *Tom Jones* empowered Tony on a scale to which few British directors even aspired. Not for him the heartbreaking haggling that most producers go through when trying to make their next film: the cash now pouring in gave him virtually a blank cheque to do whatever he wanted – with all the lack of boundaries that implied. No one was going to say no to him. 'They say that when a film does that kind of business, you're bankrolled for the next five years,' said Cilento.[8] And for the next few years, Tony wielded power with a baroque extravagance that suggested Ludwig of Bavaria on the loose in Culver City.

Notes

1. Norman Twain, author interview, 12 February 2010.
2. Susannah York, author interview, 1 December 2010.
3. Diane Cilento, author interview, 1 December 2010.
4. Lukas, Mary. 'Tom Jones Richardson', *Show*, April 1964.
5. Zailian, Marian. 'Tom Jones Romps Anew In Re-Release', *The San Francisco Chronicle*, 12 November 1989.
6. Tony Garnett, author interview, 22 June 2009.
7. Tynan, Kathleen. 'Exit Prospero', *Vanity Fair*, February 1992.
8. Diane Cilento, author interview, 1 December 2010.

CHAPTER NINE

The Red Queen and the Mad Hatter

Tom Jones was the turning point for Woodfall, which never quite retained the happy-go-lucky atmosphere of those early days. The film's success changed Tony as well: his strength always lay in his ability to get the best out of the team working under him – he made them feel their suggestions were welcome. At first, Tony seemed unaffected by hitting the jackpot. He was grateful for his double-Oscar win, despite not deigning to turn up at the ceremony in person: 'When we made *Tom Jones*, I had no idea it would win anything. I thought it would be a total disaster. You can't think in terms of winning Oscars when you set out to make a film. That way, you don't get anywhere. You must just do the film that you're excited about. Anyone who tries to go after the box office or the Oscars alone will be in big trouble and so many people seem to try. The nicest thing about Oscars is that they're genuine expressions of people's sincere views. As I say, I thought it would be a disaster. But then, I think that about everything that I do.'

Feeling generous – and in what cameraman Walter Lassally described as an 'unprecedented gesture' – Tony gave six of his key technicians half-a-per-cent share in Woodfall's profits. He also gave Oscar Lewenstein, who was nominally an associate producer, another slug of the profits. This enraged Tony's lawyer, Oscar Beuselinck, who announced Lewenstein had contributed next to nothing, but 'received riches beyond belief.'

Lewenstein, an ardent Communist, bought a house on Brighton seafront – one of only a half-dozen actually on the beach. This was in addition to his Hampstead house. He also started being chauffeured about. Asked how he could rationalise the apparent conflict between his Communist principles and his new sumptuous lifestyle, Lewenstein shot back: 'You must understand that one of the most urgent aims of the Party is to ensure that every working person in Britain will soon as possible be blessed with a house in Hampstead, a chauffeur-driven car and a villa on the beach in Brighton.'

Meanwhile, Hollywood urged Tony to capitalise on the success of *Tom Jones* and quickly make a follow-up. United Artists announced a multi-film output deal with Woodfall in the trade press: Hollywood would fully finance Woodfall's films without any interference until delivery. Six films were to be made in batches of two. As is often the way, the deal was never actually signed – it made more sense for United Artists to negotiate each film separately. The attraction for Woodfall, though, was 100 per cent financing.

Tony was elevated onto the board of state distributor British Lion, whose chairman Michael Balcon, declared: 'British films have a lot to thank Woodfall for.' For the first time, Lewenstein noticed that Tony seemed not to welcome advice or criticism from colleagues – success had apparently turned his head. He developed a syndrome that affects many artists who have achieved success. Surrounded by sycophants, he started to believe anything he touched would turn to gold. Not having to go through the same kind of struggle that other producers went through to get their films made affected his work. Orson Welles, whom Tony would later direct, summed up the situation in one of Tony's favourite films, *Citizen Kane*. 'Cheer up, Mr Kane, you're a rich man,' says the lawyer, making over Kane's trust fund to the young man. 'Ah yes,' says Kane, 'but I could have been a great one.'

For now, Tony had a blank cheque. Over the next few years he would make some increasingly bizarre choices: a black-and-white film in French with subtitles, a follow-up shot on the hoof without a proper script traipsing around Africa and the Mediterranean and a short film deemed so awful it was barely released. His Hollywood agent Mike Medavoy sometimes wondered if his client wanted to destroy his career: 'Sometimes I wondered if he even wanted to follow the success of *Tom Jones*. The way that he chose projects, it was almost as if he had a death wish.'[1]

All this lay in the future, though. Having finished editing *Tom Jones*, Tony and Vanessa flew to New York in October 1962. *The Loneliness of the Long Distance Runner* was just opening in the US. Tony loved Manhattan, saying it recharged his batteries. He'd come to discuss directing Kim Stanley in William Inge's play, *Natural Affection*. United Artists was also wining and dining Tony – the studio liked what it had seen so far of the rushes. There were interminable movie tycoon dinners with rich food and fine wines. Vanessa, who was deep into reading left-wing feminist writer Simone de Beauvoir, found all this luxury nauseous. The comfortable upper-middle-class values she'd grown up with now struck her as phoney, even repugnant.[2] Something inside her had changed: 'I know there was a breaking point then,' she said. 'I became another person – not just a woman, another person.'[3]

Hollywood was fêting Tony when the telephone rang in the couple's hotel room. Back in England, George Devine had suffered a nervous breakdown. It meant he was incapable of running the Court. Tony agreed to deputise for three months while Devine recuperated. Back in London, Tony had an almost flippant attitude towards administration: whereas Devine would stolidly plough through correspondence and the tsunami of work hanging over him, Tony would stroll in on a Saturday morning and leave after an hour of strenuous decision-making. 'My natural rhythm was quick, and his natural rhythm was measured,' Tony insisted. By all accounts, his tenure as boss of the Royal Court was disastrous and once he was well enough, Devine had to unpick most of the decisions made.

Meanwhile, Lewenstein wanted Tony to direct the London transfer of the comedy *Semi-Detached*. In the summer of 1962, the play had proved one of the biggest box-office hits in the history of Coventry's Belgrade Theatre. Leonard Rossiter had played Fred Midway, a Birmingham insurance salesman whose family derails his dreams of social advancement. Tony and Lewenstein agreed that Laurence Olivier should take over Rossiter's part. Tony surrounded Olivier with a first-rate cast: Mona Washbourne played Fred's wife Hilda, James Bolam was his son and Eileen Atkins played his daughter. John Thaw was also in the ensemble.

Tony, Lewenstein and Joan Plowright were all convinced Olivier could play the part standing on his head. He urged Olivier to 'play it wide' – almost caricaturing the conniving Midway. Instead, Olivier insisted on having an unbelievable Birmingham accent, surrounding himself with spools of tape recordings of Midland voices, which he would practise in the bathroom mirror. He and Tony then went on a tour of the Midlands to soak up atmosphere. Olivier decided to try out his accent on a Nottingham tobacconist. For a moment, the shopkeeper looked at him oddly and then turned to Tony. 'What part of America is your friend from, sir?' he asked.

Plowright and Olivier's agent Cecil Tennant joined Tony in pleading with Olivier to lose the Brummie voice. Tony said Olivier himself knew the accent wasn't working, but somehow he couldn't lose face – it was like watching someone blindly commit suicide. *Semi-Detached* opened at the Saville Theatre on 5 December 1962 after tryouts in Edinburgh and Oxford. The first night was half-empty – a dense London fog having kept the audience away. Critics found the play snobbish. The *Guardian* admitted Tony's production was unflinching – instead, it was the audience who flinched. Meanwhile, the *Daily Mail* sneered at Tony's staging: 'There is a real motor-car on the stage. There is also a real motorbike, a real lawnmower, a real television set, a real encyclopaedia and a real scale-model miniature locomotive. What is missing is a real play.' Although neither of them ever admitted it, the failure of *Semi-Detached* killed Tony's relationship with Olivier.

Not one to reflect on his misfires or flops, Tony left for New York again after Christmas. Vanessa was left alone. Rehearsals started on *Natural Affection*. William Inge said the plot was ripped straight out of the headlines – it was more like lurid soap opera. *Natural Affection* tells the story of an unmarried mother whose son comes home from reform school. The son is passionately jealous of his mother's lover, Bernie. A neighbour is also having an affair with Bernie and the neighbour's husband is also attracted to the youth. There are suggestions of incest and necrophilia. The emotional climax comes when the mother cries out to her son that she's not about to sacrifice the rest of her life for a no-good kid she never wanted. Rejected, the son randomly murders someone who has wandered in from next door.

Tony thought so highly of working with Kim Stanley, he named his second daughter Joely Kim after her. Stanley has been called 'the female Marlon Brando'. Tony compared directing her to being given a piano and suddenly finding he could play as well as Glenn Gould. She was even better than Olivier, he thought. *Natural Affection* opened on 31 January 1963 at the Booth Theatre. The reviews were pretty good, even if the *New York World-Telegram* accused Tony of falling over himself to produce the dirtiest play of the year. It closed after 31 performances. Tony claimed the producer pulled the plug because he refused to tone down the script.

Vanessa and Tony set up home at 30 St Peter's Square, Chiswick. It was a square of solid Georgian houses built in 1815 to house Wellington's victorious officers, their victory symbolised by stucco eagles on porticos of many of the buildings. Deirdre Redgrave remembered the house as enchanting. Plain, whitewashed walls were covered with valuable paintings. Next to them political posters of Castro and the Campaign for Nuclear Disarmament were pinned to the walls. Large white comfortable sofas sat on Wilton carpets. Plants trailed, spilled and blossomed everywhere. Bowls full of flowers brightened every corner. The interior was designed in Tony's exquisite taste: he had challenged Vanessa to a game of cards to decide who would decorate each room and won every hand.

What first attracted Tony to the house was the sleepy, overgrown garden with its ornamental pond and magnolia tree. The garden was created by the Scottish botanist John Claudius Loudon and, according to Tony, was one of the most celebrated small gardens in England. There was an extraordinary variety of trees, evergreen and deciduous shrubs, perennials and bulbs to ensure colour all year round. Tony demolished the garage to make way for a 30-foot high indoor glass aviary. A Miss Anns came in every day to look after his collection of tropical birds. Altogether, he had between 30 and 40 of them, which she fed on Swiss rolls, oranges, grapes and stale cake. A toucan and several mynah birds jabbered constantly whenever you walked by.

Woodfall employee Michael Deeley remembered Tony waiving a £10,000 directing fee in exchange for a huge exotic blue parrot (Deeley thought the parrot was nicer than paying tax). In addition to the birds, there was also a caged marmoset monkey in the drawing room, which was at least the equal of the one that Mrs Patrick Campbell (according to Yeats' journals) pursued so furiously through her house. Tony's whippet and Vanessa's Yorkshire terrier ('Marvellous' – supposedly named after the word Tony used most often in rehearsal) added to the household.

Mr and Mrs Richardson had a tidal wave of newspapers and magazines posted through their front door each morning. They took five daily newspapers – *The Times*, *Daily Mail*, *New York Times*, *New York Herald Tribune* and *Le Monde* – as well as four weekly magazines: *The Spectator*, *The New Statesman*, *Time* and *Newsweek*.

Having started married life knowing simply how to open an orange juice carton, by now Vanessa really enjoyed cooking. Rachel was an expert cook, while Lynn could have turned professional. Vanessa felt it part of her womanly attributes to provide for those she loved. In time, she became a very good cook indeed, especially Italian food. She also insisted on not having live-in staff. With Tony away so often, and her own acting commitments, she didn't want anybody intruding on their privacy. Neither of them wanted to rein in their career yet they couldn't be a proper husband-and-wife team with that punishing schedule.

Corin's wife Deirdre noticed how worried Tony was about Vanessa burning herself out. She would arrive home from Stratford exhausted in the early hours of Sunday morning, catch a few hours' sleep and then produce enormous Sunday lunches for family and friends, playing the gracious hostess until she had to go back up the motorway again. Diane Cilento remembered that Tony used to serve the strongest drinks, filling huge glasses right up with whisky.[4]

By now, Vanessa was pregnant with their first baby. On the morning of 11 May 1963, she had been asked to open the first Museum of Trade Union History in Britain. Tony was abroad again, this time away in Ireland filming. Vanessa was staying at Wilks Water and planned to be driven over to the museum. Her contractions started at about 4am on the Saturday. After waking Rachel, she telephoned for Tony's driver, Jan Niemeynowicz, to come and collect her (she had been booked into the London Clinic, a smart private hospital). She told Rachel that she wanted to go for a walk around the lake. Vanessa remembered it was the most beautiful May morning. In her dressing gown, she walked to the farthest edge collecting violets and primroses. Meanwhile, her dog Marvellous plunged before her through the dewy grass. Rachel then rang Tony, who told her that he would be flying home at once.

Vanessa was determined to try and give birth without pain relief. Once she got to London, she spent her labour politely fending off painkillers while trying to remember her Natural Childbirth exercises. In her mind's eye, she pictured Marvellous scampering through the wet grass. Tony and Vanessa's first child was born at five o'clock that afternoon: she weighed seven pounds, fourteen ounces. Tony compared the moment of birth to a flower opening – he said it was the most beautiful experience of his life. Vanessa remembered the whorls and spirals of hair on the crown of the baby's head moving like sand stirred by water. The couple decided to call the baby Natasha after the spirited heroine in *War and Peace*.

Tony said the happy chaos of 30 St Peter's Square was the moment he felt most content. Yet something was clearly wrong in the marriage. In 1965, he began an affair with a working-class Irish silversmith called Michael, who lived in nearby Ravenscourt Park. Tony would come round late at night and slip away in the early hours. Michael's landlord deplored the way Tony was cheating on Vanessa; he also worried about his friend: 'I warned him that nothing good would come of having an affair with a married man. I didn't like married men playing around in the homosexual world. The traffic of men through the flat was huge, but the one who stuck in my mind was Tony – I disliked every single thing about him. He was very full of himself. As far as I was concerned, he was just a noisy, objectionable, self-centred queen.'[5]

In 1963, London may have been on the cusp of the Swinging Sixties, but homosexuality was still illegal. Homosexuals existed in an underground world with its own special language and codes. Theatrical gay life centred around the Wardour Club, where Tony was occasionally spotted.[6] Susannah York, who played Sophie in *Tom Jones*, said it came as bit of a shock when she found out about Tony's secret life because he was married to Vanessa, 'although I recognised he could very well be bisexual.'[7] For Diane Cilento, news that Tony was gay was common knowledge: 'Everybody knew about his being gay right from the beginning, but Tony wasn't just one person.'[8] As to whether Vanessa knew her husband was bisexual like her father, Deirdre's friend Danaë Brook reckoned that Vanessa did know, but thought she could handle it. Greater freedom was in the air, the Beatles and the Stones had appeared in the pop charts. They moved in a circle where a lot of the men, who had glamorous girlfriends, were openly bisexual. Vanessa, said Brook, probably thought her husband's sexuality fitted in with her right-on politics: 'Here was a brilliant, attractive man, who she thought she could cross boundaries with. She would have supported his right to express himself. It would have been exciting in a way.'[9]

Tony, who was 10 years older than Vanessa, always liked to feel he was part of the 'scene'. He had, of course, helped nurture the generation whose ideas would lead to Britain being the most exciting place on earth and he was in his element at the epicentre of the revolution. Deirdre noticed how he would walk into a room and instantly identify those worth talking to. His energy and magnetism transformed everyone and everything around him. Whereas Tony could throw himself into whatever the latest craze was, Vanessa would remain myopically aloof. Like Michael, she preferred to watch and observe. Unlike her husband, she wasn't the least bit interested in staying *au courant*.

That summer, Tony once again rented La Baumette – the farmhouse near St Tropez where he'd planned *Tom Jones* with Osborne and Devine. United Artists was releasing *Tom Jones* that August, traditionally a dead month at the cinema. It showed what little confidence UA had in the film. Lynn (by now a member of the new National Theatre company) came to stay. Vanessa got up every two hours to feed Natasha, while Tony prepared his next film script, three plays for Broadway and two for London the following spring. He also managed to read a book a day. Vanessa and Lynn would do cabaret turns and sing 'Let Me Entertain You', which made Tony laugh until it looked as if he was choking to death.

By the autumn Tony was back in New York directing the Broadway version of *Luther*, which opened on 11 September 1963. The following month, *Tom Jones* opened in America. Once he'd got *Luther* spinning nicely, Tony moved on to his next plate. Rehearsals began on Bertolt Brecht's Hitler farce *The Resistible Rise of Arturo Ui* at the Lunt-Fontanne Theatre. Christopher Plummer was playing Ui, with Lionel Stander one of his henchmen. Stander's return to Broadway after years of being blacklisted for being a Communist was largely because of Tony. He had been kept out of work after being called before Senator McCarthy's House of Un-American Activities Committee (Harry Cohn, the boss of Columbia Pictures, called Stander, 'a Red sonofabitch').

With *Arturo Ui*, Tony felt he was on to a hit. Preview audiences went wild for it. Those already familiar with Brecht gave the play standing ovations. Then came opening night, on 11 November 1963. The usual Broadway audience of bridge-and-tunnel out-of-towners were the kind of theatregoers Brecht despised and the feeling was mutual: indeed, the hostility of those first-nighters was palpable. If anything, Tony's production was too imaginative. 'With all admiration for Tony Richardson and the frequent proofs in New York and London, on stage and in film, of his intelligence and imagination, I cannot condone his maltreatment of *Arturo Ui*,' wrote the *New York Times*. The *New York World-Telegram* said: 'Virtuosity gets in the way, so this Arturo Ui becomes mainly an electrifying display of theatrical invention. It is a prodigious mounting of a less-than-prodigious play.'

Producer David Merrick, disappointed by the lukewarm critical reception, closed the show after just eight performances. This triggered a public outpouring of support. Disappointed theatregoers wrote to critics who'd given the production bad reviews. Merrick's office was deluged with phone calls, largely from students begging him to keep the play open. When his secretary passed on their pleas, his response was blunt: 'Sylvia, tell them to buy tickets.'

That autumn, Corin and his new wife Deirdre came out to New York. Corin was playing the pilot officer in Arnold Wesker's *Chips With Everything*, which had been his second Royal Court part after *A Midsummer Night's Dream*. The show had transferred from the Court to the Vaudeville Theatre and then on to Broadway. Corin and Deirdre stayed in Manhattan right through Christmas, only returning to England in the spring of 1964.

Lynn, who had also been in *A Midsummer Night's Dream*, made her first West End appearance in November 1962, in *Billy Liar*. She then joined the repertory company of the new National Theatre under Laurence Olivier the following October, playing a lady-in-waiting to Michael's Claudius in the inaugural production of *Hamlet*. That inaugural National Theatre season was held at the Old Vic theatre, where Olivier had first announced Vanessa's birth. She curtsied to her father as he walked past. There, with increasing unease, she watched Michael's starring roles as Uncle Vanya and the cantankerous father in *Hobson's Choice*.

Michael's first and only season at the National was unhappy. Olivier tore into him backstage after the first night of *The Master Builder*, telling him how rotten he was. This destroyed what little confidence Michael had left in his own acting ability and, from then on, Lynn watched helplessly as what Michael described as 'the wall of fear' began closing in around him. During *Hamlet*, he found himself transfixed by props and would tremble with fear as he came over Waterloo Bridge to play *The Master Builder*.

Michael began to wonder if he was ill. He became paranoid that the rest of the company was whispering about him. Being on stage with him was an anxiety-making experience for his co-stars Maggie Smith and Joan Plowright as well – you never knew if he might need a prompt. Michael was so alarmed by his memory lapses that he sought medical help. What neither he nor Olivier could have known is that

Michael would be diagnosed with Parkinson's disease nine years later. In the intervening period he would appear mainly in films, returning to the theatre only with great difficulty and with unhappy results. Parkinson's disease, a degenerative disorder characterised by tremors and muscular rigidity, would slowly and inexorably remove Michael from stage and screen.

Meanwhile, he still felt confident enough to perform *Uncle Vanya* in an official National Theatre visit to Moscow, though. The company was billeted in the vast Ukrania hotel, where the KGB requisitioned two bedroom floors as listening posts. Every troupe members' bedroom was bugged. Each morning, Lynn would be woken early by an incomprehensible talk on Marxism-Leninism blaring into her room. One morning, she pretended to be asleep in bed while a Russian woman went through her things, reading her letters.

Not pausing for breath, Tony immediately plunged into his next play for David Merrick. The Broadway impresario had agreed to stage a revival of Tennessee Williams' *The Milk Train Doesn't Stop Here Anymore*. *Milk Train* tells the story of Flora Goforth, a rich widow living on a private Mediterranean island, who is visited by the Angel of Death disguised as a handsome young poet. The play already had a spotted history: it had first been performed at Italy's Spoleto Festival in the summer of 1962 and then played on Broadway, where a newspaper strike meant there were no reviews and no advertisements. It had closed after 69 performances. Williams had since rewritten it and desperately wanted a second chance.

Merrick saw *Milk Train* as a way to get his hands on Williams' next play. He was certainly taking a risk in reviving a play that had stalled only the year before but he appealed to Tony's vanity, telling him only he could turn failure into success. This was not the first time Tony had directed Tennessee Williams. Five years previously he'd staged the English premiere of Williams' *Orpheus Descending*. Like *Milk Train*, *Orpheus* followed a drifter who wanders into the life of an older woman. Isa Miranda played Lady Torrance, a role Vanessa herself would take on, some 30 years later.

Williams used to arrive at Court rehearsals looking as if he'd just crawled out of bed with a hangover – which he probably had. Asked what he'd been up to last night, he would admit, 'Up to no good.' One of the places visited by Williams was the Rockingham Club in Soho's Archer

Street, a private establishment for well-heeled homosexuals frequented by John Gielgud and Ralph Richardson. Not that Tony needed much persuading to stay in New York: he loved the city. Everybody he spoke to – from the waitress bringing him his morning orange juice to the bellhop and the taxi driver – were all interested in Broadway. New York, more than any other place in the world, had a sense of theatre. Tony read the play and telephoned Williams, heaping what the playwright called 'the most frighteningly extravagant praise' on his script.

By now, Tony had entered one of the most enduring working relationships of his life. Neil Hartley, who had been Merrick's production manager, began working for Tony full-time. The two had already worked together on *Luther* and he performed an important function for Tony, that of hatchet man. Neil would be the one who delivered bad news, enabling Tony to keep his hands clean.[10] Tony admired Hartley's thoroughness and tact. The mesmerically handsome Hartley also became Tony's lover.[11]

Williams insisted on having Tallulah Bankhead star as Flora Goforth. He was convinced *Milk Train* would resurrect Bankhead, just as people still talked about Laurette Taylor's comeback in *The Glass Menagerie* in 1947. Bankhead had been outrageous as a young woman, introducing herself at parties by saying, 'Hello, I'm a lesbian. What do you do?' Wildly promiscuous, with both men and women, she once tried to list all her lovers and got to 185 before the doorbell rang. Bankhead was also an exhibitionist: she liked taking off all her clothes at parties, or flashing the fact that she wasn't wearing any knickers on set (Alfred Hitchcock said he was never sure whether to refer the matter to hairdressing or the costume department).

By the time Tony met her, Bankhead was a mess: she was drinking heavily – adding 'spirits of ammonia' to her tea – and using massive doses of barbiturates to help her to sleep. Her maid used to tape her wrists together to stop her taking more pills in the night. Tony's sister-in-law Deirdre was appalled by Bankhead's dreadful hands, burned to the bone by forgotten cigarettes. One burn on her wrist was so deep she had to wrap chiffon around it on stage so the front rows wouldn't be distracted. She mumbled and slurred her words, and didn't make much sense.

Tony, understandably, had misgivings – he didn't want anything to do with Bankhead because of her appeal to the gay crowd. In his autobiography, he said he'd always disliked camp – this from someone who had one of the fruitiest voices in the business. Instead he offered the part to Katharine Hepburn, but she declined.

Tony's first choice to play 'Angel of Death' Christopher Flanders was Anthony Perkins, star of *Psycho*. Perkins recommended his old boyfriend Tab Hunter instead. Hunter was a Hollywood 'sigh guy', whose screen romances included Natalie Wood, Debbie Reynolds and Lana Turner. He was also a pop star and had his own television sitcom, all while still in his twenties. Although his screen image was as wholesome as a glass of milk, everybody knew that Hunter was gay. After a decade as Hollywood's golden boy, he was becoming tired of what he called 'the hot fudge sundae life' – he wanted to stretch himself as an actor.

Tony went back to Merrick and Williams, telling them that he had two conditions. First, that he should be allowed to fly back to London for Christmas before the play opened (his marriage was already getting rocky). Second, that he'd accept Bankhead, provided they allowed Hunter – Tony said obliquely that he owed Hunter 'a moral obligation' to the role. Williams could only surmise what that could be and was reluctant to say yes because he couldn't see Hunter having the mystic and ambiguous qualities the part demanded. Tony insisted he'd make the critics sit up and take notice of Hunter's acting. One cast member bitched that Tony was out to make Hunter in every sense of the word. In hindsight, Hartley knew Bankhead and Hunter were 'camp casting' but both names were box-office draws.

Bankhead promised to be on her best behaviour. Tony was, after all, the hottest director in the world right now. 'If I get a director I respect, I'm grateful for his advice and I will certainly follow it,' Bankhead told a Baltimore radio station. And she kept asking co-star Marian Seldes: 'Tell me, darling, tell me the truth. Is he a genius?'

Bankhead offered to host a get-acquainted dinner party at her East 57th Street apartment. Once everybody was assembled, she hollered in her gravel voice, 'Cunty!' A massive Negro maid ambled in, carrying a tray of canapés. With theatrical flourish, Bankhead pulled her maid's face down towards hers and planted a smacking wet kiss on her mouth. She wanted everybody to know she was still the outrageous Tallulah, the woman who famously said, 'Say anything you like about me, dahling, as long as it isn't boring.'

Tony gamely tried to explain his kabuki-like vision of the play over the continual barking of Bankhead's poodle, Dolores. 'I don't want to say much' – bark – 'it's a play about death' – bark – 'They are all fighting against death' – bark. Tony looked as if he was dangerously close to picking up Dolores and throwing her out the window. Tallulah shouted, 'I can hardly hear you, darling? What are you saying?' Williams giggled through dinner, chain-smoking until his suit was covered with ash. The evening ended with Tony telling Bankhead to 'f**k off.' Not the most propitious of starts.

Rehearsals began on 20 November 1963 at the tiny Lunt-Fontanne Theatre, off Times Square. Ned Rorem was hired to write the score (Tony liked to involve the composer as early as possible). At first, Rorem found Tony a civilised collaborator. However, he quickly became disenchanted. Tony disliked what Rorem had written, leading the composer to carp, 'The month-long confabs with Tony Richardson have been artistically a waste, which the token fee and dubious prestige do not restore.'

Hunter arrived in New York fresh from filming *Operation Bikini*. He was very serious about his role and became convinced Bankhead was waging a campaign, 'intentional or not, to drive us all crazy.' They clashed at rehearsals, mostly because Bankhead never stopped talking (what her biographer called 'the monologue Tallulah imagined was conversation'). There were still flashes of her old wit, though. Asked whether she thought Hunter was gay, Bankhead replied, 'How do I know, darling? He's never sucked my cock'.

At one point, Flora Goforth was supposed to sneeze. Bankhead broke character and asked Tony, why did she sneeze right at that moment? Hunter said: 'Because I'm the Angel of Death, Tallulah, and I guess one of my feathers just flew up your nose.' Williams couldn't stop laughing at that.

They were on the third day of rehearsals when Tony heard a low wailing offstage: it sounded as if another actress, Ruth Gordon, was in pain. Gordon and Bankhead were terrible rivals, always trying to upstage each other. A stage manager whispered in Tony's ear that President Kennedy had just been assassinated. Tony announced what had happened to everybody on stage. Hunter remembered leaving the theatre and watching the news crawl in Times Square. Bankhead rose from her chair and yelled, 'So that's what that bitch has been wailing about!'

She flung herself forward onto the stage edge and began howling. Not to be outdone, Gordon flung herself onto her knees beside Bankhead. Even in their grief, they had to outdo each other. Williams, standing beside Tony, pulled at his little hip flask and giggled half-hysterically, 'There, I told you Tallulah should have a frontal lobotomy!'

Cast member Konrad Matthei called rehearsals, 'a train wreck to hell.' Bankhead didn't bother remembering Tony's blocking or learning her lines. He would suggest brilliant notes to her but Tallulah would merely gaze back through those heavy eyelids and say, 'Loud or soft – how do you want it?' Slowly, but surely she was grinding Tony down. Williams – known to like a drop himself – became alarmed at how much Tony was drinking.

Tony called Bankhead the most unpleasant person he'd ever worked with and compared her to a hideous old vulture. One of her more unattractive habits was asking Seldes to run through her lines with her while she defecated on the toilet. In turn, Matthei wondered if Tony got 'some strange amusement' from antagonising Bankhead. Assistant stage manager George Hyland said that Tony seemed to take pleasure in ignoring her. 'She was begging for direction,' said Hyland. 'Begging for direction and not getting it.' Bankhead in turn complained that Tony always behaved as if he was just about to rush out the door. On this, Williams sided with Bankhead: Tony was good-natured and gifted, but also irresponsible. During one rehearsal, Bankhead told her director she could perform a scene on her head, on her back or doing a cartwheel, but he must give her direction. 'You're the actress,' he shrugged.[12]

Actress Marian Seldes, who played Goforth's secretary in the production, remembered the following exchange:

> Bankhead: This is the speech that everybody loathes.
> Tony: It's my favourite speech in the play.
> Bankhead: It would be.

Seldes thought Tony's direction was strong and imaginative but the two just couldn't hear each other. Even Bankhead admitted as such the one time she did things the way Tony wanted. But the effort of unlearning all her shtick proved too much for her. Bankhead would simply do what Vanessa would call her usual 'stencil'. 'With that old Georgia charm?' sneered Tony. He gave up on the production.

Merrick, too washed his hands of *Milk Train* before it even opened. Preoccupied with *Hello, Dolly!*, he rarely came to rehearsals. Tryout runs were limited to a few days in Wilmington, followed by one week in Baltimore. After that, *Milk Train* had to fend for itself.

Hartley remembered audiences at those out-of-town tryouts consisting of 'middle-aged women who felt emancipated by Tallulah, and gay young men imitating her. The critics all mentioned the audience. They picked up on the, as it were, homosexual cloud that hung over Tallulah.'

Merrick was dismayed by what he saw, but it was too late to change anything (Tony had already flown back to England). Indeed, he cancelled the play's New York run only to reinstate it an hour later. There was just a one-night preview at the Brooks Atkinson Theatre on Broadway. Half the seats were empty. The other half was filled with screaming queens, who shrieked with laughter at every possible gay double-entendre. Playing shamelessly to the crowd, Bankhead ignored everything Tony had told her. Her gay followers loved it. Merrick, seeing dollar signs, told Williams: 'If we had this audience every night, we'd have a smash.'

Milk Train opened on New Year's Day, 1964 to terrible reviews. *Newsweek* said Tony had 'chastened the play to a Brechtian coolness which made it wholly alien to Williams' sensuous imagination'. *New York World-Telegram* and the *Sun* said that *Milk Train* had become 'a gross hybrid of a play, hideously directed. Richardson has made *Milk Train* a spectacularly unsuccessful display of theatrical gimmicks.'

This time around, the play closed after five performances. Bankhead's biographer Joel Lobenthal blamed Tony for its failure, saying he should have spent less time on his 'private tutoring sessions' with Hunter and more with Bankhead. Williams also blamed Tony and his 'curious behaviour'. Ironically, Bankhead herself told Seldes how much she admired Tony's work over supper one night during the brief run. Seldes wished he had been there to hear it.

This was the last time Tony worked for Merrick: the impresario was so disenchanted with Tony that he decided not to pay him. Reckoning Tony would sue, Merrick's plan was to let him dangle for a while and then offer to pay half his fee – he knew Tony would jump at the offer. And that's exactly what happened.

One journalist took a snapshot of Tony at this point in his life. Despite the wreck of *Milk Train*, he was still the hottest film and theatre director in the world. Pictured in his suite at the Algonquin Hotel in New York, *Milk Train* had just opened on Broadway the night before. Five weeks before, Tony's version of *Arturo Ui* premiered, while *Luther* had been playing to packed houses in New York for the past three months. Meanwhile, people were queuing four abreast to see *Tom Jones* at an arthouse cinema, a few blocks south on Fifth Avenue. One eyewitness said Fifth Avenue resembled the evacuation of Dunkirk with people queuing round the block.

Now, Tony was returning to England to oversee editing on a film and direct a short season of three plays, all starring Vanessa, at the Queen's Theatre on Shaftesbury Avenue. Two appointments are waiting downstairs while Tony finishes his current one. The phone jangles incessantly. A room service trolley rushes purposefully in and out. In the midst of all this, Tony conducts a wickedly ingenious Sheridan Whiteside-ish campaign to frustrate his secretary from quitting. Oh yes, and somehow he's making final arrangements for a three-day holiday with Vanessa, which somehow must be squeezed into the diary before he flies back to London.

'Tony is only really happy,' a friend said, 'when he's doing 30 things at once. The thing most people don't realise is that he really can do several things at once. I've seen him really absorb the Sunday *New York Times* in 12 minutes' flat without missing any of the conversation in the room. I've found him able to recount word for word a long speech aimed at him, while he was deeply involved in reading a script. Simultaneously, he can rehearse one play, cast another, plan a third, cut a film, and still – when he is interrupted or when he interrupts himself – be the most casual, easy and pleasantly gossipy creature on earth.'

The film Tony had to go back and edit was *The Girl With Green Eyes*, an adaptation of Edna O'Brien's first novel, *The Country Girl*. It had all begun one day during the filming of *Tom Jones*. Tony, acting in the imperious manner of the grand impresario, tossed a book towards camera operator Desmond Davis. 'Catch!' said Tony. 'You said you wanted to be a director? OK, here's your film.' Davis read the novel and loved it. O'Brien's book told the story of a lonely young Irish girl who has a brief and unhappy affair with a middle-aged author. Tony decided that O'Brien, who had never had any contact with film before, should write the screenplay with Davis. Rita Tushingham was cast as the eponymous heroine and Peter Finch as the writer. Lewenstein was roped in to produce. Once again, Tony was taking a chance on people who'd never made a film before.

Davis shot *The Girl With Green Eyes* on location in Ireland in April 1963. Tony's willingness to take a risk in three first-timers was duly repaid. 'This enthusiasm, with the know-how of Richardson behind it, has given the film its keen vitality, despite the leisurely theme,' said *Variety*.

What was laughingly called the British film industry was dominated in the early Sixties by American producers taking advantage of the domestic production quota. Cinemas had to show a percentage of British films – that's how *Saturday Night* got its window at the Warner Leicester Square. Past-it American actors would be shoehorned into low-budget English films. Woodfall changed all that: you never heard an American voice in a Woodfall production. It really was the Beatles of the movie business. For a moment it seemed as if Woodfall would take its place alongside Rank's outsize gong or even Columbia's neo-Grecian lady with the torch. 'The British film industry was as affected by the Royal Court, as had been the theatre,' said playwright and screenwriter Christopher Hampton. Shirley Anne Field said: 'I loved Woodfall and still do. Tony Richardson did so much for British cinema.'

Woodfall's office in Curzon Street, Mayfair was the epicentre of what would become Swinging London. Profile writers noticed the battery of phones – red, white and black – next to a copy of *Le Monde* on Tony's desk. One reporter was told to wait until Tony had finished his private judo lesson. Woodfall even owned five Rolls-Royces, although who actually drove them was a mystery.

Oscar Lewenstein never felt that Tony was a great director. He was, Lewenstein believed, a wonderful impresario. 'His huge forte was finding extraordinarily talented people and showing them off to their best advantage,' agreed Diane Cilento. 'He always had a very good team of people, which was a sort of gift.'[13] Tony was a fantastic organiser: he understood the finance side as well as how to make a script better – an unusual combination. Most of all, he was persistent. Persistence is the single greatest quality you need to be a movie producer. British television producer Tony Garnett said: 'There might be some question as to whether he was a good director or not, but he was a bloody good producer. He deserves a lot of credit for how brilliant he was at putting films together. He made a lot of other films happen.'[14]

A born manipulator, Tony was convinced that directors had to create their own opportunities if they believed in a project strongly enough. After all, no one was going to create them for you. He also liked the power of being a producer. Most directors are just hired hands brought in to wrangle actors. 'Too many directors have a producer complex: either they cast him as a monster or they expect some God-like creature who will create ideal conditions for them,' he said. 'But it's no use looking for a Diaghilev now – you've got to get the thing together yourself.'

Woodfall announced its first three productions under the United Artists deal. All three were low-budget, as if to show the company hadn't grown giddy with success. *The Girl With Green Eyes* would cost £140,000, *One-Way Pendulum* £50,000 and *The Knack* was £125,000. What nobody knew was that Tony and Osborne treated the Woodfall company bank account like a piggy bank. Each of them would take out chunks of money whenever they felt like it. Neither cared what the other spent. For a while this was fine while the *Tom Jones* money was flowing, but that tap would slowly be turned off as Tony made one disastrous film choice after another.

Woodfall's second film, *One-Way Pendulum*, didn't do very well. Lewenstein described it as, 'the sort of flop we could afford to have.' The third non-Tony production was *The Knack ...and How to Get It*, an adaptation of Ann Jellicoe's Royal Court play. Richard Lester, director of *A Hard Day's Night*, was hired to direct. Michael Deeley watched as Tony trod carefully between his own sensibility and ambitions and what United Artists was prepared to finance. Rita Tushingham, who'd become something of a leading lady for Woodfall, starred as a girl caught between Michael Crawford and his flatmate. Deeley, meanwhile, found Woodfall's almost obsessive insistence on using real locations irksome.

Released in June 1965, *The Knack* caught Swinging London at its zenith. This little film grossed $2.5 million during its American release. Even more surprisingly, it won the Palme d'Or at that year's Cannes Film Festival. It really did seem as if Woodfall could do no wrong.

Tony often went out of his way to assist younger filmmakers. Throughout his career, he helped those trying to get up the ladder. One of his assistants, Andrew Mollo, had been making an amateur film at weekends. *It Happened Here* was a pseudo-documentary about England under Nazi occupation. One day, Tony asked Mollo how his film was coming along. Mollo admitted they'd run out of money. The next day, Tony and Lewenstein watched the footage and liked what they saw. Tony promised them £3,000 (£47,100 in today's money) if the footage they'd shot in 16mm could be blown up to cinema-quality 35mm. Mollo and Brownlow were so thrilled, they called their company Long Distance Films in homage to Tony.

The season of three plays all starring Vanessa came about because the Court had to close for repairs and a refit in March 1964 – the Sloane Square theatre would be out of action for three months. Tony agreed to stage a trio of plays, the first of which would be Chekhov's *The Seagull*. Vanessa starred as the daughter, Nina. Peggy Ashcroft played her stage mother Madame Arkadina and her real mother, Rachel, was Polina. Peter Finch, fresh from *The Girl With Green Eyes*, played the older writer, Trigorin. Tony's direction was typically loose: he was not concerned if actors strayed off their marks just as long as they kept captured the elusive Chekhov spirit. The cast often rowed with each other, though. 'The atmosphere,' said Finch, 'was barometric. Sometimes without any storm warning, we'd be in the middle of a hurricane and the next moment, flat, dead calm, peace, harmony, and we'd move forward.'

The Seagull opened on 12 March 1964 to a rapturous reception. It was the biggest theatrical triumph of Tony's career. 'The chief compliment that can be paid to Tony Richardson's production is that the cast has been orchestrated with such meticulous care that nothing jars and nothing is superfluous. On the whole, a sensitive and understanding production of an exquisite classic,' said the *Evening Standard*. Harold Hobson in the *Sunday Times* described the production as 'beyond price.' John Gielgud, having sensed Tony's throw-it-against-the-wall-and-see-if-it-sticks approach, thought the whole production hastily thrown together: 'It was a company that didn't know each other very well, which isn't good for Chekhov.' The play ran for 12 weeks.

Now that *The Seagull* was flying, Tony began rehearsing Bertolt Brecht's *St Joan of the Dockyards* with mostly the same cast. Vanessa would star as the Salvation Army do-gooder opposite Lionel Stander, the American actor whose career Tony had resurrected. Rachel was also in the cast alongside Donald Sutherland. Brecht's little-performed play was about the confrontation between bosses and unions in Chicago's meatpacking district of the 1920s. Tony, usually averse to anything which smacked of masks and mime, decided that the (verse-speaking) bosses should be covered in blood-red grease-paint while the (prose-speaking) packers and wholesalers should wear grotesque half-masks. Jocelyn Herbert, who'd designed *The Seagull*, agreed to design this second production as well: two gaunt, revolving towers surmounted her pop art design.

Tony had only four weeks to rehearse and even he realised this time he'd bitten off more than he could chew. He enlisted the help of Lindsay Anderson, George Devine and Anthony Page to help him direct. Soon, every part of the Queen's Theatre was filled with actors rehearsing bits of the play. Vanessa may have appreciated the way that Tony turned to others for advice – he was self-confident enough not to feel insecure when actors made suggestions – but it was a disastrous decision: there was no agreed vision of the play as the four directors themselves hadn't discussed the work. Instead, actors shuttled between four directors with clashing styles.

Devine rightly suspected *St Joan* was to be a disaster and then calamity struck. Pregnant with her second child, Vanessa collapsed during rehearsals and had to drop out. The entire Queen's Theatre season had been built around her, the advertising campaign was in full swing – it was too late to cancel. Lewenstein had put on the play in Dublin starring Siobhan McKenna and he persuaded the Irish actress to replace Vanessa. The critics hated it. Bernard Levin condemned 'this pitiful Agitprop rubbish' in the *Daily Mail*, grudgingly admitting Tony was a 'towering master of stagecraft.' The *Evening Standard* said: 'Tony Richardson's juggling with masks, choruses and intricate sets cannot disguise the fact that Brecht's play is a crude, badly-written, naive Marxian leaflet.'

Tony claimed this critical drubbing was only to be expected, given they were putting on such a radical play in the heart of London's theatreland. 'Well, what did you expect?' he said. Ticket sales were so poor that the play had to be taken off after three weeks. The Court made a loss of around £15,000 (£231,000 in today's money). Because Vanessa had to cancel the third play too, the Court was obliged to scrap the season. This marked the end of Tony's association with the Court. He was certain the Big Bang of *Look Back in Anger* was fading: one by one the stars exploding from it were fizzling out. The revolution was over. Theatres that had previously closed their doors to new

English playwrights were scrambling for them. 'But the vitality wasn't the same. It seemed to me that people were treading water, repeating themselves, without a great deal of feeling,' he said.

In the summer of 1964, he and Vanessa flew out to Los Angeles to start work on his next film, a follow-up to *Tom Jones*. Based on the 1948 novel by Evelyn Waugh, *The Loved One* was a satire on the funeral industry in Hollywood. Tony wanted to update it, weaving in his own experiences of making *Sanctuary*, four years previously. Now he was coming back to Hollywood on his own terms. It would turn out to be his greatest disaster yet.

Notes

1. Mike Medavoy, author interview, 22 June 2009.
2. Stephen, Andrew. 'Enter Stage Left', *Observer*, 25 January 1987.
3. Evans, Peter. 'Vanessa: The Years That Made Her What She Is', 4 October 1966.
4. Diane Cilento, author interview, 1 December 2010.
5. Author interview, 24 June 2009.
6. Author interview, 24 June 2009.
7. Susannah York, author interview, 1 December 2010.
8. Diane Cilento, author interview, 1 December 2010.
9. Danaë Brook, author interview, 8 December 2010.
10. Norman Twain, author interview, 12 February 2010.
11. Gerber, Gail and Lisanti, Tom. *Trippin' With Terry Southern: What I Think I Remember*, Jefferson and McFarland & Company, Inc., North Carolina and London, 2009.
12. Lobenthal, Joel. *Tallulah!*, Aurum Books, London, 2005.
13. Diane Cilento, author interview, 1 December 2010.
14. Tony Garnett, author interview, 22 June 2009.

CHAPTER TEN

Thirty-Two Faggot Acts

Tony was coming towards the end of shooting *Tom Jones* when two American producers came to see him. Documentary filmmaker Haskell Wexler and John Calley, an executive who would go on to run Sony Pictures, had bought the rights to Evelyn Waugh's novella. Tony had long admired *The Loved One*, which the novelist wrote after a Hollywood trip to discuss the film rights to *Brideshead Revisited*. In the end, the film was cancelled but Waugh wrote to Nancy Mitford that he'd found a 'deep mine of literary gold' in Forest Lawn cemetery, a kind of Disneyland of death.

Tony was intrigued: his hero Luis Buñuel had at one time wanted to adapt the book himself. *The Loved One* is about the muzak of death: an English writer arrives in Los Angeles, mingles with the starchy British colony and falls in love with a dedicated young cosmetician who works at the necropolis of Whispering Glades. He woos her by passing off classic English poems as his own. Her boss, Mr Joyboy, also courts her, taking her to visit his hideous mother. But Miss Thanatogenous commits suicide when she discovers that her poet boyfriend has plagiarised everything he's written to her.

Tony had already turned down one version to star Richard Burton and Elizabeth Taylor. This time around, he was to give Waugh's novel the same kind of cosmetic titivation that Mr Joyboy bestows on a loved one. He hired Terry Southern, screenwriter of Stanley Kubrick's *Doctor Strangelove*, to adapt the novel. Southern was riding high on *Strangelove*'s success; Tony encouraged him to go further with his maniacal humour on *The Loved One*. Tony, Southern and his co-writer Christopher Isherwood didn't so much as adapt Waugh's novel as rewrite it. For the most part, they abandoned the icy Latinate demeanour of the original. Southern tried to cap Waugh by inventing a deal between Whispering Glades and NASA to blast remains of the deceased into space. Jonathan Winters, playing the funeral business entrepreneur, shouts the countdown into the PA system: '... 4, 3, 2, 1 ... Resurrection *now*!' No doubt they all thought it was hysterical, baby.

Tony picked one of the campest casts ever assembled on screen, including Liberace, Tab Hunter and Roddy McDowall. John Gielgud was cast as an English expatriate, something the actor had reservations about. For some reason his bone-dry delivery, although perfect for Waugh, never translated well on screen. Rod Steiger was cast as Mr Joyboy, a lisping monster under a wig of blond kiss-curls. Tony cast American actor Robert Morse as the English poet – an odd choice considering Terence Stamp, David Hemmings and James Fox were all available. Morse, who'd never been in a film before, was unable to maintain his northern English accent during filming. Tony eventually resorted to dubbing all his dialogue with Morse reading his lines into a microphone.

Tony cast another unknown, Anjanette Comer, as Miss Thanatogenous. He said she was the only actress he'd seen who could possibly be in love with death. Later, he came to regret his casting decision: Comer was far too bland and he wished he'd cast Pamela Tiffin instead. And he stood up to MGM when the studio told him he couldn't cast Lionel Stander as a newspaper agony aunt. Stander was Tony's second choice after Lenny Bruce. Tony threw a temper tantrum – at least that's what the studio called it – when MGM refused to let him hire Stander. 'Why? Put it in writing!' he demanded. But of course MGM couldn't put it in writing because the McCarthy anti-Communist blacklist was illegal. Once again, Tony got his way.

Calley and his partner Marty Ransohoff gave Tony complete creative autonomy, thinking it was the only way they could get him. He insisted on shooting the film on location and in sequence. The budget was one third higher than that of *Tom Jones*. However, they'd struck Tony's directing deal before *Tom Jones* came out. MGM refused to budge from paying Tony Directors Guild of America scale and he therefore decided to punish them by charging as much as he could to the production. He worked at a snail's pace, shooting as many takes as possible and wasting time between set-ups: the film ended up 20 days behind schedule and wildly over budget.

The day would start with Tony opening a magnum of Dom Pérignon. He would then toast both cast and crew with a raised glass at the beginning of the morning's shooting. Dailies were shown in the screening room of the Beverly Hills Hotel, with plenty of canapés laid on. Long tables groaned with salmon, fat shrimp, cold meats and every gourmet treat you could imagine. Champagne flowed. Everybody was encouraged to drop by what became a nightly cocktail party.

Southern, who nicknamed his director 'Tip-Top Tone', said Tony's power over actors bordered on the hypnotic. 'It is fascinating to watch Tip-Top Tone work with an actor. Coddling, cajoling, pummelling – whatever is required for eliciting their best – he is always there,' Southern wrote. Gielgud found Tony delightful to work with, writing to a friend: 'Tony lets me improvise lines and chatter so that I seem natural in a way I have never been before on the screen.' However, one actor who didn't get on with Tony was Robert Morley, who'd been cast as the panjandrum of the Hollywood Raj. Morley couldn't stand Tony's working methods: he complained that any room small enough not to get the lights, camera and five actors inside would be the one Tony chose. In fact, Tony took the opposite view: the more awkward the set-up, the more realistic the sequence.

Things came to a head when Morley refused to appear in drag in a gay bar scene – even though this was written into the script he'd signed up for. 'Tony and I didn't quite agree what I was playing – I thought I was playing an elderly English actor, he thought I was playing a transvestite,' the actor said. He subsequently quit and revisions were made to the script. What was left on film was heavily edited down. Tony also provoked a mass walkout from ballet dancers hired to pose as robotic statues in one scene: the naked dancers, painted to look like marble, were supposed to come to life in erotic poses. The real-life owner of Forest Lawn had such a collection of life-size erotica. When Tony instructed them to be more lewd, the dancers burst into tears and ran off the set. Their choreographer, who'd just arrived as dancers were running past him, realised what had happened. Wagging a finger at Tony, he told him that he should have just said, 'Darlings, just do a plié facing each other.'

Tony, who loved the gypsy life, would stay out late or come back to the house he'd rented on Sunset Boulevard with a crowd of friends. It was important to him that everybody remained focused on making the film – he loved being what he called 'within the cocoon.' However, he avoided Hollywood parties where, as he put it, 'all the knife and fork work is done more on the guests than on the food.' He needed to go out or bring people home as a way of coming down from the filmmaking high. Socialising was his way of taking the edge off the adrenalin. Once again, he neglected Vanessa, who was now pregnant with Joely. She herself had been working on stage during the filming of *Long Distance* and *Tom Jones*. This time, however, she was stuck at home all day. She felt depressed and unattractive, but Tony was oblivious to her feelings.

Tony fell out with Calley and Ransohoff after they refused to give him more money following his *Tom Jones* success and banned them from the set – he wouldn't even let them see the rushes. They offered to buy him out as his contract was watertight and they couldn't get rid of him. Instead, brimming with cheek, he offered to buy *them* out. One tabloid journalist who'd flown out from London to do a set visit quickly got the measure of what was going on. 'What's all them f**king chains and strings around Richardson's neck?' he asked. 'From what I've seen of this production, one of them may bloody well be a noose.'

Eventually allowed back into the editing suite, Ransohoff said that he and Calley had argued with Tony over the film. The first assemblage of footage ran over five hours: Tony was therefore forced to delete entire performances. A segment with Jayne Mansfield as a travel receptionist ended up on the cutting-room floor. Calley was bitter about what Tony had done. '*The Loved One* is a reflection of the director's taste, not mine,' he said. 'Richardson thinks it's just great – I don't!' Privately, he described the finished film as 'thirty-two faggot acts all in a row.'[1]

Tony also managed to fall out with Waugh, who was then living in Devon, over what he'd done to his novel. In a letter to Nancy Mitford, Waugh complained: 'The film of *The Loved One* is a great annoyance to me. One of the few occasions when Peters [his agent] has let me down. He sold it a few years ago to a mad Mexican [Buñuel] for a paltry sum with the assurance it would never be produced. The next thing I heard was that an American company had bought the rights from the Mexican and were producing an elaborate travesty.' Tony let slip that he thought the novel, 'a bit thin and dated.' Waugh's agents subsequently wrote to MGM in an attempt to get him taken off the picture. Tony was embarrassed enough to write a letter of apology to Waugh. The author sent back a postcard, hoping the film would never find its way to the Odeon cinema in his local town Taunton.

Tony persuaded MGM to let him do post-synching work back in London. Vanessa was due to give birth in January 1965 and she moved into a nursing home in Welbeck Street. She remembered sitting in front of a gas fire strumming chords on her guitar and wondering if the baby inside her could hear the chords. Tony stayed beside Vanessa during labour: he stroked her hair and told her that she looked like his favourite pin-up Monica Vitti, which did her morale no end of good. He took photographs of the baby as it was being born, which embarrassed the nurses; neither he nor Vanessa cared what they thought.

Joely Kim Richardson was born on 9 January 1965. Originally, Tony had wanted to call the baby Kim after the actress Kim Stanley, but Vanessa thought Kim sounded too harsh as a first name for such a vulnerable creature. Back in California, one-year-old Natasha had been taught to swim by an instructor whose daughter was called Joely. It struck Vanessa as such a pretty name. Vanessa immediately put Joely to her breast and watched fascinated as her tiny fingers opened out like a sea anemone. Typically, Vanessa managed to turn Joely's birth into a political issue. She criticised powdered formula milk in the press, maintaining: 'It's not fresh and it doesn't taste like breast milk. I know because I have drunk my own.'[2]

Meanwhile, MGM – nonplussed as to what to do with *The Loved One* – came up with the tagline: 'The motion picture with something to offend everyone!' Indeed, it turned out to be an acquired taste. Tony had made the camp classic a decade too early and it would be another 10 years before John Waters started directing films; *The Rocky Horror Show* was also another decade away. *The Loved One* is probably best enjoyed smoking pot in the stalls of a repertory cinema, the exquisitely precious Gielgud becoming more hysterical as the screen gets cloudier and cloudier. Kenneth Tynan thought there were moments of fleeting brilliance, such as Liberace's coffin salesman discussing the onset of what he calls 'rig-mo' or Gielgud teaching English pronunciation to a cowboy star who gets 'dicey' confused with 'dykey', a shot of a Mynah bird pecking the eye out of a roast pig while Steiger's mother – a vast, bedridden object ('Every inch a queen,' Steiger drools) – tears into a side of pork. Most critics, though, viewed it with incomprehension. *Variety* thought the film's appeal would be restricted to circles who prefer their entertainment to be downright weird and the *New York Times* shrugged that although it was disastrous as a satire, it should at least live up to its advertising campaign. In London, *The Times* conceded that although Tony had always been capable of terrible miscalculations, he was incapable of doing anything lifeless or dull. In the end, MGM released *The Loved One* on one screen in London's West End. There was no danger of it ever coming to Taunton.

That summer, Tony again rented La Baumette, the old farmhouse outside St Tropez where he'd planned *Tom Jones* and Vanessa had nursed Natasha. Now they had Joely too, with all the broken nights and exhaustion having a new baby entails. Tony invited John Osborne and Penelope Gilliatt to join them once more. His driver Jan Niemeynowicz met the couple at Nice Airport. Osborne braced himself for the worst when Niemeynowicz began complaining about Vanessa: 'Oh, Mister Osborne, is so good you are here! Mister Richardson, he so unhappy! I never seen him like it before – he need you so badly but he never bring himself to tell you. He loves you, but he can't say that. Mister Osborne, please help him, is only you can do it!' Niemeynowicz seemed on the verge of tears as he hesitated on the track leading to the house. 'That woman, she is a bitch, Mister Osborne, she is not a kind person and she makes Mister Richardson so unhappy!'[3]

That night, the four of them went out to dinner because Vanessa was 'so tired'. Niemeynowicz drove: Tony and Vanessa sat in the front, the Osbornes in the back; nobody spoke. The poisonous atmosphere was broken by Tony and Vanessa beginning a vicious row in the front seat, following which Niemeynowicz stopped the car. Tony and Vanessa got out and continued the row outside. In silence, the other three waited in the car until they got in without saying a word and Niemeynowicz drove on.

The atmosphere at La Baumette was not helped when George Devine, another house guest, collapsed with another nervous breakdown on arrival. This took the form of uncontrollable weeping, inability to make decisions and paranoia that his friends were patronising or attacking him. Tony found a doctor, who gave him powerful tranquillisers. After ten days in bed, he started getting up to sit in the sun and swim in the pool. After three weeks, he had recovered sufficiently for Jocelyn Rickards to drive him back home to London in Tony's Thunderbird. His own doctor told him to take three months off. He required careful nursing until his sanity was glued back together again.

Tony talked about what he might do next. Christopher Isherwood was adapting Carson McCullers' *Reflections in a Golden Eye* for him. McCullers' story about a married army officer consumed with guilt over his homosexuality resonated for Tony. Because the book was so fully visualised, it lent itself to the screen with little alteration. Isherwood duly submitted his screenplay in September 1964. In the end, Tony decided not to go ahead with it – the subject matter was a little too close to home. Instead, he decided on a new project, *Mademoiselle*, based on a script by Jean Genet. Tony was infatuated with all things French, something Osborne found almost comical.

Oscar Lewenstein first brought *Mademoiselle* to Tony's attention when he was finishing *The Loved One*. Genet had begun writing the script, then called *Forbidden Dreams* or *The Other Side of the Dream*, in 1951. The screenplay was full of references to Genet's own childhood. He offered it as a wedding present to the actress Anouk Aimée (Genet was her husband's best man). However, the author kept rewriting it over the next five years. *Mademoiselle* follows an outwardly demure, but inwardly twisted and sexually frustrated teacher living in remote France. When not teaching, she secretly opens floodgates, poisons cows and sets fire to barns. She also manages to frame an itinerant Polish woodcutter, whom she shamefully lusts after (he is eventually battered to death by shovel-wielding villagers).

Tony had forgotten all about the project until one night when he was having dinner with fellow director Joseph Losey (*The Servant*). Losey mentioned that he wanted to film Genet's old script with Romy Schneider as Mademoiselle but his producer (Sam Spiegel) was balking at paying the $50,000 Genet wanted. There was no hurry as far as Spiegel was concerned – the script had been lying around 'for centuries.' In his duplicitous way, Tony pounced that weekend.

He tracked Genet down to a hotel in Norfolk, England, where he was having an affair with a married racing driver. When Lewenstein and Tony arrived, they were informed that 'Monsieur Jeanette' was in his room. Tony transferred Genet to the Park Lane Hilton, just up the road from the Woodfall office and together, they began work on the script.

Genet would turn up punctually every morning at eleven and Tony would go over the previous day's work – he thought Genet's script was wonderful and regarded him as a great erotic poet, going into taboo areas of sexuality. For Tony, Genet's story was almost classic Greek tragedy. Then he made the mistake of complimenting Genet on his reliability: Genet disappeared. Apparently, he only responded to being berated. Tony was forced to bring in French critic Michel Cournot to help him finish the screenplay.

Tony was infatuated with François Truffaut and Jean-Luc Godard. Like the Court, the French New Wave had turned everything upside down, providing a space for new directors, writers and actors. 'The action, as far as movies were concerned, was in France,' Tony wrote, 'where a few years earlier, the *nouvelle vague* had broken with all its vitality, force and freshness.' He screened Truffaut's love story *Jules et Jim*, starring Jeanne Moreau, on a home projector. Having lifted Truffaut for his own films, he now expropriated his leading lady.

Tony first met Moreau in 1964 when she was shooting a film called *The Yellow Rolls Royce* on location in London. He proposed that she should star in a revival of Frank Wedekind's *Lulu* at the Royal Court. Often how a relationship will end badly is right there at the moment of first meeting: Wedekind's Lulu spreads despair, ruin and death among everyone with whom she comes into contact and so Tony really should have paid heed. The pair met again by accident in Paris and immediately hit it off. Moreau had never seen any of Tony's films but she was strongly attracted to him because he seemed a bit mad. She said that she only worked happily with directors like Tony whose personalities were strong enough for her to submit to. A factor for her was the urge to mentally seduce and be mentally seduced in return.

Tony telephoned and recounted the *Mademoiselle* story. Moreau accepted at once. She later said: 'I had great faith in Tony – absolute faith. He had a mysterious quality, which is hard to define and when he said I should do the film, why, I just did it. I feel the same with Truffaut, with Buñuel, with Orson.' Vanessa had a presentiment that Moreau represented a threat to her marriage when Tony got back home after another meeting. 'Tony came back literally elated,' Vanessa told her sister-in-law Deirdre. 'It frightens me because I recognise that feeling: I've felt it myself. She must be extraordinary – Tony seemed transformed, set alight.'

Marlon Brando, who admired Tony, was keen to play the woodcutter but he was forced to drop out when a scheduling conflict arose. Italian actor Ettore Manni replaced him. Tony always regretted losing Brando. With him, *Mademoiselle* could have been the *Last Tango in Paris* of the Sixties.

Tony decided to shoot the film in one of the bleakest villages in France, strangely named Le Rat. He'd searched all over France for the right location. Costume designer Jocelyn Rickards remembered Le Rat as being without any kind of softness and totally bereft of charm. There were only 23 inhabitants, most of whom were over sixty-five. Filming began in the summer of 1965. Tony had the idea of shooting two versions: one in French and the other in English. He'd been criticised for his haphazard approach in the past. This time around, he set himself some tough rules: there was to be no camera movement and no music, only the amplified sounds of nature. The result would be uncharacteristically glum.

As usual, Tony found the actual filmmaking process magical. Moreau, however, said she detested her part and took no pleasure making the film. She arrived on location at the beginning of the second week. Tony never had long discussions with her about what he wanted – a couple of words would suffice. 'When I know how Tony sees the scene, I generally feel instinctively what he wants from me,' she said. Tony's almost telepathic relationship with Moreau triggered the crisis that finished his already precarious marriage.

To Tony's sister-in-law Deirdre, Moreau appeared independent and invulnerable while at the same time suggesting ecstasy to any man male enough to conquer her. Tony was truly fascinated. 'She's the greatest cinema actress in the world,' he raved. 'There's nothing she can't do. She works on an astonishing level of intuition – one word can set off that fantastic talent, that absolutely sure instinct. And her precision is uncanny, nothing superfluous.' He announced that he was to make a series of films with Moreau. 'He has never done that with me,' Vanessa grumbled.

Tony eventually confessed that he'd fallen in love with Moreau: he'd never met anybody like her before. 'I was absolutely infatuated,' he admitted. 'Jeanne was very exciting sexually, very interesting and unlike other people – she was just a totally different kind of woman.' For her part, Moreau didn't think any leading actress could make a film without the director falling in love with her. 'He knows so much about you, watches you so closely, he's got to understand every hidden spring of your personality. He needs, if he's a great director, to make the best use of you. His fascination with you inevitably becomes a sort of "love" relationship,' she said.

Vanessa tried to make the best of it, trundling the pushchair with Natasha and Joely through the woods, but instead found herself walking through a solid wall of pain. She couldn't believe the agony she was going through as if she and Tony were separated by a glass wall, each of them mouthing words the other was unable to understand. They slept in separate bedrooms, which came as a relief.

When the *Mademoiselle* production moved to Rome to shoot interiors, Tony rented a flat on the Via Attica for Vanessa and the girls. At this point, Vanessa had a one-night stand. She confided in Jocelyn Rickards, asking her to intercede with Tony. Rickards told Tony about the affair only to find herself shunned by the pair of them. In hindsight, she bitterly regretted acting as go-between: 'I just wish Vanessa hadn't confided in me about youthful affairs and marital problems caused by her and Tony's lack of real concern for each other, and their inability to cope with each other's complexities.'[4]

Vanessa decided to flee to China, leaving the girls in the care of a nanny. She had a long-standing invitation as part of a delegation of intellectuals and artists. In 1965, Westerners rarely visited China – it was the great unknown, the last frontier. Vanessa was a sponsor of the Society for Anglo-Chinese Understanding. By publicly supporting SACU, she was affiliating herself with Chinese Communism. It was another step leftwards. But she only got as far as Moscow, where, overwrought and remorseful, she decided to make a grand gesture and hurry back to Rome. She and Tony could make a fresh start, she thought. Everything was going to be all right. Russian officials were bewildered. Vanessa, crying and blowing kisses as she ran through the departure gate, boarded an Air India flight back to London. Robert Bolt, playwright of *The Tiger and the Horse*, took Vanessa's place on the trip. Back in Rome, she flung open the door and shouted, 'I'm back!' Vanessa's big entrance left Tony unmoved, however. She should have just stayed in China, he told her. 'She was still in love, and I was not,' he observed.

Tony was just a couple of days away from wrapping *Mademoiselle* when he was told that George Devine had suffered a massive heart attack. Devine had been playing the cross-dressing Baron in Osborne's Royal Court play, *A Patriot For Me*. Osborne had first asked Tony to direct it. 'Frankly, Johnny, I'm a bit mystified,' Tony told his friend when Osborne arrived in Los Angeles with the script. 'I mean, you'll have to explain it to me. What's it all about?' Osborne wondered how Tony could be so obtuse. Here was a play about a closeted homosexual whose life is ruined because he never admits his sexuality: he failed to recognise any parallels with his own life. The highpoint was a grand drag ball, where Devine had to dress up as Queen Alexandra.

Feeling tired in the swelter of an unusually stifling London summer's night, Devine collapsed in his office. Still in costume, he was rushed to St George's Hospital. Tony hurried back to London to find his friend in a noisy public ward at St George's, but he was too ill to be moved. Tony and Devine's doctor John Henderson was away on holiday. Tony immediately took charge, demanding that Devine be given Propranolol, an experimental heart drug (it would either arrest the damage or kill him). Devine slowly recovered and was able to receive visitors, including Rachel, whom he warned not to let Michael work himself to death.

By mid-October, Devine had recovered sufficiently to be discharged, although everyone knew he was living on borrowed time. Doctor Henderson attacked Tony for interfering: it would have been better had Devine died there and then, he insisted. Tony never spoke to Henderson again. Devine died three months later, on 20 January 1966. After his death, the Court group fell apart. 'George was the glue that held them together,' said Diane Cilento.[5]

When *Mademoiselle* premiered at the Cannes Film Festival in May 1966, the audience laughed during the sex scene between Moreau and Manni. Then they booed. Deirdre Redgrave thought cinemagoers were so embarrassed by the primitive sexuality onscreen that they laughed derisively, unable to handle the passion. 'The fact that he could evoke such a performance from his star and put on film such subtle, but ferocious sensuality spoke volumes of their feelings for each other,' she said. In London, the *Spectator* magazine published a damning review based on the Cannes screening, accusing Tony of incompetence. Tony subsequently sued for libel and won. Not that he thought much of Cannes anyway: 'It's exactly like a great heap of refuse that lots of terrible old dogs are smelling over, trying to pick up some bones with a tiny bit of meat on it.'

The *New York Times* complained that Tony had made *Mademoiselle* grotesquely solemn. *Evening Standard* critic Alexander Walker thought he had made a 'remarkable film ... Richardson's direction has great visual power and in its original French version it had a lot of atmospheric power too'. Like *The Loved One*, United Artists didn't know what to do with it. The poster outside the London Pavilion in Piccadilly Circus tried to tempt punters in with, 'Genet's story shows what can happen to a woman who is loveless.' Not the most enticing movie tagline.

Meanwhile, the divorce lawyers got to work with a momentum of their own. Vanessa said that the reason why the marriage failed was because each of them wanted to pursue their careers and neither would countenance the suggestion that either should do less. In turn, Tony believed that they had begun to take each other for granted once they had married. He blamed the institution of marriage itself for ruining the relationship.

The divorce was devastating. A great actress, Vanessa had always managed to maintain a façade of near indifference. Now for the first time, she was visibly unhappy. She wanted to run to Tony for comfort – yet it was he who was causing her all this pain. Vanessa took the girls to stay with Rachel at Wilks Water, needing to be looked after herself. Tony came to visit and as he left and walked to his car, Vanessa (who was watching from the front door) said: 'Oh, the if-onlys! If only I had gone about things in a different way.'

Tony agreed to pay Vanessa £200 a month (nearly £36,000 a year in today's money) to bring up the girls. She would continue living in St Peter's Square with the children, which was to be kept in trust for them until they were old enough to want it for themselves. The couple were both intelligent enough to realise they had to maintain a working relationship for the girls – divorce was merely a piece of paper. Tony would remain close to Vanessa, friends even, for the rest of his life. 'If you've loved someone, it really is a very stupid thing if all that goes, just because the things that made you want to live together are gone. There ought to be something left,' he said.

Of course, the divorce hurt the girls. Three-year-old Natasha had fantasies about her parents getting back together. She thought that if she saved up all her pocket money, she would send Vanessa red roses, pretending they were from Tony. Vanessa remembered both girls sobbing when Natasha asked why mummy and daddy didn't live together anymore (Joely was just a year old then).

Still infatuated with Moreau, Tony appeared untouched by the divorce.[6] His regret about wishing he'd done things differently would come later. For now, he moved on to his next film. Barely six weeks separated wrapping *Mademoiselle* and the start of *The Sailor of Gibraltar*, which was based on Jeanne Moreau's favourite novel (she'd persuaded Tony to film it). He immediately agreed – anything to prolong the time spent with her. 'It was a period when Tony was madly in love with me,' said Moreau. Author Marguerite Duras had told Moreau that she reminded her of the book's heroine and gave the actress the film rights for free. Once again, it was Joseph Losey who had originally wanted to film it with Moreau.

Duras' allegory follows an American divorcée who roams the globe in search of a sailor (her late husband had hired the sailor as a deck hand on their yacht). The heiress had embarked on a passionate affair with the young sailor she is desperate to find again. A young British tourist dumps his girlfriend for the heiress and the two of them ply the Seven Seas together – with the heiress auditioning candidates for the sailor in her bed. Christopher Isherwood, whom Tony engaged to write the script, doubted its suitability for the screen but Tony chose to ignore his friend's misgivings. The mid-Sixties were the highpoint of the film director as auteur. Tony arrogantly decided the script was the least of his concerns. Moreau recalled: 'There was no real script and Tony did it far too quickly.'

He cast Ian Bannen, who starred opposite Vanessa in *As You Like It*, as Moreau's English boyfriend. Orson Welles would play a Sidney Greenstreet character in the African souk. The rest of the cast included John Hurt, Eleanor Bron and Hugh Griffith, with whom Welles spent a lot of time drunk. Inexplicably, Tony cast Vanessa as the 'other woman' betrayed for Moreau – it was as if he couldn't get enough of humiliating his former wife. Not only had he publicly embarrassed her, now he had to victimise her on screen, too. Even more inexplicably, Vanessa agreed. One epiphany came when Moreau, overwhelmed by the intensity of Vanessa's acting, burst into tears. Unbeknown to the both of them, she'd crept up and watched Tony film a scene with his ex-wife sitting in a cafe.

Bannen called the production 'a nightmare' – Tony did not do enough preparation. He whisked both cast and crew off to locations in Italy, Greece, Egypt, Ethiopia and even a jungle near the Sudan. The weather was often terrible and they spent days holed up in hotel rooms. Moreau had suggested Tony work with Truffaut's cinematographer Raoul Coutard, who decided to use an un-soundproofed Arriflex. The camera whirred so loud, Bannen could barely hear himself speak, let alone Moreau. Meanwhile, Tony argued with Coutard all the time. Watching Tony at work, Welles remarked, 'Is this director from outer space?' Tony, in turn, accused Bannen of behaving in the most bizarre, infantile way. His male star was often incoherent with drink. He once struck Moreau hard across the face and nearly had himself and Hurt killed in a taxi when he grabbed the driver's genitals. Later, he smashed up his hotel room and an airport gift shop en route to the Ethiopian leg of the shoot.

Then, in a marvellous example of life imitating art, Moreau tried to leave Tony for a young Greek sailor. The thirty-nine-year-old actress began an affair with Theodore Roubanis, a naval cadet 13 years her junior. Tony had hired him to play one of the sailors on Moreau's yacht. Tony spread the rumour that Roubanis had been a gigolo for older women when he lived in New York.[7] Photographers snapped the couple coming out of Athens nightclubs. Tony went insane with jealousy, trailing them incognito at night. All that was missing was for him to play the rich, besotted husband. It's doubtful his agony impinged much on Moreau, though: there was a streak of selfishness about her. Later, she admitted that she had never been in love – she'd never given herself totally to anybody: 'There are many men for whom I had very strong feelings, that I had passionate love for, but I don't believe I ever experienced what I think is love. Love in the absolute.'

'It's just like a movie,' the hero comments at one point in *The Sailor From Gibraltar*. Would that it were. Moreau walks through this pseudo-romantic nonsense like a somnambulist, occasionally draping herself against the rigging and gazing sleepily at Bannen. Vanessa's touching performance is the best thing in the film. The *New York Times* called *Sailor*, 'utterly wayward twaddle'. '*The Sailor From Gibraltar* was a failure – a total failure,' agreed Tony. 'It could have been a much, much better film if I'd just spent more time on it – I messed it up.'

Bitterly hurt by Moreau's rejection, Tony spent Christmas 1965 with Vanessa and the children. He then fled to Bora Bora, trying to put as much distance as he could between himself and the French actress. Bora Bora was supposed to be the most beautiful place in the world and it was a good spot for Tony to lick his wounds. Later, he said that he'd been under no illusion that it was to be a long relationship. Of course it was Vanessa he turned to when he was in such pain: she was supportive. Meanwhile, Tony parlayed his relationship with Moreau into friendship. She would often come to his lunch parties and the pair remained friends despite his heartache.[8]

The philosopher Kierkegaard once talked about something being as meaningless as the tears of an actress. Tony had some interesting views about why actors and actresses have such short, intense relationships. According to him, actors feel an emotion and act it out at the same time. They have millions of roles – friend, lover, mother – and can play each part with marvellous intensity in their own lives. For them it is real, even though they're acting. The problem is that an actor can discard each role and walk into another with equal intensity while the people they leave behind – those who cannot change masks so easily – are left feeling bewildered and hurt. 'It's terribly difficult to know where the centre of an actor is,' he mused. 'They don't quite know who they are.'

Notes

1. Greenfield, Pierre. 'Limeys In Lotusland', *Movietone News*, 3 March 1980.
2. Munson, Donn. 'With All the Sex Appeal of Snow White: Vanessa In the Raw', *Daily Mail*, 12 December 1968.
3. Osborne, John. *Almost a Gentleman*, Faber & Faber, London, 1991.
4. Rickards, Jocelyn. *The Painted Banquet*, Weidenfeld & Nicolson, London, 1987.
5. Diane Cilento, author interview, 1 December 2010.
6. Norman Twain, author interview, 12 February 2010.
7. Richardson, Tony. *Long Distance Runner*, Faber & Faber, London, 1993.
8. Mike Medavoy, author interview, 26 June 2009.

CHAPTER ELEVEN

Hail, Vanessa

Long after the era of Betty Grable and well before that of Kate Moss, a most unlikely pin-up girl reigned on the walls of men's college dormitories across America. She was ravishing, of course, and half-naked but she had none of the doll-like passivity common to most male fantasies. Her arms were crossed at defensive angles across her bare breasts and her forlorn gaze spoke of someone disinterested in pleasure – it was almost as if she was warning you off.

Taken in Hollywood in 1967, Victor Skrebneski's photograph of Vanessa resonated in the collective consciousness of an entire generation. Skrebneski had been taking publicity photos for Vanessa's first Hollywood movie; he asked her to pose separately for this one. Emblematic of the turbulent Sixties and the rise of feminism, it became one of the most memorable – and most often reproduced – images of the decade.

Vanessa made an electrifying impact in her first film, *Morgan: A Suitable Case For Treatment*. Directed by Karel Reisz, *Morgan* was about a madcap artist (David Warner) who increasingly believes that he's a gorilla. Vanessa played his loving but desperate ex-wife, who regards him with a mixture of motherly love and total exasperation. Morgan goes on to sabotage her wedding to a rich art dealer (Robert Stephens). Vanessa was tantalisingly ambivalent as the debbish Mod who half-wants an Establishment life but hates giving up the explosive surprises of life with Morgan. 'She married me to achieve insecurity,' actor David Warner tells his rival.

David Mercer's script reflected the then fashionable views of psychiatrist R.D. Laing that schizophrenia was an act of rebellion. Mercer suggested that thousands of people sought refuge in mental hospitals and prisons because the world was trying to destroy them. Critics were queasy about the zaniness of the comedy – today, *Morgan* feels as dated as a Carnaby Street jacket – but they all raved about

Vanessa. 'Leonie is given a positively celestial radiance by Vanessa Redgrave. Her performance transmutes the intelligent actress into a great star. Hail, Vanessa! Like it or not, you have won the world,' salivated Felix Barker in the *Evening News*. Clive Hirschorn in the *Sunday Express* agreed, adding presciently: 'It is a beautiful performance which I feel sure will turn one of our brightest stage actresses into a film star of considerable importance.'

In the spring of 1966, still deeply hurt from her divorce, Vanessa began rehearsing *The Prime of Miss Jean Brodie*. The play was adapted from Muriel Spark's novel about an Edinburgh schoolteacher and her hold over a class of teenage schoolgirls. Peter Wood, the director, was fascinated as he watched Vanessa at work: she put on and discarded several Jean Brodies before settling on the right one. There had been the crypto-fascist version she'd played for three days, then the camp comedy lady she'd acted for another few days. Finally, all the different versions came together into one blend. What was fascinating was watching her progression through her different interpretations, said Wood. The play became a West End hit and it was almost impossible to buy tickets. It was typical of Vanessa that, right at the height of *Brodie*'s success, she paid for 40 of the best seats for a party of East End pensioners out of her own pocket.

Vanessa was still starring in *Brodie* when she was offered a small part in *Blow-Up*, Michelangelo Antonioni's puzzle of a film. Shooting during the day, Antonioni had to film round her two matinee performances as well. The inscrutable Italian director seemed uninterested in Vanessa's opinions – he just complained that he couldn't see enough of her breasts. Turning to Tony for advice as to how to deal with Antonioni, her ex-husband told her to remember the director was always right. When Vanessa questioned why, Tony said: 'Because for better or worse, the film is his and it better be his vision. If there's a tussle at any point, you may be right, but you're only going to muddy things.' Future directors including Joseph Losey would wish that Vanessa had heeded her ex-husband's advice. Indeed, many would be driven mad by her constant questioning and wilfulness. Vanessa said *Blow-Up* was about 'the unity and difference of essence and phenomena, the conflict between what is, objectively, and what is seen, heard or grasped by the individual.' Blimey. The public took it as a Swinging Sixties exposé of photographer David Bailey and his E-type Jaguar lifestyle. Vanessa played one of two dolly birds cavorting in his photographer's studio. Although she was only on screen for 10 minutes, romping topless with Jane Birkin, it was enough for Hollywood to sit up and take notice. Her agent began getting calls.

Six weeks before the end of her star turn in *Brodie*, Vanessa had some sort of nervous breakdown. One night she was waiting in the wings, ready for her entrance – 'Good morrrning, girls!' 'Good morning, Miss Brodie' – when she suddenly became self-conscious about what she was doing. This is fatal for any actor. In this case, she became frightened of actually going mad on stage. Vanessa's Knightsbridge doctor John Henderson – the same physician who had treated George Devine and later became Mrs Thatcher's doctor – prescribed Librium and gave her a shot of vitamin B12. 'I lost myself in a very literal sense in the part. I was just split right open with panic,' she said. 'It took the form of my being terrified that I would forget all my words. It happened just before I went on and that fear never left me until I was finished, not for one second.'[1]

Now Tony could put his director-is-always-right theory to the test. Staggeringly, Vanessa agreed to replace Jeanne Moreau in the short he was now making. United Artists' original idea was to have the three Free Cinema directors – Tony, Lindsay Anderson and Karel Reisz – combine their talents. Shelagh Delaney would write three short films to be shown together. Early in his career Anderson had directed occasional episodes of television's *Robin Hood*. Critic Philip French compared the three directors to something out of Sherwood Forest – Reisz the gentle, tonsured Friar Tuck, Anderson a somewhat menacing Sheriff of Nottingham and Tony as heroic Robin in his Lincoln-green tights.

Reisz dropped out of the project early because he was still in post-production on *Morgan*. Peter Brook was brought in to replace him. Brook immediately diverged from the plan and devised a story of his own about a Wagnerian opera singer played by Zero Mostel. Tony also digressed. Moreau loved the work of French songwriter Boris Bassiak, having sung one of his songs in *Jules et Jim*. She'd also trilled another of his compositions in *The Sailor From Gibraltar*. Tony, still infatuated with Moreau and all things French, wanted to direct her in an entire musical based on Bassiak's songs. He started filming his segment, *Red and Blue*, on 3 October 1966. Michael York, playing a circus performer, described the atmosphere as 'bizarre'. The first day of shooting coincided with Vanessa and Tony's divorce coming through.

Tony was also influenced by Jacques Demy's *The Umbrellas of Cherbourg*, aping Demy's film down to its crying Pierrot awfulness. With characters named 'Acrobat', 'Millionaire' and 'Trumpeter', *Red and Blue* was barely one up from street performance. What was so bizarre was that in his personal life Tony had tuning-fork-perfect taste yet his choice of subjects and filmmaking style was so random. The *New York Times* called Bassiak's songs 'hilariously awful'. United Artists decided to rename the feature *Red, White and Zero* – referring to Zero Mostel.

The studio then lost patience with Brook never finishing his short and in October 1968, released Tony's short on its own with *The Graduate*. 'Now *The Graduate* was the latest thing in risqué cinema at that period,' said *Red and Blue*'s editor Kevin Brownlow, 'and *Red and Blue* was so out of date, it was laughed off the screen.'

Michael York went to see *Red and Blue* at his local Odeon. As he entered the cinema, a man was not only vociferously demanding his money back but threatened the management with violence unless *Red and Blue* was immediately taken off. Lindsay Anderson thought Tony's segment was 'unshowable.' UA yanked it after two or three days. The headline in *Variety* read, 'RANK ORGANISATION SINKS RED AND BLUE LIKE SUBMARINE'. It was never shown again.

Meanwhile, in New York on the afternoon of 4 April 1966, the teenage son of Hollywood director Joshua Logan (*South Pacific*) was queuing to see *Morgan*. His father had mentioned to him to keep an eye out for any actress he saw who might fit the description 'ravishing bitch.' That was how Logan described the woman he was looking to play Guinevere in Warner Bros' movie version of *Camelot*. The only name the studio could come up with was Julie Andrews, who wasn't what Logan wanted. Tom Logan telephoned his father from New York: 'Dad, I've found your Guinevere! Her name is Vanessa Redgrave and she's acres of beautiful, Dad.' Next day Logan flew to Manhattan to see *Morgan* for himself.

That night, Joshua Logan and Warner executive Bob Solo flew to London to meet Vanessa at Claridge's. She was so extraordinary to look at, Logan was entranced: Vanessa didn't know whether she wanted the part, though. She was about to turn it down when she asked Tony for his advice. He said: 'You'd be absolutely mad. If you do *Camelot*, everyone will want you for their films – if you don't, nobody will.' Vanessa later said that she wanted to do *Camelot*, 'because it was all about equality. I mean, they had a round table.' The problem was that she was contracted to star in *The Prime of Miss Jean Brodie* for six months and Logan would have to push back the start date to accommodate her. Jack Warner, the head of Warner Bros, was unhappy about the situation. 'Do we really have to wait for that tall Communist dame until November?' he asked.

This was no joke. In fact, Vanessa had had trouble obtaining a US visa in the past. According to Corin Redgrave, the authorities played psychological warfare with her, threatening to withhold her visa. They insisted she sign in with the US Consul once she got to Los Angeles. 'Producers have pleaded with her to keep her mouth shut for the duration of filming in case the mothers of California should picket the studios,' said Corin.

Logan persuaded Warner to let him use the delay to shoot exteriors on location in Spain. Just before he left, he received a letter from Vanessa suggesting she wear the same costume throughout the entire film. 'Wouldn't it be terribly chic and original?' she wrote. Logan had to write back pointing out that *Camelot* took place over a 25-year time period; audiences might be a little confused. Vanessa, who had jumped off the precipice of divorce and found herself miraculously intact, had become increasingly confident in her opinions.

Listening to the playback of Vanessa's big number 'Take Me to the Fair', Logan thought his ears must be deceiving him. It sounded like Vanessa was singing in French. When he confronted her, she said the audience would find her taunting Lancelot in French hilarious. 'Isn't it marvellous? I sat up all night making the translation. It's marvellously funny.' Logan gently steered his leading lady back towards Alan Jay Lerner's libretto.

During filming Vanessa decided to throw a party for the British in Hollywood. Her idea was to hold the event at The Brass Bell pub in Santa Monica, a mock-Tudor inn just by the beach. An adjacent chippie sold fish and chips that you could eat out of newspaper. Vanessa's idea was that guests could eat fish and chips while playing darts in the pub – all very cloth cap. However, she hadn't bothered to check whether the fish and chip shop was open on the night. Some of the guests wanted proper

American drinks, not pale ale. Worse still, locals drinking in the pub resented the intrusion. The evening ended in chaos with Rachel Roberts screaming at her husband Rex Harrison for making a pass at Vanessa.

Joshua Logan was present at the moment when Vanessa met her co-star Franco Nero, the man who would go on to become her second husband. One day he took Vanessa into a rehearsal room to work on her songs. Nero was rehearsing next door, so Logan introduced the two of them. The way they looked at each other, Logan realised they hadn't even noticed he was in the room. 'So help me God, it occurred to me that moment, she's been looking for somebody to have another baby with and here's this good-looking Italian!' he remembered. Another version of their first meeting is not so gallant. Nero couldn't believe this distracted, bespectacled woman with no make-up and straggly hair could be his co-star. After meeting Vanessa, he supposedly went up to Logan and said: 'That's Guinevere? She's one of the ugliest women I've ever seen!'[2]

Vanessa wrote to Nero in Italian, inviting him out to dinner. Nero did not recognise the beautiful and poised woman who greeted him that night. Many have commented on how Vanessa can seemingly switch on her beauty at will. 'But I was to meet Vanessa Redgrave,' he said ruefully, referring to her two personas: the hand-wringing activist and the diva.

Camelot finished shooting early in 1967. The Warner publicity machine described Vanessa as 'Julie Andrews with sex appeal'. 'She's the skyscrapingest screen queen in filmsville,' gushed one press release. The American press compared her to Garbo, while in Britain she was seen as the next logical step beyond Julie Christie.

April 1967 proved a momentous month for the Redgrave family, both professionally and emotionally. First, Lynn (who was starring on Broadway in a Peter Shaffer farce, Black Comedy) got married to John Clark, the former child star of the BBC Just William radio series in the Fifties. They were married just two weeks after Clark divorced his first wife. Film director Sidney Lumet and his wife helped plan the wedding, which was held secretly in their downtown Lexington Avenue apartment, decorated with ivy and white gardenias. A minister from the non-denominational Ethical Church performed the ceremony, with Michael leading Lynn into the room on his arm. Afterwards, they all had dinner at Luchow's restaurant. 'Lynn looked gorgeous,' Michael wrote in his diary, although he couldn't help tartly noting that Lynn's husband, 'at first seems brash and unattractive to me.'

Next, both sisters found themselves competing against each other at the Academy Awards, nine days later. Vanessa had been nominated as Best Supporting Actress for *Morgan*, while twenty-three-year-old Lynn was running for *Georgy Girl*, whose poster billed her as 'the wildest thing to hit the world since the miniskirt'. Ironically, this was a part Vanessa pulled out of a week before shooting was due to start. Director Silvio Narizzano had his doubts about casting Vanessa right from the outset.

Georgy Girl was the story of a cheerful but dumpy girl who is put upon by her glamorous flatmate Meredith (Charlotte Rampling). In her quest to find true love and happiness, Georgy first has an affair with Meredith's madcap husband Joe (Alan Bates) before opting to marry her father's rich employer (James Mason), with whom she adopts Meredith's baby. 'I only had one question to ask her: how was she supposed to look like the back of a bus? Vanessa was the beautiful Greta Garbo of the Sixties,' said Narizzano. Vanessa answered his question days before the start of filming.

Producer Otto Plaschkes was convinced that Columbia would cancel the picture without Vanessa, but Narizzano had another idea. It was Vanessa who first recommended Lynn to play the girl who lives in the flat below Georgy's. Plaschkes criticised Narizzano for not talking much when they met Lynn. 'How could I?' Narizzano told him. 'She should be playing Georgy.' When she was offered the lead, Lynn telephoned Vanessa to clear things with her. 'She couldn't have been nicer about it,' said Lynn. 'She said she didn't like the script, but good luck.'

Though Lynn was no Sylph, she had to gain 18 pounds for *Georgy Girl*. She spent three weeks filming with James Mason, who had a prior commitment starting in Switzerland, and then shot her scenes with Rampling and Bates. No one had much confidence in the finished product, though. Lynn remembered no one saying anything gushing, as was the custom, after the preview screening. She was practically in tears. Bates took her out for some supper, where they drowned their sorrows in Chianti and Bolognese. 'You know, you can't win 'em all,' he told her.

Meanwhile, Columbia kept on delaying the opening in America. 'Would you like to have an orgy with Georgy?' was the tagline on the coming attraction poster. 'If you saw her waiting for a bus, you'd never believe it,' Rex Reed wrote about Lynn in the *New York Times* just before the film finally opened in New York. 'Treetop tall (5' 10") and all kneecaps, with hair that never seems to have met a stylist, a little round mouth invented for devouring hot fudge sundaes and a chubby figure that changes weight according to her mood, she certainly doesn't look like a star.'

Georgy Girl was nominated for four Oscars. Watching her performance, Peter Ustinov said Lynn, 'gives the impression of knocking things down by mistake because she doesn't know her tail is wagging.' But Lynn knew that chances like *Georgy Girl* didn't come along once in a lifetime for most people, 'so in retrospect I realise how fantastically fortunate I was.' In the end, both sisters lost out at the Oscars to Elizabeth Taylor in *Who's Afraid of Virginia Woolf?*

Michael and Rachel flew home from New York back to London, where Corin's wife Deirdre was about to give birth to their first child. Jemma Redgrave was born on 14 January 1965, the day before the Oscars ceremony. Corin stayed the night at Hans Crescent on the evening of the Academy Awards. Michael came home late with his boyfriend Fred Sadoff and another friend, Lehman Engel. After seeing both men out, the conversation turned to Lehman's homosexuality. Emboldened by Corin's laissez-faire attitude, and with his tongue loosened by booze, Michael spoke about his homosexuality for the first and only time. 'I think I ought to tell you that I am, to say the least of it, bisexual,' he said cautiously. He stared at Corin defiantly, as if it was his son who had wrenched the confession out of him and what was he going to do about it. Then came three deep, heaving sobs, like von Aschenbach's mask dissolving in *Death in Venice* – 'a grief so awful that it seemed to undo him,' in Corin's words.

The emotional dam had burst: the son found himself comforting the father, sitting on the arm of his chair while Michael weeped. Deirdre said Michael's confession made Corin feel like a fool, as if he'd been betrayed. Corin said that what Michael had told him confirmed something he'd known for a long time. His admission was, in a way, a kind of growing up. Yet Michael's remark to theatre director Frith Banbury – 'Thank God none of my children is queer!' – showed how his nature still revolted him.[3]

Vanessa and Franco agreed to act together again in Italian director Elio Petri's film *A Quiet Place in the Country*. In May 1967, the couple rented the wing of a villa in the Italian countryside. Filming took place in a huge deserted house about twenty miles from Vicenza and Padua. What should have been an idyllic time was marred by ferocious rows. Both would sulk in the Casa Veronese's many rooms. The problem was that although Vanessa wanted a baby, she was eager to continue her career too. She also wanted to remain single, something which didn't sit well with the fiercely Italian Nero. Deirdre remembered Franco being fascinated and infuriated in turn by Vanessa's independence and her political commitment. 'She was too much dedicated to politics, but whether you agree with her or not, you have to respect her,' he said. What would his family think of his having an illegitimate child? Vanessa tried to be the supportive woman he wanted, becoming an expert Italian cook but it proved impossible. There was one public row in a London restaurant that left Vanessa in tears and Corin shouting at Franco to leave his sister alone. This wanting-to-be-together, yet not-wanting-to-be-together would be something Vanessa and Nero were to wrestle with for the next 40 years.

Notes

1. *Guardian*, 1 January 1969.
2. Rorke, Robert. 'Magical Redgrave', *New York Post*, 10 June 2007.
3. Grove, Lloyd. 'Vanessa Redgrave Bites Her Tongue', *Washington Post*, 27 June 1991.

CHAPTER TWELVE

O, What a Charge He Made

Tony first began thinking about making a film about the notorious Charge of the Light Brigade back in December 1964. He was putting the finishing touches to *The Loved One* in Los Angeles when he read *The Reason Why*, historian Cecil Woodham-Smith's book about the Crimean War. He'd been taken to see the 1936 Hollywood production, directed by Michael Curtiz and starring Errol Flynn, when he was a boy. Hollywood's *Charge of the Light Brigade* was a rousing romantic adventure and a classic piece of American cinema, but it bore only a passing resemblance to the truth. For a start, it took place in India, not Russia. The suicidal charge celebrated by Tennyson had in fact been a military blunder condemning 600 cavalrymen to death. The more he thought about it, the more he saw *The Charge of the Light Brigade* as a way to combine comedy and tragedy; he saw the Crimean campaign as a glorious example of the ignorance of generals, ridiculous old men arguing while the young died.

History showed Crimea to be a farce right up until the moment of the charge itself. Tony had long detested the pomp of Victoriana; there's a moment in *A Taste of Honey* where Dora Bryan tuts at a bloated statue of Queen Victoria, which summed up Tony's feelings exactly. This debunking of the old and glorifying youth chimed with what was happening in London. The King's Road boutiques had begun stocking old Victorian military costumes as the Beatles were entering their 'Sergeant Pepper' phase: the timing seemed propitious.

John Osborne started writing the screenplay in January 1965 as Tony prepared to shoot *Mademoiselle*. Crew members were spotted walking round Le Rat with copies of Woodham-Smith's book. The two men, once so close, had become fractious with each other. In hindsight, Osborne felt they were on a clearly plotted collision course. 'TR is hell-bent on making an anti-war film,' Osborne complained from Tony's yacht as it toured the Greek islands that summer. Meanwhile, Neil

Hartley set about finding a location that could be used for key battle scenes: the country also had to have a large, highly trained cavalry that might be persuaded to work for Woodfall.

Russia blocked Woodfall from actually shooting in Crimea. The official reason was that the Valley of Death where the battle took place was too near Sebastopol submarine base. Tony suspected the real reason was that the Russians had lost the war. Instead, he had to find somewhere similar elsewhere. Hartley investigated Spain, Portugal and Yugoslavia before settling on Turkey, which had the closest landscapes to the Crimea. Woodfall began negotiations with the Turkish government, but it took Tony and Hartley two years before they finally struck a deal. He learnt that a Turkish 'yes' only amounted to an English 'maybe'.

Tony brokered a deal whereby the Turkish government would provide 4,000 cavalrymen and horses and Woodfall would pay for their upkeep. The cavalry commander and Tony became great friends. Woodfall brought him over to London and provided him with boxes of cigars and black frilly whalebone corsets for his girlfriend. Friendly cooperation seemed assured. Tony noted that neither the Foreign Office nor the British Embassy in Istanbul lifted a finger to help them. He repaid the snub by insisting that shooting keep going on the day his cast and crew had been invited to an embassy party.

Two valleys, about twenty miles from Ankara, proved the closest match to the infamous Valley of Death; the steppe-like terrain controlled by two different villages. Now Woodfall had to negotiate with 700 landowners for them not to plant crops in either valley. The villagers turned out to be shrewd negotiators: they were paid about three times what they would have got for their crops. However, the locals then reneged on the deal: they ploughed and sewed the valleys at night during filming, making them dangerous for horses. They also destroyed empty sets. John Gielgud wrote in his memoirs: 'The Turks were very tough with us, did not care for us at all and made things as difficult as they could for Tony Richardson.'

Tony assembled a first-class team around him. David Watkin was hired as director of cinematography. Watkin decided to shoot the film in a soft, impressionistic style, aping early colour photographs of the period. Lila De Nobili, a theatre and opera designer, who had worked for Luchino Visconti and Franco Zeffirelli, was hired as period consultant, ensuring the film gave an authentic impression of Victorian

England. Military history expert John Mollo spent almost two years researching the 3,500 uniforms. Boston Opera Company costume head Keegan Smith took control of the further 1,000 civilian costumes needed.

Tony himself was not bothered about historical accuracy, arguing it was up to the artist to use historical figures as he saw fit. 'An artist has a right to use history as his raw material as long as he makes meaning for himself out of it, it doesn't matter how distorted his vision either of the character or the events are,' he said. 'As long as an artist makes something meaningful as a work of art out of it, I think he may do anything he likes.'

Canadian animator Richard Williams was commissioned to create hallucinatory animated sequences and Kevin Brownlow was hired as editor. Brownlow, however, had misgivings right from the start. He wrote in his journal: 'I was flabbergasted when Tony Richardson began work on his version. He was totally the wrong director. He needs a small canvas, an intimate drama. He has no feeling for sweeping spectacle, a military life.' As part of his preparation, Brownlow screened various cinematic cavalry charges for Tony. Together, they watched sequences from Raymond Bernard's 1927 silent film *The Chess Player* and Sergei Gerasimov's 1958 gloomy *Quiet Flows the Don*. 'There was a shout from the back, "That's what I want!"' recalled Brownlow. 'I thought he was nuts.'

United Artists agreed to finance Tony's vision to the tune of $6.5 million ($43 million in today's money), the biggest-ever budget for an English film. Having fixed the price, now the pressure was on Tony to deliver on time and on budget. He'd given UA his personal guarantee, facing personal bankruptcy.

Tony set about assembling his stars. Michael Redgrave was his first choice to play splenetic Lord Cardigan, but his ex-father-in-law turned him down. Trevor Howard accepted the part. John Gielgud would play the gently confused Lord Raglan, who thinks he's still fighting the French at Waterloo. Everybody who worked with Gielgud relished his otherworldliness – you were never quite sure if he was pulling your leg. John Mortimer remembered a dinner at Tony's house when he brought his baby daughter Emily along. Watching the playwright struggle with Emily's carrycot through the front door, Gielgud said, 'Why on earth didn't you leave your child at home? Are you afraid of burglars?'

Tony did, however, cast Vanessa as Clarissa, the young, romantic wife of Captain Norris and Corin was to play the snobbish army officer, Featherstonehaugh. Corin's career had been taking off of late. Flying back to London after *Chips With Everything*, he'd been cast in a forgettable West End warhorse. Their daughter Jemma had been born on 14 January 1965. Late in 1966, Corin starred opposite Susan George and Judy Geeson in *The Newcomers*, the television series that made him a household name. He was being talked about in the same group of sexy up-and-coming English actors as James Fox, Ian McShane and Michael York. Corin, now twenty-seven, signed a five-film contract supposed to make him a world star like his father Michael and sister Vanessa.

It was then that the bombshell exploded: Woodham-Smith had already sold the film rights to her book to the actor Laurence Harvey three years earlier. Harvey had been planning to make his own Hollywood version starring himself as Cardigan and Peter O'Toole as Raglan. Somehow Harvey had got hold of a copy of Osborne's screenplay. He instructed his lawyer – Lord Goodman, known as Prime Minister Harold Wilson's fixer and considered the most powerful legal mind in the land – to sue for plagiarism. Tony immediately took evasive action, bringing in Charles Wood to rewrite Osborne's script.

Tony thought Wood was brilliant and eccentric with a passion for all things military. For his part, Wood was a good choice: he had actually served in the 17/21st Lancers, a unit that had taken part in the charge. The playwright recalled being told the story by his superior officers – 'a ghastly mistake draped in a mantle of heroism.' He had already read *The Reason Why*, as well as Crimean war correspondent William Howard Russell's memoirs and the journals of Mrs Dubberly, an officer's wife who witnessed the charge. Wood first heard about *Charge* when he was re-writing *The Knack* for Woodfall. He suspected Tony had only hired him to write a script designed to bamboozle Lord Goodman. According to Wood, Osborne then asked him to take over the script completely – Wood wouldn't have taken on the project unless Osborne had given him his blessing.

Wood duly turned in 300 splenetic pages, throwing in everything he felt about Empire, the Army and Victorian England. Having read the screenplay, Tony told him, 'I think it's too long, and I don't think we can have Queen Victoria f**ked by a bear, not even a very funny Russian bear, do you?'

The plagiarism case was heard in London's High Court in February 1967. Osborne and Woodfall vigorously denied ever having read *The Reason Why*. Woodham-Smith was 'deluded,' said Osborne if she thought that only she had access to all the relevant historical material. This was a lie: there were several copies in the Woodfall office, where it was pretty much regarded as 'the bible'. Woodfall eventually lost the case because of a single line in Osborne's script. Since Woodham-Smith concocted imaginary conversations between generals that might have happened 113 years ago, there was no way Osborne could have accidentally repeated her dialogue word for word. Osborne had clearly 'filched the fruits' of another author's labours, Harvey's barrister told the court.[1] Forced into the open, Osborne mumbled something about Brecht helping himself to Shakespeare.

Cast and crew set up headquarters in an Ankara hotel on 16 May 1967. Tony decided to give his assembled team a pep talk the night before filming was due to begin. The troops gathered in the basement Ankara hotel bar, tired from the flight and most of them already drunk. Tony stood under a spotlight on the small stage. Just as he was about to open his mouth, a boom operator rushed onto the dancefloor and shouted, 'All those who can't tap dance are queer!' before proceeding to do an appalling soft-shoe shuffle. Gielgud leant towards Trevor Howard and whispered, 'Personally, I never travel with my tap shoes.'[2]

Meanwhile, Tony warned his cast and crew about the dangers of 'epic-itus'. He told them that he intended to make a story of human relationships – or rather the lack of them – and he didn't want anybody getting the idea they were making a blood-and-glory epic. Tony didn't realise it, but the nub of what was wrong with the film was right there. His aversion to the epic should have set alarm bells ringing at United Artists. The studio was trumpeting that six words were going to sell this picture: The Charge of the Light Brigade.

The resources going into making the film certainly were epic. There were 5,000 extras, 3,500 authentic uniforms, 1,000 horses and a team of 60 stuntmen under the supervision of stunt coordinator Bob Simmons, who usually worked on the Bond movies. *Charge* was more like waging war than shooting a movie, observed Tony. He wisely decided to shoot the battle scenes first, figuring he'd have most energy and enthusiasm right at the start of the production. Hung-over, everybody got up at 5.30am the next morning to drive to the location. Tony

The Redgrave family poses in the riverside garden of their London home, Bedford House, c 1947. Rachel, Corin (age 7), Lynn (age 4), Vanessa (age 10) and Michael. *Photofest*

Look Back in Anger opens at the Royal Court in May 1956, the play which made Tony famous. *Topfoto*

Corin, age 15, preparing to go on stage. He was allowed out of school to play Rachel's page in *Saint Joan* in the West End. *Hulton Archive/ Getty Images*

Ian Bannen as Orlando and Vanessa as Rosalind in the 1961 Stratford *As You Like It*. *Central Press/Getty Images*

Vanessa and Tony on their way to Athens for their honeymoon in 1962.
Express/Getty Images

Tony won two Oscars in 1964 directing and producing *Tom Jones*.
BFI

Vanessa as Nina and Rachel as Polina in Tony's 1964 production of Chekhov's *The Seagull*.
ArenaPAL

Lynn makes her screen debut opposite Alan Bates in *Georgy Girl*.
Time & Life Pictures/Getty Images

Franco Nero around the time of *Camelot*. Director Joshua Logan thought it was love at first sight when Vanessa met him.
Archive Photos/Getty Images

Feminist icon: Vanessa poses in 1967 for *Isadora*.
Photofest

Vanessa brought up Natasha and Joely on her own after divorcing Tony. *Corbis*

artoonist Jak's take n Tony banning ritics from seeing *he Charge of the ight Brigade*. *he British Cartoon rchive*

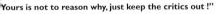

"Yours is not to reason why, just keep the critics out !"

Joely peers at her new half-brother Carlo, son of Franco Nero. *Keystone Features/ Getty Images*

Vanessa addresses an anti-Vietnam war rally in March 1968. Her growing radicalism alienated many and alarmed Hollywood. *Hulton Archive/Getty Images*

Announcing *Hamlet* in 1969: Judy Parfitt, Nicol Williamson, Tony and Marianne Faithfull.
Central Press/Getty ImagesImages

Natasha and Joely starting out as young actresses.
Time & Life Pictures/ Getty Images

Natasha and Tony in Los Angeles, where Tony lived from 1974 onwards.
Wire Image/Getty Images

Michael's autobiography launch in 1983: Rachel, Michael, Corin, Kika Markham and Corin's children Jemma and Luke.
ArenaPAL

Natasha as Sally Bowles in *Cabaret*, which she won a Tony award for.
ArenaPAL

Lynn, Jemma Redgrave and Vanessa star in *The Three Sisters*. Audiences booed Vanessa after she lambasted America during the play's run.
Dave Benett/Getty Images

Lynn wins a Best
Supporting Actress
Golden Globe for *Gods
and Monsters*.
AFP/Getty Images

Joely at the premiere of *Maybe Baby*.
The dress got more coverage than the film did.
Dave Hogan/Getty Images

Liam and Vanessa console each
other at Natasha's burial.
FilmMagic/Getty Images

Design: www.timpeters.co.

followed in his chauffeured silver Mercedes. It was the start of a gruel-
ling three-month shoot. One of the first scenes to be filmed was a huge
establishing shot of the battle. The shot had taken all day to prepare,
involving explosions and careering horses – it was the kind of shot
that you could only do once. Watkin thought it looked like a Delac-
roix painting. However, watching rushes that night back in Ankara, a
black flag marking where the explosion was to go off was clearly visible onscreen. The consensus was that the entire thing would have to
redone. Watkin argued: 'Who cares about the flag? What the hell does
it matter? It's something we could never get again. It's silly to worry
about it.' Tony's voice piped up: 'Well, Mr Watkin is obviously the only
person with any sense.'[3]

Things did not get off to a good start with the Turkish cavalry, who
were billeted under grim conditions. Only 429 Turkish cavalry officers turned up to be in the film – 171 short of the famous 600 Tony
had been promised. Things turned farcical: none of the Turks wanted
to dress up as the hated Russians and they'd slash their costumes in
protest. One colonel demanded that Tony publicly flog one of his actors
who had intervened to stop a cavalryman from stoning frogs to death
in a pond. It then turned out that most of the horses were too old. Tony
claimed that some of them were past-it mounts that had appeared in
Hollywood Westerns. Animal lover as he was, he also claimed no trip
wires were used to force the horses to keel over. However, when the
film was released on video, glimpses of now-illegal trip wires had been
removed. A visiting Turkish general then ordered his cavalrymen to
shave off the beards and moustaches they'd spent weeks cultivating to
give them a period look. A stunt demonstration went wrong and two
horses had to be destroyed; this was picked up by the Turkish press and
became a story about 10 soldiers dying on set. What was supposed to
be an epic scene of British troops landing in Crimea went terribly awry:
Turkish soldiers pretending to be Her Majesty's troops had never been
on a boat before, got seasick and began throwing up. What should have
been flotillas of barges with hundreds of soldiers passing the camera
were mysterious ghost ships – all the troops were lying out of sight,
writhing on barge decks awash with vomit. Some of the more Conservative actors were becoming mutinous at what they saw as Tony's
retelling of history. 'Left-wing rubbish,' they would mutter, or, 'slanted
nonsense.'

Still things kept going wrong. A ship carrying valuable equipment, food and costumes was held up in Athens, wigs and make-up went missing, light generators were held up at customs. Gielgud, who had always been afraid of horses, was thrown from his mount the moment he was helped onto it. Luckily, he was not badly hurt. From then on, Tony made sure Gielgud's reins were secured by extras standing just out of sight on either side. Progress seemed imperceptible. Sometimes Watkin appeared to go out of his way to stop Tony filming if the light wasn't perfect. For Tony, of course, perfection was not an aim: mindful that he faced bankruptcy if he went over budget, Tony was heard to scream, 'I must shoot – we're way behind schedule and damn the weather! I like the rain. I *want* rain! We *have* to shoot!' Watkin pointed out they were now in the lunch break. 'Of course it's f**king lunch!' shouted Tony, 'I've got Gielgud on the horse, I've *got* to shoot!'

Harvey insisted on having a part in Tony's film as part of his sizeable £60,000 settlement. He also took a share of the profits, cutting into Tony's percentage. Tony cast him as Prince Radziwill, who was in charge of the Heavy Brigade. Harvey flew out for one day's filming in Turkey: he only had 30 words to say. This was the role Osborne had been due to play. He himself was incandescent when he discovered Harvey was to replace him as the peacock-uniformed dandy and he accused Tony of complete betrayal. Tony wrote back emolliently to Osborne: what Osborne wanted from Tony wasn't friendship but sycophancy and adulation, he said. Despite this, Tony still loved his old friend.

Osborne replied with an eviscerating letter that accused Tony of callousness, sadism and 'mocking vampire contempt.' Worse still, Tony's circle was burdened with maintaining the corrosive fiction that Tony was not gay. 'I have never demanded "sycophancy or adulation,"' Osborne wrote. 'It is a bizarre accusation from you, hedged in as always by conmen, camp followers, eunuchs, pimps, procurers of all things procurable, and archetypal mercenaries and globe-trotting bum boys.' For good measure, Osborne copied his letter to his wife Jill Bennett – also appearing in the film – and Neil Hartley.

Tony thought about suing his old friend for libel. He and Osborne would never work together again.[4] Instead Osborne vented his spleen by later writing a *Waiting for Godot*-style play about his experience. Meanwhile, Tony humiliated Harvey as much as he could. His first scene involved him falling off a horse, which Tony made him do a dozen times. Then Tony got up to his old trick of not putting any film in the camera. In the end, such was his maliciousness that he cut out every scene featuring his nemesis. Although Harvey's lawyers had insisted he shoot the actor, their contract omitted that Tony had to actually keep Harvey's scenes in the film. Harvey remained sanguine about Tony's duplicity. 'After 20 years in this business nothing surprises me any longer,' he said.

The Charge of the Light Brigade is unique in that it is the only film that has had a stage play written about its making. Charles Wood was so amused by what he saw on location that he had to get it down on paper. The Royal Court premiered *Veterans* in 1970, with Gielgud playing the lead role of a septuagenarian actor stranded on location. Here was somebody playing himself playing somebody else. Wood astutely described Tony as 'tall and thin, and utterly happy ... laughing that braying laugh and slap of his legs, running on the spot without moving his heels and toes from the ground, rubbing his hands up and down his thigh.'

Actor David Hemmings, cast as the decent Captain Nolan who unwittingly brings about the tragedy, hired a three-masted schooner during the shoot. Hemmings often invited Tony and Vanessa for lunch on his yacht. In his diary, he wrote about Tony, 'His artistic flair is without question, but he can be sarcastic, with a brittle, wounding wit. He'll have his way, come what may, and suffers fools not at all.'

Brownlow noted how much pleasure Tony used to obtain from spreading malicious gossip. He loved to get relationships breaking up on set. 'He would quite happily set married couples at each other's throats,' said Brownlow. Tony himself was rumoured to be having an affair with Osborne's wife Jill Bennett. Her dressing tent was situated near the enclosure of the dancing bear used in several scenes. One day the bear pulled loose from its stake and stumbled into Bennett's tent while she was changing, taking the guy ropes with it. Bennett struggled out of the collapsed tent on all fours, followed by an amorous bear. As cast and crew killed themselves laughing, Gielgud shouted, 'Oh, Mr Richardson, how could you? And in your new motor coat, too!'

One oddity was the American tourist from Iowa who came to watch filming every day over a two-week period. The night the American was due to leave, he went up to thank Tony for allowing him to watch the production at work. 'I think you're doing a wonderful job. I hope the film is a big success and I'll be the first in line to see it,' he told him. 'It all looks so darn complicated, but then it must be incredibly difficult to make a Viking film so far from the sea.'

Back in England, Tony shot the scenes of Vanessa's character getting married at Wilks Water, the home of his former parents-in-law. He and Rachel and Michael continued to have great affection for each other despite the divorce. Rachel played Vanessa's mother, while Corin made his feature debut as a young officer. (On location in Turkey, he struck the first hammer-blow against his marriage by having an affair.) Four-year-old Natasha was cast as her mother's cinematic bridesmaid. She remembered being 'madly in love' with the groom, actor Mark Burns. Then, just as her father was shooting, a bee stung her. Natasha screamed and shouted so much that a doctor was called. Tony told her to stop being so mardy. 'But it wasn't the pain that upset me, it was the thought that I mightn't be in the film,' Natasha said. 'Already the little professional!'

Trevor Howard, used to working with meticulous directors such as David Lean, enjoyed Tony's breezy approach: 'He gave one a free hand and had ideas of gutsy things, strange things. He was very easy to work with – gave me confidence.' Watkin, too had nothing but good to say about Tony: 'Tony was very good with people. The crews also enjoyed him – we all knew how mad he was.' And Wood had nothing but happy memories of a team pulling together hard: 'Everybody felt they were doing something extraordinary. He had a genius for the kind of leadership that gets a film made. I probably had the best working relationship with Tony that I've ever had with any director before or since, but that was true, I think, of all of us.'

The crew may have enjoyed working with Tony but they were equally aware of the dangerous side of his personality – his cobra-like head swaying from side to side ready to strike. As an end-of-shoot present, they gave him a boa constrictor.

With Brownlow, Tony got down to editing the film at Twickenham Film Studios. He had bottles of champagne lined up in a wine rack next to the editing bench. Working with Tony up close, Brownlow decided there was a bitter and twisted side to him. Richard Williams, the Canadian animator whom Tony hired to create 11 minutes of animation in the style of Victorian engravers like John Tenniel, also thought Tony was a marvellous director. The problem was that Williams' cartoons were taking so long to produce: Williams and his team spent a year creating the linking scenes, working each and every day. Towards the end they were sleeping in the office. One man quit after he hadn't seen his family for a week. And still the cartoons weren't finished by the time *Charge* was due to have its royal gala premiere on 10 April 1968.

Vanessa thought that Tony was completely indifferent to his own success or failure. 'Well, what on earth did you expect?' he would say after another down-with-all-hands débâcle. This was his scornful, stoic reaction to every defeat. He shared Oscar Wilde's view that audiences could fail as well as artists. Sometimes it was as if he was waging a one-man war against the philistines.

He was becoming weary, however, of the bad reviews his films had been getting, including *Tom Jones*. There's a moment in *Waiting for Godot* when one of the tramps, trying to summon up the worst swear word he can think of, shrieks, 'Critic!' Tony thought that being a film critic was the most meaningless job in the world. Any retrospective analysis of his work was completely futile: he was enthused by a subject, made it and then walked away. Unlike Lindsay Anderson, who supported his films with a scaffolding of intellectual theory, he wasn't at all interested in writing album cover notes about his films.[5]

Tony decided to ban critics from seeing *Charge* before its royal gala premiere, arguing that he was taking a principled stand against 'a group of acidulated intellectual eunuchs hugging their prejudices like feather boas.' Critics approached their job as a frivolous exercise of obtaining easy copy, he said. They did not spend enough time considering a film's worth. Tony argued English film critics were known to be the most vicious and superficial in the world. At least, that's what he wrote to *The Times* – taking care to have copies of his letter delivered to other national newspapers.

Harry Andrews, who played Lord Lucan, thought the whole thing a cunning publicity stunt. Felix Barker, chairman of the Films Section of the Critics' Circle, immediately condemned what Tony had done, saying it denied free speech. Tony was unmoved – the critics resented being criticised, and when they were, screamed like stuck pigs, he retorted. Kenneth Tynan suspected Tony was inoculating himself against the sting of bad reviews to come. That way he could say critics were just bitter about not previewing the film. Bernard Levin, perhaps still smarting from being dumped by Vanessa, described Tony as 'flapping a limp wrist' at reviewers. Being called a eunuch by Ernest Hemingway was one thing, Levin wrote, but from Tony that should only raise an eyebrow.

Over the next few days, the letters page of *The Times* was full of correspondence debating Tony's stand. Lindsay Anderson wrote in support of Tony, as would, 'most of those who fight for a serious and authentic British cinema.' One correspondent said it was all very well for Tony to ban critics – 'it does not matter from the selling viewpoint if there are no reviews of a film in this class, or of Olivier's next production, or of Graham Greene's new novel – everyone is looking forward to them anyway' – but what about the small theatrical production or first novel which needs publicity?

Most newspaper reviewers decided to buy their own tickets to the next day's royal premiere in front of Prince Philip. Others decided to wait until the following afternoon's matinee. What's surprising is how fair and measured the reviews were. Perhaps the critics had to lean over backwards to show how unaffected they were by Tony's contempt. The *Daily Mail* described his direction as "masterly". The *Sunday Times* said *Charge* was 'uneven but often brilliant' while the *Sunday Telegraph* called it 'an audacious triumph'. Meanwhile, the Communist *Morning Star* described Tony as 'one of our most important and gifted directors who has helped raise the whole level of national filmmaking. He is, indeed, a man to admire and respect'.

Charge is one of Tony's best films, helped by Wood's pungent script. 'All this swish and tits gets my spliffin' nose up,' says Howard as upper-class women glide past him at an officers ball. 'Had my Cherrybums [cavalrymen] out today, always makes me randified.' The film is often laugh-out-loud funny, such as the moment when Gielgud looks balefully at the statue of Lord Wellington parked outside his office window. It's an illuminating period reconstruction, comparing the soft mezzotint of an officer's life to the grim Doré working-class tenements. Tony attacks the class system that produced Victorian England's greatest military blunder, portraying the Crimean campaign as a slowly dawning nightmare. He shows officers as constrained by class as Lord Cardigan was by his corset; recruits are so incompetent they cannot even tell left from right.

The problem with *The Charge of the Light Brigade* is that it lives up to everything except its title. Unfortunately, that's what people had paid to watch. Cinemagoers expecting to see the Light Brigade at its moment of tragic glory would go home disappointed. All they got was a bleak, defeatist battle that was over before it had really begun. Flies buzz around the carcass of a dead horse while generals bicker over who is to blame. According to Harry Andrews, the Turkish cavalry were suddenly recalled the day the charge was meant to be filmed: instead of the 600 Turkish cavalry officers promised, Tony had to make do with 60 British stuntmen. Trying to make them look like the 600 meant he had to keep the camera tight on the action. There were no sweeping long shots of cavalry as in the 1936 Errol Flynn version.

Brownlow blamed the failure entirely on Tony's defying audience expectations: 'Everybody was waiting for the moment, the supreme action sequence which would dominate the picture. What they did not want was a film that told the truth about war, which showed men dying of cholera, which made them depressed. It was like calling something *Ben Hur* and then not doing the chariot race.'[6] The result is an anti-climactic and ultimately disappointing film. John Mortimer thought there were moments of great visual beauty, despite the weakness of the story. Had Tony been able to shoot the charge as planned, he would have produced an undisputed masterpiece.

United Artists did its upmost to promote *Charge*. Retailers including Aquascutum designed Crimea-inspired tie-in fashions (Lord Cardigan invented the wool jacket still worn today, while Lord Raglan created his famous sleeves. Even Aquascutum got its name from the 'Scutum' General Goodlake wore during the Siege of Sebastopol.) The film did quite well in Britain, appearing in the box-office top 10 for the year alongside *2001: A Space Odyssey* and *The Graduate*. In America, however, *Charge* stuttered and failed. Trevor Howard, for one, was disappointed the film was not better received: 'It was not without its faults but I always felt that it had some marvellous moments,' he said. Despite his bitterness, Osborne named his only child Nolan after David Hemmings' character.

Tony was paid £150,000 (over £2 million in today's money) to direct *Charge*. He used some of his fee to buy a flat in Paris in the Latin Quarter, which he then rented out to his new friend David Hockney. The rest was used to carry on renovating an entire hamlet he'd bought in the hills behind St Tropez, a magical place which would become his Prospero's island: Le Nid du Duc.

Notes

1. 'Screen Firm Sues Over Osborne Script', *Daily Telegraph*, 22 February 1967.
2. Hemmings, David. *Blow Up... and Other Exaggerations*, Robson Books, London, 2004.
3. Walsh, James M. and Tibbetts, John C. *The Cinema of Tony Richardson: Essays and Interviews*, State University of New York Press, Albany, New York, 1999.
4. Heilpern, John. *John Osborne: A Patriot For Us*, Chatto & Windus, London, 2006.
5. Langley, Lee. *Guardian*, 20 June 1970.
6. Connolly, Mark. *The Charge of the Light Brigade*, I.B. Tauris, London, 2003.

CHAPTER THIRTEEN

'To Be Or Not to Be ... Oh F**k!'

It was Jeanne Moreau who first showed Tony the dilapidated farmhouse and outbuildings that would become his magical home in the South of France: it was the summer of 1966. French gossip magazines still photograph the compound from the air today – although these days, it's known as the Redgrave family eyrie. Le Nid du Duc means 'the night owl's nest'. It's difficult to find – perhaps it's meant to be. The traveller comes up through the twisting road leading up to the Provençal village of La Garde-Freinet. It was no accident that Tony ended up living near a village that historically, has always attracted revolutionaries and anarchists. The rocky dirt track leading up to Le Nid is half-hidden. Like some fairy tale, you're never sure whether the pampas grass guarding it isn't about to close up behind you. When Tony first saw Le Nid in the mid-Sixties, the buildings were in ruins: it was more a hamlet than a farmhouse. Like Sleeping Beauty's castle, the place had fallen asleep. Renovating looked a thankless, expensive task.

Happily, Tony had made a new friend that summer whom he'd met on a St Tropez gay beach. Jeremy Fry was in many ways the mirror image of Tony: a bisexual maverick with a retinue of friends and family. Tony called him the brother he'd never had. Fry was an inventor of genius, who created a four-wheel drive wheelchair and a valve for controlling oil pipelines still used today. 'He had a sense of colour and design I had never seen before,' said Natasha. 'I saw him as an impossibly glamorous, original figure.' Tony first came across Fry at dinner parties in the 1950s given by Anthony Armstrong Jones – later Lord Snowdon – who was engaged to Princess Margaret. Fry was meant to be Armstrong Jones' best man at the wedding until rumours of his secret homosexual life surfaced. He and a gang of French labourers set to work on Le Nid. Meanwhile, Tony would get panicky about how much it was all costing. Like a movie going over budget, rebuilding was spinning wildly out of control.

To supplement his income, Tony started directing television commercials. The fee from directing a 'Mr Potato Chip' commercial built the swimming pool. The pool hung off the side of the hill and faced Japanese watercolour mountains: you swam in warm water, the air crystalline. Or you baked by the poolside, melting like French cheese. David Hockney, another recent friend, was fascinated by the pool the first time he came to stay in October 1968. Unlike swimming pools in California, it was exposed to wind and weather. The ever-changing surface intrigued him. He spent hours photographing it, eventually painting 'Le Nid Du Duc' (1972) on his return to Los Angeles. Hockney had grown up down the road from Shipley in Bradford. Not only did they share northern roots and a northern sense of humour, both loved sunshine and the clear light of the South.

Tony installed his usual aviaries, a flock of 200 pigeons and around a dozen peacocks. Their ugly cawing woke people up. There were dogs and cats, chickens and ducks too. The pungent fragrance is what John Mortimer remembered most: log fires, coffee, herbs, lavender and cooking. The long table outside the kitchen never seemed to be laid for fewer than twenty. Jack Nicholson, Rudolph Nureyev, Christopher Isherwood, John Gielgud, Jessica Mitford and movie tycoon Sam Spiegel all dined beneath the mulberry tree. Tony was no snob, though. Princess Lee Radziwill, sister of Jackie Onassis, would find herself sitting next to the toothless cleaning lady. People would drop by and, like the guests in Buñuel's *The Exterminating Angel*, found themselves unable to leave. Weeks later, they would still be enjoying themselves. Lindsay Anderson was one such guest, noting in his diary: 'Peculiar atmosphere. Completely homosexual in a charming, unforced, well-mannered way. Tony is very democratic. The cook and major domo join other guests at meals.' Anderson was slightly awestruck by the lavish scale. 'The life that Tony has constructed for himself is so extraordinary – fantastic, spending *certainly* on a millionaire's level.' However, Tony was so casual about it that, 'you could almost forget how much it cost, the swimming pool that has to be continuously heated, the champagne that is opened every morning, the cars (a new Mercedes just delivered), the total hospitality of open house.' Yet today how many even acknowledge Tony's generosity? He might as well have torn up his money in the street.

Amateur theatricals became a mainstay at Le Nid. The tradition began when an Italian transvestite friend put on a drag show performing opera solos; things got more ambitious after that. Guests used to put on home-grown musicals. Natasha, probably the most sensible person around the place, would summon everybody to rehearsal. Even as a child she was very serious about acting. Hockney remembered Natasha, aged ten, gesturing histrionically and declaring, 'I'm never going to be an actress!' Fat chance, he thought.[1] Joely, her shy sister, played stripper Gypsy Rose Lee, with Natasha taking the part of the pushy stage mother. Although her striptease consisted of slowly peeling off a single long-sleeved glove, Tony remembered it as one of the most genuinely erotic moments he had ever witnessed.

Mortimer created a musical life of Saint Tropez at the climax of which a flock of doves was released from dustbins to Handel's 'Hallelujah Chorus'. Another Mortimer production somehow ended with cast and audience all jumping fully clothed into the swimming pool. Next morning, there was a competition to write the worst review possible in the style of Kenneth Tynan or one of the other London critics. The worse the review, the funnier it was.

Le Nid became the centre of Tony's life, the place he loved more than anywhere else in the world. He admitted that it had filled the hole left by the break-up of his marriage. Tony would get up at dawn, drive down to St Tropez market and come back laden with trays of *tartes tropéziennes* and *loups de mer*, melons and peaches. Sometimes he would grab his cowboy hat and drive guests to the beach in a 2CV. You could feel stones scraping as the car edged its way down the bumpy track. Tony would speed through to Gassin, the canopy of cork tree leafs jiggling in infinite perspective. There was a line of beach clubs on the road to St Tropez, the most fashionable of which was Le Club 55, where you could spot film stars. Tony, however, preferred Aqua Club, the gay beach restaurant further along the strip (its patron liked to greet customers dressed as the Pope).[2]

The weather would be crystalline. Tony and his guests would sunbathe or glance idly at the yachts of tycoons and jet skiers jumping like mechanical porpoises. Not everybody was comfortable visiting gay clubs, however. Mortimer and his very pregnant wife Penny sensed the hostility whenever they walked in.

Corin's wife Deirdre witnessed how Tony's energy and magnetism transform everyone and everything around him. Even when he wasn't directing people on stage or on screen, Tony was the puppet master – he always liked to be in control. 'After all,' he would say, 'I *am* a director – I can't do anything else.' Apart from 'marvellous!', the other favourite directing phrase Tony used was: 'I want it to be magic!' His friend the American novelist Joan Didion reflected that Tony wanted everything he did to be 'magic', from producing a movie to improvising one of Le Nid's amateur theatricals to organising a moonlit beach picnic. More than one person compared Le Nid to Prospero's island: the house was a set, filled with past and current lovers, situations full of dramatic possibility. Dinner beneath the string of fairy lights on the dirt terrace was the footage. (Tony once told Natasha that it was possible to have too much good taste – every home should have something tacky in it.)

That is not to say that life at Le Nid was always a Noël Coward play. Sometimes it felt more like Ibsen or Ionesco. According to the actor Rupert Everett, the house had a strange, feverish atmosphere. Encouraged by Tony, people were likely to go loopy there. Guests would be pushed into revealing secrets they didn't want revealed – Tony would goad them until they fled in tears. Penny Mortimer was shocked when, having just seen her husband off at Nice airport, Tony said: 'I suppose you hope the plane crashes, don't you, darling, and you'll be left a nice rich little widow?'[3] Or guests would be told to go and have dinner in the village, 'so we can all talk about you.' Canadian novelist Margaret Atwood remembered a stark-naked man running through a room, screaming at the top of his lungs. Moments later, he was followed by an equally naked Tony, holding a dead rat (the rat had transgressed one of the few house rules by biting the leg off one of his pet birds). Tony responded by plunging a skewer through the rat's heart.[4]

While Tony was sinking all his money into renovating Le Nid du Duc, Vanessa was preparing for the biggest role of her life. Universal Pictures was financing a biopic of Isadora Duncan, the dancer whose revolutionary attitudes and promiscuity had shocked America. Back in May 1962, on that Sunday afternoon when Vanessa had addressed thousands at a Campaign for Nuclear Disarmament rally in London's Trafalgar Square, one man in the crowd was closely watching her. He was Sewell Stokes, Isadora Duncan's biographer. There was something about this girl with untidy hair, wearing a white raincoat as she stood on the plinth of Nelson's Column, which reminded him of Isadora Duncan. One or two hecklers interrupted Vanessa and she answered them straight back. He began thinking about that night at Boston

Symphony Hall, 40 years ago, when Duncan had bared her breasts on stage and talked back to shocked audience members who were shouting at her. But it wasn't until he met Vanessa a couple of years later at a party that he asked her why she had never played Isadora. 'Because nobody has asked me,' she smiled.

And it wasn't until French producer Robert Hakim, who had been planning an Isadora biopic for a decade, saw Vanessa in *Morgan* during the 1966 Cannes Film Festival that he realised his search was over. Vanessa won the Palme d'Or for Best Actress. Hakim met Vanessa and Karel Reisz during a party and they agreed to do the project on the spot. Vanessa had long been fascinated by the legend of Duncan, the high priestess of modern dance and of free love (she entertained an entire Italian boxing team during one trip to Argentina). 'I would like to go down in history as a great dancer but I suppose I shall be remembered only by the number of lovers I have had,' Duncan once said.

There were so many parallels with Vanessa's own life. Like Vanessa, Isadora had dedicated herself to her Art, to Truth and to Beauty (always capitalised). The dancer's arrival back home in America was picketed by citizens outraged by her Communist beliefs – 'Red Trash Stay Away' read one placard. It was a God-given part for any actress – a combination of Camille, Joan of Arc and Eleonora Duse – and one she would have played for nothing (an admission which didn't go down too well with her agent).[5]

Vanessa started to train with Litz Pisk, the Austrian movement teacher with whom she had been working since 1961. Pisk herself had studied with Isadora Duncan's sister Elizabeth in Vienna. The only existing footage of Duncan dancing was a few minutes of scratchy Russian silent film so Vanessa and Pisk largely had to interpret Duncan's dancing. James Fox and Jason Robards were cast as Duncan's lovers, theatre designer Gordon Grieg and Singer sewing machine heir Paris Singer respectively. Reisz hired Jocelyn Herbert as production designer: it was her first film since *Tom Jones*. Filming started on 1 September 1967 on location in Yugoslavia, standing in for Russia and for Nice. Reisz remembered the stills photographer asking Vanessa to run along a castle parapet – there was a sheer drop of thousands of feet below. No sooner had the photographer asked her than Vanessa was running along the parapet in her Isadora costume, defying certain death. Reisz was stricken. 'Why did you do that?' he asked. 'Oh, I knew I wasn't going to fall off,' Vanessa replied, 'and I wouldn't have cared if I had.'

'Vanessa IS Isadora' proclaimed the thirty-foot high billboard of Vanessa, her arms crossed provocatively across her naked chest, which towered over Sunset Strip. Universal used the iconic Skrebneski portrait for the poster. Prudish Californians were shocked. Protestors, offended by Vanessa's anti-Vietnam stance, threatened to paint her out. Housewife Pamela Patrusky declared: 'It's not artistic, it's indecent! I don't want my kids riding in the school bus past it every day.' Meanwhile, Vanessa dismissed the prudes. 'I see no shame in my body,' she declared. 'For me, the body is an instrument, like the voice, the lights, the costumes. To be naked may be as easy or as difficult as reciting one's lines. And anyway, I'm used to it: all the directors ask me to undress. Perhaps it is the contrast between nakedness and my face, which is rather austere.'

The film begins with an ageing Isadora, raddled and broke, grieving in her South of France studio – ('My arms,' she mutters, 'the last of a woman's glories to fade, you know ...') – and ends with her preposterous death by strangulation when she catches her scarf in a sports-car wheel. Critics were divided about the film, which some felt was far too rambling and impressionistic. They agreed on the magic of Vanessa's performance, though. 'It does seem to me to give her an almost ideal role, a temperamental and even a physical matching so close as to be uncanny,' wrote John Russell Taylor in *The Times*.

As a dancer, Vanessa left the Isadora legend unchallenged, but what she lacked in technical skill was more than made up for in the sheer ecstasy of being: Vanessa is never less than gloriously radiant and memorable, her performance as sweeping and flowing as the woman she portrays. What she lacks is the aura that explains why Isadora took Europe by storm at the start of the 20th century when audiences in Berlin and Budapest showered stages with flowers and students pulled her carriage through the streets of Munich. With her air of invincible propriety, there's too much of the schoolmarm about Vanessa. Revolution, yes – but only after a good dose of cod liver oil.

While *Isadora* was filming in Yugoslavia, opposition to the Vietnam War was growing. US forces had first attacked the Communist Viet Cong in the summer of 1965, when Tony was shooting *Mademoiselle*. Three years on, Vanessa was becoming the Isadora Duncan and La Pasionaria of the anti-war movement rolled into one. She began speaking out. On 17 March 1968, she was at the head of a protest march handing in a letter to the American Embassy in Grosvenor Square. Thousands of hippies and left-wing agitators had come together; mounted police charged at protestors. Vanessa, wearing a fetching white headband, was bundled to safety. A hippy offering a mounted policeman a bunch of flowers was beaten to the ground. Police severely beat up one pregnant marcher and demonstrators threw marbles beneath horses' hooves, throwing police officers. The fighting continued for almost two hours.

Vanessa's anti-Vietnam stance made her unpopular in America. Universal began fretting about its investment as the December 1968 release of *Isadora* loomed. However, she was still nominated for a second Academy Award for her performance. When she and Franco Nero attended the April 1969 Oscars, protestors picketed the ceremony holding up a sign which read, 'A Vote for Vanessa Is a Vote for the Vietcong'. Vanessa had forgotten to bring her glasses: she mistakenly took the protestors for fans and started smiling and waving at them.[6]

Vanessa may have been calling for peace in Vietnam, but Corin – who was already left of his sister – wanted victory for the Viet Cong. The authorities were already aware of Corin. The telephone in his flat, which was listed in the phone book under Vanessa's name, was tapped. As public hatred of Vanessa and Corin intensified, Deirdre began getting nuisance calls. Callers, assuming Deirdre was Vanessa when she answered the phone, would make disgusting sexual suggestions. There were also death threats. Deirdre received poison pen letters telling her, 'All Redgraves are whores.'

More than a year after filming began on *Charge* – and Tony betrayed John Osborne by casting Laurence Harvey in a role meant to be his – the playwright took his revenge. Osborne attacked Tony in a two-act play titled *The Hotel In Amsterdam*. Ironically, the Court gave the work its premiere in July 1968. Screenwriter/hero Laurie and his show-biz chums bitch and gossip during a weekend in Amsterdam having fled a megalomaniac film director. Osborne based two of the characters on Tony's regular composer John Addison and his wife Pamela, although he admitted himself it wasn't a very flattering portrait. Tony, transparently portrayed as movie producer K.L., is described as 'the biggest, most poisonous, voracious, Machiavellian dinosaur in movies'. K.L. is a ruthless, relentless creature that feeds on his victims while keeping them apart. Describing the way K.L. works, Laurie says he 'insinuates his grit into all the available oysters. And if ever tiny pearls should appear from these tight, invaded creatures, he whips off with them, appropriates them and strings them together for his own necklace.' It's a devastating character assassination. At one point, Laurie/Osborne bitchily refers to K.L. as 'K.Y.', referring to Tony's homosexuality. Given Tony's litigious nature, it's a wonder he didn't sue. The vivid picture Osborne creates shows the enormous part Tony played in the lives of his friends and closest colleagues: it's almost as if he's Godot – feared of, but never arriving.

Osborne wasn't the only one whose relationship with Tony had soured. Gradually, many of his closest colleagues refused to have any more to do with him. Having grown to resent his manipulation and backbiting, they no longer trusted him. This in turn left Tony feeling that he had been badly treated by those whom he had helped. According to Robert Stephens, the play was 'about all of Osborne's hangers-on waiting for a tyrannical film director who never arrives because he commits suicide: that was Osborne's final pay-off to Tony Richardson.' Osborne had attacked Tony for being controlling, divisive and mendacious. It's ironic then that during the same summer, Tony performed one of his greatest acts of kindness.

Tony Garnett was a young BBC producer who had optioned the second novel written by Yorkshire schoolteacher Barry Hines. *A Kestrel For a Knave* told the story of a working-class schoolboy who pours all his love into rearing a wild kestrel. Garnett raised the £165,000 budget (£2.1 million in today's money) through an American distributor. Filming was just about to start in Barnsley, south Yorkshire when financing collapsed. Although Garnett went all round the British film industry trying to replace the cash, everyone said no. 'It had been turned down by everybody,' Garnett remembered. 'We went up and down Wardour Street trying to raise the money and they sniggered and said, "Wrong kind of bird!"'

Tony learned of the difficulties Garnett was having: indeed, Tony himself was part of the problem. The feeling on Wardour Street was that he had already exhausted the seam of working-class culture. One financier told Garnett, 'Oh, we've done the North.' In the early summer of 1968, he was duly summonsed to Woodfall, where Tony asked how much he needed. Garnett told him. 'Come back at five-thirty,' said

Tony. Meanwhile, Garnett tramped the streets and wondered what was so significant about half past five. When he returned to Curzon Street, Tony told him that he'd found the cash – he'd had to wait until the United Artists executive in Los Angeles that he needed to speak to had arrived at the office. Afterwards, Garnett reflected, 'People have said to me, "Oh, he just made a phone call" – but he didn't have to make that call. He was calling in a favour. I think that was very noble of him. I've never stopped being thankful to Tony.'[7]

And it was Tony who came up with the title of *Kes*. Shirley Williams thought that he was attracted to *Kes* because it resonated for him: here was a film about a lonely boy growing up in Yorkshire who, like Tony, finds comfort bringing up a bird of prey.[8] Like Billy Casper in *Kes*, Tony had nursed and fed an owl when he was a boy. Eventually he taught the owl to fly. Like Kes, the owl would alight on Tony's hand whenever he called it.

Tony gave Garnett notes on Hines' script, protecting him and director Ken Loach from fathead American executives. 'Tony told us not to take any shit from these people. He told them to f**k off,' said Garnett. And United Artists left Garnett alone until *Kes* was finished – 'I don't think they even knew where Barnsley was,' he said. However, the studio decided the Yorkshire accents were incomprehensible. One UA executive sneered as he walked out of a screening that he would have 'preferred Hungarian.' What's more, the studio told Garnett and Loach that it wouldn't release the film in North America unless they gave it a happier ending. Eventually, ABC released *Kes* on a handful of screens around Yorkshire, hoping to drum up local interest. Word of mouth spread. Today, *Kes* is regarded as a classic: the British Film Institute voted it the seventh greatest UK film of all time (Tony either directed or produced another four in the list).

Meanwhile, Tony was having his own problems: he was trying to find an actor to replace Richard Burton, who had quit his latest production. It was his new agent Robin Fox who had recommended Vladimir Nabokov's novel *Laughter in the Dark* to him. Burton was to play Sir Edward More, an art dealer who becomes infatuated with Margot, a common cinema usherette, leaving his wife for her. Unbeknownst to him, Margot is having an affair with someone her own age and the two lovers bilk the art dealer for cash. More realises what's going on and confronts both of them. Driving away, he's accidentally blinded in a car crash. Margot rents a villa for More to recuperate in and installs her lover. Finally, More attempts to shoot Margot but instead accidentally kills himself: 'It's a gripping, haunting story and it intrigued me from the first moment I read it. There are a lot of disturbing things around nowadays and if you are making films about the times you're living in, you are bound to get into a lot of subjects that deal in those things,' said Tony.

In February 1968, Burton arrived in London with his wife Elizabeth Taylor. In order to avoid paying British tax, the Burtons were staying on a yacht moored in the Thames. The first scene to be filmed was an art auction scene. Taylor offered her services as an extra. Tony agreed, only to realise that Taylor wanted £10,000 for her cameo. He refused. Taylor comforted herself by buying a Monet for £50,000. Burton also bought a Picasso drawing for £9,000.

Filming continued for a couple of weeks until the blow-up happened: Burton turned up late for filming on a Sunday. Exactly how late he was remains unclear – the papers reported the star turned up six hours late. Later accounts, including most biographies of Burton, put the actor's lateness at an insignificant half hour. Tony's autobiography says that Burton was four-and-a-half hours late. His lateness was the last straw after a fortnight of taking hours out for lunch, leaving early and sneering at the script; he was also rude to the film's crew, who were becoming demoralised. And his lateness was pushing the film further and further behind schedule. Like *Charge*, Tony was picking up the bill if *Laughter* went over budget. Either way, he bawled Burton out and the actor, feeling that Tony had humiliated him in front of his own daughter (Liza), shouted straight back. Both men reached for their lawyers. Elizabeth Taylor intervened, trying to get both of them to apologise. Tony went to see the Burtons on their yacht but the meeting ended with Taylor yelling at him with a scream so piercing it penetrated the cabin walls.

Tony, desperate to find a replacement acceptable to United Artists, tracked down Nicol Williamson in the South of France (Williamson had played Flute in Tony's production of *A Midsummer Night's Dream* in 1962). His breakthrough came two years later, when he played John Osborne's embittered solicitor in *Inadmissible Evidence*, a character based on Tony's own lawyer, Oscar Beuselinck. One theory is that Tony had wanted Williamson all along and was looking for a justification. Williamson was grateful for the part. *Laughter in the Dark* had, he said, 'flashes of joy and of bright, sometimes hilarious humour, just as life has. And you grab hold of these moments and cherish them because the film, like life, is also harrowing.' Now Tony had to persuade United Artists to keep filming going. UA, knowing the weakness of Tony's position, made him promise to repay the studio £1 million (£13 million in today's money) if the film flopped; he also had to relinquish his share of *Tom Jones*' profits.

Laughter could have been a taut psychological thriller, a successor to Joseph Losey's *The Servant* or Roman Polanksi's *Knife in the Water*. Instead, Tony had his usual problem of not being able to decide on one style. The reviews were positive, even though cinemagoers didn't share the critics' enthusiasm. 'What a relief to find a film to praise wholeheartedly and without reserve. The result is some of the most disturbingly evil scenes the cinema has ever conjured,' said the *Sunday Mirror*. The *Sunday Express* described *Laughter* as 'altogether a memorable and disturbing experience'.

By the end of 1968, London was changing again. Things were hardening on the streets. People were taking 'Lucy In the Sky With Diamonds' off their LP turntables, and putting on 'Streetfighting Man' instead (Mick Jagger's song about the Grosvenor Square demonstration led by Vanessa). Corin had come home from Turkey to Deirdre and his two children, Jemma and Luke, contrite about the affair he'd had on location. They struggled on, but the first fault line was there in the marriage for adultery is hard to forgive. 'Corin was ostensibly not very affectionate. Deirdre found that very difficult as his wife,' observed her friend Danaë Brook.[9]

Corin, who had always had a coldly analytical mind, despised the hippy-dippy nonsense of psychedelia. He dismissed the underground movement as middle-class and bourgeois. The real problem, he believed, lay in class structure – the stranglehold of the ruling class. It would take more than a bunch of stoned hippies wearing bells and nodding 'Right on, man' to change all that. Some wondered if Corin's new political consciousness sprang from his guilt at having everything so easy: a private education at Westminster School followed by a Cambridge scholarship. Excepting going to Eton, you couldn't get a more privileged start. However, his friend Rita Tushingham didn't believe his new political stance sprang from guilt so much as a realisation that there was a much bigger world beyond the cloisters.[10]

Corin and Deirdre took up the cause of poor Afro-Caribbeans living in Notting Hill. It was the era of radical Chic when Leonard Bernstein entertained the Black Panther separatist movement in his fashionable New York apartment. In Paris, Jean Seberg, another left-wing actress, introduced Vanessa to an American black activist called Hakim Jamal (his real name was Alan Donaldson). Jamal claimed to be Malcolm X's cousin, but the truth was that he came from a broken home in a black district of Boston. At fourteen, he had become a heroin addict and was committed to a mental asylum after trying to kill two people. In prison, Jamal underwent a spiritual conversion and joined the Black Panthers. He preached hatred of whites. His modus operandi was to let wealthy liberals entertain him and then make them feel guilty about being bourgeois. His English publisher Diana Athill thought that Jamal was an engaging psychopath.

Jamal's dislike of touching white people didn't extend to movie stars, though: he and Seberg were lovers. It was Vanessa who paid for his air ticket to London and raised funds for his Montessori school for black children. Calling him 'inspirational', she hung a large photo of him on her living room wall.[11] One night she brought Jamal along to a party and parked him with Corin and Deirdre, wandering off in her careless way. In London, Jamal fell in with Michael X, another black separatist described as 'the authentic voice of black bitterness'. Originally known as Michael De Freitas, Michael X had been a pimp, drugs dealer and rent-collector for notorious slum landlord Peter Rachman. The previous year, he had spent time in prison for inciting racial violence – he had called for any black woman seen with a white man to be shot. Jamal and Michael X began to feed off each other's paranoid fantasies. In fact, Jamal even started to believe he was God. Corin and Deirdre became alarmed and distanced themselves from him. Others were not so fortunate.

Gale Benson, the ex-wife of Corin's best friend Jonathan Benson, became infatuated with Jamal. They'd met at a dinner party given by Vanessa.[12] Benson, whose half-sister was said to be Jackie Kennedy Onassis, moved with Jamal to Trinidad to live in Michael X's commune. Jamal encouraged Benson to believe that he was God. She changed her name to Hale Kimga, an anagram of Gale and Hakim. One day Benson was caught snooping among Michael X's private papers. In his paranoid way, Jamal suspected her of being a spy working for MI6.

Benson, twenty-seven, was subsequently hacked with a cutlass and buried alive on 2 January 1972 – her body was found seven weeks later in a shallow grave. Her brother, Frank Benson, believed that Jamal and his accomplices murdered his sister. Jamal fled Trinidad and was in turn murdered himself shortly afterwards in his hometown of Boston, Massachusetts. Michael X was executed for killing one of the gang who murdered Benson. His body was found in another shallow grave near hers.

Lynn, meanwhile, having just had her first son Benjamin on 8 May 1968, started filming *The Virgin Soldiers*, based on the bestselling novel by Leslie Thomas. She played Phillipa Raskin and Rachel was her screen mother. It was one more example of the Redgraves appearing together (Corin had just finished playing a progressive young barrister in *A Man For All Seasons* and Vanessa had the role of Anne Boleyn). Michael always turned down many 1960s offers of American TV specials to feature some or all of 'Michael's Bloody Marvels'. Lynn said most days, somebody would contact her about a script in which the entire Redgrave family could play together. 'They all involve incest, which rules them out in my opinion,' said Lynn.

Tony decided to take a break from being a movie producer. He was becoming disenchanted with Woodfall, which had become a sort of anti-establishment Establishment. Over the years, Woodfall had grown more and more self-indulgent, ignoring tastes and public opinion. Tony was increasingly uninterested in running the company: committee meetings were tedious for someone used to making decisions with a flap of the wrist. He wanted to concentrate on directing – in particular, the theatre. And he especially wanted to work with Nicol Williamson again, directing him in Shakespeare.

Tony regarded *Hamlet* as the seminal work of all Western European culture. Williamson would bring what Tony called 'irony' to the role – Hamlet stands back from the action and comments on his own involvement in it. With one eye on the papers, Tony called his new theatrical company 'Free Theatre' in a nod to the Free Cinema days. Always one to keep up to date, he staged his new production at the Roundhouse, a 19th-century train repair shed in Camden, north London. The disused circular building had reopened a couple of years ago, hosting UFO – the psychedelic nightclub that gave Pink Floyd its break. The Doors had played the Roundhouse the year before.

Once again, Jocelyn Herbert designed the production, although it was more like designing a theatre from the ground up. The Roundhouse consisted of two concentric circles, one inside the other. Tony restricted the performance to the inner circle, building a semi-circular stage facing banked seating. Increasing the intimacy, the space was enclosed by thick black curtains. Tony called it, 'a new revolution needed to destroy, finally and completely, the form of the proscenium of the proscenium theatre and the social habits that go with it.'

Tony cast pop star Marianne Faithfull as Ophelia. The twenty-two-year-old had already appeared in two Court productions: *The Three Sisters* and *Early Morning*. However, she was best known for being Mick Jagger's girlfriend. Faithfull had been discovered naked and wrapped up in a fur bedspread when police raided Keith Richards' home in an infamous drugs bust, two years previously. There was lots of gossip that police had found Jagger performing cunnilingus on Faithfull with a Mars Bar inserted into her vagina. In fact, Faithfull and the others had been listening to Bob Dylan while coming down from an LSD trip. Richards was still so befuddled that he thought the police were a group of identically dressed dwarfs – 'very small people wearing dark blue with shiny bits and helmets' – and he welcomed them with open arms.

Introducing the petite Faithfull to the press, Tony towered over her like a flag on a high mast. '*The Three Sisters* is one of my favourite plays, but I never really understood Irina so fully until I saw Marianne Faithfull play her. Of course I chose her for Ophelia. She is innocent and vulnerable, and has a simplicity and directness. People think she has been chosen because she is a pop star and she can't be any good. She hasn't the technical background, nevertheless she is an actress,' he pronounced.

The cast was rounded out by Mark Dignam, Judy Parfitt, Gordon Jackson and Anthony Hopkins. Tony didn't like Hopkins[13] and the feeling was mutual. Hopkins described Tony as a maniac who brutalised actors. 'Richardson was one of the worst,' he said. 'Those directors, I hate them. I don't understand why actors don't stand up for themselves when they're being abused by some directors.' Hopkins found the play, 'a deadly experience. I was so bad in it. I was very erratic – I changed my performance every night.' Rehearsals began. Tony spent a fortnight just discussing the play with the cast, discovering its themes and subtext.

Hamlet became the hot ticket in town. The first-night audience included Prime Minister Harold Wilson. The play was running smoothly until Williamson flubbed his famous soliloquy, 'To be or not to be ... oh f**k!' The star walked offstage. There was an appalled silence until Tony's voice could be heard calling out from the audience, 'Come back, Nicol.' But that was only the start of it. Williamson began walking offstage with increasing frequency during the 10-week run, much to the audience's titillation. People even began buying tickets in the hope of seeing him flounce off. Harold Wilson, however, was so enthused by what he had seen that he insisted President Nixon go and watch it, too. Wilson grandly described Williamson's Hamlet as the best of his generation – perhaps of the century. Nixon said he was too busy. Still, the British Prime Minister's recommendation must have stuck in his head: Nixon invited Williamson to perform his Hamlet at the White House.

The reviews were very good. Harold Hobson in the *Sunday Times* wrote, 'I do not remember seeing this play before. By which I mean that Mr Richardson's production, like those pictures in the National Gallery which have been cleaned, is so bright, clear and vivid that one has the impression of seeing both it and them for the first time.' Its sister paper *The Times* added: 'Richardson's production uses a savagely cut text but it has a justification of force and fluid movement'. The *Daily Sketch* said it was guaranteed to make Shakespeare top of the pops. Williamson won Best Actor at the London Evening Standard Drama Awards in November 1969 for his performance.

Faithfull and Williamson began an affair, having sex in his dressing room before going on stage. Looking back, Faithfull resented Tony for what she saw as him manipulating her into a relationship with Williamson. Faithfull also decided to inject herself with heroin during the interval just before the mad scene, thinking it would add verisimilitude. It's hard to see what she thought she might be adding, except perhaps nodding off during the longer soliloquies. She began missing performances and her eighteen-year-old understudy Anjelica Huston had to fill in. Faithfull began contemplating suicide: she pictured herself floating in the Thames with flowers garlanded around her head like Millais famous painting of Ophelia.[14]

Meanwhile, Tony started to think about filming the production. He believed that all previous Shakespeare movies had taken away from the poetry – you didn't need to see what Shakespeare was describing. His solution was to just film the actors in tight close-ups. That way, Shakespeare's rhythm would exist on film. 'It's not perhaps a film really, but something like a visual LP of *Hamlet*,' he said. Martin Ransohoff, the producer on *The Loved One* with whom he'd since patched things up, found the $350,000 budget. They filmed *Hamlet* between 8am and 5pm each day with a two-and-a-half-hour break before the evening performance. This punishing schedule went on for 10 days. Tony opened out the action a little, filming in the Roundhouse cellars for the ghost scene and bringing in some horses.

Ransohoff immediately sold the film to Columbia Pictures for $500,000. *Hamlet* went on to gross many times that figure although Tony grumbled he never saw a penny of it. He dismissed the project as 'a minor experiment.' The *New York Times*, however, thought it was an experiment that had failed: 'Richardson has used the medium to close in rather than to open up the drama, and the result, though not without honor, is quite without interest.' Faithfull, too thought the film was muted compared to the actual production. 'In the live production it was f* *king great 'cause everybody just had to let rip,' she said.

Tony was also working on taking the production over to America. He had met theatre producer Norman Twain at a party in New York, which he'd attended with magazine editor Jean Stein. It was January 1959 and he had just directed *The Chairs*. Tony asked Twain to bring *Hamlet* to Broadway. The play would then travel across America on a college tour before reaching Los Angeles. Twain was familiar with Williamson's reputation: the actor was even said to have once dumped David Merrick in a trashcan. Neil Hartley and Tony assumed everybody in the cast would want to go to the States. The play was booked into a tryout run in Philadelphia before moving to the Lunt-Fontanne Theatre, where Tony had such a disaster with *Milk Train*. Tony called the cast together after the final London performance. Hopkins remembered how upset Tony was when he told him he wasn't going: 'I think it was assumed that we were all itching to go to the States, so when I told Richardson I couldn't, he was beside himself.'

Having been away at the Le Nid du Duc for most of the run, Tony hadn't liked what he saw on his return. He singled out Williamson for particular blame, attacking his star for what he considered to be shameless overacting. For Williamson, Tony had come to symbolise 'power without love'. Williamson told Tony: 'I'm not going to ask you not to talk to me like that again. You. Will. Never. Talk. To. Me. Like. That. Again.'

Tony oversaw the US transfer but left after *Hamlet* opened on Broadway at the Lunt-Fontanne Theatre on 1 May 1969, where it played for six weeks. Altogether, there were 52 performances. Meanwhile, Williamson swapped one Ophelia for another and had an affair with Anjelica Huston. Trouble began when the touring version reached Boston. On the Boston first night Williamson walked off during the play scene – which, as Tony pointed out, is hardly the most difficult scene for Hamlet. Roger Livesey, who played Archie Rice's father in *The Entertainer*, stepped forward and said: 'Normally, we'd bring the curtain down at this point, but in this production we don't even have a curtain!'

Twain went backstage, where he found Williamson stark naked. He ordered Williamson back on stage, where 'he gave the greatest Hamlet I've ever seen. Nobody's ever come close to Nicol doing Hamlet.' As the US tour progressed, Tony washed his hands of the show. By the time *Hamlet* reached Los Angeles, it literally ended in a car crash. Williamson, who'd never learnt to drive, persuaded an actress that he'd picked up at a party to let him take a drive in the twisty Hollywood Hills. Drunk behind the wheel of her car, he managed to drive offroad and landed on the roof of somebody's house.[15] Williamson was hospitalised and somehow the accident was kept out of the papers.

Faithfull came to dislike Tony as much as other people now did. 'He had a Machiavellian streak,' she said. 'He wasn't just a bisexual narcissist living his life: he was a director, which gave him licence to indulge in serious game playing. He was bitchy, sarcastic and ruthless; in other words, your typical director.' In particular, she felt that she had been used as a stepping stone. But there was somebody else in that first-night audience that Tony wanted to get to … and that person was Mick Jagger.

Notes

1. Tynan, Kathleen. 'Exit Prospero', *Vanity Fair*, February 1992.
2. Everett, Rupert. *Red Carpets and Other Banana Skins*, Little, Brown, London, 2006.
3. Mortimer, John. *Murderers and Other Friends*, Viking, London, 1994.

4. Renzetti, Elizabeth. 'This Time, No Dead Rats', *The Globe and Mail*, 5 May 2007.
5. Stokes, Sewell. 'The Legend of Vanessa Redgrave', *Kinematograph Weekly*, 8 March 1969.
6. Bosworth, Patricia. 'If I Love... And I Do Love, *New York Times*, 4 May 1969.
7. Tony Garnett, author interview, 22 June 2009.
8. Shirley Williams, author interview, 11 November 2009.
9. Danaë Brook, author interview, 8 December 2010.
10. Rita Tushingham, author interview, 8 December 2010.
11. Bosworth, Patricia. 'If I Love... And I Do Love', *New York Times*, 4 May 1969.
12. Moore, Victoria. 'Buried Alive', *Daily Mail*, 16 February 2008.
13. Norman Twain, author interview, 12 February 2010.
14. Faithfull, Marianne. *Faithfull*, Michael Joseph, London, 1994.
15. Norman Twain, author interview, 12 February 2010.

CHAPTER FOURTEEN

The Pharaoh and the Monster

Ned Kelly, the Australian outlaw who had defied the authorities while holed up in the Outback, had long fascinated the Free Cinema group. Sydney Nolan, an Australian artist, had exhibited a series of paintings about the Wild Colonial Boy in London in the early Sixties. Tony was intrigued by the brooding, armoured, solitary horseman of Nolan's paintings: 'I became interested in a man who was a criminal, a revolutionary, a dreamer, an idealist – who wrote letters to Members of Parliament from his hideout,' he explained. Kelly, an Irish labourer working in the 1870s, was persecuted by the Victoria police and eventually killed three policemen and fled deeper into the bush, from where he staged some audacious bank robberies dressing up as a policeman himself. He also burned people's mortgage deeds, making him seem like Robin Hood in the eyes of some. Meanwhile, he protested his innocence in long letters written to the Australian government. Kelly was finally captured after a shootout in the town of Glenrowan and hanged in Melbourne Gaol on 11 November 1880.

Karel Reisz originally announced that he would film the Kelly legend for Woodfall back in 1964 (it was to be Albert Finney's next film after *Saturday Night and Sunday Morning*). But Woodfall couldn't raise the million-pound budget, despite the success of Reisz's first film. Now, five years later, Tony announced it would be his follow-up to *The Charge of the Light Brigade*. His first idea was to cast Corin's university friend Ian McKellen as Kelly. For his audition, the twenty-nine-year-old actor recited part of the outlaw's Jerilderie Letter – the 8,000-word manifesto calling for an independent Victoria state which Kelly wrote to his MP. Tony shot McKellen's audition in a stable with the actor in full make-up and costume. Ian Jones, the film's scriptwriter, thought McKellen would make a superb Kelly, later raving, 'he made a beaut Ned.'

Then Tony came up with an idea he thought even better: he had long been a fan of the Rolling Stones, whom he had met through

Marianne Faithfull. Tony persuaded himself there was a way that Mick Jagger, a ballet-dancing matador type, could be transformed into the hulking, burly Kelly. On one level, like Kelly's infamous homemade suit of armour, Jagger seemed forged for the role – persecuted by the authorities, both became almost mythical figures in their own lifetimes. In any case, what was important for Tony were Kelly's inner qualities, his poetry and rebelliousness, not just his physicality. In hindsight, Tony admitted this was a mistake: Jagger's face might have been great, but his body seemed frail and at times even herky-jerky. In concert, energy snaked out of him like an urban street cobra, but on film he was flat despite his exceptional intelligence (Tony thought Jagger was far too bright to be an actor). Faithfull believed Tony had a more base reason for casting her boyfriend. 'I think the main reason Tony chose Mick was because he wanted to have an affair with him,' she said.[1]

Tony's scriptwriter was incredulous when he rang to tell him the casting news. Jones had been researching Kelly's life since the age of ten: he'd never envisaged the collar-bolt-arsed Jagger playing black Irish Kelly. 'I said, "Mick Jagger?" And he said, "Have you seen him act? He's maaaarvellous!" I said, "He's not very big." And he said, "Christ, no. He's the smallest man I've ever seen, but he's got a very, very big head."'

Jagger had his own reasons for accepting the part. Although he'd been exploring an acting career (his debut in *Performance* was still waiting to be released), getting out of the country for three months came at a good time: he had multiple problems piling up at home. For a start, his lover, actress Marsha Hunt, was pregnant with his child. Next, he and Faithfull were on remand for drug charges after police raided their home on 29 May 1969. Officers had found cannabis in a white Cartier box in the sitting room, plus a large lump of hashish in an upstairs bedroom. Jagger insisted the drugs had been planted by the police, who wanted paying off: the police officer leading the raid had demanded a £1,000 bribe, he said. (The singer was subsequently vindicated. Release, the drug advice charity, published a report in late 1969 documenting two years' worth of drugs cases where the police had planted drugs or demanded bribes. An internal Scotland Yard inquiry discovered that Chelsea drugs squad did regularly blackmail those it planted drugs on. Several years later, senior detectives of Scotland Yard's drugs squad were convicted on charges of corruption.)

Then, on 2 July 1969 (and five days before Jagger was due to fly out), Brian Jones was found dead in his swimming pool. Jones had been sacked from the band a month before. Although his death was not entirely unexpected – given the massive amounts of drugs and alcohol he ingested and his increasingly loopy behaviour – Jagger still went into shock. The Stones were due to play a free concert in Hyde Park that Saturday, the day before leaving. Jagger came down with stress-induced laryngitis the day after Jones died; he told Woodfall that he couldn't possibly make the start of production as planned. Woodfall replied by showing Jagger detailed figures on shooting costs and production schedules, insisting if he was well enough to perform in Hyde Park then he could also leave for Sydney the next day.

Jagger went ahead and performed the free concert. His tribute to Jones fell flat, though. The idea was for thousands of white butterflies to be released into the air once Jagger had recited two stanzas from *Adonais*, Shelley's ode on the death of Keats. Instead, most of the butterflies dropped dead from heat exhaustion. Next afternoon, Jagger boarded the one o'clock flight for Australia.

Relatives of the ironclad outlaw were none too impressed by the rock star's casting either. A group called Citizens for Kelly Country petitioned the Immigration Minister not to let Jagger into the country. Residents of Glenrowan, the town terrorised by the Kelly gang back in 1878, organised a 2,000-signature petition demanding Jagger be dropped. They threatened to picket his arrival in Sydney. 'I don't want Jagger's type,' said Kelly's great-nephew Paul Griffiths, 'I don't think he's a man at all.' Certainly, Jagger's arrival did nothing to allay Glenrowan townspeople's fears. According to the scandalised Australian press, Jagger 'minced into Sydney dressed like an advertisement for Carnaby Street.' The rock star wore a maroon maxi-coat, black-and-white check flared trousers, high-heeled boots and a straw hat, with a long white Isadora scarf trailing around his neck; he was also carrying a fringed leather handbag and was accompanied by the increasingly heroin-addled Faithfull, whom Tony had cast as Kelly's sister. Jagger blew a kiss to journalists before being asked, 'What sort of Ned Kelly are you going to play?' Unconvincingly, Jagger growled back: 'A violent one.'

Immediately, Jagger and Faithfull checked into the Chevron Hotel. On the 13th floor overlooking Sydney Harbour, he flopped onto the antique bed and fell asleep with his boots on. Meanwhile, Faithfull rang room service and ordered hot chocolate. She reached into her handbag for the bottle of Tuinals, a legally prescribed barbiturate she had started swallowing on the plane. Faithfull, who in her own mind now completely identified with Jones, decided to kill herself. She'd already swallowed 15 Tuinals during the flight. Now she took another 150 pills. First, she tried to throw herself off the balcony but the door wouldn't open. As she fell into a drug-induced coma, Faithfull began hallucinating. She found herself in some featureless landscape, walking through a gray limbo alongside Jones, who didn't seem to realise he was dead. Then she was in what looked like Albania, wandering down long, deserted streets with names like the Avenue of the 17th of October. People she knew and loved floated past her, their feet not quite touching the ground. Fortuitously, Jagger suddenly woke up and raised the alarm.

Faithfull was rushed to the intensive care unit of St Vincent's hospital, where she lay in a coma for six days (Tony sat with Jagger at his girlfriend's bedside most of the time). Three days after she'd taken the overdose, a spokesman admitted Faithfull was close to death. Australian tabloids were determined to splash a photograph of the star in her hospital bed across their front pages. Guards were posted around her section of the intensive care ward. However, one photographer broke through the security cordon by disguising himself as a doctor. Escaping when discovered, he managed to knock over at least one patient's intravenous drip. A local paper splashed an out-of-focus photo of an unrecognisable Faithfull with blurred tubes in her mouth and nostrils.

A couple of days later, she regained consciousness. Her first words to Jagger were, 'Wild horses wouldn't drag me away,' which became the basis for one of the Stones' most famous ballads. Faithfull remembered: 'Tony was wonderful, actually. He took it very well but it was obviously a terrible drag for him. After I came out of St. Vincent's I saw him quite a lot. We went down to the country somewhere in central Australia, some sheep farm, and it was really rather wonderful. It was all complete hell of course, but at the same time it was very interesting. Christopher Isherwood was there. They were working on the script for *I Claudius*, which I don't think they ever did, which is a pity.'

In his diary, Isherwood described Tony on location in the Australian Outback as 'looking like the Duke of Wellington, in a kind of Inverness mackintosh cape; we embraced in front of the whole crew and the actors, including Mick Jagger.' The Stones' frontman certainly made a good impression on Isherwood. Writing to his friend John Lehmann, Isherwood described Jagger as 'a very unusual person with great style, the perfect balance of introvert-extrovert, very funny, perfectly serious when he is serious, a "gentleman" according to my mother's rating, almost certainly entirely without affectation and, it seems, vanity.' But even Tony began to doubt the wisdom of casting Jagger when the singer visited Melbourne to inspect Kelly's relics and couldn't even lift his iron headguard he used in the last shootout.

Once again, United Artists was funding the film despite the disappointment of *The Charge of the Light Brigade*. Australian banks were keen to lend money to the production, but they'd been blocked from doing so by their government, which also wanted to sting Jagger for super-tax on his earnings.

Tony had decided to make *Ned Kelly* in bitterly cold mid-winter, thinking it suited the story better. As with *The Charge of the Light Brigade*, he wanted to subvert expectations. Audiences expecting blue skies and wide Australian vistas would be disappointed. Canberra in winter was bleak and cold under porridge-like gray skies. 'You would think, "Oh, Australia, like in Sydney it's all warm and lovely," but it was not warm and lovely where we were near Canberra. It was always cold and unpleasant and rainy,' said Jagger. Meanwhile, the director made up for the drab weather by cutting a colourful figure on set, dressed in white moleskin trousers, a short coat made of wolf fur, a pale-coloured silk scarf and black leather gauntlet gloves. One set visitor described Tony as, 'brilliant, if sometimes petulant ... receding into the shadows like a ballet dancer. To watch him prancing around in his dark corduroys and sneakers is to observe a man not merely confident, but blissfully content with the performance of his star.'

The production was dogged by violence, both threatened and real. 'Whenever you meet Tony after a separation, it always seems to be the same situation; he tells you with a gleeful conspiratorial air that something absolutely terrible has just happened. ("Just" is the operative word),' wrote Isherwood. First, Tony also had to deal with a threat to kidnap both himself and Jagger, holding United Artists to ransom. For 10 days, the production found itself under siege. Around half-a-dozen policemen slept in the hotel corridors outside the pair's bedrooms. This meant that Tony had to step over their sleeping bodies whenever he wanted to sneak out and smoke a joint. Then Jagger almost lost an eye when a prop gun misfired, shooting him in the hand. Tony had asked a local gunsmith to convert period rifles and revolvers to fire blanks – standard procedure when making period films. The converted guns had been inspected and approved by a firearms expert but Jagger's gun had not been properly converted. Suddenly, during a take, Jagger yelped and dropped his pistol. The misfiring gun had almost severed his forefinger, his most crucial one for guitar playing. A Canberra doctor told Jagger he would never play guitar again. Thankfully, he recovered sufficiently within a few days to sit on a tree stump and strum what would become the Stones' classic 'Brown Sugar'. At that time, with Hunt almost certainly on his mind, Jagger was calling the song, 'Black Pussy'.[2]

For the most part the shoot was an unhappy experience, the opposite of *Tom Jones*. Jagger remembered: 'I mean, it was quite a difficult time and I wasn't very prepared for the Ned Kelly part, but Tony Richardson was a good director. It was a very long shoot and hard going.' Tony himself came to loathe everything about Australia, describing it as a 'marvellous country, full of horrible people.' On arriving back in London in late September 1969, Jagger told reporters, 'It's been sort of interesting – [Australia] sort of needs about 20 million black people.'

Tony now holed himself up with the film's editor, piecing together what he saw as a sepia-tinted Victorian folk ballad as opposed to the rootin' tootin' Western UA thought it was financing. Sensing the film was going to be a flop, Jagger kept his distance. He sent his mother along to the London premiere, claiming he was 'too shy' to attend himself. 'Mick, in Tony Richardson's words, walked away from it,' said Ian Jones, the film's scriptwriter. 'I think he realised it had come off the rails a bit and wouldn't be a big hit. Tony was very, very hurt by the way Mick behaved.'[3]

'It's all gone wrong,' laments Jagger at one point. He might have been talking about the film. *Ned Kelly* is a tiresome mix of the haphazard and the self-consciously arty. Confusion takes the place of drama. Tony starts the film right at the emotional climax: Kelly hanging in Old Melbourne Gaol. This leaves little place for the film to go from there. The audience was bewildered by *Ned Kelly*'s lyrical and pastoral quality as opposed to the Outback Western they'd paid to see. There is the odd beautiful moment such as when Jagger comes across a white bull standing in a deracinated wood but for the most part, Tony seems to have an almost unerring instinct for putting his camera in the wrong place. Shots don't match. The climactic shootout seems to be taking place simultaneously in the dead of night and at dawn. Compare the nauseating, gripping tension with which director István Szabó shows Colonel Redl pacing up and down in his hotel bedroom, trying to work up enough courage to blow his brains out (based on John Osborne's play, *A Patriot for Me*) and a similar moment in *Ned Kelly*, when two outlaws casually place their pistols in each other's mouths and pull the triggers. Tony just throws the moment away. And Jagger's range of one expression means the singer is about as convincing as Ned Kelly as Austin Powers playing Jack the Ripper. Like his massive iron helmet, the burden of carrying the film seems too heavy for Jagger to bear.

The *Daily Mirror* placed the blame entirely on Tony. As the puppet on the string, Jagger could do no more than respond to the curious manipulations of his master, the paper said. However, the reviews were not all bad: the *Financial Times* described Tony as Britain's most admirable filmmaker. The renaissance of British theatre in the Fifties and British cinema in the Sixties owed more to his flair and fearlessness in chancing something new than to any other single person or historical factor, they said. The same fearlessness had marked his subsequent career: Tony never played safe or hesitated about trying something that had never been attempted before. The result was a patchy, if distinctly heroic cinema record.

Alexander Walker in the *Evening Standard* described *Ned Kelly* as 'brilliantly imaginative'. Richardson was surpassed by no other English director at defining a social scene at a distant period of history, he wrote. *The Times* praised Tony's fine eye for eccentric visual detail, the sharp period feeling and the way he got extraordinary results from inexperienced actors: 'Richardson is, above all, an aesthete: he can be brilliant elaborating a style or carrying out a decorative scheme ... as an image-maker Richardson has few rivals.' (Somerset Maugham – an author of whom Tony thought highly enough to adapt one of his novels – once wrote that homosexual artists like Tony, although they have a wonderful gift for delightful embroidery, were at the same time prevented by their sexuality from swimming down to greater depths.)

The violence that had dogged *Ned Kelly* did not let up once the film was released. Three homemade bombs exploded in Glenrowan when the film had its local premiere on 15 June 1970, shaking the town hall where it was being screened. In the end, Jagger had nothing good to say about the project. He said: 'That was a load of shit. I only made it because I had nothing to do. I knew Tony Richardson was a reasonable director and I thought he'd make a reasonable film. The thing is, you never know until you do it whether a film will turn out to be a load of shit, and if it does all you can say is, "Well, that was a load of shit," and try to make sure you don't do anything like it again.'[4] Tony himself compared the experience of making *Ned Kelly* to giving birth to a stillborn child: the shape and features were all there, but without the breath of life.

The money that UA lost on *Ned Kelly* effectively ended his relationship with the studio: from now on, Tony would have to find his own finance. UA finally managed to force him to give up what was left of *Tom Jones'* income stream to mitigate some of its losses (it had tried to do the same thing on *Charge*). Indeed, UA told Tony's agent that any profits the studio had made on *Tom Jones* had drained into the sand with his flops.[5]

By 1970, Tony was living in a graceful crescent near Brompton Oratory Church in Knightsbridge. The white stucco Egerton Crescent house was large and filled with primitive objets d'art from his travels. A great white bird was suspended from the ceiling, its black-ringed eyes staring in sightless surprise at the modish surroundings. Tony was now forty-two, but he wasn't concerned about middle age: 'Life gets more interesting and exciting all the time, and there are always new things to do and new possibilities,' he said. He had filled out a little and appeared to be enjoying his material and physical wellbeing – at least compared to the gaunt and unapproachable young intellectual he had once been. And he smiled more easily than he used to.

The dawning of the Seventies was a difficult time for Tony. Now that United Artists had stopped funding his films, he was back to putting funding together himself. Film finance has been compared to piecing together a three-dimensional jigsaw puzzle. No sooner is everything in place, than something drops out and you have to start over. It can be an intensely frustrating experience. The average length of time to get a feature going is seven years. Tony was to spend the next couple of years working on projects that kept blowing up on the launch pad.

One intriguing project that fell into Tony's lap was the screen version of John Fowles' *The French Lieutenant's Woman* (Tony was Fowles' second choice to direct after Lindsay Anderson). Published in 1969, the novel was a kind of faux Victorian tragedy: an English gentleman falls in love with the tragic woman he sees every day as she stands gazing out to sea on Lyme Regis harbour wall. What stopped the book from being a Thomas Hardy pastiche was Fowles' post-modern knowingness: the novel had three alternative endings. Anderson turned the project down. However, Tony, whom Fowles thought would have had enough of Victoriana after *Charge*, said yes. That Fowles wanted Tony to direct ahead of Franco Zeffirelli and Joseph Losey shows how highly regarded he still was. This was despite how the movie scene had changed since Tony's halcyon days. New directors such as Roman Polanski and Milos Forman were coming up. *Easy Rider*, with its trippy backwards-and-forwards editing, was released that summer. Stanley Kubrick's technically astounding *2001: A Space Odyssey* made Tony's work slapdash in comparison. Indeed, his films now seemed very old-fashioned.

Tony immediately gave the book to Vanessa and told her to get reading, double-quick. 'She, if not visually perfect, is so far ahead of every other ability from our other toyed-with names (Sarah Miles, Glenda Jackson) that I pray we get them,' Fowles wrote in his diary. However, the project foundered. Helen Mirren eventually became Fowles' favourite to play the abandoned Sarah Woodruff (it would be another decade before Karel Reisz eventually directed Meryl Streep in the title role).

Oscar Lewenstein, meanwhile, had optioned the first novel of a Canadian writer called Margaret Atwood. The thirty-year-old Atwood had only published a book of poetry before. *The Edible Woman* was a satire about consumer culture rooted in Atwood's experience of working as a market researcher. The book's heroine gives up eating altogether when she perceives consumerism to be a form of cannibalism. Her boss and her boyfriend feed off her, too. In the end, she bakes a cake of herself to feed to her fiancé. Lewenstein invited Atwood to London to work on the script. Although slight, Tony thought Atwood's screenplay 'very funny' and agreed to direct. He invited the novelist and her university lecturer husband Jim Polk out to Le Nid du Duc in May 1970 to work on the script. Polk remembered stepping out of the car in what seemed like a small village only to realise Tony owned the whole place. Waiting to meet them was John Gielgud. It was all rather dazzling. Over dinner, Polk mentioned that he was thinking of specialising in Canadian literature. Gielgud wagged a finger: 'Canadian literature? James, no. No, No! It's so boring.'

Financing *The Edible Woman* proved as difficult as *The French Lieutenant's Woman*. Summoning up all his charm, Tony would breeze into the offices of Canadian banks hoping to raise the money but the banks, risk-averse as they were, would be cautious. Tony hoped that finding a big enough star would persuade them. He briefly considered Barbra Streisand and Donald Sutherland, with whom he'd worked on *St Joan of the Dockyards*. State funding agency Telefilm Canada agreed to provide cornerstone financing and one banker offered to lend the rest of the budget. Tony began scouting locations in Toronto, accompanied by Atwood's artist friend, Charles Pachter, but things went badly wrong one night at a party when the banker made a few innocent casting suggestions. Lewenstein turned on him and humiliated the man in front of his wife. How dare he, a mere financier, presume to offer creative advice to the likes of Tony Richardson? After that, the offer disappeared swiftly. Other Canadian banks too closed ranks. Tony and Lewenstein were frozen out.[6]

Harry Saltzman re-entered Tony's life in spring 1970. Saltzman had enjoyed fabulous success since Tony sacked him from Woodfall. In one of those small twists of fate that change everything, Saltzman had bought the rights to the James Bond books. The problem was, being Harry, he didn't have the money to fly to New York to close the deal. He borrowed the airfare from another producer, a tough customer called Albert 'Cubby' Broccoli. And so the Bond phenomenon was born. Saltzman became bored once the Bond machine was up and running – he wanted to produce other films as well.

The year before, Michael Redgrave had co-starred in his *Battle of Britain*. Now Saltzman wanted Tony to direct a biopic of Vaslav Nijinsky, the Russian dancer who revolutionised ballet in pre-First World War Paris. Nijinsky also conducted a scandalous affair with his impresario Diaghilev. It was to be the first mainstream gay love story in Hollywood. Tony wasn't Saltzman's first choice as director: Herbert Ross (*Goodbye, Mr Chips*) and Jerome Robbins (*West Side Story*) had both turned him down. Ken Russell, who had made several acclaimed television documentaries about composers, was hired. Saltzman's ace was that Rudolph Nureyev would play Nijinsky. Nureyev had never acted before. Six years earlier, Luchino Visconti had tried to get him to star as Nijinsky. At the time, Nureyev wasn't interested. This time it was Nureyev who couldn't get along with Russell. Instead, the director made *The Devils* later that year with Vanessa.

Tony had already been thinking about a Nijinsky film. It's not hard to see why he identified with Nijinsky: the ballet dancer was a revolutionary who introduced sex on stage for the first time and also the first to create ballet in modern dress. Later, Tony said, Nijinsky became a hippie, railing against the world and its values. Mick Jagger was his original choice to play the dancer. Of course, this wasn't going to happen following the débâcle of *Ned Kelly*. Paul Scofield did agree to play Diaghilev, though. And Edward Albee, playwright of *Who's Afraid of Virginia Woolf?*, came on board to write the screenplay. Tony gave Albee some ideas of what he wanted to see onscreen. Albee then set to work. Tony also consulted Nijinsky's biographer, Lincoln Kirstein, who thought Dustin Hoffman would be much better to star. Albee delivered his screenplay, which everybody seemed to like apart from Nureyev, who thought it was 'terrible.'[7] Nureyev believed there was too much emphasis on Diaghilev and not enough on him.

Filming was due to start in August 1970, in Paris. Tony flew out to St Petersburg at the beginning of June to scout for locations. He travelled with Lee Radziwill, sister of Jackie Kennedy. A physicist friend of Nureyev's spent a weekend showing them around the city. In fact, this proved a dangerous thing to do: on the Monday, the KGB interrogated her about what she had been doing with Tony. Acting as Tony's tour guide affected her career and stopped her from travelling overseas – she had become a 'suspicious' person. Two weeks later, Saltzman scrapped the project. Albee said: 'It was a happy collaboration. Then all of a sudden Saltzman pulled out.' A stockmarket crisis meant the producer was unable to raise the money despite having already spent $1 million on it. Saltzman, trying to wriggle out of paying for work done thus far, claimed Albee's screenplay was amateurish because it contained some silent scenes. Tony was furious and told Saltzman so in no uncertain terms.[8]

The beginning of 1972 saw Tony direct Vanessa in his version of Brecht's *The Threepenny Opera*. The play is in itself a reworking of *The Beggar's Opera*, first produced in 1728. Vanessa volunteered to play villain's moll Polly Peachum after the star that Tony had found for Macheath suddenly dropped out. The starry cast included Hermione Baddeley, Diana Quick, Barbara Windsor and Arthur Mullard. Joe Melia stepped in to play the criminal highwayman. Tony decided to stage *The Threepenny Opera* as if in a fairground, putting a real merry-go-round on stage. Meanwhile, Vanessa made it clear that she could only appear for nine weeks due to prior commitments – her political work came first (she even missed the dress rehearsal to go on a peace demonstration shortly after Bloody Sunday in Belfast, when the Army shot dead 26 unarmed civil protestors).

The play opened on 10 February 1972 to stinking reviews. 'From a director of Mr Richardson's distinction and a cast of so many celebrities one could be forgiven for expecting more,' *The Tatler* sniffed. It was Tony's usual problem of facing both directions at the same time. The *Guardian* said he seemed in two minds about what play he was directing: something shocking and sleazy or a send-up of Brecht's play. In addition, Brecht's widow dismissed Vanessa's performance as 'a parody of a parody.'[9]

Despite the reviews, *The Threepenny Opera* sold out because of Vanessa's appearance. However, the theatre management neglected to tell advance ticket buyers that the star was quitting after a couple of months. There were some unhappy members of the audience when the curtain rose on her unknown replacement. Box-office takings dropped like a stone. Producer Michael White heaped blame on himself. 'I made a mistake I will never repeat. I agreed to have her [Vanessa] in the show for only nine weeks,' he said. 'I knew at the time that it was foolish, but I believed that Tony would be able to convince her to stay longer once we were running.'

Tony's next project was a stage version of Robert Graves' historical novels *I Claudius* and *Claudius the God*. He had long been trying to adapt Graves' novels for the big screen: they were, he said, about the fight for power and politicians who wanted to become gods. Tony commissioned playwright Edward Bond, who had caused such a scandal at the Court with his play *Saved*, to write one screenplay. Tony found what Bond had submitted to be 'pathetic and unusable.' Christopher

Isherwood wrote another script and finally, John Mortimer produced a version that Tony was happy with.

He took Nicol Williamson with him to Deia, the Spanish village where Graves lived, during the filming of *Laughter in the Dark*. Tony wanted Williamson to play the lame, staggering Emperor who was mistaken for a fool. He told Graves that Mortimer's script had 'just the right style and irony.' Financing such an ambitious project proved impossible, though. Five weeks after Mortimer had delivered his screenplay, Tony reported the industry was lukewarm about a new 'toga film.' His latest plan was to put it on stage first. Mortimer adapted what he'd written to be a manageable theatrical chamber piece with actors doubling up parts. Tony, however, kept expanding the ambition of the production. Rehearsals began around the pool at Le Nid du Duc. Tony stripped the cork trees round the house to provide the blue-pained armour worn by the ancient Britons.

By the time rehearsals continued in London, Mortimer was surprised to discover that his chamber piece had swelled to around thirty actors. Many of his lines had been transferred to characters he had left out. Still, rehearsals continued to look promising, powered by Tony's endless enthusiasm. David Warner was cast as Claudius and Warren Clarke as Caligula, the insane Emperor whose murder leads to Claudius' succession. Tony's idea was to stage the play on American-style bleachers – tiers of hard wooden seats which practically filled the stage of the Queen's Theatre. One scene, apparently historically accurate, had Caligula dancing over the steps in drag. Michael White, who once again was producing, thought the bleachers looked horrible, but was too in awe of Tony to say anything. Later, he said how *I Claudius* was a perfect example of how the wrong design could wreck a good play – which was strange considering what great taste Tony usually showed.[10]

Graves told friends that he was delighted with the way Mortimer had preserved the spirit of the original. Mortimer remembered the pre-first night party that Tony gave at Egerton Crescent. He found himself sitting on a sofa between Graves and Jo Grimond, the former leader of the Liberal Party. Tony was having an affair with Grimond's daughter Grizelda, who was working as Lewenstein's secretary. Their daughter Katherine – half-sister to Natasha and Joely – was born on 8 January 1973. (Grimond would come to marvel at the way his granddaughter commuted around the world, visiting Tony in France or in America. 'Aeroplanes are as familiar to her as cabs were to me,' he said.)

Graves told Grimond and Mortimer that he had personally won the Battle of Anzio during the Second World War by insisting the Allies direct gramophone records of women giving birth towards the Italian army. He then announced that Jesus Christ lived until the age of eighty, went to China and discovered spaghetti. 'In which Gospel do we learn that Jesus Christ discovered spaghetti?' Grimond asked mildly. Graves replied this was common knowledge.

The play opened at the Queen's Theatre on 11 July 1972 for a nine-week run. White realised he had a flop on his hands when he strolled into the bar on opening night during the interval. A lot of people he knew were standing about, obviously in no hurry to go back in. One actor, not realising White's connection, confided: 'Isn't this the biggest load of tripe you've ever seen?' Most of the notices were terrible. 'Why so many talented people got mixed up in this disaster is beyond moral comprehension,' wrote John Crosby in the *Observer*. 'Unpredictable in the extreme and yet another reminder of the fact that for sheer Barnum showmanship in the theatre Mr Richardson is still unbeatable,' said *The Tatler*.

'We didn't win,' Tony told Mortimer (who thought Tony secretly relished this kind of disaster) during the first-night party held on a boat on the river. 'I could feel the play sinking beyond hope in the red-plush sea of stalls. We used to have nights like that at the Court – it was down with all hands.'

Meanwhile, American theatre producer the Ely Landau Organisation had begun adapting stage plays as movies and Tony was asked if he wanted to take part. Eight contemporary plays were being shot for the American Film Theatre. Two had already been released to great success: Peter Hall directing Harold Pinter's *The Homecoming* and John Frankenheimer directing Lee Marvin in *The Iceman Cometh*. Tony was first offered either John Osborne's *Luther* with Stacy Keach, or Eugène Ionesco's *Rhinoceros*, starring Zero Mostel. He rejected both, instead choosing Edward Albee's *A Delicate Balance* – a play about a family's disintegration when two houseguests overstay their welcome. It had first been performed on Broadway in 1966. Two years later, Michael Redgrave had planned to star opposite Vivien Leigh in the London version until Leigh's tuberculosis forced her to drop out. Tony had been impressed by Albee's *Nijinsky* script and wanted to work with him again. For his part, Albee admired Tony's mind and was keen for him to direct: 'He was somebody with taste and integrity. He had a fully developed dramatic intelligence, which is rare in this business.'[11]

Tony decided Kim Stanley would be perfect for the role of the witch-like alcoholic younger sister. He was still terribly fond of the actress – after all, he'd named his second daughter after her. Stanley said yes. Paul Scofield agreed to play the ineffectual husband and Lee Remick his petulant, chain-smoking daughter who is touching middle age, having just busted her fourth marriage. Joseph Cotten and Karel Reisz's wife Betsy Blair were cast as the invasive, controlling neighbours.

Tony approached Katharine Hepburn to play Agnes, the tower of strength who supports the edifice of family decorum. He believed she would be perfect as the matriarch. He'd first met her when he had only just come down from Oxford in early 1952: she was appearing on stage in *The Millionairess*. Tony had written a fan letter, cheekily inviting her to tea. To his surprise, Hepburn turned up at his grotty flat. 'I didn't have enough money to buy cakes, so we had nothing to eat,' he recalled.

Hepburn had also been his first choice to play Flora Goforth in his 1964 production of *The Milk Train Doesn't Stop Here Anymore*. They'd met to discuss the part but she was already booked and in any case, Williams was insisting on Bankhead for the role. At first, Hepburn turned Tony down on the grounds that *A Delicate Balance* was too downbeat. Initially, Tony couldn't understand her resistance. 'There's a lot of that same kind of inflexible, authoritarian quality in her. She suited the part terribly well, the obsession with her home – the New England background – all very "Kate,"' he said. Later, he suspected the real reason was that she didn't want to be outshone by Stanley. Hepburn eventually came round, though. 'Tony has a good smell for the pictures and that's what matters. You need a nose for it. Some people have different kinds of instincts,' she said.

However, things went awry as soon as the cast met at Egerton Crescent to do a read-through in spring 1973. An alcoholic herself, Stanley began to roll around on the floor, spluttering and crying. Here was an out-of-control, falling-down drunk. Tony was mesmerised but the others were aghast. 'How could you let that happen to us?' Scofield hissed as everybody was leaving. Cast rehearsals continued, but it was becoming clear that Stanley couldn't remember her lines. This was even more of a problem because Tony wanted to film in sequence (most of Stanley's lines were in the first act).

Hepburn announced she would quit unless Stanley was fired. Meanwhile, the Ely Landau Organisation backed away, leaving Tony with the dilemma: rehabilitating Stanley was the only reason he'd wanted to do the film in the first place. He accused Hepburn of blackmail, but realised continuing with an alcoholic would be impossible. Scofield suggested the Canadian actress Kate Reid replace Stanley because he thought she sounded like Hepburn.

The house Tony chose for the location was The Wood, 16 Sydenham Hill. It is close to the south London suburb of Crystal Palace. The Wood was a bit dilapidated when the unit moved in and so the art department set about smartening the place up so that it could double for an expensive New England house. Once again, rather than shoot in a studio, Tony made things deliberately awkward. The rooms were too small to cope with all the cameras and equipment. Tony was crammed into a tiny room in the basement. Scofield and Cotten used one of the bedrooms as a dressing room, while Remick, Reid and Blair shared the other. Hepburn would arrive each morning in the back of her chauffeur-driven limousine. Only she had the privacy of her own dressing room. Still, the set had no running water, which prevented Hepburn from taking her constant showers. One day, she walked down the street and knocked on a woman's door to ask if she could use her bathroom. The neighbour was so astonished to find the legendary Katharine Hepburn on her doorstep that she ushered her straight in.

Tony and Hepburn fought over every scene. Hepburn refused to take direction. She admitted tormenting her director, calling him 'The Pharaoh'. For his part, Tony called her 'The Monster'. 'Kate and I fight and insult each other at times,' he admitted. Albee and Tony would watch dailies together: Albee thought that Reid, 'did a superb job. Her performance was certainly better than Kate's, who wouldn't play it the way Tony wanted her to.'[12]

A Delicate Balance is an elusive study of suburban ennui. The characters are gripped by an unnameable terror, eating away at the delicate balance of the title. Albee's epigrammatic banter stops things from becoming too grim, though and the overall effect is that of a baroque concerto. There's a feeling that the actors are better than the script. And the reviews were pretty damning. Time found Albee's screenplay, 'pompous, windy, arch; it is a series of tableaux shaped out of crushed ice'. 'Today, Albee seems diminished by time as does his rhetorical, florid, hollowly bitchy world,' was *Newsweek*'s verdict.

Increasingly desperate to have one commercial success after a decade of near misses, Tony decided to turn jockey-turned-thriller writer Dick Francis' first novel *Dead Cert* into a movie next. This time, he managed to convince United Artists to fund the production. Racing journalist Lord John Oaksey was hired to co-write the script. Scott Antony played the hero and Judi Dench – who'd known Vanessa at RADA – was the love interest. Under glorious summer skies, production began on 14 May 1973 at Aintree racecourse. This was incongruous, as anybody who knows anything about racing would have known: the steeplechase season begins in November and ends in March. Still, Tony tried to give *Dead Cert* a documentary feel, strapping a camera to a jockey's chest for a 'you-are-there' sense of excitement. And he paid homage to one of his heroes by naming one of the horses competing in the Grand National 'Buñuel'. Another in-joke was having Oaksey listed on the number-board as riding in a race, simultaneously giving the race commentary and then popping up in a cheerful cameo as a vet.

Tony soon discovered that making a thriller wasn't so easy as he imagined. Even as he was editing the film, he knew this was another also-ran. 'It isn't that a thriller script has more problems, it's just that it has a different type of problem. I don't know whether I can make one. Thrillers are very difficult. I can't direct anything if I'm not convinced of it myself,' he said. But you can see why he was attracted to the subject (police corruption eating away at the Sport of Kings sat well with his anti-Establishment attitude), it's just that the finished film is all stop-start, never building towards any climax. That's why thrillers often end with a third-act chase whereas *Dead Cert* simply ambles along.

For Tony, it was another flop. He realised the time had come for him to make a change in his life. If he wanted to continue making movies, he had to be where the money was and in 1974, he decided to move to Los Angeles.

Notes

1. Zwar, Adam. 'Mick and the Kelly Curse', *Sunday Herald Sun*, 13 January 2002.

2. Leys, Nick. 'No Satisfaction: A Previous Cinematic Incarnation of the Infamous Bushranger Famously Miscast Mick Jagger', *The Bulletin*, 25 February 2003.

3. Zwar, Adam. Mick and the Kelly Curse', *Sunday Herald Sun*, 13 January 2002.

4. Sandford, Christopher. *Mick Jagger: Rebel Knight*, Omnibus Press, London, 2003.

5. Mike Medavoy, author interview, 22 June 2009.

6. Cooke, Nathalie. *Margaret Atwood: A Biography*, ECW Press, Toronto, 1998.

7. Edward Albee, author interview, 28 October 2009.

8. Mangan, Richard. *Gielgud's Letters*, Weidenfeld & Nicolson, London, 2004.

9. Nightingale, Benedict. 'An Actress In Love With Risk', *New York Times*, 17 September 1989.

10. White, Michael. *Empty Seats*, Hamish Hamilton, London, 1984.

11. Edward Albee, author interview, 28 October 2009.

12. Edward Albee, author interview, 28 October 2009.

CHAPTER FIFTEEN

I Need You Now

Vanessa Redgrave may be the only person driven to drink by industrial relations strategy. In her autobiography, she recalled in 1972 reaching for the bottle when Prime Minister Ted Heath imposed statutory wage controls on union workers. She started drinking cheap wine in the morning, its 'fuzzy obliteration' drowning out her despair. This was despite becoming a mother again at the age of thirty-two.

Joshua Logan had been right in thinking the moment Vanessa set eyes on Franco Nero she wanted to have his baby. When the contractions started, her nanny drove Natasha and Joely across the river to stay with Lynn in Barnes. Oddly, Nero went back to Rome just when he knew the baby was due. Carlo Nero was born on 16 September 1969 after a four-hour labour during which Vanessa was assisted by her doctor and an NHS midwife. When she rang Nero to tell him he was a father, he booked the next flight back to London, burst upstairs, opened the baby's nappy and kissed his testicles. Lord Astor used an editorial in the *Observer* to attack Vanessa for having a baby with a man she 'loved, but had not married'. Vanessa was deeply wounded by this and couldn't understand why the press was making such a fuss. 'I was full of free-spirit ideas so it seemed quite hurtful and ridiculous,' she admitted. In the autumn of 1970 Vanessa miscarried her second child with Nero while filming *The Devils*. She would have liked to have more children. Indeed, her dream was to have five or even six. Sadly, this was not to be.

Vanessa's relationship with Franco continued to unravel in a series of bitter rows. He was the traditional Italian alpha male. She had causes to fight, a career to maintain and children to bring up. In 1971, Franco moved back to Paris – and to his former partner, Nathalie Delon. 'I didn't think she had the qualities to be a wife,' he said, after a parting that must have left him angry, confused and sorrowful. The couple never really separated though, partly because they had a son to bring up together, although the arguments continued.

Corin, seeing the state Vanessa was in, sat her down with volume 38 of Lenin's collective works, the daunting *Philosophical Notebooks*. At this point, he had turned his back on acting in favour of revolutionary politics. With his brilliant intellect, it was as if he was embarrassed about being an actor. Those who knew him wondered if the fencing champion with the First from Cambridge felt guilty about how easily everything had come to him. Corin told Vanessa that Lenin would answer all those political questions revolving around in her head. Once again, Corin was the teacher and Vanessa the pupil.

The year before, actress Kika Markham had introduced Corin to the far-left Socialist Labour League run by Gerry Healy. Kika was brought up as an anarchist by her actor father David and poet mother Olive. The Markham and Redgrave family lives had criss-crossed for three generations – Kika's mother had knitted Corin a baby shawl – but she and Corin didn't meet until 1970, when both were in a television love story called *Happy Ever After*, in which they played newlyweds. Corin was immediately attracted to the actress, whose views were even more left than his.

The Socialist Labour League – later renamed the Workers Revolutionary Party – represented politics of a simultaneously nasty and romantic kind. Corin's wife Deirdre said that her husband was attracted by power – he really believed that the WRP was going to run England. With his angelic good looks and astringent manner, Corin was being talked about in far-left circles as the British Lenin himself. At first, Deirdre's family joked about it. Diana Hamilton-Hill teased him: 'Darling, when you run the country and I'm like the Queen Mum, could I have Hampshire?' Like Vanessa, his new political commitment meant spending long periods away from home. 'Deirdre was very upset that Corin was never there for the children. He was an absent father. She took over all the parenting,' said her friend Danaë Brook.[1] Back in Chelsea, he would criticise Deirdre for doing such bourgeois things as putting wine in a stew. Their mansion block flat became a crash pad for the hard left. 'Their family life was invaded by politicos,' said Brook.[2]

When Vanessa eventually signed up to the WRP's Trotskyite cell in Clapham – 'a small room, very simply furnished' – it was with the relief of the alcoholic taking the pledge. As George Orwell observed of young writers who flocked towards Communism in the 1930s, 'It was something to believe in. Here was a church, an army, an orthodoxy, a discipline.' In Orwell's time, Stalin was the father figure. For Vanessa, it was WRP leader Gerry Healy.

At first glance, Healy didn't appear at all charismatic: he was a squat and ugly man. Deirdre Redgrave thought that what Healy represented was the strong father figure Vanessa and Corin had been missing all their lives. Healy was just three years younger than Michael but unlike Michael, he was strong and unwavering in his faith. Corin had even greater need of a father figure since Michael had revealed his homosexuality. 'Vanessa and Corin both thought of Healy as a father figure, not because Michael wasn't around very much, but because they knew he was gay, which must have been extraordinarily difficult for Corin because he was such a masculine alpha male,' said Brook.[3]

Like all cults, which the Socialist Labour League was, Healy maintained his personal domination by isolating members from their families and the outside world. Anybody or anything that might question his teachings was closed off. Acolytes couldn't see the imminent revolution he promised was as far away as ever. Michael Banda, Healy's successor as WRP leader, said Healy was a classic example of a paranoid schizophrenic – in the morning he could be nice, and in the afternoon he would be plotting against you. Healy was also a brutal man: he once ordered his cohorts to beat up a husband who dared confront him after Healy ordered the man's wife to sleep with a union leader. Women were 'made round to go round,' Healy said dismissively.[4] Healy also had homosexual leanings, going to bed with Labour MP Tom Driberg after a party at John Schlesinger's flat. Driberg was involved in the springing of Soviet spy George Blake in 1966, whose escape Vanessa may have unwittingly financed.

Because WRP members invested vast amounts of time in the party, Vanessa began spending longer periods away from home. Joely and Natasha would cry and cling to her as she tried to get out of their shabby front door.[5] Around this time, six-year-old Natasha appealed to her mother to spend more time with her. Vanessa tried to explain that her political struggle was for Natasha's future and that of all children of her generation. 'But I need you now. I won't need you so much then,' Natasha said.[6] Later, Vanessa came to regret spending so much time away from her daughters. They 'certainly suffered,' she admitted. 'I came to see that was a big mistake.'[7]

Vanessa gave so much of her money away to the WRP that they were short of cash at home. The house in St Peter's Square began to look unloved, the garden overgrown. 'The WRP took our mother away from us and that really hurt,' Natasha remembered. 'She gave a lot of money to them, and it did alter our lifestyle, radically.' Meanwhile, Joely wished she could live in a more conventional family. Deirdre remembered Natasha and Joely and her own daughter Jemma sitting around talking about how much they hated the Party. 'All those scruffy people marching around our house as though it was their home and not mine,' Joely would say, exasperated. Natasha was left to fend off barbed remarks in the school playground: 'I didn't like the way she [Vanessa] was perceived – it was hurtful to me,' she revealed. The way that Vanessa put the People ahead of her own children angered Lynn. In the end, she gave up talking to her. It was useless trying to reason with her sister because it was not like arguing with somebody who could be swayed.[8] Lynn knew people expected her to be able to shed some light on Vanessa's rigidity, but she was unable to do so.

Vanessa's politics ended her romance with a young actor called Timothy Dalton. Their relationship began during the filming of *Mary Queen of Scots* in 1970 with a six-hour-long argument about the true meaning of Hamlet's 'To be or not to be' speech. It continued to be a stormy relationship. Deirdre thought Vanessa's Pauline conversion to the Hard Left sprang from her turbulent relationship with Dalton. Here was something fixed and unwavering she could pour her roiling emotional energy into. Brendan Martin, a WRP member, said that Healy extended special privileges to Vanessa because of her role as internationally emissary and party fundraiser – 'most particularly' said Martin, 'the privilege of having a lover, Timothy Dalton, who was not in the Party.' Healy allowed Vanessa to retain some private life: she was permitted to continue working, to have a part of her life which did not belong to the WRP.

Corin, on the other hand, found his whole life subsumed by the WRP. A beautiful young man with a striking presence, he had seemed set for big things – he and Anthony Hopkins were secret agents in the 1971 film of Alistair MacLean's *When Eight Bells Toll* and he was a First World War air ace that same year in *The Red Baron*. Healy forbade him to continue his acting work. Corin's role, according to Martin, was to become 'a hack organiser' – not a job he was particularly suited to. Martin asked rhetorically, 'Was Vanessa's career sacrificed? No. Was Corin's? Yes. Do you think that is a coincidence?'

Corin seldom had time for his children. His radicalism was also driving a wedge between himself and Deirdre. One night, about fifty WRP members barged into their flat wanting to rehearse a fund-raising cabaret. At the same time, their Algerian au pair was having religious hallucinations in her bedroom. The evening became like a scene from a Marx Brothers movie. In one room, Deirdre found an actor dressed as Lenin rehearsing a rousing speech to the proletariat. In another, she discovered a buxom revolutionary practising a lubricious striptease for an agitprop cabaret. Meanwhile, her au pair ecstatically proclaimed that she was pregnant with the new messiah. She herself had refused to join the WRP and was personally summoned by Healy to explain why. Deirdre told him that she had two young children to bring up and she didn't want them growing up disturbed – WRP members seldom saw their kids. Corin and Deirdre's rows became increasingly bitter. Once, in the middle of an argument, Corin threatened to shoot his family if they impeded the revolution.[9]

Unknown to Vanessa, in April 1976, Corin flew out to Tripoli where he signed a secret pact with the Libyan government, headed by Colonel Gaddafi.

Libya agreed to pay the WRP hundreds of thousands of pounds to spy on prominent British Jews. For the next eight years, the WRP handed over 'intelligence' reports to Tripoli: the information centred on Jews who the WRP believed were part of a 'powerful Zionist connection'. These included MPs, businessmen and those in the media. The Libyan money was mainly used to finance the party's daily newspaper *Newsline* and to buy equipment for the 'coming revolution'.[10] However, some of it was also used to open youth centres in Brixton and Liverpool. The Conservative government feared the WRP would use these centres to indoctrinate youngsters in its campaign to smash capitalism. Home Secretary William Whitelaw leaned on the Charity Commission in 1981 to block Vanessa's youth training scheme.

Tony became so alarmed by Vanessa's behaviour that he made her sign a legal document promising not to take the children to political meetings. Adding to the tension was that they'd decided to work together again. In July 1973, they began rehearsing a modern-dress adaptation of *Antony and Cleopatra*. Tony said it was a play the two of them had quarrelled over and argued about for years. 'We're trying to get down to what the real conflicts are,' he said.

Tony first approached Richard Burton to play Antony and the actor was taken aback by his cheek, given the falling out they'd had over *Laughter in the Dark*: 'That man must have the thickest skin in and out of Christendom,' Burton wrote in his diary. 'This is his second offer to me this year – the other being to do the film of *I, Claudius*. After our bitter débâcle about Nabokov's *Laughter in the Dark*, one would think that he would be scared witless to approach me to play Scrabble. But not our Tony.' In the end, Julian Glover was cast opposite Vanessa.

Tony's modern-dress version was presented at the Bankside Globe, a tent-like structure on the South Bank site of Shakespeare's original Globe Theatre in London. It was not a happy production. Tony had the cast wear costumes that suggested a time warp in which Nazi soldiers rubbed shoulders with pirates and silent film stars. When Vanessa met with a messenger telling her about Antony's marriage, she ended up threatening him with a soda bottle.

'It's a long time since I've seen a major Shakespeare play so mangled and I'm genuinely sorry to see so much acting talent wasted on such a trivial footling production,' sighed the *Guardian*'s critic. The play's short three-week run ended several days early when a storm collapsed the tent. Tony hurried back to Los Angeles.

Tony always felt vastly more at home in Los Angeles than he did in England. He found he could live the life he wanted in California, something he hadn't been able to do in rain-sodden Britain. Los Angeles was probably the only major Western city where you could live entirely in the open air, he said. No wonder the British, brought up in rain and cloud, found it such an awakening; everything was somehow so much easier and more equal under the sun. He had originally flown out to Los Angeles trying to raise money for a project titled *The Bodyguard* that American playwright Sam Shepard had written for him (Jack Nicholson was keen to play the lead). Tony found himself in the typical bind of an independent producer: just when he'd get the money lined up, the cast would fall apart. And vice-versa. He decided to stay on in the City of Angels.

Lindsay Anderson said Tony quit England because he couldn't stand the English. Looking round London 20 years after he'd directed *Look*

Back in Anger, Tony was dismayed at how little had really changed. It was still a 'them and us' society, he said. California, on the other hand, was all about cars and mobility. 'You just don't find the divisions that cut through society [in Britain],' he observed. 'I've never liked England – I don't like the whole English attitude, I don't like English society, I don't like anything about it, really.' Tony's agent Mike Medavoy once asked why he chose to live in Los Angeles rather than London. 'I mean, he sounded like an English aristocrat,' said Medavoy. Tony replied that he loved the freedom of living in Hollywood.[11]

John Mortimer felt that Tony exaggerated the conveniences of American living. In America, Tony assured him, they have deep-freezers and cordless telephones and washing machines. In vain Mortimer told him that you could get all those white goods in England, too. Mortimer thought Tony made a mistake in relocating to Los Angeles: the British, he felt, did best in the Hollywood system when they could be summonsed and hired. If you're there all the time, you're not thought of as hard to get and therefore not worth having. Tony's other friends also believed he'd made a wrong decision. His Oxford friend Shirley Williams wrote to him, urging him not to move there. 'I thought it would be the end of him as a director and it was. The gilt came off the gingerbread. Tony had a strong social conscience in his earlier films and Hollywood just doesn't work like that,' she said.[12] Jocelyn Rickards also regretted Tony moving to Hollywood, which she called his 'demon bitch.' Rickards felt that Tony would have realised his promise as the one really creative English film producer more fully had he stayed.

In 1974, Tony rented a house above Sunset Boulevard from porn star Linda Lovelace. The red wooden house was perched on a steeply vertiginous street called Kings Road. It was a Tudorish ranch house on a half-acre plot surrounded by a large, jungle-like garden. The winding paths of the garden were planted with citrus, orchids, crepe-myrtle, palm, pepper and jacaranda trees. Tony nurtured the orchids in particular with loving care. The house was in a dilapidated state when he moved in – there were holes in the roof. 'Then I suddenly realised it was a marvellous home,' he said. What Tony loved about 1478 Kings Road was the light. David Hockney once said that the light in Los Angeles reminded him of Canaletto's Venice. The sun moved around the house all day: the great sitting room window overlooked downtown, where dawn broke over a city which seemed like Brecht's Mahagonny.

The sun would move over the Palos Verdes Peninsula and then across the ocean before setting behind the Santa Monica mountains.

Tony bought the house for a bargain price and started doing renovation work. Excavating the hill to create a second swimming pool, he discovered the dead bodies of a couple in a Cadillac who had been forgotten in a landslide. He also uncovered an old tennis court in the undergrowth. Tennis soon became his new passion: having scorned sport at Ashville College and Oxford, he came across tennis in middle age. He was now forty-six. Tony recognised tennis immediately for what it is: a mirror you hold up to yourself, magnifying every fault and virtue. He told his daughters that tennis was life: it showed you who you really were. He became as proselytising about tennis as Vanessa was about Trotskyism. Despite having a lesson every day for 20 years, he never learnt to play very well – his great stork-like legs and fitful movements meant coordination was terrible. According to Natasha, he just crashed about, smashing balls and making himself depressed: he was once easily beaten by a one-armed player who had to throw the ball into the air and then grab his racket from between his knees to serve.

And then of course there were the birds. On arriving at Kings Road, the first thing you saw was an enormous toucan with a gigantic beak guarding the front door. Inside, you would be greeted by a large, very colourful parrot on his perch, which went upside down clinging to the ceiling. Dozens of birds, in an array and variety of colours, flitted about aviaries running through the house. Exotic golden pheasants strutted about the garden.

Tony lived in Los Angeles like the prince of some small and magical country. In Hollywood, where originality is often flattened by executive fiat, his breezy intransigence was liberating. 'He was Hollywood royalty at that time. He could get through to anybody,' said Norman Twain.[13] Actress Fiona Lewis thought of 1478 Kings Road as the cultural centre of Los Angeles. She remembered Tony presiding over lunch and dinner parties where guests included Prime Minister Edward Heath, Peter Hall, Jack Nicholson, Isherwood and Hockney – the last two also British exiles, who loved Los Angeles. Tony would preside over these meals like a giant treetop bird, one eyebrow permanently raised in anticipation of some diverting catastrophe. He would deliberately provoke arguments between guests. Lewis remembered Tony publicly humiliating Lindsay Anderson for about ten minutes, telling him how ridiculous he was.

'You have absolutely no taste, not a clue,' he told Anderson, who sat mutely on a paisley cushion as Tony rained abuse on him.

Tony loved to play host: Kenneth Tynan's daughter Roxana observed that he was one of the few adults in Hollywood who enjoyed having children around and he would arrange an annual Easter egg hunt for them. Talking about her parents, she said: 'Tony was one of their friends who actually liked kids.' Joan Plowright recalled Tony organising one such Easter Sunday egg hunt. The idea was for each adult to accompany a small child and help them understand clues, if necessary. The hunt became fiercely competitive. Theatre impresario Michael White grabbed Matthew Tynan, who was clearly the brightest child, ensuring he came back first with the coveted prize.

Sheridan Morley, the biographer, thought that Tony's move to Los Angeles had more to do with the sexual intolerance of England. John Osborne begged his former friend not to forsake England for the 'blue skies and buggery in California.' Another colleague also believed the sun, drugs and easy availability of boys ruined Tony.[14] It was around this time that the 11-year-old Natasha became aware of her father's homosexuality: somebody told her that her father was gay. There were never any physical displays of affection, but she put two and two together. 'That was very difficult. I had a growing awareness of it, which I voiced to my mother when I was about eleven. I'm not sure why I was so upset by it – I suppose because it wasn't the norm and that made me feel isolated.'[15]

Natasha was confused by Vanessa's explanation of her father's bisexuality. 'He was never in the closet, but he was never open about it,' she said. Joely, on the other hand, took her father's sexuality in her stride. 'He was very much the central influence in my life,' she said. 'I was brought up in the sort of environment that completely accepted homosexuals, bisexuals and lesbians.'

Tony's detractors said he was simply a closeted homosexual. However, the actor Rupert Everett, who later became a friend, thought Tony was more complicated than that: he was neither gay nor straight. Tony introduced several of his lovers to his screenwriter friend Gavin Lambert, although there was an unspoken rule between friends never to discuss his sexuality. Lambert thought Tony far too intelligent to be ashamed of being bisexual. Rather, he was of the generation that still had to be guarded about it. Throughout the Angry Young Man years and the Court, being gay had been a criminal offence: exposure could have ruined him. Indeed, homosexual acts between consenting men only became legal in 1967. That's why Tony placed female lovers such as Vanessa and Grizelda Grimond centre stage, relegating his boyfriends to the wings.

Tony's male lovers were always shadowy figures – he never allowed himself to become deeply involved with them. The nearest he came to acknowledging his own conflict was in 1984 when he directed *Dreamhouse*, a play largely about homosexuality. 'Some people have chosen to be gay, some people are in conflict with it,' he said. Lambert never knew how much this tension cost Tony emotionally; he wondered if Tony ever did. Tony wasn't a particularly self-reflective man – he claimed he was too busy to be introspective. Ironically, it was he who accused Lindsay Anderson of being repressed. 'The price of repression,' he used to say, 'is extremely high.'

'Some kind of ongoing conflict is a driving force behind every artist,' Lambert wrote. 'Tony's whole life was a high-wire act, and he seems to have handled his sexual identity as one of the trickier parts of the act.' Occasionally, Tony would let his guard down, though. Actor Peter Allen remembered Tony asking him during an audition if he could, 'pass for straight.' Taken aback, Allen replied, 'Can you?' Tony smiled like the Cheshire cat and purred, 'I do.'

In the autumn of 1974, Tony began rewriting the script for *The Bodyguard* with screenwriter John Byrum (Sam Shepard had written the first draft that summer while staying at Le Nid du Duc). His collaborator was also rewriting a script for record mogul Berry Gordy of Motown Records. Another friend of Tony's, Broadway composer and lyricist Bob Merrill, had written the first draft of the Motown script. It was to be the next vehicle for Diana Ross, who had recently won an Oscar nomination for her movie debut in *Lady Sings the Blues*. *Mahogany* was to be an old-fashioned rags-to-riches women's picture, set in the world of haute couture and updated for an African/American audience. Ross was to star as a secretary who becomes an international fashion model and designer. Motown was putting up half the money for the $3.5 million film. Paramount was providing the rest. Gordy's twenty-five-year-old in-house producer Rob Cohen – whom Gordy referred to as his 'little white nigger' – suggested Tony help Byrum rewrite the *Mahogany* script.

Tony remembered driving to Bel-Air with Byrum to meet Gordy. They were met at Bel-Air's west gate by two cars filled with guards. The three cars travelled in a motorcade to Gordy's mock Tudor estate, which was being renovated into half-fortress and half-*Playboy* mansion. The walls, floor and ceiling of Gordy's bedroom were made of quarter-inch thick steel; the windows were of bulletproof glass. The atmosphere was exactly like *The Godfather* – senior members of the entourage even kissed Gordy's ring. Adding to the surreal atmosphere, llamas, deer and peacocks wandered about the lawns. Byrum remembered Tony remarking that they were the quietest peacocks he'd ever known – they were so silent. 'Oh, *them*?' said Gordy, waving to one of the birds, 'I had their fuckin' voiceboxes cut out – I hate the way those little f**kers squawk!' Tony told Gordy how much fun it was going to be working with him on the movie. Gordy assumed this meant they would be working together as a team – it was an assumption that Gordy got wrong.

On 18 November 1974, filming began in one of the toughest neighbourhoods on Chicago's Southside. The crew was a few blocks away from a housing project known as the 'Bucket of Blood'. Onlookers jeered Tony when he arrived on set wearing an expensive fur coat and he got off on the wrong foot, behaving high-handedly with locals. He barked at them to get out of shot, even when all they were doing was sitting on their own front porches. The wary atmosphere at Gordy's mansion extended to the Chicago shoot. Word on set was that the Detroit underworld had forced Gordy to flee to Los Angeles. Now that he was back in Chicago, home of what was once Al Capone's gang, he wasn't taking any chances: four bodyguards would surround him whenever he walked down the street, two in front and two behind.

Billy Dee Williams, who would later become famous in *The Empire Strikes Back*, was cast as Ross's lover and Anthony Perkins as her fashion photographer Svengali. Byrum didn't get the impression that Ross and Williams liked each other very much. Being Motown and being the music business in the early Seventies, there were a lot of drugs on set. Anthony Perkins in particular, angry at his agent for getting him into this Harold Robbins/Jacqueline Susann nonsense, was doing a lot of coke and the drugs were affecting his performance. Tony informed Gordy who ordered his staff to watch over Perkins, even to the extent of sleeping in his bedroom.

Diana Ross was thrilled at the idea of being directed by the brilliant, articulate and extremely witty Tony Richardson. She and Tony worked well together. He consulted her over where he was putting the camera and encouraged the singer to add her own decorative touches to the heroine's apartment. Ross had never enjoyed this kind of trust before: Gordy normally just told her what to do. Tony was struck by the Motown boss's proprietorial attitude towards his star. Gordy felt he owned her. 'Tony, you've got to understand – Diana isn't a personality, she's a product,' Gordy told him. Tony thought there was an element of truth in this.[16] Ross may have thought she and Tony had a good working relationship, but one observer said he didn't know what to make of her. He regarded Ross and Gordy like monkeys in a cage, '… these weird animals he couldn't make head nor tail of.' Rob Cohen believed that underneath all his lubricious charm, Tony was a racist: he seemed to think of black people as charming little imps he could treat like children. Indeed, Williams lost his temper when Tony referred to blacks as 'you people.'

Tony tried poisoning Ross against Cohen, who would go on to become one of Hollywood's biggest producer/directors. Cohen was too inexperienced to be in charge of a production this ambitious, he told her. However, this time Tony's usual divide-and-conquer tricks backfired on him. Ross was loyal to Cohen. 'If Rob is so goddamn stupid, then why'd he pick you?' she snapped back. Shooting became increasingly tense; Tony and Gordy clashed practically every day. Eventually, Tony stopped speaking to both Gordy and Cohen. Things became so bad that Ross begged her Motown boss to go back to Los Angeles. Gordy thought the dailies were lifeless – Tony wasn't capturing the drama. For him, it seemed just another gig. But for Gordy, this was his life – and his money. Gordy began rehearsing scenes with Ross and Williams behind Tony's back. Tony, who'd never encountered such insolence before, was incandescent. It was obvious to everybody that Gordy had really wanted to direct. This was fine with Tony as he was beginning to wonder what he was doing there; he'd catch Gordy looking over his shoulder while he worked. Tony began joshing Gordy about his directing ambitions.

They were about halfway through shooting when the confrontation happened. Tony was unhappy with an actor who'd been cast as a rapist and had found somebody who looked more menacing. What he didn't know was that Gordy had been rehearsing the scene with the original actor and insisted Tony use his first choice. There was a standoff. Most of the British crew went on strike in support of Tony. Meanwhile, he repeated his suggestion that Gordy take over. Gordy suspected Tony wanted to be fired and the whole casting argument was his way of getting out of the movie.[17] He told Tony what he wanted to hear. Afterwards, Tony turned to the other Brits and drawled, 'I've just been fired. Berry Gordy has fired me.' Then he turned back to Gordy. 'OK, it's all yours,' he told him and walked off. Not that Tony cared: he got a $200,000 payoff and didn't have to make a film that he knew was completely wrong for him. The official line was that Tony 'didn't quite capture the feeling of blackness – the black point of view'.

Even though Tony shot half the film, *Mahogany* remains mediocre throughout. Given such appalling material, the only sensible approach would have been – in Dorothy Parker's words – 'to kid the living tripe' out of it. Instead, every inane word of the script was treated with solemnity. The silliness level rises even higher when we get to the scenes Gordy directed in Rome. Anthony Perkins reprises Norman Bates who clearly developed a career as a fashion photographer after running a motel didn't work out for him. Despite this, *Mahogany* broke box-office records when it opened in October 1975. It's a pity Tony's name wasn't on the credits.

Notes

1. Danaë Brook, author interview, 8 December 2010.
2. Ibid.
3. Ibid.
4. Behan, Brian. 'How Vanessa Was Fooled By a Communist Gangster', *Mail On Sunday*, 27 February 2000.
5. Ross, Deborah. *Daily Mail*, 26 April 1996.
6. Cohen, Nick. 'Of Cults and Conmen: Vanessa Redgrave's Unblinking Allegiance to a Discounted Leader Offers a Pointed and Topical Lesson', *Observer*, 8 May 2005.
7. Cohen, Nick. 'Of Cults and Conmen: Vanessa Redgrave's Unblinking Allegiance to a Discounted Leader Offers a Pointed and Topical Lesson', *Observer*, 8 May 2005.
8. Simpson, Anne. 'How Fiery Vanessa Ruffled Comfy Lynn', *Glasgow Herald*, 31 May 1978.
9. Redgrave, Deirdre and Brook, Danaë. *To Be a Redgrave*, Robson Books, London, 1982.

10. Ellis, Richard, Craig, John and Weir, Andrew. 'Far Left Party Paid to Spy By Gaddafi', *Sunday Times*, 7 February 1988.
11. Mike Medavoy, author interview, 22 June 2009.
12. Shirley Williams, author interview, 25 November 2009.
13. Norman Twain, author interview, 12 February 2010.
14. Author interview, 27 January 2010.
15. Bevan, Emily. 'Prime Time for Natasha', *Sunday Telegraph*, 27 April 2003.
16. Taraborrelli, J.R. *Call Her Miss Ross: The Unauthorised Biography of Diana Ross*, Sidgwick & Jackson, London, 1989.
17. Gordy, Berry. *To Be Loved: The Music, the Magic, the Memories of Motown*, Headline, London, 1994.

CHAPTER SIXTEEN

Zionist Hoodlums

Corin spent the early Seventies preparing for a fascist coup d'état that never arrived. Early in 1974 the British Left whipped itself up into a frenzy over what it saw as the proto-fascist tendencies of the Edward Heath government. Its biggest fear was that the Establishment would form an alliance with the Army and become a military junta. Vanessa warned that Britain was being prepared for dictatorship and concentration camps.[1] She called for workers to take power through armed insurrection.[2] 'The WRP genuinely believed that the revolution was about to happen,' said former trade unionist Roy Lockett. 'They thought troops were being mobilised and were taking over airports. I remember Waterloo Bridge was closed for repairs and this was believed to be the first move to seal off London. It was crazy, barmy, barmy.' Lynn was in no doubt as to how serious Vanessa was: 'When the revolution comes, if it does, if I were in her way, I'm sure she'd walk right over me, much as she might love me. It would upset her, I think, but you know, onwards brothers to the ... to the final goal.'[3] Some childhood habits died hard, though – Vanessa still shopped at Harrods.

Having polled a miserable 572 votes as the WRP candidate in Newham, east London during the 1974 general election, Vanessa decided to focus her political-consciousness raising efforts on other actors. This was a ludicrous idea when one considers the innate selfishness of the dramatic profession. Just as the WRP had virtually taken over the technicians' union, the Association of Cinematograph, Television and Allied Technicians (ACTT), so Vanessa and Corin campaigned for the actors' union Equity to control all theatres and television stations. Brother and sister would turn up at West End theatres shortly before curtain call to explain WRP policy within Equity to other actors. Deirdre Redgrave said the young middle-class actresses who attended Party meetings would gaze up at Gerry Healy and Corin with the same kind of adoration that groupies had for rock stars. Actor Simon Callow remembered one meeting where actors shuffled into a theatre to find Corin sitting onstage, looking every inch the political commissar. He sat at a book-laden trestle table under a naked lightbulb, working away on some document and was dressed in a Gestapo-like trench coat. (Sometimes it seemed as if the Far Left and Extreme Right were so far round the circle, they met each other again. The Fascists' black leather uniforms were always sexy.) The ashtray was filled with cigarette butts, each stubbed out with peculiarly venomous intensity; the tension palpable. Finally, Corin took off his spectacles and rose. He began almost inaudibly. Little by little, the volume increased and the quotations from Friedrich Engels and Antonio Gramsci were hammered home. By the time he reached his peroration, Corin was shouting: the Heath government was about to surround Heathrow airport with tanks as a prelude to a military coup, he screamed. He then slumped back into his chair, lighting another cigarette.[4]

Back then the actors' union was a closed shop, but you had to belong to the union if you wanted to go on stage. This meant Equity had political muscle. At the height of its popularity it was estimated that about 60 of Equity's 23,000 members belonged to the WRP; around 30 of these were truly active. Theatre managers were rumoured to be circulating a blacklist of those who belonged to the party. Corin said the BBC blacklisted him too, keeping him off television screens.

Indeed, walking back into a BBC studio in 1994, for a BBC production of Shakespeare's *Measure For Measure*, Corin remarked: 'How strange, here I am again! I was last here in 1970.' For those 24 years, he said, he worked only one play a year, most often at the Young Vic. 'Even then, the theatre got a little bit of a backlash for employing people like me.' It wasn't his decision to work less, he explained, 'what determined it was the sense that to a degree I was excluded by other people from activity.'

In the spring of 1975, Vanessa and Corin decided to open a school for revolutionaries. First, they needed to find a suitable property. White Meadows Villas was a redbrick Edwardian mansion in two acres of land near the Derbyshire Peak District village of Parwich. Vanessa bought it for £23,000. Fellow actors were charged £30 each for a two-week course in revolutionary indoctrination. The course aimed to produce a trained cadre of about 1,500 revolutionaries yearly. Guards patrolled the perimeter and inmates spent every waking minute imbibing Healy's thoughts – the local pub was out of bounds. Inside, the atmosphere was of Spartan discipline. A child crying outside the lecture hall would be left to wail: the lecture came before parenthood and bourgeois concerns of family life. Intense paranoia about MI5 agents within their midst reinforced the belief that the rest of society couldn't be trusted – safety lay in absolute loyalty to the group. The WRP renamed the place, 'The Red House'.

On Saturday, 27 September 1975, 100 policemen stormed the Red House. Switching on powerful floodlights, they raided the building with 14 vehicles, two power generators, dogs, metal detectors, handcuffs, truncheons and flares. Members of the Special Branch, the Special Patrol Group and Regional Crime Squad took six hours to search the place. Healy and the others were interrogated with police guards stationed at the door. While no arrests were made, the police claimed to have made an interesting discovery: nine .22-calibre bullets were found in a stairway cupboard (but no guns). The WRP insisted the bullets were planted: the police raid was the biggest provocation against a working-class political organisation since the war, they claimed, designed to whip up red-baiting hysteria.

The police raid happened after the authorities were tipped off by the *Observer* newspaper: Special Branch had been watching the Red House ever since Vanessa had bought it – her membership of such an extreme political group alarmed the government. Irene Gorst, twenty-eight, a television sitcom actress, had gone to the *Observer* to complain that she'd been the victim of an interrogation. Gorst told the newspaper of the 'ordeal' she had suffered at the hands of the Redgraves. As she told it, she arrived late for the beginning of her fortnight course because an old boyfriend had whisked her off to Maidenhead for lunch – the boyfriend was determined to break the Party's hold on her. This infraction of Party discipline upset Corin, who had been having an affair with Gorst.

The Redgraves and two other party members, according to Gorst, spent seven hours interrogating WRP Recruit No. 5005, accusing her of being a Special Branch spy. Corin called her 'bourgeois, middle-class and arrogant' and when she tried to leave, Gorst claimed, Vanessa pushed her back into her chair.[5] At one point, she was even forced to empty her handbag. Television producer Roy Battersby seemed particularly interested in her eyebrow pencil – 'He kept peering down at it as if he expected to discover a hidden microphone,' Gorst recalled.

When the *Observer* informed Vanessa of Gorst's allegations, she denied the substance of the story and said she was taking legal action. The *Observer* published its story the next morning: 28 September 1975. Corin's response was that the newspaper story and the raid were a set-up: according to him, the police and the newspaper had worked together to frame the party.

It took three years and 11 days for the Red House case to come to court. Vanessa's friends warned her that she was being naive if she thought she would get justice. One of the tenets of the WRP was that the law treated people of different classes differently. By now, Deirdre and Corin had separated (Deirdre had become involved with a King's Road boutique owner called Mickey). Corin was now living with Kika Markham, the actress who'd first introduced him to the WRP, yet he still asked Deirdre to accompany him to court (he thought it would look better if his wife was supporting him). Later, Deirdre admitted that supporting Corin during the court case was the hardest decision of her marriage. Gorst testified that her six-hour interrogation had left her with screaming nightmares. It was Vanessa who soothed her back to sleep, saying, 'Don't worry, comrade – it's only a dream.' After a 13-day hearing in the High Court, Vanessa, Corin and four other WRP members lost their libel action. The verdict was a bizarre one. Although the jury decided unanimously that the *Observer* article was generally true, parts of the story were untrue. However, they refused to award Vanessa damages because she apparently had no reputation to lose. And so although Vanessa and Corin had proved parts of the *Observer* article were defamatory and wrong, they were now saddled with the newspaper's legal bill. One legal expert pronounced the finding to be 'very unusual.'

The judge ordered Vanessa and Corin to pay costs officially estimated at £70,000. Vanessa immediately claimed victory: 'It would appear that we have to pay the *Observer* for the privilege of defaming us,' she said. 'Not so,' said the *Observer* – the jury had accepted the general truth of Gorst's allegations, if not every word of the article. Vanessa was quite mistaken to say that she had been 'cleared' of anything. Indeed, the verdict was the opposite of that. *Observer* editor Donald Trelford said: 'Her statement that the jury cleared her is ridiculous. The *Observer* won, with no ifs and no buts.'

Vanessa and Corin gave a press conference on Friday, 11 November 1978 to announce the launch of a £70,000 appeal fund. Corin said the case set a dangerous precedent for victims having to pay the costs of a libel action after they'd proved newspaper allegations to be untrue. The *Observer* libel fundraiser took place on 28 January 1979 at the Lyceum theatre in London. Fifteen minutes from curtain up and the theatre doors were still bolted. 'You can go home, if you don't like it,' snapped a WRP member as the audience shivered in the rain.

The fundraiser was supposed to be a Redgrave family affair but Michael announced he was not well enough to appear. Four years earlier he had been diagnosed with Parkinson's Disease, which in a way came as something of a relief – it explained his blank moods and the difficulty he had in remembering lines. Lynn, too dropped out at the last moment because she was rehearsing for *The Muppet Show* (her husband John Clark was always careful to insulate her from the rest of the family in case it damaged her career). The tabloids chortled at how Vanessa had been upstaged by Miss Piggy.

Standing barefoot on stage, Vanessa exhorted the 1,000-strong audience to be as generous as it could. She said she had already received a 'very generous' contribution from Warren Beatty. 'Come on now, who'll be the first?' she asked. A small boy opened the proceedings with a £5 note. She and Corin then performed an emotional scene from *Antony and Cleopatra*. The concert raised just £3,000 towards the WRP's £70,000 legal costs. Corin made no mention of the hundreds of thousands of pounds Libya was paying the WRP to spy on prominent British Jews.

On 27 January 1976, Vanessa spent her 39th birthday sitting round a small wooden table in a New York apartment. With her were seven-year-old Carlo and his nanny. The single actress celebrated with a bowl of Rice Krispies. Once again, she had left her two girls behind. For three months, thirteen-year-old Natasha stayed with a school friend while Joely (now eleven) was parked with Corin's ex-wife Deirdre.

Vanessa had come to New York City to star in Tony's production of Ibsen's *The Lady from the Sea*. The play was being put on at the Circle in the Square, the closest Manhattan had to subsidised theatre. It marked Vanessa's first Broadway appearance and seeing the pressure David Merrick had put Tony under made her wary. Nobody could accuse Vanessa of not having integrity: the $1,000 a week she was getting was less than half of what she'd earned the last time she worked with Tony on *The Threepenny Opera*.

The Lady from the Sea was in many ways a reinterpretation of the themes of Ibsen's previous play, *A Doll's House*. Vanessa played Ellida Wangel, an unhappily married woman haunted by the ghost of a lover she thought drowned at sea years before. One day during rehearsals, actor Pat Hingle, who played Ellida's doctor husband, said he simply couldn't tolerate Vanessa's character and her interminable suffering. Tony urged him to think what he would do if Vanessa really was his wife. Hingle exclaimed, 'If she was my wife, I'd hit her!' Tony laughed and clapped his hands as if this was the funniest joke ever, then urged Hingle to do just that. 'Go on, *hit* Vanessa! Hit her *hard* – it'll do her good!' he said.

Natasha remembered it as being a spare, intellectual production. 'I don't have specific memories of my mother doing the play when I was a child, but I remember the mood of the production was very cool,' she said. She herself was to play the role of Ellida Wangel nearly 25 years later.

The reviews were mixed. '*The Lady from the Sea* is a silly and ridiculous play, not merely third-rate Ibsen. I cannot imagine what possessed the Circle in the Square to produce it, except perhaps the willingness of Vanessa Redgrave to appear in it. Tony Richardson's production solves none of the play's soapy problems while creating others,' wrote the *New York Post*. The *New York Times* was enthusiastic, though: 'Mr Richardson has captured both the wildness and peace of the play. He never misses a trick … he uses theatre exceptionally well.'

What drew audiences was the intensity of Vanessa's acting. 'I give myself to my parts as to a lover,' she explained. 'It's the only way.' The play ran for 77 performances. Writing in his diary, Peter Hall marvelled at what Vanessa had achieved: 'You could see right through the skin to the emotions, the thoughts, the hopes, the fears underneath. But here's the paradox. What Vanessa says politically is, to me, insane, and I believe that to her, lies are truth if they support her ideology. So, how can she express such truth, such sincerity, such lack of hypocrisy in her art? In life, which is true, she is false. In art, which is false, she is true.'

Coming off *The Lady from the Sea*, Tony was in even more urgent need of success. Although money was still dribbling in to Woodfall, he was a spendthrift living beyond his means. Tony had spent most of his vast profits from *Tom Jones* on his own films; he also needed to retain his 'bankable' position in Hollywood, a city where, as his friend Joan

Didion observed, status is minutely calibrated. The movie business had changed since Woodfall began. In the Sixties, it could afford to have the occasional failure. In the era of *Jaws* and *Star Wars* saturating the screens, now the pressure was on: hit the jackpot or go bust. 'The last three or four years haven't been too good,' he admitted to the author and journalist Sheridan Morley.[6]

He decided to adapt *Joseph Andrews*, the novel Henry Fielding wrote seven years before *Tom Jones*. Comic epic was always his favourite genre. The ingredients were much the same: bedroom romps, misunderstandings of parentage and amorous adventures. Joseph is a sturdy country lad treading a path of righteousness through a rollicking world of bottoms, bed and bawd. Tony couldn't explain why he'd suddenly become infatuated with Fielding again – it was inexplicable, like falling in love. 'It was always in the bank of projects in one's head as something one would like to make at some time,' he said.

This time around, Tony persuaded Paramount to stump up the modest $3 million budget. He assembled a cast headed by Peter Firth and featuring Peggy Ashcroft, John Gielgud, Michael Hordern, Beryl Reid and Jim Dale, plus others from Tony's repertory company (Norman Rossington, Murray Melvin). He also cast one or two familiar faces from *Tom Jones*: Peter Bull and Hugh Griffith (Tony was shocked to see what booze had done to Griffith – it was only by spoonfeeding him brandy that he could get any performance out of him at all). Asked why he cast American-Swedish actress Ann-Margret for the role of Lady Booby, Tony replied somewhat ungallantly, 'Well, there aren't all that many stars around with really big boobs.' He made a rare misstep in casting seventeen-year-old drama student Natalie Ogle as Joseph's sweetheart, Fanny Goodwill. Tony predicted great things for Ogle but she never became the star he thought she might be. He also assembled his usual technical collaborators, including lighting cameraman David Watkin, producer Neil Hartley, composer John Addison and production supervisor Roy Millichip, who'd worked on *Tom Jones*.

Shooting began on 26 April 1976. The first scene that Tony shot was the opening May Day celebration involving pagan rites and climbing up a greasy pole. Once again, Natasha played a cameo as a village maiden – she had to dance around the maypole in torrential weather dressed in a sodden cotton shift: 'And I thought, I want to be a star when I grow up, so I can have a Winnebago like Ann-Margret and not be in the pouring rain,' she said. Tony was noticeably happy, back working outdoors in the West Country he'd captured in *Tom Jones* (he had shot that film at a clip in 14 weeks). This time around, he had just 10.

Tony and his crew covered 61 separate locations in a fleet of 43 vehicles. The production roamed through villages with olde-English names such as Newington Bagpath, Stow-on-the-Wold, Chipping Norton and Norton St Philip. Television aerials and any other signs of modernity were removed. The crew started work at 6.30 in the morning until late at night, but 'they do it for Tony Richardson. He is a remarkable man,' said art director Michael Annals. That summer, Britain was in the midst of a sweltering heatwave. Make-up artists fought a running battle with cosmetics dripping in 90°F-heat. The props department hastily constructed a leaning board so that Ann-Margret, who gamely persevered with her weighty crinolines, petticoats, wig and a picture hat measuring two feet across, could rest between takes.

Over a sparse lunch of chilled white wine and Cheddar cheese, Tony said he'd set out to produce a film that would simply make people laugh. Taking a swipe at Lindsay Anderson, he said other directors preferred talking about their films after they made them, whereas he pretty much forgot about them once he was finished – 'You have to do what you believe in and hope audiences like it, too.'

Writing in the *New Yorker*, John Osborne's ex-wife Penelope Gilliatt (the couple had separated on 12 June 1966 and divorced a couple of years later) gave *Joseph Andrews* a glowing review, saying it could only have been made by somebody like Tony who, although he lived abroad, knew England and English literature backwards. Most critics, though, slammed Tony for cynically trying to revive his slumping career. Derek Malcolm in the *Guardian* said *Joseph Andrews* resembled nothing so much as a heavily tarted-up *Carry On* film. The *Financial Times*' Nigel Andrews called the film's relentless knockabout hysteria 'a disaster', while *Variety*'s critic found himself backing away from the film, 'not from any sense of outrage, but rather in the way one retreats from bad breath.'

Tony blamed *Joseph Andrews*' failure on people expecting another *Tom Jones* – all the books really had in common was the same author, he said disingenuously. Later he admitted it was his fault for making a film so similar that it wasn't judged on its own merits. Tony had made a fundamental error; he had also made a film completely out of step with Britain in 1977 – Lady Tattle and Mrs Slipslop larking about in the West Country had nothing to do with punk rock and the Brixton riots. As with *Red and Blue*, it all seemed hopelessly out of date. Then again, Tony thought oblivion was the price of being fashionable. *Joseph Andrews'* failure meant his long, dry spell wasn't over yet. In fact, *Joseph Andrews* was Tony's last British film. 'Sure, he got frustrated,' said his agent Mike Medavoy. 'There's nothing worse than not being hot. You don't get your calls returned, no matter how talented or bright you are.'[7] But if Tony's career was still in the doldrums then Vanessa's was glowing white-hot. She had just been nominated for an Oscar for a small part she'd played in a Fred Zinnemann film.

The same month that Tony was starting production on *Joseph Andrews*, Vanessa made a momentous decision: she decided to sell the house she lived in with Natasha and Joely at 18 St Peter's Square. She wanted to use the money to make a pro-Palestinian documentary titled *The Palestinian*. At the same time, she also sold another house she owned round the corner. Vanessa was literally selling the roof from over their heads. Both houses sold for £65,000, of which all but £5,000 was spent making *The Palestinian*. The girls both became frightened. Joely had great difficulty sleeping. Natasha, for one, felt very uncomfortable with it all.[8]

Vanessa disappeared for nearly two months filming her documentary. Altogether, she was out of contact for seven weeks. With the support of the family nanny, Silvana Sammassimo, fourteen-year-old Natasha was left in charge of eleven-year-old Joely and seven-year-old Carlo. The girls had to organise installing a new kitchen and an inside lavatory. Natasha pinned a rota to the fridge for the three of them to do the shopping, cooking and washing-up. 'That was a nightmarish period in my life,' Natasha remembered. 'There were some dark times.'[9]

There was a storm of controversy in June 1977 when Vanessa showed her pro-Palestinian documentary. Jewish groups were outraged. Dore Schary, the former boss of MGM who chaired the anti-defamation league of B'nai B'rith, said that Vanessa's anti-Israeli film was, 'very dull, fortunately.'

At the same time 20th Century Fox was casting Fred Zinnemann's next film, *Julia*. Based on playwright Lillian Hellman's memoir *Pentimento*, *Julia* told the supposedly true story of Hellman's childhood friendship with a young woman called Julia. Hellman's sense of injustice was sparked by Julia, whom she later encountered living in Nazi Germany. Jane Fonda was to play Hellman and Jason Robards her lover, Dashiell Hammett. The role of crippled Julia, fighting Nazi oppression, seemed tailor-made for Vanessa but Fox was strongly opposed to casting her because of her politics. Zinnemann stood firm and Vanessa immersed herself in research, reading all the background material she could find. By the time she arrived on set, she knew Lillian Hellman's work and history thoroughly.

Filming their scenes together, Fonda was thrown slightly offbalance because she never knew what Vanessa was going to come up with next. 'Her voice,' wrote Fonda, 'seems to come from some deep place that knows all suffering and all secrets. Watching her work is like seeing through layers of glass, each layer painted in mythic watercolour images, layer after layer, until it becomes dark – but even then you know you haven't come to the bottom of it.'

Vanessa's performance was truly brilliant. Edward Fox, the actor whose younger brother, Robert, would marry Natasha on 16 October 1990, said she was completely believable as the one-legged victim of Nazi persecution: she became Julia.

Vanessa's performance was so extraordinary that she was nominated for an Academy Award. Her Oscar nomination inflamed Jewish campaigners. Militant Jewish groups called for Academy voters not to vote for Vanessa because of her documentary about Palestinian refugees. 'I say straight out that Vanessa Redgrave is an anti-Semite,' said Rabbi Abraham Cooper, associate dean of the Wiesenthal Center. The Jewish Defence League warned it was organising about 400 people to picket the Academy Award ceremony: it had already told 20th Century Fox there would be trouble unless Vanessa was dropped. One speaker waved a fistful of dollars at a meeting and asked, 'Who is willing to rid the world of a Jew-baiter?' Eli Spira, one of the organisers of the Jewish protest, told a news conference that Vanessa supported, 'murder, terrorism and destruction of innocent people.' Meanwhile, the Palestinian Liberation Organisation said it was organising a counter-demonstration in support of her stance.

As Vanessa drove up to the Dorothy Chandler Pavilion on 3 April 1978, there were dense crowds behind police barriers. Protestors were burning Vanessa in effigy as 'Arafat's Whore', dancing and shouting around the smouldering heap. Police sharpshooters were posted on the roof. Two groups of helmeted police kept both groups apart. Even the Nazis turned up: Jewish protestors attacked three men dressed in Nazi uniforms, striking one man on the head.

Tension was high inside the building as well. Armed plainclothes security milled around backstage. *Star Wars* and *Close Encounters of the Third Kind* had carved up the technical awards between them. Alvin Sargent had collected his Oscar for Best Adapted Screenplay. Now it was Vanessa's turn. Seventy million television viewers watched her face as John Travolta read the nominations out: she was competing against Tuesday Weld in *Looking For Mister Goodbar* and Melinda Dillon in *Close Encounters*. The place erupted with applause as Vanessa's name was read out. On stage, she used this moment to answer the picketers outside. Praising Academy voters, she said: 'You have stood firm and refused to be intimidated by a small band of Zionist hoodlums who have insulted Jews all over the world in their struggle against fascism and Nazism.' There were boos and hisses: she meant to refer to the picketers outside but all audience heard was 'Zionist hoodlums'. Smiling happily, Vanessa descended the steps, gave Fred Zinnemann a big kiss and sat down – 'In thirty seconds the temperature had dropped to ice,' Zinnemann noted.

Meanwhile, screenwriter Paddy Chayefsky was applauded on stage when he told the audience: 'I'm sick and tired of people exploiting the occasion of the Academy Awards for the propagation of their own personal political propaganda. I would like to suggest to Miss Redgrave that her winning an Academy Award is not a pivotal moment in history – it does not require a proclamation. A simple "thank you" would have sufficed.'

Like two stones cast into a pool of water, the words 'Zionist hoodlums' rippled out to affect everybody. Natasha remembered being in a physics class at school when a kid pointed at her and said, 'Your mother is a Commie.' Natasha ran away, sobbing.[10] One friend of Vanessa's observed that had it not been for her Oscar speech, she might have become the greatest star of all time, as well as the greatest actress. 'As it is, her films have too often been character parts,' said the friend. Vanessa believed that one day the Jews would realise their firmest allies against anti-Semitism were the Palestinians. Her dream, however unlikely, was for Jews and Arabs to live together in a United

Socialist States of the Middle East. It was an argument that went over the heads of most people. Even before her infamous Oscar speech, Vanessa said she'd been 'subjected to numerous attacks by British Zionists and capitalists, in particular Jews, who tried to destroy my career.'[11]

In fact, those two words gave birth to an ineradicable belief that Vanessa Redgrave regarded all Jews as 'hoodlums'. For the next decade, she would find herself blacklisted, bringing her close to ruin. Tony said it was not surprising that most Jews perceived her as being anti-Semitic – she'd created this image for herself, which made her almost uncastable in a leading role. It had cost her lots of jobs and all kinds of problems and harassment. Admittedly, Tony didn't think she necessarily understood the political issues she tried to deal with. He said: 'She's totally unrealistic in her attitude when she says "Zionism" – she thinks she isn't talking about Jews.' Her approach, continued her ex-husband, was an instinctive, emotional one – which was why she was such a great actress. 'Vanessa may have made mistakes, but there isn't a drop of anti-Semitic blood in her body,' he maintained.

Vanessa stood as a candidate in the 4 May 1979 general election as candidate for Manchester Moss Side. The WRP was fielding 60 prospective MPs nationally, 50 more than it put up in 1974. Corin was standing as a candidate for Lambeth Central, south London. Looking quite exhausted after touring the constituency in an S-registration Ford Fiesta and gray donkey jacket, Corin insisted that he hadn't abandoned an acting career. 'Like so many actors, I just don't have one,' he said. One day he led a door-to-door canvassing team, marking down those interested in voting for the Party. He spent some time talking to one couple apparently keen and ready to join – 'They called me "brother,"' he enthused. It was gently pointed out to him that the couple were Plymouth Brethren religious revivalists who called everybody 'brother'.[12]

Although Vanessa was fighting to become an MP, she said Parliament was merely a 'façade to hide the conspiracies taking place inside.' Vanessa campaigned to smash capitalism, abolish the Monarchy and replace the police with a worker's militia but her first priority, she declared, was to stop the 'Thatcher menace.' She was standing as a far-left candidate in a Britain that had been brought to its knees by union militancy. Striking dustmen left refuse to rot in the street, even the dead were left unburied. In what became known as the 'Winter of Discontent', people were ready for change. Vanessa faced an uphill struggle in convincing them that the answer lay in going even further Left. In the end, she won only 225 votes and lost her deposit. Corin fared even worse, taking just 152 votes. Indeed, every single WRP candidate lost their deposit.

In the late spring of 1979, Tony was asked to direct a three-hour television drama for CBS. Arthur Miller had adapted the autobiography of concentration camp survivor Fania Fénelon. *Playing For Time* told the story of the woman's orchestra formed from prisoners inside Auschwitz. Tony wanted Vanessa to play Fénelon (Jane Fonda and Barbra Streisand had already turned the role down). Jewish groups reacted vociferously when the casting of the PLO's highest-profile overseas champion was announced. One rabbi told CBS that Vanessa's casting showed 'utter, callous disregard' for Nazi concentration camp victims. Vanessa's portrayal would 'desecrate the memory of the martyred millions,' said Rabbi Marvin Hier of the Simon Wiesenthal Center for Holocaust Studies. Dore Schary also called for Vanessa to be dropped: casting her would degrade and mock the memory of Auschwitz survivors and victims alike, he said. Other Hollywood executives, including producer David L. Wolper, also complained. Sammy Davis Jr said that Vanessa playing Fénelon would be like him playing the head of the Klu Klux Klan. Fénelon too objected to Vanessa playing her. Calling Vanessa a 'fanatic', she told more than 200 protestors that she was determined to block the television movie. Fénelon planned to sue CBS if it broadcast the programme. Protesters petrol bombed a US television station and set fire to an effigy of Vanessa outside CBS Studios. Vanessa herself received death threats.

Some wondered if CBS was cynical in agreeing to Vanessa's casting – the network must have known giving her the role would arouse horror and anger. As one CBS executive said, 'Our business is showbusiness.' CBS broadcast a confrontation between Vanessa and Fénelon at prime time to whet appetites for the show. Both women were painfully polite to each other and close to tears. But it wasn't the reaction of Jewish groups that forced Tony off the project: it was the television movie's chaotic management and apparent lack of financing. After *The Sailor from Gibraltar*, he'd learnt his lesson never to embark on something without adequate preparation. Tony's successor – Joseph Sargent – also dropped out. In the end, Daniel Mann was the director.

CBS took fright as controversy built, slashing prices for advertising spots during the show. The network usually charged $50,000 for the cheapest 30-second television commercial. Ad spots during *Playing For Time* were a rock bottom $30–35,000. The network also kept a tight lid on which companies were sponsoring the programme. CBS was concerned Jewish groups would pressure sponsors to withdraw if their names got out. *Playing For Time* went on to win several Emmy Awards, including Outstanding Actress for Vanessa and Outstanding Drama Special.

Five weeks after *Playing For Time* aired, Vanessa was quoted in a Palestinian magazine on 3 November 1980, questioning whether 'there is any room for a state of Israel,'[13] but reiterating that she was against Zionism, not Jews as a race. (In 2005 Vanessa was concerned to emphasise to interviewer Larry King that she supported Israel's right to exist.)

The Emmy success of *Playing For Time* might have rejuvenated Tony's career. Instead, he was back to square one, developing original projects no studio was interested in. For some time he'd wanted to make a movie about illegal Mexican immigrants. In 1977, the *Los Angeles Times* ran a series of exposés about cross-border traffic, the border patrol and its tragedies. Every day, thousands of Mexicans attempted to cross the US border, some of them smuggled illegally by human traffickers. Tony wanted to create a 'documentary fresco' of the exploiter and the exploited. He had lots of notes and story ideas – the problem was finding a hook.

Universal, meanwhile, had commissioned him to remake Graham Greene's thriller, *A Gun for Sale*. Deric Washburn, who would shortly be nominated for an Oscar for *The Deer Hunter*, was hired to write the script. Washburn mentioned he, too was working on a project about illegal Mexican immigrants for Edgar Bronfman Jr, scion of the Seagram liquor empire – Bronfman had read the *Los Angeles Times* articles as well. All three started collaborating but Tony and Washburn fell out about the script (Tony turned to David Freeman and later, Walon Green for help).

Tony took his finished screenplay to Jack Nicholson, who became keen to star as Charlie, an El Paso border patrolman who abandons his dreams of living simply to satisfy his wife's avaricious demands. Strangled with debt, Charlie uncovers an illegal baby-smuggling racket with the tip of his dusty cowboy boot – his problem is the criminal enterprise is run by other policemen.

Tony and Nicholson had known each other for 14 years, having first met in Cannes in 1966. They had reconnected through Nicholson's girlfriend Anjelica Huston. In 1977, Tony and Nicholson had dinner with Roman Polanski the night before he was sent to Chino Prison after drugging and sodomising a thirteen-year-old girl. With Nicholson on board, Universal suddenly became keen on *The Border*, tripling its budget from $4.5 million to $14.5 million. *The Border* would be the first movie to bear the RKO label for 30 years. Tony was excited to be working with his old friend: 'There's a fineness about Jack's taste as an actor that there never was, for example, with Larry Olivier's,' he said. 'Larry was a very stupid man with wonderful instincts, but he never surprised me.'

Tony found Universal's extravagance mind-boggling. The studio, which reminded him of the Kremlin in the top-down way it operated, would rather build entire shantytowns and a cathedral on the backlot than go on location. Tony, as usual, got his way: filming began on 7 July 1980 in El Paso, Texas. Seventeen-year-old Natasha came out for several weeks and worked as an assistant director, shepherding extras. Eventually, the budget swelled to $23 million.

Much of the ballooning came from the Screen Actors Guild strike called within weeks of the start of production. The strike went on for nearly three months, which meant that famed cinematographer Vilmos Zsigmond had to drop out because of prior commitments. The temperature plummeted from 110°F at the start of filming to near-freezing by the end. This played havoc with continuity. The Rio Grande, which figured so prominently in the film, had almost burst its banks by the time filming stopped.

Adding to Tony's problems was that Nicholson's co-star Valerie Perrine was tetchy and irritable with the crew. She and Nicholson did not get on at all. Nicholson also turned out to be a disappointment: Tony expected collaboration between director and star in the way he'd coaxed great performances out of Olivier and Finney. Instead, Nicholson was polite, professional and somewhat offhand, as if he just wanted to get back to his trailer. Cleverly, Tony put him in mirrored sunglasses for much of the film, stopping him from doing his usual eyebrow waggling at the audience. Nicholson enjoyed baiting Tony, seeing how far he could push him. Tony came away feeling that his star didn't enjoy acting as much as he once did. Nicholson, though, had nothing but praise for his director – at least in public. 'Tony has a very subtle, quiet control – and at the same time, is consistently trying something new with each take of the same scene. Which most directors don't do, but that's exactly what I try for in my work,' he said.

Universal executives didn't like what they saw when Tony showed them the rough cut and the studio ordered extensive changes. The original ending had Charlie going berserk, blowing up his police station and ending the film behind bars. According to Tony, it was his idea to reshoot the ending – he wanted a gentler, more upbeat finish. Universal previewed the movie and the test scores were divided: half the audience wanted more of a wham-bam ending, while the other half wanted something more reflective. 'I decided I just didn't like the ending we had – it was too violent, too Clint Eastwood, if you like. I decided it was important to allow Jack's character to do one good little thing – that is the message of the movie. So I called the studio and I said, "Listen, I've got this new idea" and they said, "Fine." I was amazed because it was a costly operation,' Tony said. One year later, he went back to El Paso with Nicholson and original cinematographer Vilmos Zsigmond. They shot for a month and the new ending cost the studio another $1.5 million.

The Border protests against the atrocities because of deceit and exploitation on either side. Tony said: '*The Border* is a very serious film, about an amazing circumstance – there's no situation like it anywhere. You've got the richest, most powerful country in the world side-by-side with one of the poorest. It's a classic confrontation – the most amazing juxtaposition of the Third World and the West that one could imagine.' There are moments when the script is as sharp as barbed wire. The film comes most alive when Tony's doing what he does best: the documentary 'fresco' scenes of border-town life, acidly contrasting desperate immigrants with complacent American suburbia. No other director felt more out of step with the early Reagan years. The problem is the film just doesn't seem to go anywhere – characters cross and re-cross the border without any sense of urgency.

Critics were divided. *Films* dismissed Tony's handling of the material as weak and half-hearted; there was nothing for the audience to respond to, nothing to draw it in: 'This is a film which should, in theory, build in intensity until Nicholson goes on his crusade to find the abducted child and then explode with violence and bloodshed, leaving the audience exhausted, purged and fully on the side of the hero. In Richardson's incapable hands though it bumps and grinds along. Richardson hasn't made an effort, or if he has then it doesn't show'. *Variety* described Tony's direction as 'uninspired', but *The Hollywood Reporter* said the cast worked flawlessly together under his direction and the film had an expansiveness that came from judicious use of the Texas terrain. *Rolling Stone* found its 'depiction of the corruption rife in the border patrol [to be] devastating and damning'. Michael Sragow declared this 'Goya-like mural of bloodshed and corruption' was Tony's 'most powerful piece of filmmaking yet', adding never before had 'this British filmmaker worked so comfortably in an American milieu'.

The moderate success of this studio picture at last gave Tony a flame to warm his hands by. He now had a bit of heat to make the film he really wanted to do next, an adaptation of John Irving's *The Hotel New Hampshire*.

Notes

1. *New York Times*, 20 February 1974.
2. Wallace, Mike. 'Vanessa Redgrave Interview', CBS News: *60 Minutes*, 3 June 2007.
3. Wallace, Mike. 'Vanessa Redgrave Interview', CBS News: *60 Minutes*, 3 June 2007.
4. Callow, Simon. 'The Talented Mister Redgrave', *The Times*, 10 April 2010.
5. 'Vanessa and the Red House Mystery', *Observer*, 28 September 1975.
6. Morley, Sheridan. 'Tony Richardson's West Country Vaudeville', *The Times*, 16 March 1977.
7. Mike Medavoy, interview, 22 June 2009.
8. Rose, Tiffany. 'When Death Was Too Lifelike For Natasha', *Express On Sunday*, 16 September 2007.
9. Young, Lucy. 'Tasha Takes Off', *Sunday Independent*, 4 September 2005.
10. Hamill, Dennis. 'Her Life Is a Cabaret: Showgirl Natasha Richardson, Heiress to a Showbiz Legacy, Is Now a Broadway Star', *New York Daily News*, 15 March 1998.

11. 'Now It's Vanessa, Scourge of Desperate Dom's Enemies', *Daily Mail*, 22 February 1978.
12. Harding, Norman. *Staying Red: Why I Remain a Socialist*, Index Books, London, 2005.
13. Michelson, Judith. 'Vanessa Redgrave Still Seeks...', *Los Angeles Times*, 19 March 1985.

CHAPTER SEVENTEEN

The Floating Houseparty

Natasha always wished that her crazy childhood had been different: the pattern of benign neglect that Vanessa herself had suffered as a child was repeated as her political work took her away from the family, leaving the girls to fend for themselves. Looking back, she realised the children suffered; her justification was that she could only concentrate on one thing at a time and she just didn't know how to juggle all her responsibilities.[1] In truth, she simply wasn't a good mother – she could not cope with the children. Rehearsing *Daniel Deronda* in Manchester when Natasha was six and Joely was five, Vanessa admitted: 'Actually truthfully, I'm glad I haven't got them at the moment.'[2]

After the divorce in 1966, the girls had a schizophrenic childhood. During weekdays, they were with Vanessa in their plain Hammersmith semi-detached. Life was mundane. At weekends, they were transported to a whirl of social activity and drama at Egerton Crescent – Tony was always slipping his daughters huge sums of money to go and blow at Harrods.

From the age of six, both girls attended the Lycée Français in South Kensington. 'The Lycée was my father's decision – he was very clever in insisting that we go to that school because he wanted us to both to have a second language under our belts before we had time to realise we'd learnt one,' said Joely. Every weekday morning Vanessa and the girls would cram into the back seat of a Morris Traveller, with Carlo strapped into a baby seat in front. At the time Vanessa couldn't drive so the nanny would take the girls to school. Natasha then transferred to the smart, private St Paul's Girls' School in Hammersmith, leaving Vanessa open to criticism that in calling herself a Communist, she was a hypocrite. The oscillations became wilder once Tony moved to Los Angeles: life there seemed one long party, the opposite of being shut up in a drab, unkempt semi-detached in west London.

A short and plump, domestically minded child surrounded by unpredictable adults, Natasha became the pivot of a fragmented family, stubbornly fashioning order out of chaos from the age of twelve in a reaction to all the uncertainly surrounding her. 'When I was younger, I always thought of myself as older than my years, or wanting to be older,' she revealed. She also began comfort eating and would sit in front of the television, working her way through packets of chocolate biscuits. Tellingly, her favourite programme was *The Waltons*, the saccharine American series about a close-knit family: she wanted to be a member of the Walton family, living a routine, normal existence.

By the time Natasha was seventeen, she weighed nearly 12 stone and this in turn affected her self-esteem. In her heart, she always remained that frumpy, overweight teenager longing to be glamorous and sexy.[3] 'I turned my anger into sadness and eating,' she recalled. And because she was greedy, she learned to cook: Natasha started to read cookbooks the way other pubescent girls read Jilly Cooper novels. Family friends remember the teenager cooking massive and regular meals for the floating houseparty at Le Nid du Duc. 'She would go down to the market at St Tropez, bring back boxes of food, and suddenly there would be roast lamb and potatoes for thirty people,' recalled author Fiona Lewis.

Natasha also developed an allergic reaction to Vanessa's chronic lateness – she remembered her mother as always being terribly late for everything. It was another manifestation of what Tony called Vanessa's 'absent-mindedness', but others interpreted this as her selfishness. This in turn made Natasha pathologically early for things: 'I can't bear being late – it seems very rude,' she admitted.

Growing up, Joely also craved a normality that she simply could not have. She didn't enjoy her gipsy-like existence shuttling between Tony and Vanessa. Furthermore, she didn't want her mother to be wild, extraordinary and difficult – she just wanted a cosy mum.[4] Joely savoured a dream of belonging to a more humble dynasty, the Bisto Kids. Gravy adverts on television used to show a family getting together over the Sunday roast. 'I wanted to be born into the Bisto family, drinking Horlicks, laughing round the fire. Who doesn't?' she shrugged.

Joely dropped out of the Lycée – which during the Seventies was a notoriously tough school – in the autumn of 1975 when she was nine, joining Natasha at St Paul's. Like lots of little girls, her first two obsessions were for gymnastics and skating. As a teenager, she developed Tony's passion for tennis. A middling student, she quit St Paul's when she was fourteen and wanting to become a Wimbledon champion, she transferred to the prestigious Saddlebrook Tennis Academy in Tampa, Florida. She stayed for two years before Tony, alarmed at how badly she was doing academically, moved her to yet another boarding school in artsy Ojai (as in 'Oh, hi'), half an hour from Los Angeles.

If Natasha was the homebody with her lists and cookery books, then Joely was the tomboy. Just as Corin was jealous of Vanessa and Michael, Joely resented how close her sister was to their father. They were so close, she felt an outsider.[5] And Tony was the one from whom she sought approval – his opinion counted above all else. Tony, though, made no secret of his preference for Natasha and Joely never got over her feelings of being second best; she used to think he wished she was more like Natasha – less rebellious, less obnoxious. 'Natasha was the golden girl in his eyes, the firstborn. I think I irritated him a lot of the time,' she said. She and Tony had some blistering rows. People said they were too similar and that was why they clashed. Joely also argued with Vanessa.[6] Looking back, Joely surmised that Tony didn't think she had the right attitude. Her father explained that the reason why he was so hard on her was because he wanted her to be perfect. 'The trouble was that I wanted to be perfect for him. And, of course, there's no such thing,' Joely revealed.

Meanwhile, Vanessa was still away campaigning a lot of the time. She herself estimated that out of the six months she was on the road promoting the second documentary she'd made, *Occupied Palestine*, she only spent 17 nights at home (Carlo was twelve and Joely and Natasha were fifteen and seventeen respectively). In fact, her mother being so political put Natasha off politics for the rest of her life – not that she was a Conservative just that she was not politically active or motivated.

Acting jobs dried up for Vanessa following her Oscar speech but she remained unrepentant. 'I don't regret what I said,' she insisted, 'but one regrets enormously that people would not wish to employ me because of my support for the Palestinians.'[7] The phone stopped ringing. Considering she was at the height of her powers, this was a terrible loss for theatre and film. Lynn was appalled by the way her sister had been blacklisted.

But then came a call from the Boston Symphony Orchestra early in 1982, hiring Vanessa to narrate Stravinsky's opera-oratorio *Oedipus Rex* between 15 and 17 April. The orchestra offered to pay her $31,000. However, two weeks before the concert was due to take place, the BSO announced it was cancelling the performances: the management felt it had no option but to cancel, given the opprobrium surrounding Vanessa. There were rumours of threats and protests from Jewish groups. Some of the orchestra, many of whom were Jewish, signed a private petition in support of Vanessa's right to hold her opinions, but criticised the management for picking her in the first place. The BSO offered to pay Vanessa a $27,500 cancellation fee.

Four days later Vanessa announced that she was to sue the BSO for breach of contract for $5 million (the sum was eventually lowered to $1 million). She charged that her orchestra appearance was cancelled because of her support for the PLO. 'If such threats and tactics are successful, it can happen to others,' she declared while claiming the cancellation had caused her, 'substantial pain and suffering, emotional distress and turmoil.' At the same time, she also accused prominent Boston businessman Irving Rabb, a leader of the local Jewish community and a member of the orchestra's board of trustees, of hatching the plan to dump her. Rabb and another unidentified man had exerted pressure on the Symphony's general manager, argued Vanessa's lawyer.

Two years later, the case went to court. Vanessa's lawyer Daniel Kornstein sought to heighten the sense of drama by depicting the case as being one between 'one of the world's greatest symphonies and one of the world's greatest actresses'. Kornstein contended the BSO had called off her performance after Rabb objected to her pro-Palestinian views. The courtroom took on something of the atmosphere of the theatre as Vanessa sat erect at a table next to the witness box. Dressed in a simple gray wool coat, she listened intently. The BSO countered that she had deceived the orchestra's management – they were unaware she had not performed in the US for six years because of previous threats against her. Her support for the PLO meant she was constantly surrounded by turmoil. Taking the stand, Vanessa testified that she'd earned no money as an actress since the BSO's decision and revealed how her acting fee had dropped to $60,000 (before she'd earned $200,000 for *Camelot*, $125,000 for *Julia* and $100,000 for *The Devils*). As she described the financial cost of her personal beliefs, she began to cry and a recess was called so that she could compose herself.

The jury of one man and four women took eight-and-a-half hours to reach its verdict at the end of the three-week trial, awarding Vanessa

$100,000 in damages. But they rejected her second contention, that the orchestra had violated her civil rights by blacklisting her for political reasons. Once again, both sides claimed victory. Vanessa's lawyer argued she'd struck a blow by standing up for the rights of artists. Meanwhile, the BSO crowed that the jury had found the orchestra innocent of hounding Vanessa for her beliefs. However, it was ordered to pay her original $27,500 cancellation fee. Four months later, in February 1985, a Federal judge threw out the $100,000 jury award, ruling the BSO could not be held liable for damages to Vanessa's career. US District Judge Robert Keeton also ordered her to pay the BSO's court costs. The irony was that it was Vanessa herself who had appealed the original decision. Now she was left with even less than if she'd just accepted the BSO cancellation fee in the first place. Still she would not back down. In October 1987, a three-member panel of the US First Circuit Court of Appeals restored $12,000 of the original $100,000 thrown out by Judge Keeton. The three-man panel also agreed with Vanessa that her civil rights had been violated under the never-used Massachusetts Civil Rights Act. The BSO appealed again and on 31 August 1988, the full US First Circuit Court of Appeals listened to Vanessa's case. This time the appeals court ruled by three to two that the BSO had not violated her civil rights. Bob Sullivan, the orchestra's lawyer, expressed relief that the case was finally over – the First Circuit Court of Appeals had done a rare thing in reversing its own earlier decision. Undaunted, Vanessa took her argument over a $31,000 fee all the way to the Supreme Court. On 23 January 1989, the Supreme Court declined to review the Federal appeals court ruling, though.

The Boston Symphony Orchestra case left Vanessa to face legal bills of £250,000 (£492,500 in today's money) and she didn't do anything for her public image by accepting a donation of $150,000 from a Saudi Arabian prince. Film parts, though, began slowly trickling back. One of her first was in James Ivory's *The Bostonians*, in which she played a Boston bluestocking that she based on Cousin Lucy, the Kempson cousin she had stayed with during the war. Ivory remembered that during the meeting where they discussed the role she was to play, Vanessa abruptly changed the topic to the WRP, hitting him for a donation. 'Her voice got deep and remote,' said Ivory. 'It was like an oracle coming out of a cave. I found myself in this grotesque position of writing out a cheque for $50 for a political party whose whole mission was to overthrow practically every institution in Western civilisation, but there was no way around it.'

Corin too noticed the funny blank look that Vanessa gets in her eyes, as though a light has been flicked off inside her head. 'She just switches off,' he said. 'It's a very strange thing – she's done it for as long as I can remember.'

Then, in February 1984, Vanessa was cast opposite Sarah Miles and Diana Dors in an adaptation of Nell Dunn's play *Steaming*, directed by Joseph Losey. However, the two did not get on. At one point, Losey became so enraged that he threw his script in Vanessa's face.[8] One day, Vanessa announced she would not be turning up for work the following morning because she had to attend a political meeting. Losey lost his temper, drawing her attention to the conditions in her contract. What was heartbreaking was that Losey was so clearly dying of cancer and he was directing from a wheelchair, attended by a doctor and two nurses. This was to be his last film: on 22 June 1984, he died of liver cancer.

Vanessa attempted to regain some control when it came to filming one of the final scenes: all the cast were to strip off and enter a plunge pool together. She refused. Losey and Vanessa began arguing again. At one point, he became so frustrated he tried to push her in himself. After much wearisome haggling, Vanessa stripped and took the plunge. Losey's friend Dirk Bogarde wrote to film critic Dilys Powell that despite being so 'beastly' to Losey, she had once again turned in a radiant performance. 'Why is she such a ninny?' Bogarde wondered.

Lynn too was in litigious mood: in October 1981, she sued the Hollywood studio Universal for firing her after she breastfed her baby in a dressing room. Lynn claimed she'd been sacked from the sitcom *House Calls* because she had suckled her then infant daughter Annabel during filming hours. Rachel too had appeared in the show – cast, inevitably, as Lynn's mother. Universal, however, said the dispute was really about money: the studio claimed Lynn was trying to double her salary. Lynn said she was certain Vanessa supported her stand. 'I disagree with her views on almost everything but acting and motherhood,' she said. The Hollywood Women's Press Club, though, nominated Lynn for a Sour Apple award for 'confusing motherhood with publicity.' The case mired her in a legal wrangle that cost her half a million dollars ($754,516 in today's money) in legal fees. Her suit became a Dickensian tangle of cross-complaints, countersuits and allegations of malpractice. In the end, she lost the case and the 13-year legal battle bankrupted her. 'It has been an absolute nightmare from the beginning, with us running into a series of legal roadblocks at every turn,' admitted her husband, John Clark. For her part, Lynn revealed the case had damaged her career: 'It wasn't exactly that I was blacklisted, but Hollywood is the smallest town in the world and Universal is the most powerful studio in the world, and it just became more convenient not to hire me.' Yet for all Vanessa's dreary earnestness, it was Lynn who affected the greatest change in working women's lives: her case became a cause célèbre for American mothers and she was called on to give evidence to Congressional committees. From then on, American politicians were mindful to include pro-breastfeeding statements in their election manifestos.

While Vanessa was suing the Boston Symphony Orchestra and Lynn was suing Universal Pictures, Tony was trying to raise money for his next film. *The Hotel New Hampshire* was John Irving's follow-up to his bestselling novel, *The World According to Garp*. Irving's book tells the story of the Berry family. Win Berry, the head of the family, is a heedlessly dreaming father who makes a disastrous investment in a New England hotel. The second half of the book follows the family's misadventures when it migrates to Austria to run a hotel there. One way or another, all of the characters have been wounded sexually – indeed, one lesbian character, abused as a child, disguises herself as a bear. The narrator is Win's son John, who has an incestuous affair with his sister Franny; his brother Frank is gay, while his younger sister Lily is a precocious dwarf who eventually commits suicide.

Tony believed Irving to be one of the most original and talented of contemporary writers, a storyteller in the tradition of Fielding and Dickens. He immediately saw *The Hotel New Hampshire* as a movie – for him it sprang off the pages as a natural film. The extended Berry family, consisting of homosexuals, incestuous siblings and dwarves appealed to him enormously. What particularly attracted him to the book was that it was an affirmation: 'It's about going on. It says that, however vividly you've imagined your dreams, life is never as good but you must live with everyday life.' Tony shared his enthusiasm for the novel with Norman Twain, the theatre producer who had overseen the American tour of *Hamlet*. Twain ran into Irving by chance and communicated Tony's enthusiasm. In turn, Irving was flattered that a filmmaker as eminent as Tony wanted to adapt his novel – he loved his films. Neil Hartley borrowed $200,000 to buy the rights and Tony set about adapting the novel himself. Some critics had recoiled at the degree of sexual farce in the novel. Not Tony: for him, it couldn't be sexual or farcical enough – he saw the novel as a sexual can-can.

Twain then introduced Tony and Hartley to Gene Bicknell, a pizza tycoon who eventually owned the world's largest Pizza Hut franchise. Bicknell had already put money into a couple of films, including *Rooster: Spurs of Death!* in 1982. The Pittsburgh-based pizza entrepreneur was represented by a lawyer who said he used to work for 20th Century Fox and mentioned he represented a family trust fund which might also put money into the movie. Bicknell repaid the money Hartley had borrowed to buy the rights – so far, so good.

Elizabeth McGovern was originally cast as Franny and Timothy Hutton her narrator brother. Mel Brooks was talked about as playing Freud, Win Berry's mentor who owns a performing bear. At this point, Tony wanted Twain out of the movie. Despite having only introduced the parties, Twain expected to be paid. Such intermediaries – who often call themselves 'executive producers' – are common in independent film financing. This was, however, a new world for Tony. 'I'd secured the rights and brought the money, so he didn't need me anymore," said Twain. Tony summoned Twain to dinner at New York's Algonquin Hotel, where he told him that McGovern was unable to work with him. This came as a surprise – Twain had never even met the actress. In turn, Twain pleaded with Tony he needed the fee as he'd only discovered that day his wife was pregnant. 'Tony showed as much remorse as O. J. Simpson,' said Twain.[9]

Tony then went to see his old friend Arthur Krim from United Artists, who had set up again with Orion Pictures, essentially United Artists Mk II. Krim offered to put up two-thirds of the budget in exchange for the North American rights (Tony would have to find the other third of the budget himself). At the airport following the Orion meeting, Bicknell's lawyer accepted with alacrity the offer of a free seat back to Los Angeles in exchange for taking a later flight. Not the action of somebody who controlled millions of dollars, thought Tony. Alarm bells started ringing inside his head. Although Bicknell was just the financier, he started offering Tony advice. 'Even the pizza man has an opinion!' said Tony.[10] Back in Los Angeles, the lawyer tried to get Tony to sign a document handing control of the project to Bicknell. Tony refused and following this, the lawyer turned up at the 1478 King's Road accompanied by a strong-arm heavy. The goon threatened to break Tony's legs but Tony stood his ground. Eventually, the pair retreated, half-heartedly smashing up Tony's office on their way out. It emerged that the lawyer had inveigled Bicknell into a pathetic scam, making him believe he would own a $12 million movie for an outlay of a couple of hundred thousand dollars.

Realising the family trust fund was just fantasy, Tony went back to Orion having shaved one-third off the budget. The distributor could now have the whole film for the same outlay, he offered. However, nobody at Orion apart from Krim had any enthusiasm for the project. Krim, however, stuck to his word: if Tony could find the other third of the budget, then Orion would cover the rest. Tony was now thrown into the shark-infested water of indie film finance. For the first time in his life, he could not rely on a studio to fully finance his movie. He approached London-based sales agent J&M Entertainment, whose job it was to sell off each distribution territory in advance. Slowly, this patchwork of cash advances would be sewn together, moving the film into production. Hartley once tried to explain to Irving how the film was being financed. 'He might as well have been describing the pleasures and perils of hang-gliding to a mole,' Irving commented drily.

Tony began assembling his core team around him: David Watkin was once again cinematographer and Jocelyn Herbert production designer. Tony told Watkin that this time he wanted 'a Norman Rockwell look.' He and Hartley had decided to shoot *The Hotel New Hampshire* in Canada because it was cheaper there. Herbert's job was to somehow make various Canadian locations stand in for parts of New England, Manhattan *and* Vienna.

Production was looming and the finance kept collapsing. Tony plugged the last bit of the budget with $2 million of his own money. He took out a mortgage on King's Road to keep production going, reassuring his cast and crew that everything would be all right. In truth, the production could fall apart at any moment. 'It was the one time I saw him in such an uncertain situation,' said Watkin. The sheer effort of appearing upbeat all the time was draining. When shooting eventually began, Tony estimated the lawyers and brokers had been paid double what the cast were getting and he himself was still several hundred thousand dollars out of pocket by the time the film was released.

Jodie Foster agreed to play Franny. It was her first role after the trauma of being stalked by John Hinckley. He had become obsessed with Foster after watching her play a teenage prostitute in *Taxi Driver* (1976), a film in which Robert De Niro plays a loner who is determined to impress her by assassinating a politician. Hinckley followed Foster to Yale University where she was studying, slid poems and messages under her door and plagued her with phone calls. He then tried to assassinate President Reagan on 30 March 1981, describing his assassination attempt as 'the greatest love offering in the history of the world.'

She loved how joyous Tony's script was and stuck by the production even when she had to lower her fee. 'Tony's an incredibly interesting, fascinating man, and very funny,' she said. However, Foster rowed with him when he asked her to appear naked: her contract stipulated no nude work. Tony fixed her with his bird-of-prey eyes. 'Someday when you're ready to really be an actor, then you'll be completely free to be who you are,' he told her. At the time, Foster thought Tony was behaving like a jerk and it was only later when she realised that he was trying to encourage her self-confidence. 'He'd get you into trouble,' she recalled. 'He'd force you to laugh too loud, take big leaps off big buildings. I felt that he was asking too much of me because I couldn't make art that fun. Looking back, I just wasn't ready.'

Rob Lowe was eventually chosen to play John after Tony tested dozens of actors. Nastassja Kinski was cast as Susie the Bear after Tony heard that the German-born actress considered herself unattractive. Eighteen-year-old Joely made her screen debut in a cameo as a hotel waitress. The cast stayed in a small Montreal hotel, eating meals together in the disused convent the unit had taken over. Everyone soaked up the quirky, offbeat atmosphere Tony engendered. Between takes, Foster, Lowe and Kinski eased the long hours by playing practical jokes on each other. They shot a fake porn video and gave it to Tony, who encouraged the fooling around.

Charming and utterly mad, one can see why Tony was so drawn to *The Hotel New Hampshire*. Irving's fanciful and dreamlike attack on American respectability provided him with his most personal material. More than any other of his films, *Hotel* reflected his personality. Gavin Lambert thought the reason why the finished film felt so rushed was because it was made on the express orders of Tony's subconscious. This oddball family and its tangled sexual relationships reflected the Redgraves themselves; it was as if the characters represented Tony's ideal family, his dream of a group which embraced their different sexual orientations with an openness he admired but could never really share. Lindsay Anderson thought *Hotel* was 'tremendously redolent of Tony's wilful, extravagant personality – in other words, much better than it was taken to be. If only he had not had those ambitions to write his own scripts. But there was a strange arrogance about him, which preferred to fail on his own terms rather than succeed on anyone else's.' Meanwhile, the author himself thought that Tony had captured the book's fairy-tale qualities. 'He had a good time with it,' said Irving. 'It's a book that I wrote for people to have a good time with.' Irving was also of the view that Tony was 'too original to be nice, not concerned with good taste, nor careful whom he offended.'

Once again, Tony's vision of an alternative America was completely out of step with Reagan's White House. *Hotel* celebrated a rainbow tent of sexuality – interracial and incestuous, as well as gay and lesbian at a time when Republicans were slashing funding for gay rights. The Sixties seemed a long way away. 'This is the film equivalent of a hippy picnic,' wrote critic Chris Auty, 'rambling across the landscape in a slight daze, and finding it beautiful and sad.' However, most critics hated it. 'Richardson packs too many sardines into the tin; the movie looks squeezed, shapeless, jumbled,' wrote David Denby in *New York* magazine. Others were more kind. Surprisingly, the right-leaning *Daily Mail* said that Tony had returned to '*Tom Jones*-like form' after too long a run of indifferent movies. The *Sunday Times* agreed: 'Richardson has the rare ability to sum up a person or a relationship with a telling phrase or gesture. The film is directed with intelligence and cunning'. And its sister paper, *The Times*, enthused, 'Tony Richardson, with a skilful and skilfully selected cast, manages a formidable juggling feat in sustaining the multiplicity of characters and incidents. He still retains, though, his old capacity to surprise with sudden banalities. Such failings though were always concomitant with the ambition and nerve which makes Richardson one of the most valuable British figures of his generation'.

By now, Natasha and Joely had both entered the family business, so to speak. In the early Eighties, they were studying at drama school – Natasha was attending Vanessa's alma mater, Central School of Speech and Drama, while Joely was at RADA. Tony joked that he bred his daughters like racehorses to become champion actresses. Now it was his turn to step back and let his daughters move centre stage.

Notes

1. 'Dear Natasha', *New York Post*, 22 March 2009.
2. *Guardian*, 1 January 1969.
3. Pacheco, Patrick. 'A Play Against Type', *Los Angeles Times*, 18 April 1999.
4. Crampon, Robert. 'Sleeping Beauty', *The Times*, 24 July 2004.
5. Vincent, Sally. *Independent Magazine*, 25 September 1993.
6. Thwaite, Jazz. 'Truth Behind My Pap Pix – "I've Come a Long Way Since Being Called a Bag Lady" – Joely Richardson', *Sunday Mirror,* 12 January 2003.
7. Sheridan, Peter. 'Vanessa Redgrave – Grief And No Regrets But Now the Rebel Bully May Finally Be Forgiven', *Daily Express*, 20 February 2010.
8. Hastings, Chris. 'Attenborough's An Idiot, Redgrave's a Ninny', *Sunday Telegraph*, 18 June 2006.
9. Norman Twain, author interview, 12 February 2010.
10. Irving, John. *My Movie Business: A Memoir*, Bloomsbury, London, 1999.

CHAPTER EIGHTEEN

Family Business

Sometimes it seemed as if Natasha and Joely Richardson were not so much born into the theatre, as given birth by it. Natasha inherited that hesitant, throaty, absurdly familiar voice which, like a grandfather clock or a necklace, had been handed down from her mother. She herself had known she wanted to be an actress since the age of six, although she went through a phase of wanting to become an airline stewardess during her unhappy early teenage years when she craved normalcy. 'Like any person whose family is involved in a particular business, you either go along with it or you rebel against it,' she explained.

Natasha was quite single-minded about her career: she dropped out of St Paul's when she was sixteen so that she could sit her A-levels in one year at a crammer and then go on to drama school a year early. In 1980, Natasha followed her mother to the Central School of Speech and Drama. Once there, she didn't think much of the teaching. She took classes like 'Animal Study', where she would observe an animal and then reproduce its movements in class: she picked a potoroo – 'the most obscure animal I could find' – and spent most of her time in the zoo cafe drinking coffee and smoking cigarettes. When the teacher came around, Natasha did a doubletake of her hand and made a funny hand movement. Animal Study did not seem to have much to do with becoming somebody else and so she turned to Stanislavski in her spare time, just as her mother and grandfather had done before her.

Leaving drama school and looking to get her first job in regional theatre, she found her rarefied childhood more of a hindrance than help. 'Having met Jack Nicholson doesn't do you a whole lot of good,' she said ruefully. Her first professional acting job was at the Leeds Playhouse in 1983. After performing three plays in as many months she obtained her Equity card. 'The "family profession" thing used to tense me up before auditions because I found that you're put under the microscope even more,' she said. Her first London acting job was playing Helena in a Regent's Park production of *A Midsummer Night's Dream*, the role in which Lynn made her stage debut.

Briefly in England, Tony attended the first night. He then asked Natasha to drive him to Heathrow early the following morning. In the car, he said: 'I'm pleased to see you've got talent, and I'm pleased to see you move very well, but that's not all there is to it.' He then proceeded to shred her performance all the way to the airport. 'And I'd thought I was so wonderful,' Natasha remembered. 'I cried, made excuses – and tried to keep the car on the road. He said I must find something more interesting than myself in the character.' The next day she received a Fed-Exed copy of the Shakespeare play, which Tony had marked up with suggestions.

Natasha said that Michael was a very shadowy figure in her childhood. When she did see her grandfather, she always felt slightly in awe of him. Now enfeebled by Parkinson's Disease, he was taken in a wheelchair to watch a matinee performance of the Young Vic *Hamlet* in which Natasha played Ophelia. He sat at the back, watching the play unfold. By then he could hardly speak, although he managed to tell Vanessa, after a painful silence which lasted the whole way home: 'She is a true actress.' The very last play Michael watched was *Hamlet*, the play in which he'd had the role of Laertes when Olivier announced Vanessa's birth, 48 years ago. Having anointed another generation, Michael died the following week in a nursing home on 20 March 1985, one day after his 77th birthday. Lynn was happy that she'd made her peace with Michael before he died. 'It meant a fantastic amount to me, and was important to him, too, I think,' she said. 'I was able to reach out, and he accepted it.' The Redgraves may have rejoiced in each other's achievements, but they still left his ashes unclaimed for eight years in the crematorium.[1]

Then there was Michael's shadow: it was as if Corin couldn't get past his father's reputation when he was still alive. Only after his death could he come into his own. The collapse of the Soviet Union in 1991 speeded up Corin's rehabilitation; being a Trotskyite now seemed as quaint as being Amish. Within a few years, Corin's rebirth was complete. Some people, including his sister Lynn, saw the connection. 'Now there's a power in knowing that what Corin does on stage is his own thing,' she said. Corin had found having one of England's greatest actors as his father cripplingly inhibiting – everything he did was compared to him. 'Corin grew into the most wonderful actor. It must have been so difficult for him having such a brilliant actor as a father,' said Rita Tushingham.[2] Intriguingly, some of his later stage successes were in roles associated with Michael, including Crocker-Harris in *The Browning Version*, Frank Elgin in *The Country Girl* and *King Lear* for the RSC. How could Corin have possibly surpassed his father when he was alive? He also played Coriolanus at the Young Vic opposite Rachel as Volumnia, fulfilling a teenage dream of Michael's to play the role opposite his own mother, Daisy. (Vanessa in turn played Volumnia in the movie version.)

Theatre critic Michael Billington agreed with Lynn: 'If he enjoyed a golden theatrical rebirth from the late 1980s onwards, it may have been less to do with politics than with his determination to inherit the mantle of his revered father.' Corin too acknowledged Michael's death was liberating. 'Psychologically, there is a great problem for sons about being better than their fathers. If you surpass your father, in a way you kill him. I know that I consciously never took on, if I could avoid it, any part he had made his own,' he revealed. 'When someone is dead, you no longer feel any sense of rivalry. It's much more troubling, oddly enough, to think you might do something better than him. It's an Oedipal thing to feel as if you're killing him. So, subconsciously, if there's likely to be any comparison, you always just scale your performances that much below the level at which they would become murderous to your father. Once they're dead, you have no such inhibitions.'

A twenty-two-year-old Natasha made her West End stage debut in 1985. She was playing Nina in *The Seagull*, the part in which Vanessa had scored such a triumph directed by Tony, 21 years previously. She was even performing in the same Queen's Theatre. Eerily, Vanessa played her stage mother, actress Madame Arkadina. It was another instance of what the Redgraves' critics would dismiss as stunt casting – family members appearing with each other. Over the years, all the Redgraves would play opposite each other. Vanessa was not in the original touring production and it was only when Samantha Eggar dropped out that she unexpectedly joined the cast – the play was transferred from the Lyric Hammersmith in May to the Queen's Theatre at which point Vanessa replaced Eggar and Jonathan Pryce replaced John Hurt as the dissipated novelist Trigorin. According to Natasha, Vanessa rehearsed like a tornado: 'I was scared and very intimidated,' she recalled. She remembered watching dumbfounded as her mother rolled on the floor in some scenes. 'She just threw herself in at the deep end, like an abstract artist who's painting big, bold stripes of colour. I realised, watching her, that if you do dive into the deep end, all you have to do is swim to the shallow end. Back then, I was the opposite way around, doing baby steps toward the deep end.' The play's director Charles Sturridge was also taken aback. 'Vanessa throws the character around the room and gets into every conceivable corner of the part, not all of them logical. It's very noisy and adventurous and terrifying to watch, but it does fill you with ideas. It gives you 17 directions to go and 27 not to go in.'

As the first night approached, Natasha was terrified of being on stage with her mother: 'I was suddenly aware that I'm on stage with this overwhelming actress. It made me want to run and hide,' she admitted. Even worse, Natasha overheard a member of the first-night audience saying how she had copied her mother's mannerisms. Still, the audience applauded wildly. Vanessa couldn't resist a sideways glance and a beaming smile as Natasha stepped two paces in front of her – she said her pleasure in seeing Natasha play what had been her part was 'almost indescribable.' Critics compared mother and daughter in terms of their emotional strength and deep, un-actressy stage presence. However, being daddy's girl, it was Tony's praise that meant the most to her. 'My God,' he told her, 'you were better than your mother.' Natasha won that year's London Theatre Critics Award for Most Promising Newcomer.

Joely too was waiting in the wings. Although she had always joined in the theatricals at Le Nid du Duc, as a girl she had wanted to become an athlete. It was Tony who encouraged her to go into acting. Vanessa, meanwhile, tried to put her off – she knew what a tough business it could be.[3] As with Michael discouraging his youngest daughter Lynn, perhaps Vanessa subconsciously didn't want the competition. Joely applied to all the major English drama schools and was offered places at nearly half of them: she decided to go to the Royal Academy of Dramatic Art, London's most prestigious drama school. Other students resented what they saw as her easy ride through family connections. 'Oh well, you're a Redgrave,' said one. 'You'll get it all handed to you on a plate sooner or later. I suppose Mum will be helping you get a job when you finish here?'

Joely graduated from RADA in September 1985. Two months later, Vanessa took the train up to Liverpool to see her play the lead in Strindberg's *Miss Julie* at the Liverpool Playhouse. Considering it was her first acting job, this was an incredible break as well as a prestigious and difficult part – doubtless helped by her family name but Joely always insisted that being a Redgrave was more of a hindrance than anything else. Had she come from any other family, people would have congratulated her on how well she'd done. Instead, she'd always had more to prove. 'People think I had everything laid out on a plate, but everything I've achieved has come despite my family rather than because of it,' she said. Of course, her mother and her grandfather were a mighty hard act to follow and she admitted that if she thought about it too much, she'd just curl up in a foetal position. 'I've had to fight so hard, doubly hard, to establish any kind of career,' she said. 'There's no way I've gotten the work I'm getting because of my family – it's the reverse.'

In one of those strange connective moments, stretching back through the generations, Joely was living in digs just like the place where Vanessa herself had stayed in 1958 when she and Michael were playing *A Touch of the Sun*, where Michael and Rachel had first fallen in love 50 years previously and beyond that where Daisy Scudamore had stayed when she was touring the provinces of Edwardian England.

Just as Joely was making her stage debut in *Miss Julie*, Vanessa was blindsided by a sex scandal that split the Workers Revolutionary Party in two. Gerry Healy, seventy-three, had been accused of 'gross sexual misconduct' and had been expelled by the party he founded. Michael Banda, the WRP's new leader, said Healy had abused his position by having sex with at least 26 party comrades. 'He told the girls it was their revolutionary duty and they said, "I understand that, Gerry, but why dog fashion?"' said trade unionist Roy Lockett.[4] Healy, in the words of the party's West Croydon branch, turned the women, 'into his sexual slaves.' Banda said the figure probably represented only a fraction of what had gone on. *Newsline*, the party newspaper, accused Healy of the 'cruel and systematic debauchery' of women recruits and members. Healy's own secretary said he used the party offices for sexual liaisons and it transpired that Healy had slept with the daughter of two of his closest friends and then beaten her up, leaving her almost crippled.[5] One woman declared she had lost her faith when Healy forced his way into her bedroom. 'Everything I believed in was proved, in one revealing second, to be false, lies. I, my husband, my children, my comrades, had sacrificed so much for this animal,' she said.

Meanwhile, Vanessa and Corin rallied to Healy's defence. On 4 November 1985, Vanessa held a press conference during which she accused Healy's victims of lying (he himself had already denied all allegations to the Party's central committee). She said: 'These allegations are all lies and the women who are supposed to have made them are all liars. I don't care whether it's 26, 36 or 236, they are all liars.'[6] In turn, Banda blasted the Redgraves for defending 'the corrupt sexual practices of a "leader" who thinks nothing of abusing his political authority to degrade women and girl comrades.' Both sides met for one last time. Corin insisted what Healy did in his spare time was his affair and must be separated from his politics, adding that he was 'neither for, nor against rape' but 'for the social revolution.'[7] And so the Redgrave faction expelled Banda and one of his aides. Banda and his supporters, in turn, expelled the Redgraves. The new WRP leader described Vanessa's breakaway faction as a 'bogus WRP bereft of all credibility, detested and reviled by the vast majority of members.' So now there were two Workers Revolutionary Parties, each with its own newspaper and each fighting for control of the party's £1.5 million war chest, the majority of the funds having been donated by Arab supporters including Libya, Iraq and the Palestinian Liberation Organisation.[8] The WRP aligned itself with Islamists because it saw them as the shock troops of anti-Americanism. In the end, Vanessa and Corin were among the 150 WRP members who stuck by Healy, blaming MI5 propaganda for his downfall: they renamed their breakaway faction 'The Marxist Party'.

Corin said his political beliefs resulted in him being blacklisted by the BBC for 20 years. However, his longed-for Revolution never happened. Instead, the Berlin Wall came down and the Soviet Union collapsed. Work at the BBC trickled back. Corin said: 'People discovered that Marxism was no longer frightening; it didn't have to be something which was threatening so I was able to resume acting.' Film director Roger Michell believed that once the Berlin Wall came down, Corin put the dogmatism to bed. Corin may have stopped being so doctrinaire with other people, but he never gave up on his Marxist ideals. However, after Healy died suddenly, aged seventy-six of a heart attack while working at home in his study, he organised the funeral so that his mentor could be buried near Karl Marx in Highgate cemetery. 'If artists, actors, musicians and writers felt they ought to be celebrities and shut up, then the world would be a pretty awful place,' he said.

Corin's marriage to Deirdre collapsed and the couple divorced in 1974 (Jemma was nine and Luke was seven at the time). His wife had reached the point with his unforgiving politics where she had snapped. Corin moved out and started living in Vanessa's basement. 'Corin had become a completely other, detached person. Just as some people aren't there through drink or drugs, so it was with Corin and politics,' said her friend Danaë Brook.[9]

The divorce meant that Corin, like his father before him, was estranged from his children, both of whom reacted badly. Like Joely, Jemma just wanted a normal upbringing. Corin began living with Kika Markham, the actress who'd introduced him to the WRP in the first place (the pair met in London in 1976 at a mutual friend's flat). Their eldest son Harvey was born in 1979 and a second son, Arden (again, in a nod to *As You Like It*) arrived four years later. The divorce had been bitter: at one point Corin even tried to claim money from Deirdre, who was by then a single mother bringing up two children on her own.

After nearly a decade together, Corin secretly married Kika Markham in October 1985. Only family and close friends attended the Balham register office ceremony, including Rachel, Vanessa and Natasha. Kika's mother, children's writer Olive Markham, hosted a small reception at her Ashdown Forest, East Sussex home. Jemma eventually went to live with Corin and his second wife for four years before attending the London Academy of Music and Dramatic Art and for a short while afterwards. 'I was very grateful for that because it meant I could spend time with Jemma, unlike my father who didn't have any time for me,' said Corin. Their rundown terraced house in south London looked almost derelict from the outside, like a student squat. Inside, the heaps of dirty dishes covering every surface showed people who didn't have time for bourgeois niceties.

Norman Harding, one of their WRP comrades, always thought Kika was a better actress than Vanessa. She was more sensitive and warm compared to Vanessa, whom he found cold and humourless. When Harding told her this, Kika warned him never to say such a thing within Vanessa's earshot.[10]

That same year, Vanessa and Joely worked together for the first time. Joely played a younger version of Vanessa in David Hare's film *Wetherby*. Hare found directing Vanessa maddening. Because she did profound things so easily, Hare suspected she got bored: she was always fiddling with cups, flowers or pens in the naive belief they made her more authentic. She spent one long speech eating peanuts. When Hare asked her why, she said: 'Real people eat peanuts all the time.' Hare told Vanessa that she was the greatest emotional actress he had ever seen, so why mess herself up with props? After two takes, he became really angry. 'Put down those bloody peanuts!' he shouted.

Hare decided that Vanessa had a late-Victorian cast of mind: she believed in nouns with capital letters, words such as 'Youth', 'Art', 'Hope' and 'Oppression'. Sometimes it seemed as if she was trying to portray the history of Oppression through the female roles she chose, from Cleopatra to Mrs Alving in Ibsen's *Ghosts*. There was so much to do, so little time: she was so preoccupied with injustice that individuals didn't seem to register. Tony charitably described this as her 'absent-mindedness'.

Given Vanessa had burst into tears in court over how much distress and hardship she'd endured since her Oscar speech, one might have thought she would have had enough of Zionist-baiting. Not a bit of it. In April 1986, she urged Equity to blacklist Israel after its invasion of Lebanon following international condemnation of its actions. She circulated a petition asking Equity to tell its members not to perform there. This was not the first time that Vanessa had tried to organise an Equity boycott of Israel: she'd tried once before in June 1978, right in the middle of the *Julia* furore. That time, Hollywood producers and writers unreservedly condemned her. Nine years later, Israel labelled her proposal 'cultural terrorism'.

Hollywood actress Jane Fonda said how appalled she was by Vanessa's attempt to try and stop Western films and television shows going to Israel. Fonda described what Vanessa was doing as 'a vicious act'.[11] Meanwhile, Linda Yellen (an American producer who had made two television movies with Vanessa) said she felt utterly betrayed. Yellen ventured Vanessa just could not help stirring up trouble – it was her nature: 'It is just abhorrent that Vanessa is using the forum she has developed as an actress to spout these hateful political ideas,' she said.

By the mid-Eighties Tony was finding it more and more difficult to persuade anyone to fund the movies he wanted to make. His old studio United Artists had become a label of MGM, which itself was being passed from owner to owner like a game of pass the parcel, and the BBC wasn't at all interested when he tried to get work there as a jobbing director.[12] By this stage of his career, he couldn't even convince the box office of the Royal Court to cash him a cheque. He had no option but to start working in television – it was the only place where he could find work. Unlike many film directors, Tony never admitted that television was a comedown. Rather, he believed that TV was the future and approached it as another adventure (he called television, 'the medium of reality'). As far as he was concerned, film and television were just images on the screen. Working in television also allowed him to take a more discursive approach: it was the era of the television movie and miniseries – slower pacing and more limited resources actually suited him better, he said. 'You approach a movie for TV so differently than for the big screen – you give yourself more to TV. The pace can be more leisurely than a film. In a cinema, the audience wants instant and total entertainment,' he explained. The other great thing about television was that it gave him an audience again. No one would go and see your movie if it wasn't a must-see hit: in contrast, millions would watch a television show regardless. Television was as much a part of life as a freeway or an airplane, he said.

Tony had first ventured into television back in the winter of 1977, making a TV movie for CBS. For some time, he had been keen to make something on a small scale with American actors. A Death in Canaan told the true story of Peter Reilly, a seventeen-year-old boy manipulated by police into confessing that he had murdered his mother. People who knew Reilly banded together, believing the boy to be innocent. Local Connecticut celebrities including Mike Nichols, William Styron, Candice Bergen and Arthur Miller also spoke up. Finally, the verdict was reversed. Paramount first sent producers Bob Christiansen and Rick Rosenberg an article Miller had written about the case for the New York Times with the idea of making a feature film. One year later, Warner Bros. Television approached the duo again, this time with the idea of having Tony direct it for the small screen. The producers sent Tony a copy of investigative journalist Joan Barthel's bestselling book, A Death In Canaan, about the case. Rosenberg recalled: 'We sent off the Joan Barthel book and a preliminary script to Tony in the South of France. To our astonishment, he said he'd love to do it.' What attracted Tony to the project was that the long interrogation scenes – which had to be shot word-for-word – could only be done on television (a cinema audience would have become fidgety).

Stefanie Powers was to play Barthel. With its $1.5 million budget and tight 23-day shooting schedule, *A Death in Canaan* presented Tony with the limitations and challenges that had inspired his best work. He jettisoned some of the screenplay and went back to his Free Cinema roots, shooting scenes based on actual court records and lie detector transcripts; he also shot fast. He would block out elaborate scenes, rehearse them completely and then film them in just one take, murmuring at the end, 'Oh, fantastic, very good. Now, let's have a clear-out please and go on.' His cast certainly liked working with him. One actor was overheard exclaiming: 'I would die for that man!' The reviews were good, with critics fulsome in their praise of Tony for returning to the documentary feel of his Free Cinema days and the sense of injustice of *The Loneliness of the Long Distance Runner*. 'Underlying the whole production was the steady hand of Tony Richardson. Richardson turned in a standout job and much of the credit for the program's effectiveness seems the result of his sensitive helming,' said *Variety*. 'Tony Richardson's direction is qualified and composed of controlled substance, having a strong sense of latent indignation yet allowing the events to ensue at their own prodded pace,' agreed *The Hollywood Reporter*. *A Death in Canaan* was nominated for an Emmy at the 1978 Emmy Awards ceremony.

In 1986, Tony returned to television and made another TV movie for CBS in which Peter Strauss played a judge faced with the dilemma of freeing a convicted murderer when he realises the police may have violated the rapist's rights (the script was written by a judge serving in Orange County). However, *Penalty Phase* was not such a success. *The Hollywood Reporter* criticised Tony for making too much of the material – every sigh, utterance and aside was treated with 'portentousness, which sometimes edged into pretentiousness,' it said.

Still, his *Death In Canaan* star Stefanie Powers and producer Tamara Assayev were so impressed by Tony's speed and the way he handled actors that they asked him to direct *Beryl Markham: A Shadow on the Sun* the following year. Based on a *Vanity Fair* article by James Fox, *A Shadow on the Sun* told the story of Markham's torrid life and loves, including her historic East-West transatlantic flight. Tony spent the winter of 1987 shooting on location in and around Kenya. He brought the $11 million production in on schedule and under budget. *Variety* praised his shrewd direction, while the *New York Times* called the four-hour CBS miniseries, 'nearly always intriguing'.

In the summer of 1989, Tony began shooting a two-part, four-hour version of *The Phantom of the Opera* for US network NBC. Arthur Kopit who wrote the libretto for the Broadway musical *Nine* adapted the story – originally he had written his own musical version of *Phantom* only to be pipped to the post by Andrew Lloyd Webber. Instead, Kopit rewrote his version as a drama. Like *A Death in Canaan*, *Phantom of the Opera* was inspired by real events: in 1896, a massive seven-ton chandelier fell into an opera house audience, killing one woman and injuring many others. About the same time, author Gaston Leroux read about the mysterious kidnapping of a young singer and combined both events in his 1910 novel, *Le Fantôme de l'Opéra*. By the time Tony began filming in Paris, there had already been a dozen film versions.

Teri Polo, the actress who played the Phantom's opera singer inamorata, thought she'd flubbed the audition. Tony kept interrupting her, saying: 'No, no, no, darling, not so fast!' Charles Dance was cast as the Phantom and Burt Lancaster was to play the Phantom's father, a former manager of Opera (Lancaster nicknamed Tony 'the surgeon' because of his tendency to wring and flap his hands a lot).

Tony's production was all cloak and swagger: he saw *Phantom* as a big romantic love story rather than a horror movie and chose never to show the Phantom's disfigured face. Better to leave the horror to the imagination, he decided. Unfortunately, Dance's mask hugged his facial contours exactly, his sharp cheekbones glinting alluringly in the half-light, that the Phantom seemed to have come disguised as Charles Dance. Tony's was the first version to actually shoot at the Paris Opera and the director, who was not fond of heights, filmed the climax on the opera house roof, 160 feet above the street. The Phantom's watery lair was re-created at a stone quarry outside Paris. The $10 million budget may have been lavish by television standards, but Tony still had to shoot at a clip. Filming lasted for three months in the summer of 1989, with only three days off. Despite this, Tony appeared the opposite of the typically high-strung, pressured TV director: he seemed to move in slow motion. Wearing his trademark white jeans low on his hipless form, he would cajole the actors in his singsong voice and improvise changes in the shooting schedule when it suited him.

Like John Huston, Tony would listen carefully to his actors' ideas and might even try one but then he'd try the thing he had in mind all along. 'Marvellous director, brilliant ideas,' said Lancaster. And still he managed to bring the production in significantly under budget. The *New York Times* praised Tony for deftly capturing the fairy-tale aspects of the story. *Phantom* was eventually nominated for five Emmy Awards and two Golden Globes.

Tony found the pressure of television, the low budgets and short schedules, stimulating in a familiar way; the problem lay in the obtuseness of television executives. This was why it was important, he believed, that television should be freed from the corporations that had seized it. One of the problems with television, he said, was that you had to keep re-summarising the plot for those who had only just tuned in after the ad break. He was wary, however, of just being pigeonholed as a television director. Yes, it had been a good experience but there were few stories that lent themselves well to television movies, he said. Also, he probably didn't want to be seen as having moved permanently down the Hollywood totem pole: he had to re-establish his feature film credentials. Anyway, it was an open secret that everybody who worked in television really wanted to migrate to movies.

Tony's final work for television was an adaptation of Ernest Hemingway's story *Hills Like White Elephants* for pay-television channel HBO in December 1989. Very little happens in Hemingway's tale – a man and a woman sit talking in the restaurant of a Spanish railway station. Although nothing is spelt out, we realise the man is pressing the woman to have an abortion. Whatever she decides, the woman knows the relationship is doomed. Tony's friends Joan Didion and John Gregory Dunne had adapted the story for the mini-series *Women and Men: Stories of Seduction* (1990). James Woods and Melanie Griffith starred as the couple. Woods said most of the scripts he was sent were such nonsense that he jumped at the chance of working with Tony. But Tony felt so ill during shooting – for reasons that only later became apparent – that he couldn't talk to the press. One reporter was palmed off with the excuse that he was suffering from shingles. The reality, as would become clear, was far worse.

Notes

1. Roberts, Glenys. 'A Dynasty Where Dramas All Happen Offstage', *Daily Mail*, 4 March 1999.
2. Rita Tushingham, author interview, 8 December 2010.
3. Terry, Clifford. 'Family Business: Joely Richardson Found Becoming an Actress Was Relatively Easy', *Chicago Tribune*, 6 June 1991.

4. Turner, Adrian. *Robert Bolt: Scenes From Two Lives*, Hutchinson, London, 1998.
5. Pulan, Anna. 'Vanessa, Red Drama Queen', *Daily Express*, 22 December 2007.
6. Horsnell, Michael. 'Vanessa Redgrave Denies WRP "Lies"', *The Times*, 5 November 1985.
7. Harding, Norman. *Stay Red: Why I Remain a Socialist*, Index Books, London, 2005.
8. Ellis, Richard, Craig, Jon and Weir, Andrew. 'Far Left-Party Paid to Spy By Gaddafi', *Sunday Times*, 7 February 1988.
9. Danaë Brook, author interview, 8 December 2010.
10. Harding, Norman. *Staying Left: Why I Remain a Socialist*, Index Books, London, 2005.
11. 'Redgrave Campaigns for Actors' Boycott of Israel', *Los Angeles Times*, 9 April 1986.
12. Tony Garnett, author interview, 22 June 2009.

CHAPTER NINETEEN

Exit, Prospero

For his last film Tony returned to one of the recurring themes in his work, that of an unusual family. *Blue Sky* was a love story between a soldier and his sexy but unbalanced wife set against the background of an atomic-test cover-up in 1960 and within the closed society of military life. Like mother and daughter in *A Taste of Honey* or the Berrys in *Hotel New Hampshire*, the Marshalls are not your average nuclear family.

The script was sent by producer Robert Solo, the first person screen-writer Rama Blum submitted her unsolicited screenplay to – she had based the script on her own childhood growing up in the Army. Solo liked what she'd sent him and optioned the screenplay. He then got in touch with Tony and hired two more writers, Arlene Sarner and Jerry Leichtling. 'Tony felt very strongly that the film was a very personal story about a family rather than the subplot, which deals with atomic testing,' said Solo. Sarner and Leichtling were experienced profession-als, who largely re-wrote Blum's first draft. Sarner said of working with Tony, '[He] was relentlessly inquisitive about people's personal lives and the kind of writing you gave him was really much more personal than you wanted.'

Tony would talk to Blum about regrets in his own family life. 'Because it was a family story, there were times when he'd talk about his own marriage and family,' she remembered. 'He'd talk about major mistakes he had made in the past, and he admitted that at times he had been the culpable party.'[1]

Tony cast Jessica Lange, an actress whom Jack Nicholson once described as 'a delicate faun crossed with a Buick', as Carly and Tommy Lee Jones as Hank, her army scientist husband. Lange said that find-ing parts as good as Carly were 'as rare as hen's teeth.' The essence of Carly's character was her sexuality, she continued, describing her as manic-depressive or borderline crazy. 'Crazy women are always easiest to play. There's something in the playing of madness: it's very liberating.'

Filming began in Selma, Alabama in July 1990 – nine months after Solo first received the script. The budget was $15.6 million. Filming in the uncomfortable heat lasted for 10 weeks during which the temperature hit 95°C with 80 per cent humidity.

Lange liked the way Tony made her character complex enough so you didn't know whether to like or dislike her. 'I think that's brave on a director's part,' she said. 'Too many times people try to simplify.' She also admired how he staged scenes that crackled with energy. He was one of the few directors she'd come across who never used a monitor: he would stand right next to the camera and watch you. And she also enjoyed his fast way of working – he didn't have to do fifteen takes trying to figure out what the scene was all about. 'It was economical,' she said. 'He was one of those rare directors who knew what he wanted and knew how to get it.'

Tommy Lee Jones felt that Tony was perceptive about people and about actors. He didn't need to waste a lot of words to establish communication – he would just come over and whisper something like, 'Faster and funnier'. Jones described him as an artist full of surprises. 'It was a pleasure to keep Tony's company,' he said. 'He was a very funny man and a happy man. The last time I saw him, he was heading north out of Van Horn, Texas, toward Carlsbad in New Mexico because he wanted to see the caverns and never had.'

Tony's editor Robert Lambert remembered how important accuracy was for his director. 'At times, Tony could be painstakingly intense in his desire for realism,' he said. 'He liked non-perfectionism because he viewed the world as imperfect. In a sense, despite all his acclaim, he never felt he belonged. He was never truly accepted.'

Blue Sky was finally released three years after Tony finished editing it. The project was dealt a blow when the US distributor Orion Pictures declared bankruptcy: the film was locked in a bank vault in New York. Lange remembered her frustration: 'In the beginning it was very disappointing, then I quit dwelling on it because it was so completely out of my hands. There was no studio to even have a conversation with any more.' Orion only emerged from Chapter 11 bankruptcy protection in October 1992. It had several films gathering dust on its shelves, of which *Blue Sky* was one. 'Orion went through a really bad period of time, and when we came through the bankruptcy, we had nine films [waiting to be released],' Susan Blodgett, senior vice-president of marketing for the company, said later.

Blue Sky was very well received. Todd McCarthy of *Variety* praised it as 'a solid melodrama from the 1950s,' in which 'a small number of characters define themselves in terms of their interaction within well-proscribed physical and social limits'. *Newsweek*'s David Ansen wrote that *Blue Sky* felt 'like a Hollywood film from another era because of its belief that character can drive a movie. There is nothing more fascinating than the complexities of the human heart'. However, Orion did not have enough money to release the film widely, nor did it have any major publicity behind it and so *Blue Sky* was in and out of American cinemas within a couple of weeks. Blink, and you'd miss it.

It really is Jessica Lange's movie. Her energy level rivals the film's nuclear tests and she clearly relishes every wiggle. There's one sequence in particular when the family arrives at its new base posting and we see them drive past married quarters declining in grace and spaciousness until they pull up outside the glorified hut earmarked for them. Lange, whose mood has darkened throughout this parade of other people's status, explodes into a torrent of abuse and hysteria: indeed, her performance is so superheated it almost goes into meltdown. Carly Marshall herself becomes a bomb, spreading sexual fallout across the base. As Tommy Lee Jones observes, what he's dealing with here is unstable nuclear material. At the climax, she even dares a real atomic bomb to out-blast her.

Despite her amazing performance, it was still a surprise when Lange was nominated for Best Actress at the following year's Academy Awards. The Oscars are usually about studios thanking movies that have made them lots of money and the 67th Academy Awards were watched by almost a billion people in 100 countries worldwide. Tom Hanks opened the envelope and announced that Lange had won. Onstage, Lange gushed, 'Oh, I want to thank the Academy so much. This is such a wonderful honour, especially for a little film that seemed to have no future.' She received applause when she thanked Orion and again, when she praised Tony. 'He loved actors and he was the perfect person for me to work with, he just kept nudging me over the edge,' she later said backstage.

Natasha had come out to work as an assistant director herding extras during the shooting of *Blue Sky*. Once filming was over, she flew back to London to be with her fiancé, theatre producer Robert Fox. She had first met Fox five years previously during his production of *The Seagull* when she starred as Nina. Fox started his career as an assistant director at the Court. Natasha was twenty-two when they met, Fox thirty-three. He was also married with three children. Natasha anticipated trouble when she told her father that she and Fox were getting married. 'Why ruin a perfectly good four-year relationship with a vow that changes everything?' he asked. Tony and Vanessa both claimed they would still be together if they hadn't married.[2]

Fox, meanwhile, was producing John Osborne's latest play *Déjàvu* – his sequel to *Look Back in Anger*. Already, the National Theatre had rejected it. The obvious thing to do, thought Fox, would be to ask Tony to direct it. After all, the pairing of the original Angry Young Men and debuting *Look Back in Anger II* at the Royal Court would have enormous publicity value. 'Better the devil ...' Osborne muttered. Fox casually mentioned *Déjàvu* to Tony during one of his prospective father-in-law's rare visits to London. Tony read the script overnight. He then telephoned Osborne, telling him portentously: 'I think you've written the best play since *Look Back in Anger*.' Buddhists have a saying that you must never re-cross an old bridge: *Déjàvu* was a sad attempt by both men to revive the past. Max Stafford-Clark, the Court's artistic director, turned the play down. 'Hasn't he got any entrepreneurial flair?' Tony groaned when Fox informed him. Who should play Jimmy Porter then sparked another falling out. By October 1989, Tony was off the project.

In any case, Tony had his hands full organising Natasha's wedding. He treated it as another production to be mounted: the bride and groom would arrive on elephants and, as they hove into view, you'd cut back to the guests, all in fancy dress. Tony would be dressed as the Mad Hatter and Vanessa, no doubt, as the Red Queen. Natasha and Robert would drift away in a hot-air balloon (no run-of-the-mill going-away car for them). Natasha listened to her father's plans and got on with making her own arrangements – she knew it was all a fantasy inside Tony's head.

But father and daughter had a bust-up when he realised she wasn't taking him seriously: he began phoning her up and forced her to listen to him breathing down the phone in silence. The night before her wedding in December 1990, Natasha asked her father how she should behave. 'For God's sake, don't cry. It's not a day for parading your emotions,' she was told.

Natasha and Fox were married in the New York apartment of Joan Didion and John Gregory Dunne. She wore a creamy, ivory pant-suit with a décolletage down to her navel. After the civil ceremony, around ninety guests gathered at a nearby Italian restaurant on Lex-ington Avenue. Apart from the Redgraves and the Richardsons, other guests included Lauren Bacall, Paul Schrader and Buck Henry. Vanessa read a poem written by Lynn. Afterwards, an accordionist played, and Vanessa – not one to remain in the wings – tied a napkin around her head while she and Rupert Everett treated everybody to an impromptu duet of 'Edelweiss'.

Looking back, Natasha knew that throwing herself into a relation-ship so young was, like the comfort eating and the obsessive tidying, a reaction to her chaotic childhood. She had faced profound insecurity as a child, never knowing what was going to happen next. Perhaps she was in love with the idea of security as much as with Fox himself. On the other hand, she was little more than a child herself. 'I was with him for eight years and took on some responsibility for his three children,' she said. 'I was desperate to be thought of as older and as more inter-esting than I was, to be the good grown-up wife, trying to get the flow-ers right, the socks in the correct drawer. I did not spend my twenties out exploring or partying – I know that worried my dad enormously.'[3] A friend of hers described Natasha's married life at home as intimidat-ing: 'The china just so, drinks at six, dinner at eight.'[4] Tony's misgivings about the institution of marriage proved correct: Natasha's marriage would collapse less than two years later.

The same month that Natasha got married also saw Lynn back in London starring opposite Vanessa and their niece Jemma in Chekhov's *The Three Sisters*. The two sisters had first performed the final scene in a charity concert in New York to celebrate the collapse of the Berlin Wall; Corin also took part in 'The Wall Breaks' concert. Vanessa said: 'It was a very special moment that we were there in this scene playing real sisters.' The Chekhov production was first announced in March 1990. Joely was originally meant to play Jemma's part, but opted to appear in the Hollywood movie *King Ralph* instead, which filmed over the summer. Others thought having three Redgraves appear on stage together for the first time smacked of gimmickry: 'After 30 years of screaming about the inequities of British society with its inherited privilege, old-school ties and jobs for the boys, Miss Vanessa Redgrave has the nerve to flog her second-rate name five times over in a pathetic attempt to get bums on seats,' opined the *Daily Mail*. In fairness, the Redgraves had, over the years, rejected many offers for them to appear together. It shows how distant Vanessa and Lynn were that it was only during a dinner to discuss the production that they realised it was the first time they had ever been out for a meal together.[5] 'It's hard to understand, but my sister and I have a good relationship, only it's an unreal one,' observed Lynn.[6]

The First Gulf War began soon after *The Three Sisters* opened. Vanessa – who shook with unfeigned emotion when speaking her character's final lines in which she prayed for the advent of peace – flew to Barcelona on 13 January 1991 to address a rally on her day off. She called for, 'the withdrawal of US, British and all imperialist troops from the Gulf,' and added, 'We must unconditionally defend Iraq against American, British or Israeli troops.' A scandal ensued. People watching Vanessa in *The Three Sisters* started booing her on stage and the remark prompted Lynn to say she was thinking of changing her name from Redgrave in case people confused her with her sister.

One year later, Lynn had still not forgiven Vanessa for attacking her adopted homeland when she arrived in London to promote her book, *Diet for Life: How I Lost Weight and Learned to Stay Slim*. 'There are so many people here to thank,' she said, 'but most of all, I'd like to thank my sister Vanessa and my brother Corin for not being here.'[7] Meanwhile, Israeli audiences snubbed *Brecht In Exile*, an evening of work by Bertolt Brecht (Vanessa was to have played a Jewish woman living in Germany during the rise of the Nazis). One Israeli pundit said Vanessa's hatred for Israel was unprecedented, even among Western radical leftists. 'For decades, the famous English actress has missed no opportunity to condemn Israel. She opposed, with ruthless consistency, the very existence of the state of Israel,' wrote Yosef Lapid.[8]

Meanwhile, Vanessa accused British internal security service MI5 of bugging her private conversations. She had discovered a listening device hidden in an electrical socket in the Clapham house she shared with Corin. Vanessa called a press conference, where she said it was common knowledge that the security services bugged left-wing activists. She complained to the European Commission that MI5 had violated her rights but the human rights watchdog sided with the British government, saying that bugging radicals such as Vanessa was 'necessary in a democratic society.' Even if it had bugged her, MI5 would have been justified in doing so.[9] In any case, it turned out the bug had nothing to do with MI5 monitoring her as a subversive: a rival left-wing faction had planted the bug in her study.

Natasha said it never bothered Vanessa that she wasn't liked, which gave her mother enormous freedom.[10] 'It's very, very unrelenting,' sighed Robert Fox. With most actors, he said (referring to Jane Fonda), 'it's a phase, and then they marry Ted Turner.' With Vanessa, her activism was an identity that had ossified into hard, unrelenting granite.[11]

Meanwhile, the New York-based theatre group the Shubert Organization dropped Vanessa from its US national tour of *Lettice and Lovage*. She herself had suggested the idea of a touring version of Peter Shaffer's London hit play, which had starred Maggie Smith. When Smith refused to travel around America with the play, Vanessa stepped forward – perhaps that's what she'd had in mind all along. However, big protests were being planned to 'greet' Vanessa on each stop of the tour. Normally, the Shubert Organization wouldn't pay much heed to this kind of intimidation – all publicity was good publicity. How seriously they were taking the threats was summed up by one wag: 'The Shuberts would tour Hitler if he sold tickets.' However, the Shubert Organization was getting cold feet: the company had been considerably underwhelmed by box-office takings for Vanessa's most recent Broadway production, *Orpheus Descending*. The Tennessee Williams' play had closed earlier than expected. It therefore cancelled the tour.

Vanessa believed she'd been dropped for what she had said about the Gulf War. Equity rules state an actor's political belief should not be a factor when deciding whether to scrap a play, she argued (she has always had a touching faith in articles of association and international law). Concerned whether she would be allowed to work in the US again, Vanessa asked Equity to intercede. The actors' union had to determine whether she had what was known as a 'grievable claim' against the Shubert Organization – oh, and against her son-in-law Robert Fox, who was helping to organise the US tour as well. She wasn't afraid to take legal action against her daughter's husband.

If Equity sided with Vanessa, then it would file a grievance with the US theatre producers' association. And if the dispute was not settled there, it would go to arbitration.[12] In the end, the arbitrator sided with the Shubert Organization: Vanessa had not been discriminated against when she was dropped from the US tour.

Meanwhile, Vanessa was facing more legal problems at home. Corinna Gilbert, a woman who had lost her job as Vanessa's personal secretary, had gone to a London industrial tribunal to claim unfair dismissal. Gilbert told the tribunal that she had spent the previous five years working seven-day weeks up to 100 hours long as the sole employee of Vanessa Redgrave Enterprises. She said that she had been sacked for showing an actor round the actress's office in Clapham, the same study that had been bugged. Gilbert was only told that she'd lost her job when she walked out into the Arrivals Hall at Heathrow Airport after a holiday in Greece. She also received a letter from the international committee of the Marxist Party expelling her for one year for being 'a proved agent provocateur'. When she went to collect her belongings, Corin 'behaved like the Gestapo,' Gilbert said, going through her personal letters and medical records. Vanessa had put the phone down on her.

Corin told the tribunal that the Clapham study contained Vanessa's 'lifetime's archives, irreplaceable documents and valuable possessions.' Gilbert had admitted Cork Hubbard, an actor linked to the CIA and FBI, Corin testified. This posed a security threat to the Marxist Party. When remonstrated with for allowing a security breach, Gilbert had become abusive, Corin said, screwing papers into his face and calling the Redgrave brother and sister Stalinists. Gilbert denied calling Corin a 'stinking aristocrat'.[13] However, the tribunal sided with Gilbert in deciding that Vanessa and Corin had acted unfairly and awarded their former employee £8,925 in compensation. Vanessa had lost yet another court case.

While her mother was embroiled in legal disputes, Natasha was increasingly concerned about her father's health. Natasha started worrying about Tony's lifestyle when rumours of AIDS first began circulating in the early Eighties. 'There's nothing ascetic about me – I enjoy every possible pleasure,' Tony once told an interviewer. 'I was worried about him,' Natasha said, 'but it would have been unthinkable to say anything.' Tony was never a face in the gay LA bar scene in the Seventies or Eighties – you never saw him in the usual Santa Monica

Boulevard gay watering holes. He was, after all, well known and had a wide circle of friends.[14] His male lovers were shadowy figures alluded to, but kept in the background. Nevertheless, Tony was diagnosed as HIV-positive in 1984.

For a long time Tony managed to work without people realising. Jessica Lange said she wasn't aware of anything being wrong while filming *Blue Sky*. 'Tony was very strong still when we were shooting the film. You know, it wasn't something that everybody was conscious of when we were working. He had tremendous energy and wit,' she said. Tony never discussed his illness – he would carelessly mention that he had been to hospital, at the same time challenging his friends not to enquire further. He told people that doctors believed he was suffering from some new form of Parkinson's, the same disease that had killed Michael. He was back to his old tricks of divide-and-conquer. Such was his control over his friends that they were mesmerised into dumb acquiescence.

Tony started a course of chemotherapy, which caused his feet to swell up to five times their normal size. Yet he still stood firm on his beloved tennis court, bashing away at tennis balls hour after hour, unable to move one way or the other with his elephantine, bandaged feet. His hands were covered in blue marks, which he valiantly covered in make-up. He wore a long-sleeved sweater to cover lesions on his arms.

Tony carried on as if nothing was the matter. In the spring of 1991, he commissioned a screenplay of Joan Didion's best-selling novel *Democracy* and tried to raise finance for its production. And he himself adapted *The Magician*, Somerset Maugham's roman à clef about Aleister Crowley. He also planned to direct Natasha in his own adaptation of Elmore Leonard's 1987 novel, *Touch*. She was to play a record promoter who falls in love with a faith healer, who is in trouble with local gangsters. Finance was all lined up and shooting set to begin in July 1990 before Tony felt too ill to continue. He also daydreamed about putting on a double bill of *The Cherry Orchard* and *Hamlet* – Vanessa was to co-star with Tony's new young friend Rupert Everett, then the swoony heartthrob of *Another Country*. Robert Fox was roped in and calls put in to the best theatres all over the world, from the Odeon in Paris to Sydney Opera House. Because of Tony's illness, everyone knew this was just a dream. 'Right up until the last moment, we were all keeping up the charade that this production was going ahead, even though it was clear that absolutely nothing was going ahead,' said Joely. 'I remember him having jokey conversations on the phone with my mother about the play.'

To Everett, Tony's shrunken neck and his head with its giant brain looked more than ever as if he had recently stepped off a spacecraft. Everett remembered a dinner at Spago's during Christmas 1990 when somebody went around the table with a video camera, asking people what they were hoping for in the New Year. 'Death,' was Tony's blunt reply. Gavin Lambert wrote to Lindsay Anderson about Tony's illness: 'The immediate visible symptom is Kaposi's sarcoma. I think he's been covering up the lesions on his body for some time but now they're on his hands and just starting on his face. He doesn't refer to them and his whole attitude is one of heroic denial. His energy is undiminished, as far as I can see. He plays tennis, talks about his next picture, and by silent mutual understanding his friends (at least the ones I know) make no reference to it. Well, if anyone can beat it, Tony can. Triumph of the Will has always been his specialty.'

Tony became bedridden at King's Road in October 1990. Marianne Faithfull and Lindsay Anderson were shocked at how awful he looked when they came to visit (Tony wouldn't allow Anderson to take any photographs). Natasha and Joely flew in from Los Angeles, pretending they were just passing. Soon afterwards, Tony was admitted to the AIDS ward at St Vincent's Medical Center in Los Angeles and swore the medical staff to secrecy about what was wrong with him (at the time, AIDS patients were treated as if they had some alien contagious plague). Row upon row of skeletal men was waiting to die. Nurses would shove trays of greasy hamburgers under doors and stumble away as hastily as their protective moonsuits would allow. Tony's daughters found themselves pressed into becoming nurses – neither had nursing skills and Joely was heavily pregnant to boot. Children dressed in witches' hats and horrific masks ran up and down the corridors at Hallowe'en, adding to the surrealism. At first, Tony seemed to rally: he was still editing *Blue Sky* from his hospital bed, discussing the way he wanted final scenes cut.

Natasha and Joely nicknamed one doctor 'Springtime for Hitler' because every time he saw them, he'd mouth, 'London in January' – trying to give them hope that Tony would go home after Christmas.

Natasha said Tony allowed his daughters to take care of him in ways so intimate they would have horrified him when he was able to look after himself: he had to endure his daughters giving him bed baths. If someone had told Natasha she would have to deal with his soiled sheets, she would have recoiled. It was only when confronted with how abject he was that she realised what was needed was a practical proof of love. For once the Redgraves weren't just acting out what it meant to be a family. 'There's nothing, no state they can be in, nothing too disgusting or too abhorrent. You just do it, unthinkingly,' she said.

Relatives of AIDS patients would beg doctors to give dying men more morphine. Instead, the physicians would stand over those bed-ridden skeletons and warn of the dangers of addiction – as if it mattered. Seeing the agony Tony was going through caused Natasha to support assisted suicide. 'I could never have imagined the horror he went through during the last weeks he was alive,' she confessed.

Tony developed a serious fever on 9 November before lapsing into a semi-conscious condition two days later. His three daughters held a bedside vigil. Vanessa spoke to Tony during his final lucid moments just before she boarded a plane to Los Angeles. Surrounded by his daughters – Natasha, Joely and Katherine – together with Vanessa, Grizelda Grimond and Robert Fox, Tony died at 1.30pm on 14 November 1991.

Family and friends went back to Tony's house that same afternoon. There were lavish white flowers everywhere. Above the fireplace was a blown-up photograph of Tony wearing a Stetson while directing a movie. Natasha remembered a lot of laughing, a lot of crying and a fair amount of both at the same time. Tony had told his family that he didn't want a funeral or a memorial service. He had been particularly fond of a small tank of tropical fish in his hospital room, though, and so huge coloured fish paper fish were hung from the living-room rafters. Someone made a trip to a balloon shop and they released a flotilla of bloated-fish balloons.

Tony had lived in Los Angeles like deposed, but flamboyant royalty – a king who relished his own exile. John Mortimer compared him to Prospero living in his enchanted magical island of Le Nid du Duc. At the heart of Tony, as at the heart of Prospero, was a mystery: were these magicians proud of producing happiness or victims of their own power to manipulate other people's lives? Both loved their daughters. Mortimer wasn't sure how much Tony loved anybody else. King's Road was eventually sold in November 1992 to Barbet Schroeder, director of *Single White Female*, who had enjoyed a long affair with Tony's friend, Kathleen Tynan. In 1992, Tony's ashes were scattered at his beloved Le Nid du Duc. 'There is only one pleasure in life,' Tony once wrote to a friend, 'and that is to make a film.'

Fifteen years after her father's death, Vanessa still talked about how much she missed him. Natasha said her father's death was the first major loss she had suffered. Tony's death also brought her back together with Vanessa.[15] Natasha said: 'There's no guidebook on how to deal with grief but with time, it eventually heals. I took a lot from him: he was incredibly strong and opinionated and he opened all sorts of windows for me. I learned from him that when you're in professional difficulties, you should go on failing but fail better.'

Sorting out Tony's things at King's Road after his death, she came across the manuscript of his autobiography in a downstairs cupboard. She remembered him telling her it had been 'something to do' but according to him, what he'd written was worthless. The person who had typed up the manuscript for Tony presented his daughters with the typescript on the day of his death. In fact, Tony's autobiography, which Natasha pushed to have published two years later, was penetrating and well written, just as one might expect from somebody of his far-reaching intellect. There were huge gaps in what he wrote, though. John Osborne archly called it 'the authorised version.' Reading through, you would never have thought that Tony behaved badly in his life, whereas many of those who suffered under the lash of his tongue – with its sing-song, taunting tone – called him 'a real bitch.' And you would never have known he was gay.

Although many in showbusiness were by now openly homosexual, Tony was of the generation who couldn't quite admit who they were for fear of damaging their career. When the reviews came out, Joely was irritated at how the press harped on about Tony's being gay, ignoring how he had reinvented British theatre and cinema in the early Sixties. 'I don't mind if people reference his sexuality,' she said, 'but to headline it is reductive given the weight of his achievements. He was a renaissance man who believed that life and art are multifaceted. Not bad for the son of a chemist brought up in Shipley.' Joely never paid any attention to her father's work when he was alive – it was only after his death that she watched a lot of his films. She wished she could have talked to him about them. Now it was too late.

David Picker, the United Artists executive who had given Tony the green light to make *Tom Jones*, remembered him as 'a consummate filmmaker, sometimes destroyed by his choice of material.' Tony acknowledged his work was difficult to pigeonhole because his output was so varied. Unlike some directors who kept exploring the same world from different angles (Alfred Hitchcock, Woody Allen), Tony explored different worlds from the same angle (location shooting, improvisation on set). Tony Garnett, the television producer whom Tony helped with *Kes*, said he had a profound effect on British television and film. No one had ever shown working-class lives before or the poetry of a rainswept gasworks. Without Tony, there wouldn't have been any *Coronation Street* or *EastEnders*. His influence can still be felt in the work of Ken Loach, Mike Leigh and Shane Meadows. Garnett said: 'Most British cinema and television before Tony was class-ridden, people coming in through French windows saying, "Anyone for tennis?" Tony gave a voice to people whose voices had never been heard. It was Tony who changed that – it wasn't Pinewood and the rest of the Establishment.'[16]

Notes

1. Aronson, Tara. 'Richardson's Final Film/"Blue Sky" Premieres After Three-Year Delay, *San Francisco Chronicle*, 24 August 1994.
2. Vincent, Sally. *The Independent Magazine*, 25 September 1993.
3. Adams, Tom. 'My Family and Other Actors', *Observer*, 27 April 2003.
4. Lane, Harriet. 'Natasha Richardson – Dynasty', 6 December 1998.
5. Lister, David. 'Versatile, Vivacious and Underrated', *Independent*, 4 May 2010.
6. Adams, Cindy. *Daily Mail*, 21 February 1991.
7. Callow, Simon. 'Lynn Redgrave – Obituaries, *Sunday Times*, 9 May 2010.
8. Webb, Gervaise. 'Vanessa Is Warned of Angry Israel Protests', *Evening Standard*, 20 June 1994.
9. 'MI5 "Justified" In Watching Actress', *Guardian*, 11 April 1994.
10. Macchins, Gray. 'Natasha Richardson Goofs Off At Last', *Toronto Star*, 11 September 1991.
11. Bruni, Frank. 'Under a Bare Bulb', *New York Times*, 16 February 1997.
12. Witchel, Alex. 'Redgrave Says She Was Dropped From "Lettice" for Gulf Stand', *Chicago Tribune*, 28 March 1991.

13. 'Corin Redgrave Used "Gestapo Tactics" On Me', *Evening Standard*, 15 July 1991.
14. David Ehrenstein, email to author, 22 June 2009.
15. Young, Lucy. 'Tasha Takes Off', *Sunday Independent*, 4 September 2005.
16. Tony Garnett, author interview, 22 June 2009.

CHAPTER TWENTY

Dancing Naked in the Rain

In 1992, Natasha began spending longer periods in New York – in Manhattan, nobody cared about the Redgrave baggage, she said. Her American career started to take off, too. Funnily enough, it only started happening for Natasha once she'd had a nose job to reduce her Tony-sized, parrot-style beak. Casting directors had been put off because it did not photograph well. Natasha was urged to think about surgery to avoid becoming stuck as a character actress. 'I'd never considered changing my nose,' she told *Tatler* magazine. 'It was part of me and any issues I had about myself were to do with my weight.'

When Natasha broached the subject with Vanessa, her mother told her not to be so silly – after all, having a big nose hadn't harmed Barbra Streisand's career. Natasha thought, 'Bloody hell, I don't want to be like Barbra Streisand!' She then asked her father's advice and he cooed, 'Oh, I'm so pleased, darling! I've been meaning to say something for some time.' Soon after she had surgery in the late 1980s, the parts began rolling in.

Her first movie role was for director Ken Russell. While Vanessa had played a hunchbacked nymphomaniac nun for the director, Natasha was the relatively demure Mary Shelley in *Gothic* (1986). Afterwards, she began to carve out a peculiar niche playing victimised women. In 1988, she played heiress-turned-revolutionary Patty Hearst for director Paul Schrader, followed by a submissive sex slave in Volker Schlöndorff's *The Handmaid's Tale* (1990), based on Margaret Atwood's novel. Natasha then played another passive victim for Schrader, co-starring with her pal Rupert Everett in *The Comfort of Strangers* (1990). These roles were so unlike her spunky real self. In 1993, she appeared as Zelda Fitzgerald in the television movie, throwing herself into fountains and flinging platinum necklaces out of train windows. 'Self-destruction, right up my street,' Natasha reflected with humorous grimness. 'It could be my *Isadora*.'

Starring as Nina in *The Seagull* in September 1985, making her film debut with Russell, playing self-destructive hedonists ... sometimes it seemed as if she was subconsciously mapping Vanessa's own career. Schrader believed Natasha was afraid of doing just that: 'Her mother was never a commercial star – she was never hot, not on the A-list.'[1]

In the spring of 1993, Natasha, now aged twenty-nine, recreated her Old Vic role of Anna Christie on Broadway. Three years previously, she had won the London Theatre Critics' Award for her portrayal of Eugene O'Neill's heroine. Director Richard Eyre said that Natasha had inherited Tony's ability as a fantastic organiser: it was she who discovered the Criterion Center Stage Right theatre in Manhattan, fixed the dates and invited David Leveaux to direct.

Anna Christie is a prostitute who enters a steamy liaison with a strapping Irish sailor in the New York docks. Natasha decided that Irish actor Liam Neeson would be perfect for sailor Mat Burke. She called him once a month until he accepted the role – Natasha had also inherited Tony's persistence. 'I think O'Neill wrote that part for Liam Neeson,' Natasha said. 'He's a young guy with all this history behind him. He's had a girl in every port, lived a rough life, so there's that feeling of experience and manliness while at the same time, he has this boyish vulnerability. He's got passion and strength. And he's at a point in his life when he wants to settle down.'

It was unclear whether she was talking about O'Neill's sailor or indeed, Neeson himself. When they finally met, Natasha said 'something magic happened.' They started rehearsing and 'it was like walking on air, coming home. You know how somehow the cosmos is working? I never felt more alert.' As rehearsals progressed, the two became closer. They developed a little ritual together: she took over the task of painting a lurid scar on Liam's back – part of the make-up required for his role. She described it as 'a bonding thing.'

Liam – Gaelic for William – Neeson was born into the Irish Catholic minority in Ballymena ('Middle Town'), 16 miles from the coast of Northern Ireland. Ballymena was an ultra-Protestant country, a stronghold of the Democratic Unionist Party. It's a dour Scots-Irish town, the atmosphere reflective of the Scots and English settlers imported by the English Crown in the 17th century to dominate local Catholics. Liam was a mixture of two heritages: industrious Presbyterian

Scots – he says 'canna' for 'can't' – and romantic Irish through his mother Kitty, who was born south of the border in Waterford, County Cork.

Kitty Neeson was a school cook, while his father Barney was the school's caretaker. Barney was a quiet man who spent much of his time in his greenhouse talking to his canaries; it was Kitty who had all the energy and drive. Growing up in Ballymena in the Sixties, Catholics and Protestants rubbed along together, although Neeson was aware that his family were poorer than their Protestant neighbours. Liam and his three sisters lived with their parents in a tiny Housing Trust flat. His former girlfriend Helen Mirren said that growing up Catholic in Northern Ireland gave Liam a sense of insularity. As a boy, he was lanky and shy; also lacking in self-confidence. He became an altar boy at the local church. When the parish priest announced that he was starting a boxing club, Liam joined in. For three years running, he became Irish youth heavyweight champion and Ulster champion. An opponent broke his nose when he was fifteen. At the same time, Liam – who put on pretend plays with his sisters when he was a child – also joined an amateur acting group run by his English teacher. The group performed works by Irish playwrights J. M. Synge and Brian Friel, among others. 'Something clicked,' said Liam. 'I thought, this is what I want to do for the rest of my life.' However, he was pushed into attending Queen's University in Belfast, where he studied maths and physics – he hated it. At the same time he was offered a place at London's prestigious RADA acting school but he didn't have the money to go there. Instead, he dropped out of university and drifted through jobs as a forklift truck driver and an architect's assistant. On a dare, he auditioned for an acting job at Belfast's Lyric Theatre: he got it. Soon, Belfast became too small for him and he moved to the Project Arts Centre in Dublin, where he met directors Neil Jordan and Jim Sheridan as well as actor Gabriel Byrne.

In the early Eighties, Neeson lived for five years in London with Helen Mirren. When he moved to Los Angeles, he spent two years with Julia Roberts. His other girlfriends included Brooke Shields, Sinéad O'Connor and Barbra Streisand. However, Liam's reputation as a ladies' man didn't deter Natasha in the slightest. Rather, it was a source of pride. 'I'm pleased that women fall in love with him,' she said, 'because I know why.'

Anna Christie opened on 14 January 1993 to breathless reviews. 'Not since Brando tossed meat up to Stella in *A Streetcar Named Desire* has flesh made such a spectacular entrance,' wrote John Lahr in the *New Yorker*. Neeson was a 'sequoia of sex,' Lahr panted. Richardson and Neeson's scorching sexual chemistry gave O'Neill's play new heat and life. *Newsday* said Natasha's performance as tough but vulnerable Anna was 'complicated and captivating,' while the *New York Times* said she was giving 'what may be the performance of the season'. Both actors were nominated for Tony awards but the person whose opinion mattered most, of course, was her mother. Natasha begged Vanessa to tell her what she thought of her acting. Usually Vanessa was reluctant to say anything, afraid of being hurtful. When her daughter pleaded with her to tell her the truth, Vanessa – with her eye for detail and needing to know everything she can about a character before playing them – suggested the suitcase Anna stuffs all her belongings into should be more beaten-up. Then she went quiet. 'I hope you know what's in the suitcase?' she asked.

Natasha's marriage to Robert Fox was souring even before she met Neeson. Fox criticised her for the amount of time she was spending away from home.[2] 'Natasha was focused at 14,' said her friend Polly Vaizey. 'At 22 she was mature, capable and shared a huge amount of interests with Robert. But at 30, you're a different person. As the Eighties went on she became clear that she wanted to live in the US, and he wanted to live in the English countryside. That caused problems.'[3]

Anna Christie's sell-out Broadway run ended on 28 February 1993 after 54 performances. Natasha wasn't sure where she stood with her co-star. Neeson flew to Poland to begin shooting *Schindler's List*, a role that would secure him an Academy Award nomination. The timing of Liam filming in Poland and Natasha flying back to London would have provided the perfect opportunity had they wanted to forget what had just happened. Instead, Liam sent Natasha a note on the eve of her 30th birthday. 'You're catching up with me,' he quipped, signing off with the name of his philandering *Schindler's List* character: 'Lots of love, Oskar'. It wasn't quite the message Natasha had been hoping for. Her response was to grasp the nettle: 'This is like a letter from a buddy,' she wrote. 'What is our relationship?' The response stopped Liam in his tracks. This was the moment when Liam realised he was in love with Natasha. He thought, 'This is real and genuine and is something that has to be protected.'[4]

Rather than fly back to London for the first night of her husband's West End revival of *The Importance of Being Earnest* – and also his 41st birthday (Fox was seen having lunch in trendy Italian restaurant San Lorenzo with his three children) – Natasha flew out to Poland, spending a week there while Liam finished shooting. She was said to have told Fox that she 'wasn't coming back', to which he replied, 'Well, don't bother.'[5] Natasha did not believe marriage was necessarily for life – the way that her own parents had remained friends showed her that divorce did not necessarily mean failure and misery. 'I thought it was perfectly normal and OK for people to be married for a few years and then to break up if it wasn't working out,' she explained.

Having smashed up Robert's first marriage, Natasha now took a hammer to the second. She admitted the timing was bad, perhaps inevitable – she'd spent so long bottling everything up and keeping everything under control required a great effort. 'It was a very painful time realising I was in an unhappy marriage,' she admitted. Natasha saw herself as a hopeless romantic searching for grand passion and someone for whom the everyday sometimes didn't seem like enough – she once said that she wanted to dance naked in a thunderstorm while Liam liked to stay in bed and read.

Natasha and Liam decided to live in upstate New York. Relocation suited them both – Liam had never felt at home in London. Being Irish in London during the IRA bombing campaigns of the early Eighties made him feel like a Negro growing up in the racist Deep South. And living in New York helped Natasha escape from the Redgrave shadow – as well as, no doubt, the disapproval of the Fox family, a theatrical dynasty themselves.

Natasha and Liam were married at their white 1810 clapboard farmhouse in Millbrook, a pretty village 90 miles north of Manhattan. Millbrook was close enough to New York to be within commuting distance of Broadway, yet it was also remote and patriotic Heartland. Their neighbours included Mary Tyler Moore, newscaster Katie Couric and scions of the DuPont and Johnson & Johnson families. Yet the owner of Millbrook's diner waved celebrity hunters away when Matthew Broderick, a friend of Liam and Natasha's, was trying to eat undisturbed. The wedding took place on Sunday, 3 July 1994. Two minibuses of guests got lost and arrived late, as did several individual stragglers. Natasha and Liam exchanged vows in a 40-minute Catholic ceremony during which a priest conducted mass and a choir sang 'Morning Has Broken'. Seventy guests including Lauren Bacall, Mia Farrow, Ralph Fiennes and Emma Thompson were seated in a marquee beside the 180-year-old barn.

Vanessa was unable to attend because she was busy in Italy filming *A Month By the Lake* – produced, ironically, by Robert Fox. She sent a letter to the newlyweds wishing them well, in which she also managed to slip in a reference to Palestinian liberation. Steven Spielberg was also unable to be there but sent Neeson a 1950s Harley Davidson as a wedding present. The evening ended with Natasha and Liam dancing to Irish jigs and the Beatles. Liam chafed when people asked what it felt like to be marrying into the royal family of theatre. 'Aristocracy is a term my wife and I hate,' he insisted. 'When you use words like that, you think of tea served on a croquet lawn at two-thirty. We jokingly talk about us royals. Natasha and her sister Joely had a tough upbringing, with Vanessa filming somewhere and their father making a film somewhere else.'

Not everybody wished the newlyweds well, though. One friend told Natasha that her new marriage was cursed. 'You will never be happy,' he declared. 'Your marriage will end in disaster.'[6]

Their first son Michael was born the following year in Dublin on 23 June 1995. Named after Natasha's grandfather, Michael's second name was Antonio after Tony's hated middle name. His younger brother Daniel Jack was born 14 months later on 27 August 1996 in New York City. Daniel was named after Father Daniel Berrigan, the priest who had officiated at their wedding. Natasha said it was comforting to see little pieces of Tony in both boys.

Most women wouldn't mind being married to James Bond –Vanessa had, after all, gone out with Timothy Dalton. Early on in their marriage, the franchise producers asked Liam to be the next 007. Natasha advised him not to take the part, thinking he would be typecast; his growing fame was becoming a problem for her. After Daniel was born she went into therapy partly because she felt so overshadowed by Liam and the rest of her family. She suffered a crisis of confidence. 'People kept asking me how I managed to get him – never the other way round,' she revealed. 'I had a slight feeling of losing what was special about me and becoming "Mrs Neeson". I have a famous mother and it took me years to get over that. Now I have this really famous husband.'[7]

Vanessa too had embarked on a new friendship. David Harewood, a young black actor, joined the repertory theatre company that Vanessa had founded on a shoestring with Corin. His agent thought him mad for turning down television roles in lieu of the £200 a week the Redgraves were paying him. When they first met, Harewood was twenty-nine and Vanessa a sprightly fifty-eight (Harewood was nearly 30 years younger). For two-and-a-half years, Vanessa and Harewood toured Britain, Brazil, Spain and America as Antony and Cleopatra. They got on so well that he even moved into her mansion flat in Chiswick at the end of 1996. There was speculation as to whether the relationship had gone beyond mere mentoring and become a sentimental education in the Flaubertian sense. Harewood said he was never conscious of any age difference, only the experience gap. He thought Vanessa had been mistreated by the media and undervalued by the theatre Establishment because of her politics. 'People think she's cold and distant,' he said, 'but she's not. She's a very, very funny person, she's got a great sense of humour.'

If he'd lived five months longer, Tony would have become a grandfather. Joely, now twenty-five, had met the man she would marry: Tim Bevan, head of Working Title Films, the most successful film company in Britain. At the time, Working Title was still in its early days and it would go on to make Notting Hill, Bridget Jones's Diary and Bean. In total, films made by Bevan and Working Title have grossed nearly $5 billion to date. Before she met Bevan, Joely had one affair with Randal McDonnell, son and heir to the Earl of Antrim. Then she met theatre producer Archie Stirling, forty-eight, producer of the play in which she was appearing. Stirling was married to Diana Rigg, the actress who stood next to Vanessa in the crowd of Tony's Othello. Like Natasha, Joely was having an affair with someone else's husband. Stirling and Rigg tried to reconcile at his family home, a 5,000-acre Scottish estate but it was too late, the hurt was too deep. Their daughter Rachael was thirteen years old at the time.

Joely and Bevan were secretly married in January 1992, a couple of months after Tony's death. Their daughter Daisy was born two months later. Now that he was part of Britain's greatest theatrical dynasty, Bevan admitted that he did feel slight positive discrimination to casting family members. The couple bought an imposing house in west London. She started nest-building, painting walls and cooking for dozens of friends at a time. Joely believed she had finally found the stability she had craved all her life.

Joely may have inherited her mother's tall, slender build, fair hair and gray-blue eyes but her acting career got off to a stuttering start. She went back to work when Daisy was just six weeks old to shoot Ken Russell's *Lady Chatterley's Lover*, playing the sensuous lady of the manor. Some laughed at her performance opposite horny-handed Sean Bean; others were aroused. Critics said that Russell filmed Joely unflatteringly considering she had only just given birth. However, the production broke all records for a BBC television period drama, which Joely helped promote by posing naked with some strategically placed flowers – that got her into the tabloid *Sun* newspaper. Afterwards, she became a tabloid fixture, something that she herself exploited when she appeared at a movie premiere in a plunging backless gold lame dress. The tabloid coverage did not help her career, though: all she was offered were television mini-series (she turned down $2 million to play Princess Diana shortly after her tragic death). Slowly, so-so Hollywood movie roles began coming back. In American-slob-turned-British-monarch comedy *King Ralph*, she played a Finnish princess with a voice, as the *New Yorker* put it, 'pitched so low that it could summon deep-sea creatures from the North Atlantic'. She was an astronaut in jogging bra and Lycra shorts in sci-fi horror movie *Event Horizon* (1997). Then came the wholesome love interest in Disney's *101 Dalmatians*, a role she likened to 'mainlining fudge.' Somehow Joely never seemed to break through – she had been groomed for stardom once too often, overshadowed by puppies and black holes.

The Chinese have a saying: once everything is perfect in the garden, a wind will come and knock everything down again. So it proved. Disaster struck after less than five years of marriage. Bevan left Joely. 'Divorce, for anyone, is a nightmare, a real trial. You have to completely re-assess your whole life. Having lived with someone for so many years and gone through so much, then suddenly there's this great big hole. But you get through it. Life goes on, even if your husband has run off with a much younger woman, which is what happened to me,' she said.[8] At the same time, the agent whom she'd had for a decade retired and she had to leave the west London house she loved; she also felt that she was no longer seen for parts in Working Title films such as *Bridget Jones* or *Elizabeth*.[9] Bevan and Joely's divorce was only finalised four years later, in July 2000, perhaps a sign of how much she wanted to hang onto the relationship.

Sam Mendes, creative director of the Donmar Warehouse, cast Natasha as Sally Bowles in the Broadway transfer of *Cabaret* in early 1997 (the play opened at London's Donmar Warehouse in March 1997). For his London production, he went back to the original Sally Bowles of Christopher Isherwood's *Goodbye to Berlin*. Audience members were served drinks at small tables, inches away from the ripped stockings and bare flesh of KitKatClub girls in a seedy Berlin nightclub. It had always struck him as odd that in the Hollywood movie version Liza Minnelli was supposed to be singing in a Weimar Republic dive bar. 'I mean, she's a Broadway star,' said Mendes. He wanted to go back to the original idea of Sally Bowles being someone who never quite made it at home.

Natasha, of course, had known Isherwood in her younger days. As a teenager she'd played the *Cabaret* soundtrack over and over again. Family friends told the *New York Times* that Tony and Isherwood would have been thrilled to see their 'Tasha' play Sally. Natasha still had singing lessons, despite Mendes wanting authenticity. She was reminded of how nonplussed Laurence Olivier was when he was complimented on how well he got across the second-rate hoofing in *The Entertainer*. 'But that's what happens when I give it 100 per cent,' Olivier said.

As rehearsals began, Mendes noticed how addicted Natasha was to tragedy. 'I was really struggling with the funny, bright, perky scenes,' she explained. 'He said, "You know, you're just the opposite of most actors – you just want to splash around in the dark, painful areas and you get really frightened of doing the confident, comedy stuff." It's where I'm drawn.' It was also because she'd learned from her father not always to take the safe and easy road: if you were going to do good work, you faced the risk of failing badly. Natasha spoke about the high she got from being on stage – indeed, she talked about acting as if it was a drug: 'The best moments are when you're on stage or you have one take in a movie, and suddenly you feel totally free. You don't always know what's going to happen next and yet you're in control – it's the best feeling in the world. And you always want to get it back. It doesn't happen very often, it comes only in flashes.'

When Natasha asked Vanessa for her advice it was typically practical: first, look into people's faces, not up at the lights and second, treat Sally's fur coat as if it were her most treasured possession.

The Broadway version of *Cabaret* opened after 37 previews on 19 March 1998 at the KitKatClub, housed in what was previously known as Henry Miller's Theater. One night, Liza Minnelli herself came to see how Natasha had interpreted the role that the Broadway diva was so identified with. The audience stood up and clapped when Minnelli entered the auditorium. Natasha, who was peering through the stage curtain, burst into tears. But she needn't have worried: she won a Tony award for Best Actress. *Cabaret* transferred to Studio 54 later that year, where it remained for the rest of its 2,377-performance run. The show became the third longest-running revival in Broadway musical history, third only to *Oh! Calcutta!* and *Chicago*.

The following April, Natasha was back on Broadway to play the female lead in *Closer*, Patrick Marber's bleak play about infidelity. Natasha played Anna, a photographer who cheats on her husband. She based her performance of what it's like to be betrayed by remembering how she felt as a child when she realised she came second best to Vanessa's politics. Ironically, one of the show's producers was her ex-husband Robert Fox. She admitted it was embarrassing and awkward at first to be on stage confessing her adultery with Fox in the audience. 'He came to a run-through at one point and I thought to myself, "I don't think I can do this in front of him." It was so raw, so lacerating,' she said.[10]

Notes

1. Conrad, Peter. *Feasting With Panthers: Or, The Importance of Being Famous*, Thames & Hudson, London, 1994.

2. Maddins, Craig. "Natasha Richardson Goofs Off At Last', *Toronto Star*, 11 September 1991.

3. Howell, Georgina. 'In the Name of the Father', *Sydney Morning Herald*, 21 May 1994.

4. Huguenin, Patrick. 'A New York Love Story: Magical Marriage Takes a Tragic Turn', *New York Daily News*, 18 March 2009.

5. Dempster, Nigel. 'The Importance of Being Natasha', *Daily Mail*, 29 March 1993.

6. Phillips, Martin and Smith, Emily. 'Natasha Said: We're Cursed', *Sun*, 19 March 2009.

7. McDonald, Peter. 'How Natasha Casts Off Her Family Baggage', *Evening Standard*, 10 August 1998.

8. Convey, Olivia. 'No Striptease For Joely', *Belfast Newsletter*, 22 December 1998.

9. Mottram, James. 'Interview Joely Richardson – "I'm Failing Better Than Ever"', *The Times*, 21 May 2009.

10. Pacheco, Patrick. 'A Play Against Type', *Los Angeles Times*, 18 April 1999.

CHAPTER TWENTY-ONE

Offstage Drama

By the late 1990s, things were going well for Lynn. Her film career had revived with roles such as *Shine* (1996), which won her a BAFTA nomination, and *Gods and Monsters* (1998), for which she was nominated for a second Oscar and won a Best Supporting Actress Golden Globe. She enjoyed a beautiful $5 million five-bedroom home in Topanga Canyon, Los Angeles with a swimming pool and tennis courts. And she had one of the most stable marriages in Hollywood, having been happily married for 32 years to John Clark, the man whom she'd wed in 1967. Perhaps everything was too perfect in the garden. On Thanksgiving Day 1998, Clark exploded a bombshell that cratered his family when he told Lynn that her grandson was in fact his child: their former daughter-in-law had given birth to his baby. Lynn had brought up the now eight-year-old Zachary as her grandson.

Back in 1990, Lynn had taken on Nicolette Hannah, an attractive brunette, as her personal assistant. Clark and Hannah began having an affair and she fell pregnant. Neither of them told Lynn what had been going on. Instead, Hannah informed Lynn that the baby was the result of a one-night stand. Lynn assumed the baby's father was 'a shit who never paid any attention to him.' Worse still, Hannah went on to marry Lynn's airline pilot son Ben in 1996 (the pair divorced in 1996). Lynn said: 'It was right beneath my nose for eight years – I thought this child was my surrogate grandchild.' After hearing the news, Lynn nodded and went back into the kitchen to take the Thanksgiving turkey out of the oven.

The affair might have remained a secret but for Clark's extraordinary behaviour: Hannah and Ben Clark split up and he started pursuing her again. This time, however, Hannah was not interested – she had fallen in love with a plumber whom she'd met through Lynn. She and Zachary were living with him in his mobile home. But Clark would not stop pestering her: at night, he would go over to her mobile home and shout messages of love. In the end, Hannah was forced to take out a restraining order against him. Lynn said: 'He harangued them in the most appalling way, and she threatened to tell me [what had happened] if he didn't stop. So he told me, but then he carried on.' Meanwhile, Clark seemed completely unrepentant: 'I've been a naughty boy,' he said, 'but I don't regret anything.' Astonishingly, he added: 'My kids were so slow giving us grandkids, I had to go out and make our own. To say this is a dysfunctional family is an understatement – we seem to lurch from crisis to crisis – but considering the Redgrave family history, this recent dose of heterosexuality should be considered a step in the right direction.'[1] Sometimes it seemed as though all the drama in the Redgrave family happened offstage.

The December 2000 divorce, messy even by Hollywood standards, was front-page tabloid news for months. Clark even blamed Lynn for enjoying the scandal in some way. 'She's glorying in this, and she resents that if there is a star, it's me rather than her ... so what if I like sex?' he demanded.[2] Meanwhile, the pair fought bitterly over their estate: he claimed that for 12 years they'd had a 'sexless' marriage and agreed to tolerate each other's infidelities.[3] He also claimed that Lynn had had affairs with actors Brian Dennehy and Brandon Maggart.[4] She then accused him of being penny-pinching and controlling: he made her wear second-hand clothes, clean the swimming pool herself and do the gardening. In turn, he accused her of turning his children against him, destroying his directing career and refusing to try and save their marriage.

Lynn contended that Clark had salted away money in various bank accounts without her knowledge. She urged the divorce judge to send him to prison on his 68th birthday for failing to produce financial documents in court. When the judge pointed out that sending Clark to jail would not help retrieve the documents, Lynn's lawyer replied: 'No, but it would give me a great deal of satisfaction.' In the end, the court ordered Lynn to pay around $20,000 a year in alimony to her former husband. She compared her pain to having 'open heart surgery without an anaesthetic.' The stress probably contributed to the cancer that would eventually kill her. 'In many ways my marriage wasn't perfect,' Lynn reflected, 'but I loved him deeply. My heart rose when I heard his footfall in the kitchen.'

In October 1999, Corin was starring as Sir Hugo Latymer in Noël Coward's play, A Song at Twilight. The plot had a subject matter that touched Corin's private life: it is about a visit to an elderly artist who never had the courage to admit his homosexuality – shades of Michael. Of course, Michael and Coward had been lovers. The sense of A Song At Twilight being a Redgrave family affair was only increased as Corin's wife Kika was playing Sir Hugo's long-suffering wife and Vanessa was his former lover. Coward's official biographer Sheridan Morley was the director. Vanessa and Morley just did not get on: Morley derided what he saw as her pretension and her antiquated political views and judged her performances over-indulgent and hysterical. Vanessa wrote a barbed letter to Morley in which she expressed doubts about his directing pedigree and told him how irritated she was by his habit of giving her notes relaying what audience members had said during the interval. Vanessa apologised if she had been rude, explaining that she could not work properly in chaotic rehearsals. She suggested the problem lay with Morley's inexperience. During one rehearsal, Morley shrieked, 'This woman is driving me to an early grave! She never does the same thing twice.' Indeed, he became so overwrought that he had to be taken home. For his part, Morley wrote to Corin about his sister's performances: 'I could never quite understand how she could be so breathtakingly wonderful some nights and almost embarrassingly terrible others, and not quite understand the difference.'[5]

Joely, meanwhile, had found a new boyfriend after the collapse of her marriage three years previously. Jamie Theakston was a television presenter whose previous girlfriends included pop singer Natalie Appleton, actress Anna Friel and model Sophie Dahl. Their first date, however, ended up as four hours in the A&E at Paddington Hospital. Theakston had arrived at the appointed hour to find Joely's house temporarily unnumbered because it was being painted. Joely had stood on a table and leaned out of the window to call out that he was at the right place, but she didn't realise the table had a hairline fracture in it and crashed right through it. Theakston walked in to find her shaking with a gash in her leg. He ended up holding her hand and making her laugh while she had her leg stitched up. The relationship ended a year later when Theakston was caught visiting a Mayfair brothel, where he had sex with three prostitutes. Theakston admitted that he had been 'foolish' to visit the brothel, which featured a 'bondage dungeon'. 'It is extremely embarrassing and I would like to apologise to my close friends and family,' he said. Days after describing Joely as the 'love of his life', he found himself dumped, however.

That same summer, Liam was almost killed in a motorbike accident. He'd gone out to pick up muffins from the local store and was riding home on his Harley-Davidson when a deer suddenly shot out of the trees and tried to jump over him. But the deer landed on Liam and he swerved off the road. 'The deer came out of nowhere. Front paws straight up the handlebars,' he remembered. Liam, the bike and the deer slid down a twelve-foot embankment and hit a couple of saplings. He pulled himself back up to the side of the road, where he sat laughing and crying. Then he noticed that one of his legs was swelling. His pelvis was twisted by 90 degrees and he couldn't move for months. His local doctor arranged for him to be transferred to Lenox Hill Hospital in Manhattan. Natasha was filming *Haven* in Canada when she was told the news and she could not get a flight home. Hysterical, she was driven to Liam's bedside. Doctors told Natasha that Liam was going to die that night. Nine years later their situation would be fatally reversed. Throughout that autumn, Liam hobbled on crutches with Natasha by his side. Slowly, he began to heal. The couple would be seen at Cafe Luxembourg, an upper West Side bistro near their Manhattan apartment, or taking the boys to swimming lessons. Life slipped back into reassuringly mundane and cosy domesticity.

Crunching up the Millbrook farmhouse drive on a Friday afternoon, visitors would be met by Natasha with a jug of frozen cocktails (she was taken with exotic drinks, from lychee martinis to pomegranate margaritas). There would be swimming and tennis; also delicious things to eat – Natasha remained a fabulous cook whose shelves of cookbooks were marked with curling Post-Its marking her favourite recipes – followed by gossip late into the night. In the morning, visitors would get up to find the house immaculate, a plate of fresh croissants and a pot of steaming coffee on the table alongside the *New York Times*. A mug drained of builder's tea standing by the sink would be the only evidence Natasha had already been downstairs. Later, she would be seen wandering round the house with an electronic labelling machine in one hand and a long, slender cigarette in the other. She never quite overcame her childhood fear of disorder: everything had to be labelled from kitchen drawers ('Potatoes, onions') to shelves in the hall ('Boys' gloves').[6] The strain of trying to keep everything under control must have been immense.

Natasha and Joely had been worrying about Vanessa. By the turn of the century, she'd given away so much money to good causes there was hardly anything left in her bank account. Her home, which she shared with eighty-nine-year-old Rachel, was an unremarkable two-bedroom flat in Hammersmith, west London with a bare bulb dangling in the hall. Adding to Vanessa's fears, Rachel began suffering from dementia. One friend, the pianist Katharina Wolpe, said Vanessa hadn't a penny to her name. Actress Eileen Atkins, another chum, said that Vanessa knew she needed to have more personal funds. 'At 60, you begin to get worried about whether you have anything in the bank,' said Atkins.

Vanessa, though, had a new *and* distant cause to fight for: this time it was defending human rights in the Russian province of Chechnya. Just as the IRA had done in Northern Ireland, Chechen rebels were fighting for an independent state. The Russians clamped down hard on the breakaway republic and Vanessa raised money for refugees. Quick to denounce Russian human rights abuses, she was determinedly blind to horrors committed on the Chechen side. Labour politician Roy Hattersley, one of those on Vanessa's side, said there seemed to be a filter in her brain that holds back facts inconvenient to her view of life – or at least allows her to interpret them in a way which confirms her prejudices.[7] When Chechens kidnapped and then beheaded a group of British phone engineers, Vanessa blamed the atrocity on Russian black propaganda. Moscow had to be secretly responsible, she rationalised, because it showed Chechens in such a bad light.

She became friendly with Akhmed Zakayev, a former actor-turned-soldier in the Chechen rebels. Zakayev, who was now Chechnya's deputy prime minister, once warned Chechnya might attack Russian nuclear power stations, potentially killing thousands. In December 2002, he was arrested at Heathrow Airport after arriving from Denmark – Moscow had tried to extradite him during the five weeks he spent in jail there. The forty-three-year-old was fighting extradition from Denmark to Russia, where he stood accused of a variety of terrorist crimes dating back to the 1990s. In particular, Zakayev was suspected of being involved in the 1996 Moscow theatre attack in which 169 people died.

On 12 December 2002, Vanessa put up £50,000 bail for her friend. 'The evidence on which this extradition warrant is based is all fabricated,' she said.[8] The Russian government reacted angrily, branding Vanessa a friend of terrorism; they accused her of providing 'moral cover' to a man Russia compared to Osama Bin Laden. *Isvetzia*, the Russian newspaper, dismissed Vanessa as 'childish'. The paper accused her of supporting the IRA and Libya's Colonel Gaddafi, adding: 'As often happens to young revolutionaries who could not raise their compatriots to fight against local oppressors, she started trying to find a use for her political passion outside her motherland.'

That night, Vanessa appeared at the Royal Court to call on the British government to save Zakayev from extradition. Court actors gave up their rehearsal room for an impassioned performance by Vanessa in support of the man known as 'Chechnya's Laurence Olivier'. Far from being a terrorist, Zakayev had been the one man who negotiated directly with Russian authorities and he had signed every peace declaration since 1995, she said. 'The truth hasn't arrived here in London yet, but it will,' she assured those in the rehearsal room.[9]

Vanessa's intervention caused a rift between Downing Street and the Kremlin. Britain resisted pressure to imprison Zakayev by agreeing to extend his release on bail pending an extradition hearing. On 11 December 2002, Vanessa entered the witness box at Bow Street Magistrates Court to say she was prepared to continue her guarantees. Zakayev's solicitor told the court there was no evidence to link the Chechen politician to the infamous Moscow theatre attack. As Chechnya's deputy prime minister, Zakayev would be at risk if deported to Russia, his solicitor argued. Once again, Vanessa had been proved right: Zakayev was eventually allowed to stay in Britain.

Vanessa's meddling infuriated the Russian government. Demonstrators in the pay of a militant group linked to Russia's security service, the FSB, and to Russian president Vladimir Putin made her the target of an intimidation campaign: hundreds of demonstrators mounted a picket near her Chiswick flat. Demonstrators waved pictures of Vanessa, Osama Bin Laden and Saddam Hussein as well as Zakayev during one Trafalgar Square rally. It emerged that most of those taking part had been paid £15 to turn up and many of them had little idea who Vanessa was. Somebody even tried to smash the front door of her block of flats. Scotland Yard had already installed a panic button after Vanessa was targeted by neo-Nazi group Combat 18: this time around, she sought advice on personal protection from anti-terrorist police and asked for closed-circuit television to be installed. Vanessa said: 'I don't think the KGB will stop at anything.'[10]

This time, Vanessa's paranoia proved correct: Zakayev and Alexander Litvinenko, a former KGB intelligence officer granted asylum in Britain, both had petrol bombs thrown at their homes in the same north London street. Litvinenko was hospitalised in November 2006 after being secretly poisoned with radiation. He suspected that he'd been poisoned in the restaurant of a London hotel and died later that same month. MI6 uncovered a plot by a Russian hitman to also assassinate Zakayev at a London hotel. Intercepted phone calls revealed that the FSB, successor to the KGB, was planning to shoot Zakayev in the back of the head.

That December, Lynn started to worry about a lump in her breast. At first, she was in denial and it took two weeks before she did anything about it. 'I thought maybe it would go away and I kept feeling it in the wrong place and think, yes, it's gone and realised it hadn't,' she admitted. By now she had moved to Connecticut on the East Coast, distancing herself from the past. Happening to be in Los Angeles, she visited her old doctor who diagnosed breast cancer; she was booked in to have her right breast removed the following month. After that she would have to start chemotherapy, which left her feeling wretched and made all her hair fall out. 'Please, dear God, dear life, I'm being demanding, but let me please have more. Let me not have to cut it short. More time please, to love, to learn, to act, to write, to enjoy my family. Please,' pleaded a frightened Lynn in her journal.

Vanessa, doubtless pleased to be getting out of Britain for a while, swapped flats with Natasha in the spring (she was opening on Broadway in A Long Day's Journey Into Night in May 2003). At the same time, Natasha was starring in London as Ellida Wangel in The Lady From the Sea, the role for which her mother had won such admiration 25 years previously. Trevor Nunn was directing the new Almeida Theatre production. In her New York office, Natasha kept a picture of Tony directing Vanessa in The Lady From the Sea. Vanessa gave her some thoughts about how to play the role. Natasha conceded that she based her interpretation of a woman torn between her husband and her phantom lover on the pain she felt at being caught between Liam Neeson and Robert Fox.

With Vanessa in Manhattan, Rachel, now ninety-two, went to stay with Liam and her great grandchildren as Long Day's Journey Into Night prepared for opening. Lynn in nearby Connecticut was close by.

Vanessa and her mother arrived in New York on 15 March. Corin came out to Manhattan as well, having finished a run at the National Theatre. The three siblings were having lunch together at a restaurant on 16th Street when Vanessa started getting phone calls that Rachel had suffered a massive stroke. Four days later, early on Saturday morning, 24 May 2003, Rachel died at the Millbrook farmhouse. Vanessa sent Lynn a text: 'Our darling has gone.'

Natasha said that Rachel's death still came as a great blow to Vanessa, who'd looked after her mother for years. Lynn, who had kept the news she was suffering from breast cancer from Rachel, saw her mother's body after she died – 'It made me look at death differently because I had never seen a dead person until I saw my mum,' she admitted. 'It made me less scared.' Presciently, Lynn noted in her journal that she wanted to be buried by Rachel in the pretty Lithgow cemetery when the time came: she had just seven years left to live.

But Lynn was not the only sibling battling cancer: Corin had been diagnosed with cancer of the prostate. 'Did I ever say to Dad, "Slow down"?' said his daughter Jemma. 'There was no point, because he would always reply: "Yes, yes, I will, I will, I will." And of course he never would – politics is part of him, he will always want to be active in humanitarian causes.' Corin's sense of injustice was inflamed by Essex councillors trying to evict gyspies from an illegal Billericay campsite. He called them Britain's 'most deprived community' and said he was prepared to put a human shield around the camp to save the travellers, who had exceeded a two-year deadline to vacate. In June 2005, he was giving an impassioned speech at a public meeting in Essex when he faltered and fell unconscious to the floor: Corin had suffered a heart attack. Police officers, who had been at the meeting to provide security, tried resuscitating him and used defibrillators to shock his heart into restarting. They got a pulse on the second attempt and then one of the gypsies started to give him mouth-to-mouth resuscitation. Corin was rushed to Basildon hospital, where he was put on life support; he was not breathing and was being kept alive by the machine. Fearing the worst, the Redgraves gathered around his bedside. 'All the family were there in the intensive care unit, like Orpheus waiting for Eurydice to come back from the underworld,' recalled Jemma. Corin was on life support for three days and then in other hospitals after that. 'We were all praying for him to step back into the world, and he did,' said Jemma.

Joely, who felt she had been cold-shouldered by the British film industry after her divorce from Tim Bevan, now had an unexpected offer: she was offered the plum role of a neurotic surgeon's wife in the US television series *Nip/Tuck*. She laughed that she was so unknown her co-star Julian McMahon couldn't remember her name, calling her 'honey' and 'sweetie' during the first year of filming (she filmed the pilot for US cable channel FX early in 2003 and the first 13 episodes were commissioned in March). The first series of *Nip/Tuck* became the highest-rated show on US cable television. For the second series, Vanessa was cast as Joely's malevolent bitch of a mother – it was the tired old trick of having the Redgraves appear together on screen. Vanessa co-starred in a total of 10 episodes as Julia's mother, a child psychologist who constantly belittles her daughter. The show earned Joely two Golden Globe nominations and a rumoured £3 million-a-year salary.

Being in a long-running US television show meant that Joely's daughter Daisy had to divide her time equally between her mother and her father, shuttling between London and Los Angeles. Eleven-year-old Daisy would fly out to be with Joely during boarding school holidays. However, Joely found trying to dovetail her filming commitments with looking after Daisy impossible. Like many a single parent, she discovered that work and childcare went together like oil and water: she had to choose one or the other. 'It just got to a point where I couldn't make it work anymore,' she explained. 'It all got too much – I couldn't juggle any more. I've worked hard for many years and *Nip/Tuck* was a great job but I couldn't carry on with it for the sake of my conscience or for my desires as a mother.'

Five years into her seven-year contract, Joely announced that she would be quitting the show: she was about to start filming the fourth season. On the face of it, what she was doing looked like professional suicide. Joely then explained that Daisy (now fourteen) had suffered from a rare medical condition affecting her circulation since she was a baby – she had a vascular problem in one leg. The condition had weakened the valves and walls of Daisy's veins, making them less efficient at circulating blood back to her heart. 'Surgeons and hospitals have been a big part of our lives,' she said. 'We were always told that Daisy would have more surgery when she got older. The time has come. I love my work but I had to be in two places at once and I thought, "If it were all over tomorrow, what would I regret?" It would be not being there for

Daisy.' However, Joely was also afraid that Time Warner would sue her for dropping out of the show (the studio had a reputation for defending its interests and would make a particularly determined opponent for anybody in the entertainment industry who crossed it. 'If a company sues you, it can affect the next ten years of your life,' said Joely.

In the end, Joely missed shooting just four episodes. She told a friend there was so much competition for roles that she couldn't risk not taking work when it was offered to her. Perhaps she realised that for all her grand gesture, money melts quicker than butter in the frying pan. The best thing she could do for Daisy was to keep the cash coming in. Joely continued to star in the FX network show right up until its final 100th episode aired in March 2010.

Not only was Vanessa playing Joely's mother on television, she was also doing the same thing with Natasha in the film *Evening* (2007), based on the Susan Minot novel. Vanessa starred as a dying woman who looks back on her life, while Natasha played her on-screen daughter. When Natasha read Michael Cunningham's screenplay, she noticed one large gap: there was no scene between mother and daughter. She insisted on one being written, taking advantage of what she saw as a unique opportunity to see both of them onscreen. Summoning up her Stanislavsky sense memory, once again she drew on how she felt rejected by Vanessa in favour of politics. 'I sort of remember the feeling as a child of wanting her back,' Natasha explained. 'It was a time in her life when she was very politically active and it took her away from her family. I think we felt somewhat abandoned.' Cunningham talked to Vanessa, heard the story of 'I want you back' and incorporated it into the screenplay. In the film, Natasha sits by her mother's bedside and says, 'I want you back now, just for five minutes.' Natasha later admitted how emotionally painful she had found the scene: 'It evoked so many thoughts, resonances in my life, my past and my future.'[11]

Vanessa, meanwhile, had rekindled her relationship with Franco Nero. They had grown closer over the years, although contact was often limited to phone calls because Nero still lived in the Rome flat overlooking St Peter's Square that Vanessa had chosen for him years ago. They had never really lost touch, although there had been times when they weren't speaking or just shouted at each other. 'Getting back together, there's that bonus of discovering that I was right to fall in love with him in the first place,' she said. Surrounded by family and friends, Vanessa married for the second time at the age of sixty-nine on 31

December 2006. The couple decided not to be legally married because that would have involved lawyers and money. Instead, there was dancing and grandchildren running around. Carlo, now aged thirty-seven, put a gold band on Vanessa's finger and she took to wearing her wedding ring, on- and offstage. 'I think after 40 years you know who you love and respect,' she said. 'And I do love him and respect him very, very much.' However, she was still unconventional enough to accept that her new husband might want other relationships, especially with younger women – this was something she could live with.[12]

During this period there was growing public unease at what America was doing incarcerating Muslim prisoners in its Guantanamo Bay prison camp. Suspected al-Qaeda terrorists from all over Europe and the Middle East were captured and sent to Cuba. Nightly TV news bulletins showed images of orange jumpsuited prisoners forced to kneel in the dirt. Human rights groups protested that some had been illegally kidnapped and flown to Guantanamo. There were allegations of brutality while the Bush administration parsed the legal definition of torture. Like Hungary and Vietnam, here was another faraway cause for Vanessa: images of death camps in Nazi Germany had seared her brain when she was a child and the flashpoint came when two former Guantanamo Bay detainees wanted in Spain on terror charges returned to Britain in December 2007, having been incarcerated for five years. Within hours, they were re-arrested because of a Spanish extradition request. The authorities in Spain claimed they were involved in an al-Qaeda terror cell, recruiting volunteers to fight in Afghanistan and Indonesia.

Jamil el-Banna, forty-five, was alleged to be an associate of radical preacher Abu Qatada, ostensibly Osama Bin Laden's right-hand man in Europe. Spain alleged el-Banna had distributed extremist propaganda, some of which had been produced by Bin Laden himself. El-Banna was also linked to Iraqi insurgent Abu Musab al-Zarqawi, who had organised the televised beheading of British hostage, Ken Bigley. Omar Deghayes, thirty-eight, allegedly featured in a terrorist training video found in the home of one of the Madrid train bombers who had killed 191 people three years previously. El-Banna and Deghayes appeared at the City of Westminster Magistrates' Court.

Palestinian-born father-of-five el-Banna, reported to have entered Britain illegally in 1994 on a fake Kuwaiti passport, lived in Dollis Hill, north London. He spoke in Arabic to the court and his answers were translated into English. Deghayes squinted through one eye: he was said to have lost the other during his time in captivity. Vanessa flew into action, paying £65,000 towards their £100,000 bail. Campaigners said both men were innocent individuals who had been kidnapped and tortured. She described it as a 'profound honour' to help el-Banna, whom she called a 'hero.' Vanessa said: 'Guantanamo Bay is a concentration camp. It is a disgrace that these men have been kept there all these years.' The right-wing British press gnashed its teeth. Conservative MP Patrick Mercer said: 'This is yet more publicity seeking by someone with a long track record of backing just about every fashionable radical cause going.'

In March 2009, Spain's leading investigative judge, Baltasar Garzón, ruled the two men were unfit to stand trial because both had mental health problems after their incarceration. His decision was reputedly based on medical reports provided by the British authorities.

While this was going on, Joely had found a new love. Joely, forty-three, was seeing Evgeny Lebedev, the twenty-six-year-old son of Russian billionaire and former KGB agent Alexander Lebedev. The Aeroflot heir's previous girlfriends included Geri Halliwell of the Spice Girls. His father's London representative Justin Byam Shaw was the great nephew of Rachel's lover Glen Byam Shaw. Paparazzi flashbulbs blinded Joely and Lebedev whenever they turned up together at glitzy events.

Softly spoken, Lebedev grew up in England during the time his father worked for the KGB. He attended a Church of England primary school and then schools in Holland Park and Mill Hill, after which he studied for a degree at the London School of Economics and took a history of art course at Christie's. Among his interests Lebedev was a film producer and a production of his had won the Silver Lion at the Venice Film Festival. In one of those connections that stretched back through Redgrave family history, Lebedev owned a stake in the Moscow Arts Theatre made famous by its founder Constantin Stanislavski, the drama teacher who had inspired Michael, Vanessa and Natasha in turn.

Now with the wound of Joely's divorce healing to an almost imperceptible scar and with Vanessa finally married to the man she had loved for 43 years, it seemed as if almost everything was once again perfect in the Redgrave family garden.

Notes

1. Boshoff, Alison. 'The Love Child Who Broke Lynn Redgrave's Heart', *Daily Mail*, 8 May 2010; 'Lynn Redgrave Finds Out Her Husband Is a Naughty Boy', *Daily Telegraph*, 5 March 1999.
2. Boshoff, Alison. 'The Love Child Who Broke Lynn Redgrave's Heart', *Daily Mail*, 8 May 2010.
3. Clark, John and Gallagher, Paul. 'Redgrave and Ex-husband Sue Mistress', *The Scotsman*, 30 November 2001.
4. Whittell, Giles. 'Redgrave's Husband Names Her "Lovers"', *The Times*, 8 March 1999.
5. Hastings, Chris. 'The Actor's Crush On the Rock Rebel Is Among the Secrets Uncovered in the Papers of his Biographer Sheridan Morley', *Sunday Times*, 5 July 2009.
6. Weinberg, Joanna. 'Goodbye, Gorgeous Tasha', *Sunday Times*, 22 March 2009.
7. Hattersley, Roy. 'A Life In Parts', *Guardian*, 6 May 2000.
8. Laville, Sandra. 'Redgrave Speaks Out for Her Chechen Olivier', *Daily Telegraph*, 7 December 2002.
9. Ibid.
10. Fielding, Nick. 'Redgrave Targeted By Russian Rent-a-Mob Over Chechen Support', *Sunday Times*, 2 January 2005.
11. Stone, Jay. 'On-screen Mother and Child Reunion', *Ottawa Citizen*, 30 June 2007.
12. Clinton, Jane. 'I've Fallen In Love With My Franco Again Says Vanessa', *Express On Sunday*, 9 April 2006.

CHAPTER TWENTY-TWO

A Thin Streak of the Irrational

Natasha once said that she always got frightened as soon as everything was going great: she knew something was always coming round the corner. By the spring of 2009, Natasha and Liam's two boys were becoming teenagers. Natasha wanted to make sure their upbringing was as stable as possible compared to her own crazy childhood: she was determined to keep them away from danger, always making them feel loved and supported. Neither Michael, thirteen, nor Daniel, twelve, was ever left for any length of time without either Liam or herself being there and she was always careful to spend time with each of them separately.

In the spring of 2009, Natasha visited London with Daniel – that was why she decided to take Michael skiing in Canada, where Liam was filming *Chloe* in Toronto. She and Michael booked in to the hotel Quintessence in the ski resort of Mont Tremblant. Natasha was not a fan of winter sports and she'd never learned to ski. Indeed, she even told shoe designer Kenneth Cole that skiing was dangerous. Vanessa mentioned to a friend: 'Natasha is off skiing. I don't understand – she doesn't even like to ski.'[1]

In one of those small twists of fate that decide things for generations – the thin streak of the irrational which runs through everything – on 15 March, Natasha noticed a smell in her suite. The hotel moved them to another room, offering one free night by way of apology. Natasha, who had been about to check out, decided to stay on for one more day. The next morning, 16 March, she made another decision that affected everything when she declined the offer of a helmet in the ski rental shop. 'She said she wasn't a good skier and was a little nervous,' said a shop assistant.

By noon, Natasha was at the bottom of a nursery slope known as The Flats when she took a tumble. This was an accident that happened hundreds of times a day on nursery slopes all over the world. As she went down, the left side of her face hit the snow. She got up laughing. A fellow skier said: 'She just fell over, picked herself up and laughed – it didn't seem serious at all. She joked: "I need more practice at this." She seemed absolutely fine.' Her instructor, though, decided to do things by the book: he called an ambulance, which arrived minutes after the fall. However, the ambulance was turned away – Natasha even signed a medical form saying she did not need help. What she didn't know was that a chunk of ice had impacted her temple, tearing a blood vessel beneath the skull: blood was slowly leaking into her brain.

The instructor and two ski patrol members accompanied Natasha to her hotel room. Within an hour, she began to complain of a headache, nausea and dizziness. At 3pm, an ambulance was called to take her to the local Hospitalier Laurentien. Inside the ambulance, Natasha had no idea where she was, what day it was or what had happened to her. Her condition deteriorated rapidly. Hospital brain scans revealed a tear in the temporal artery on the left side of her brain. By 6.38pm, Natasha had been medevaced to Hôpital du Sacré-Cœur de Montréal. By now her pupils were unresponsive – a sign of advanced brain damage. Meanwhile, word had reached Liam on set – the colour drained from his face the moment he was told. Liam immediately flew to Montreal. But nobody knew who he was when he got to the hospital. Staff wouldn't let him see his wife. Bewildered, Liam went outside where he came across two nurses having a cigarette. They pointed to a back door where he could slip in. 'I was so fucking grateful – for the first time in I don't know how long – to be recognised,' he said. 'So I get there, just in time. And these young doctors, who look all of eighteen years of age, they tell me the worst. The worst.' As the enormity of what had happened sank in, he broke down in tears and had to be comforted by hospital staff. Meanwhile, steroids were injected to reduce the bleeding inside Natasha's skull but scans showed that her level of brain activity was minimal. They operated to remove the blood clot but shortly afterwards, Natasha suffered a devastating stroke on the operating table when the artery tear widened: she was brain dead.

The decision was taken to fly Natasha by private jet to Lenox Hill Hospital, New York so that her family and friends could say goodbye to her. With tubes covering her face, she lay in an intensive-care bed in the plane. Liam sat in silence holding his wife's hand and caressing her pale cheeks as they drove from New Jersey to Manhattan. The press was frantic to report on Natasha's condition but with their customary hauteur, the Redgraves refused to comment. There was a sense that nobody really knew what was going on. Paparazzi asked impertinent questions as Vanessa and Joely entered Lenox Hill. Lauren Bacall, Meryl Streep and Joan Didion were among those close friends who visited Natasha in hospital. On the morning of 18 March, Liam and the boys gathered at Natasha's bedside with Vanessa, Lynn, Joely, Robert Fox and Daisy Bevan for her final moments. Michael was still wearing his Mont Tremblant sweatshirt. Vanessa is reported to have crooned the lullaby 'Edelweiss', the song she had sung at her daughter's wedding, while tenderly stroking Natasha's face. She collapsed in shock when the life support machine was switched off.[2]

The following night, Broadway dimmed its lights in Natasha's honour. Liam, Vanessa and Joely stood at the heart of New York's theatre district at 8pm as theatre lights began switching off. Liam seemed close to tears. Looking pale and gaunt, he could only bear to watch for a few minutes before walking away. One by one, theatre marquees along the Great White Way darkened.

The next evening, Natasha's body was loaded into a hearse at Greenwich Village Funeral Home in Lower Manhattan and driven to the American Irish Historical Society on Fifth Avenue. On Friday, 20 March, Natasha was given a wake in the traditional Irish manner. Liam received every single person at the viewing, hugging them. Rupert Everett came to pay his last respects, as did director Mike Nichols, television host Diane Sawyer, Ralph Fiennes and Uma Thurman. Liam was the last to leave: he shook off the paparazzi and walked home alone across Central Park.

Natasha's funeral took place the next morning at St Peter's Episcopal Church near her Millbrook home. Clouds obscured the sun as her coffin was carried in to the tiny white clapboard church. The bell tolled. Her casket was carved with the centuries-old Irish claddagh symbol of hands holding a crowned heart said to mean 'With my hands I give you my heart, and crown it with my love'. Liam, in a dark suit and sunglasses, was one of the pallbearers. A flurry of snowflakes rested on her casket as it went inside. The pews of the 19th-century American Colonial church were packed. Vanessa, Joely and other family members stood together in a bent row, some blessing themselves with the sign of the cross as the coffin went past.

After the service the Redgraves walked hesitantly to the graveyard further down the road. Natasha was laid to rest a little way off from where her grandmother Rachel was buried. Looming trees stood guard over her final resting place. A single bouquet of lilies was placed on her grave. Vanessa stood wraithlike over her daughter's grave. It is hard to comprehend the fathomless grief she must have felt: a parent outliving a child is a terrible thing – it's just not meant to be that way.

Joely said that Natasha's death had shocked her down to a cellular level. The appalling tragedy of her sister's death made her think more often about Tony, too. 'So much of who I am is who Tasha was, and I think, sharing all those formative years, there is a level of merging. I still think of my father daily.'[3] For Liam, the grief still came in waves. 'It hits you in the middle of the night ... I'm out walking. I'm feeling quite content. And it's like suddenly, boom.' Liam twisted both fists in opposite directions. Speaking for the first time about the tragedy, Vanessa said: 'Nothing can help, absolutely nothing.'[4] She compared bereavement to walking into another country, 'the country of having lost the one member of your family whom you just adore. It's a very strange country and it does strange things to your mind.'[5]

Notes

1. Young, Toby. 'Tasha Takes Off', *Sunday Independent*, 4 September 2005.
2. 'Redgrave Collapses', *Northern Territory News*, 23 March 2009.
3. Hadley-Dent, Ticky. 'Joely's Journey', *Tatler*, January 2010.
4. Sheridan, Peter. 'Vanessa Redgrave – Grief And No Regrets But Now the Rebel Bully May Finally Be Forgiven', *Daily Express*, 20 February 2010.
5. Vanessa Redgrave interview, *Woman's Hour*, BBC Radio 4, 10 June 2010.

CHAPTER TWENTY-THREE

The Undiscovered Country

When I was eighteen, I was invited abroad on my first proper foreign holiday. The father of a school friend was renting a house in the South of France and did I want to come? Never having really been out of the Midlands before, I leapt at the chance. I took the overnight train from Paris and remember watching the gray lunar-dawn landscape change to copper-red rocks as we plunged deeper through Provence. By the time I finally reached St Tropez, I was so exhausted that I slept on the beach.

The house was hidden in the hills inland and was difficult to find, almost as if it did not want to be discovered. As in a fairy-tale, you could imagine the dirt track leading to the farm sealing up behind you. I remember walking down the rocky track with my bag and glimpsing a farmhouse between the trees. Mountains stained the silence and the scent of pine and lavender was overpowering. The gnarled, desiccated trees, their barks like crocodile skin, looked as if they had every drop of moisture sucked out of them; the air throbbed with sullen heat. However, the almost tactile absence of sound was broken by somebody diving cleanly into water and then followed by laughter.

It was not really a farmhouse, more a small hamlet with cottages converted into guest rooms. We ate meals at a long table at the side of the house sitting beneath a string of coloured lights. Nights were spent playing cards in the sitting room, which had a hippie feel to it, like the hangover of an acid trip. We played the LPs that the owner's teenage daughters left stacked against the windowsill. Lou Reed and David Bowie played out into the night and down along the valley. It was truly a magical place. The house itself was called Le Nid du Duc (or The Owl's Nest). I discovered that it belonged to an English film director called Tony Richardson, although I'd never heard of him. It showed how diminished his reputation had become by the early Eighties. The more I found out about Tony, the more I realised you couldn't understand him without describing his relations with the rest of the family, who circle each other like a solar system. There was his turbulent marriage to Vanessa, the products of which were his adored Natasha and more strained relationship with Joely. Circling Tony's immediate family were Corin and Lynn. And beyond them grandparents Michael and Rachel, extinct stars which still exerted a gravitational pull.

'We are,' Vanessa has said of the Redgrave acting dynasty, 'the sprigs of a great and beautiful tree.' Family is important – her flat is full of photographs of other Redgraves, although intriguingly, there's none of Vanessa herself to be seen. Snaps of her parents, Michael and Rachel, flank the mantelpiece; Tony looks out from a frame on the table. There's a dramatic shot of her son-in-law Liam holding her grandson. Vanessa has always denied that this great and beautiful Redgrave tree is in any way a dynasty. A dynasty implies power, she said, while the Redgraves are just a family of professional actors. The only power they have, she said, is to try and do the best work they can.

Natasha also dismissed this talk of a dynasty – 'What a load of crap! We're a family of working actors. It's like coming from a family of carpenters or plumbers who work in the family business, generation after generation, that's all. Because it's acting, it makes it more public,' she said. Corin too rejected the idea that the Redgraves' acting ability was something genetic. 'I don't particularly like the word dynasty,' he said. 'I can't put an embargo on it – it's not something I think any member of my own family is pleased with. I don't think there is any such thing as an acting gene, and no evidence that a talent for acting is inherited.' Rather, it was because Natasha, Joely and his own daughter Jemma grew up absorbing acting and saw how, at its best, the stage could be a delightful life. Also, none of the girls were ever discouraged from going on stage, whereas most parents react with horror.

But the Redgraves are being disingenuous here: they are a dynasty, and a powerful one at that. They've been called a dynasty where all the drama happens offstage. Natasha first married one of Britain's leading theatrical impresarios and then a big Hollywood star. Joely's first marriage was to the man who pretty much controls the British film industry. At the time of writing, she is going out with the son of the Russian millionaire who owns the *Evening Standard* and the *Independent* newspapers. The Redgraves have influence. Furthermore, generations of plumbers and carpenters don't write books mythologising themselves. Back in the early Sixties, Michael considered writing a book about Roy and Daisy. Corin actually wrote a radio play about his grandparents that broadcast in 1998; he also penned a biography of Michael. Lynn wrote and performed three plays about her family. The first, *Shakespeare For My Father*, tried to understand and come to terms with her feelings towards Michael, and how much of his indifference was driven by his own demons. *The Mandrake Root*, her second, was about a distinguished actor whose homosexuality causes his actress-wife to take up with a lover. (Vanessa was said to be furious with what she saw as Lynn's betrayal; she consulted lawyers, who insisted on script changes.)[1] Lynn next played her maternal grandmother Beatrice Kempson in *Nightingale* (the British premiere was at the New End Theatre in Hampstead, north London, in January 2006).

Rachel did see traits running through the family. 'I suppose if there's any link between the generations, it's in their extreme sense of individualism, of personal freedom and self-will,' she said. Acting runs through the Redgraves, as does musicality in other families: it's like someone being able to draw well or not – you can't teach it, it's inherited. Lynn said there was a gene running through the Redgraves with a proscenium arch attached. That's one way of looking at it. Another way would be to recognise adultery and homosexuality as twin strands wrapping around the Redgrave DNA. Vanessa's grandfather Roy was, after all, an adulterer and bigamist who walked out on two separate families to further his own career – selfishness being another part of the Redgrave genetic code – while Vanessa's mother and father were both unfaithful.

Her daughters' first important relationships were both with other people's husbands. Natasha's first marriage was ended by her having an affair. Michael, father of Vanessa, was of course famously bisexual, having affairs with Noël Coward and Edith Evans. The first person we associate with love and care is our parent peering over our cot; Vanessa went on to marry a bisexual herself. Of all the family, only Lynn seems to have noticed a pattern of a family acting out the same things again and again. Corin was estranged from his young children, just as Michael was absent from his own life. Vanessa left Natasha and Joely for months at a time to go off and make pro-Palestine documentaries. The consequences for those around them have been so much unhappiness. And for all the Redgraves' outward concern for humanity in the abstract – Michael too described himself as a 'red hot Socialist' – Norman Harding, a WRP member who really was from the working class and the family's driver in the Eighties, experienced a different side. One night the Redgraves invited him to have dinner with them in a hotel. At the table, Harding said it was as if he didn't exist: 'You see films featuring an aristocratic family having dinner, the servants standing a few paces from the table, upright and staring into space. They only existed when their "betters" wanted another potato putting on their plate,' he said.[2]

Vanessa may have described the Redgraves as a family who rejoice in each other's achievements, yet they can be curiously remote with each other. Lynn said that although she and Vanessa were sisters, they were never close. She never really knew where her sister's severity came from. Journalists who queue to interview Vanessa have compared it to waiting outside the headmaster's study. You shuffle and fidget. You go first. No, *you* go first. An interview with Vanessa – fixed by those vatic blue eyes – is more akin to a lecture, impervious to interruption, probably on the Universal Declaration of Human Rights. Her hands knot with earnestness. She parses her sentences with taxonomic precision. It's hard for Vanessa to got across what she really means. Opponents find her tone wearyingly doctrinaire, and cannot abide what they see as her constant hand-wringing. You just wish she'd be more human and less humane, said one. Others, such as journalist John Walsh, have found her just too perfect in her radiant humility, a little too Christ-among-the-Wretched. So many people, so many plights. 'I feel it,' she once said, 'like a physical pain.'[3]

Supporters, though, have compared her to the Statue of Liberty ('Give me your poor, your huddled masses'). And nearly every cause that Vanessa has taken up – from ending the Vietnam War and apartheid in South Africa to campaigning for the closure of Guantanamo Bay prison camp – has become accepted middle-class, middle-thinking. Like Trollope's heroine, she knew she was right.

And yet, watching Vanessa's anguish in *A Long Day's Journey Into Night*, unable to prevent her family from being sucked down by alcoholism, or Corin blazing with righteous anger as *King Lear*, or Lynn clucking her disapproval as the German housekeeper in *Gods and Monsters*, nothing else seems to matter. The Redgraves have a magic possessed by all the great actors, there's a sense of mystery and radiance in their presence. Whenever they appear on stage or screen, it's as if someone just turned up the light in the room. Your skin begins to prickle. Sometimes Vanessa is so good on stage that she seems on a different plane to the actors around her. The Redgrave power springs from the spontaneity Michael instilled in his three children when they were learning the craft. At best, there's seemingly no distance between them, the writer's ideas and the audience. Somehow a good Redgrave performance fuses all three; it's as if what they're saying really has only just occurred to them. Corin or Natasha could communicate a character's entire history in one evanescent moment. It's a rare gift and why the Redgraves are so highly regarded. Vanessa herself believes the purpose of acting is to reach out and make every person watching feel they're right by her side. She wants everyone in the audience to understand what she's feeling. That's not pretending – it's something deeper than that.

In February 2010, while waiting for Vanessa backstage at the Royal Opera House in London – where she once queued overnight as a ballet-mad teenager – I reflect on her long journey. Prince William is on stage presenting her with an Academy Fellowship. For most of her life, Vanessa would have been more likely to call for the royal family's abolition, not accept awards from it, but then the Establishment's soft embrace is hard to resist. Finally, she comes backstage to face the press. Her large, mannish hands hold a tissue. Immensely tall, luminous and yet somehow sorrowful, there's something anguished about her. Her startlingly blue gull's eyes search out the first question. The voice, like rough velvet, is a little more papery than it was but the impression you're left with is of her rather lovely smile.

The line from *Hamlet* that 'when sorrows come, they come not single spies, but in battalions' certainly rang true for Vanessa. Her beloved brother Corin died, aged seventy, on 7 April 2010 peacefully surrounded by his family. He had never fully recovered from the heart attack suffered five years previously. Vanessa said that of all the things she missed most, it was her darling brother's wacky sense of humour. The funeral took place on 12 April 2010 at The Actor's Church, St Paul's in Covent Garden, where Michael was eventually buried. Vanessa and Corin's widow Kika led hundreds of mourners at the service. Joely and Liam were also there. A desperately frail Lynn, dying of breast cancer, was carried from the car into a wheelchair and conveyed into St Paul's. She was expected to speak, but it seemed impossible – her body was so emaciated, despite the puffy face. A black scarf covered her head.

Jemma Redgrave read from *Uncle Vanya*. She said her father gave her a copy of the complete works of Chekhov when she was a teenager. Although she would have preferred an album by The Clash, it had become a lifelong companion. Vanessa read from *Antony and Cleopatra*, saying her brother had read the passages to her and she wanted to return the gesture. Lynn was brought, with great difficulty and infinitely slowly, to the lectern, which she leant against almost insouciantly, as if in a bar. 'Sorry to stagger up like this,' she drawled. 'These things happen.' The service ended with a recording of Corin singing 'Goodbye' from the film *Oh! What a Lovely War*. As the hearse carrying his coffin left the church grounds, the congregation gave Corin one last standing ovation.

Lynn died the following month at home in Kent, Connecticut. She was working on a new family play, *Rachel and Juliet*, about her relationship with her mother. Rachel had a lifelong fascination with Shakespeare's heroine. Alas, the breast cancer she so bravely fought came back virulently. One week later, she was buried. Pallbearers carried a basket-weave casket adorned with flowers through a light drizzle into the First Congregational Church of Kent. Vanessa, Joely and Liam gathered together once again, four weeks after Corin's funeral. Lynn's casket was then driven to the rural cemetery in Lithgow, New York, where her mother and Natasha were buried.

To reach what has become the Redgrave family cemetery, you must take the train to Poughkeepsie from Grand Central Station, whose baroque marble hall Michael once compared to the size of Vanessa's conscience. The train slides past the poorer, emptier streets of Harlem and the ugly industrial hinterland of The Bronx; you slide past bricked-up warehouses and apartment blocks that look like prison watchtowers, then a real prison with searchlights and barbed wire. The guard rattles off the destinations in his 'fuhgedaboutit' voice: the horn-blowing assonance of Yonkers, the childlike Tarrytown and the Indian-sounding Mahopac. Suddenly, you're out of the tunnel and running alongside the wide, flat Hudson River. You can see why Natasha wanted to live here: the peaked hills are oddly reminiscent of those surrounding Le Nid du Duc, while the delightful bluffs and coves resemble St Tropez Bay. It's almost paradisiacal.

Sitting in St Peter's Episcopal Church, the church where Natasha's funeral took place surrounded by the Good People of Millbrook, I reflect on moments from the Redgraves' lives: Corin giving an impassioned speech on behalf of gypsy rights, Lynn taking a Thanksgiving turkey out of the oven and Vanessa tying a napkin around her head while singing 'Edelweiss' at Natasha's wedding. Then there's Vanessa lifting her Oscar in triumph and a scorpion-hot summer at Le Nid du Duc, Tony getting the phone call telling him he'd won three Oscars and Laurence Olivier stepping forward to announce that, 'Tonight, a great actress has been born.' Rainbow light from a stained-glass window falls across the organist's back and the vicar says, 'Give to the departed eternal rest.'

Poor Lynn – even in death she is overshadowed by her mother and niece and is buried next to Rachel in a far corner of Lithgow cemetery. The cemetery stands on a hill overlooking cornfields. This is farming country; cows amble past a stars-and-stripes painted barn. It feels like the last good day of summer, so lovely it catches at the back of your throat. Yet there's a pang because you realise there won't be a day of such surpassing loveliness for another year. Tall stalks of green-gold corn guard both graves. Rachel's headstone is a broken Doric column, ringed with statues of her three children holding hands. The inscription reads: 'Rachel Redgrave 1910–2003. Beloved wife of Michael. Dearest Mother of Vanessa, Corin and Lynn.'

A little further off, Natasha's headstone is even grander: an idealised bronze statue of herself kneeling, bearing a plate with the words 'Cast your bread upon the water and it will be returned tenfold'. Running along the marble base is the inscription: 'Beloved daughter, sister, niece, aunt and true friend. Though your days were brief, your spirit was alive, awake, complete'.

The looming trees are turning a coppery-red, russet, tawny gold … Butterflies skim over the fallen leaves. The grating of the crickets is reminiscent of the South of France and, as at Le Nid Du Duc, there's a throbbing, almost liquid stillness. You get the feeling that nothing bad could ever happen here: there's a sense of everything coming to rest.

Notes

1. Moore, Toby. 'Play Turns Redgraves Into a Family At War', *Daily Express*, 13 March 2001.
2. Harding, Norman. *Staying Red: Why I Remain a Socialist*, Index Books, London, 2005.
3. Driscoll, Margaritte. 'Odd Bedfellows for Redgrave, Rebel With a New Cause', *Sunday Times*, 26 March 2000.

Acknowledgements

First, I want to thank all those individuals who helped and offered me their advice during the writing of this book. They include Margaret Atwood, Candida Crewe, Hugo Davenport, Mike Downey, Duncan Heath, John Heyman – who so generously introduced me to Natasha Richardson – Luke G-Jones, Sandra Lousada, Leon Morgan, Patty Mayer, Agnès Poirier, Christopher Robbins, Roger Smith and in particular, investigative journalists Anthony Summers and Robbyn Swan, who sat me down after my last non-fiction book and taught me the process of how to write a biography properly. My teacher June Beavers taught me a valuable lesson trying to write this book while holding down a demanding full-time job. 'Little and often,' she would say, which is probably the secret to trying to finish any big project. Nikki Finke, my editor-in-chief at Deadline Hollywood, passed on her secrets for writing entertaining copy – every day, I learn something new.

Second, my gratitude extends to all those who agreed to be interviewed about their memories of the Richardsons and the Redgraves: Edward Albee, Danaë Brook, Diane Cilento, Nigel Davenport, Tony Garnett, Sandra Lousada, Mike Medavoy, Rita Tushingham, Norman Twain, Baroness Williams and Susannah York. And to others who agreed to speak to me but only on condition of anonymity.

Sean Delaney, chief librarian at the British Film Institute library along with the rest of his staff, was, as always, immensely helpful as were their colleagues at the British Library and British Library Newspapers at Colindale, north London. And thanks also to Erin O'Neill at the BBC Written Archives Centre in Caversham.

Graham Coster, my editor at Aurum, gave me insightful notes on the first draft, pushing me deeper to explore why some of the protagonists in this book sometimes behaved in the way they did. My agent Laura Morris was unfailingly cheerful, even when at times I felt Eeyore-ishly overwhelmed by the amount of work left to do.

I want to thank my two sons Jack and Theo for providing me with such happy, simple pleasures: riffing away after coming down off from a hairy ascent of Tryfan (which I think must translate from the Welsh as 'bastard mountain'), Theo's cheeky sideways-glance as he glided out of Canterbury Cathedral Quire as one of the cathedral's chorister ducklings and Jack laughing his head off surrounded by other teenagers dangling his legs in a swimming pool. I can't wait to find out what happens next.

After some initial correspondence with Vanessa Redgrave and a phone conversation with Natasha, representatives of the Redgraves later made clear the Redgraves would not co-operate with this project. They have not done so, and they do not authorise it in any way.

In writing this book I have tried to be mindful of Vanessa Redgrave's own discomfort in reading about herself. 'Public figures', she has said, 'must be prepared to cope with all manner of intrusions into their lives and psyches, whether or not they seek out the limelight. It is difficult reading intimate or negative things about oneself.'[1] I have also been mindful that the very final words of Vanessa's autobiography were, 'We must know the truth.' Quite.

Note

1. Haddad, George M. 'Tea With the Red Queen of Hearts', *After Dark*, October 1978.

Index